Readings in
Organizations
STRUCTURE, PROCESSES, BEHAVIOR

Readings in Organizations

STRUCTURE, PROCESSES, BEHAVIOR

Edited by

JAMES L. GIBSON comp.
Associate Professor

JOHN M. IVANCEVICH
Associate Professor

JAMES H. DONNELLY, JR.
Associate Professor

All of the
Department of Business Administration
University of Kentucky

1973

BUSINESS PUBLICATIONS, INC.
Dallas, Texas   75224

IRWIN-DORSEY INTERNATIONAL   London, England   WC2H 9NJ
IRWIN-DORSEY LIMITED   Georgetown, Ontario   L7G 4B3

© BUSINESS PUBLICATIONS, INC., 1973

First Printing, June 1973

ISBN 0-256-01456-6

Library of Congress Catalog Card No. 73–77025

Printed in the United States of America

Preface

The study of organizations is of vital concern to many groups in society. Behavioral and social scientists have led the way in observing that modern man works, learns, plays, worships, heals, and governs in larger and more complex institutions than his ancestors. Modern society is characterized by the existence of intricately organized firms, universities, clubs, churches, hospitals, and agencies, each carrying out specialized social functions through the combined efforts of individual specialists. The effectiveness of these organizations determines the quality of modern man's life.

The achievement of effective organizational performance is the essence of the managerial process. As a consequence of history and tradition, society delegates authority to use its scarce resources to the managers of its institutions. And, in return, it holds managers accountable for their actions. Thus, managers of organizations are crucial to the manner in which a modern society functions. More particularly, the decisions of managers determine to an important degree the effectiveness of society in achieving its economic, educational, leisure, religious, health, and political goals.

Thus, our perspective in this book is the management of organizations. Our purpose is to bring together a selection of articles which bears directly on the process by which managers achieve effective organizational performance. The contributors of these articles are representative of a variety of behavioral and social sciences, including psychology, sociology, and social psychology. Though diverse in background and training, the contributors share a common interest in bringing their theory and research to bear on the practical problems of managing organizations.

The framework which we use to present the articles identifies three aspects of organizations: *structure, process, and behavior.* Organizational structure refers to the relatively fixed relationships among tasks and it derives from managerial decisions which define jobs, group jobs into departments, and assign authority. The important features of structure are job descriptions and chains of command. Organizational processes are the activities of people in the organization. These activities consist of two important elements—communications and decision making. Organizational behavior emphasizes the human element of organizations and relates to the elements of motivation, groups, and leadership. The analysis of organization is enhanced through an understanding of each of these aspects.

However, analysis of organizations implies some definite purpose. Our point of view is that the modern manager's purpose must be organizational improvement. Thus we identify a fourth aspect: modification of organizations. This aspect refers to the process by which managers improve the organization's effectiveness through the development of structure, process, and behavioral elements. Organizational development requires knowledge of these three elements; the bases for acquiring this knowledge are provided by the articles that appear in this book.

The introductory section contains four articles which preface the entire collection. Here we provide examples of behavioral science theory and research which have implications for management. Part II includes five articles, each dealing with one or more aspects of organizational structure. This section includes two articles dealing with nonbusiness organizations, universities, and hospitals, which facilitate interorganizational analysis. Part III is comprised of five articles which discuss problems and strategies of communications and decision making. Part IV contains seven articles dealing with individual, group, and leadership behavior. Motivation theory, job satisfaction, intergroup conflict, and leadership theory and style are discussed by the contributors. Part V presents six articles which discuss the climate and modification of organizations. Finally, Part VI integrates the material through three case studies of organizations which utilized behavioral science concepts in some aspect of management.

The articles which we included in this book were selected for a number of reasons. Of particular importance is that they are recent discussions of fundamental managerial and organizational issues. Moreover they are of high professional quality and readable by students. Yet, ultimately we had to make choices and in numerous instances, excellent articles were omitted which would have been included in a larger collection. Although not arbitrarily selected, the articles do represent our judgment.

We wish to thank the authors and publishers of the included readings. We also wish to acknowledge Virginia Scott and Patricia Scott for handling all the typing details.

May 1973

JAMES L. GIBSON
JOHN M. IVANCEVICH
JAMES H. DONNELLY, JR.

CONTRIBUTORS

Anderson, G. Lester
Barkdull, C. W.
Beer, Michael
Bowers, David G.
Buchanan, Paul
Bucklow, Maxine
Davis, Louis E.
Delbecq, Andre L.
Duncan, W. Jack
Gibb, Jack R.
Greiner, Larry E.
Harrison, Roger
Hill, J. W.
Hobbs, Walter C.
Holder, Jack J., Jr.
Hunt, J. G. (2)
Huse, Edgar F.
Indik, Bernard P.
Johnson, Alton C.
Lawler, Edward E., III
Lippitt, Gordon L.
Lorsch, Jay W.
Mintzberg, Henry
Nord, Walter R.
Sales, Stephen H.
Schulz, Rockwell
Seashore, Stanley E. (2)
Starkweather, David B.
Swinth, Robert L.
Walker, Arthur H.
Wickesberg, A. K.
Yuchtman, Ephraim

Contents

CROSS-REFERENCE TABLE

For Relating These Readings to the Authors'
Organizations: Structure, Processes, Behavior
and Other Organizational Behavior Type Textbooks

Parts in *Organizations: Structure, Processes, Behavior*

Selected Organizational Behavior Oriented Textbooks	Part I Introduction	Part II Structure of Organizations	Part III Processes within Organizations	Part IV Behavior within Organizations	Part V Climate and Organizational Development within Organizations	Part VI Application of Structural, Process, and Behavioral Concepts
Athos, Anthony G. and Coffey, Robert E. *Behavior In Organizations: A Multidimensional View* (Englewood Cliffs, N.J.: Prentice-Hall, Inc., 1968).	Chaps. 1, 2	Chap. 12 (219–232)	Chap. 12 (224–226 and 233–237)	Chaps. 3, 4, 5, 6, 7, 8, 9, 10, 11, 13, 14		
Davis, Keith, *Human Behavior At Work* (New York: McGraw-Hill Book Co., 1972).	Chaps. 1, 26	Chaps. 2, 11, 12, 13	Chaps. 20, 21, 22	Chaps. 3, 4, 6, 7, 8, 17, 18, 19, 23, 24, 25	Chaps. 5, 9, 10	Cases 1–10
Filley, Alan C. and House, Robert J., *Managerial Processes and Organizational Behavior* (Glenview, Ill.: Scott, Foresman and Co., 1969).	Chap. 2	Chaps. 4, 6, 7, 8, 9, 10, 11, 14	Chap. 5	Chaps. 3, 13, 15, 16	Chap. 17	Chap. 19

Source						
Gibson, James L., Ivancevich, John M., and Donnelly, James H., Jr., *Organizations: Structure, Processes, Behavior* (Dallas: Business Publications, Inc., 1973).	Chaps. 1, 2	Chaps. 3, 4, 5	Chaps. 6, 7	Chaps. 8, 9, 10	Chaps. 11, 12, 13	Chap. 14
Hampton, David R., Summer, Charles E., and Webber, Ross A., *Organizational Behavior and the Practice of Management* (Glenview: Scott, Foresman and Co., 1968).	Chaps. 1, 2	Chap. 4	Chap. 4 (189–91)	Chaps. 3, 5, 6, 7, 9	Chaps. 8, 10	
Kast, Fremont E. and Rosensweig, James E., *Organization and Management* (New York: McGraw-Hill Book Co., 1970).	Chaps. 1, 3	Chaps. 5, 6	Chaps. 12, 13, 14, 15, 16	Chaps. 4, 8, 9, 10, 11		Chaps. 17, 18, 19, 20
Kelly, Joe, *Organizational Behavior* (Homewood, Ill.: Richard D. Irwin, Inc., 1969).	Chaps. 1, 6		Chap. 11	Chaps. 2, 3, 4, 5, 7, 8, 12	Chaps. 10, 13	Chap. 14
Kolasa, Blair, *Introduction to Behavioral Science For Business* (New York: John Wiley & Sons, Inc. 1969).	Chaps. 1, 2, 3	Chaps. 11, 16, 20	Chaps. 9, 14	Chaps. 4, 5, 7, 8, 10, 12, 13, 15, 17, 18, 19	Chap. 6	

Selected Organizational Behavior Oriented Textbooks	Part I Introduction	Part II Structure of Organizations	Part III Processes within Organizations	Part IV Behavior within Organizations	Part V Climate and Organizational Development within Organizations	Part VI Application of Structural, Process, and Behavioral Concepts
Lawless, David J., *Effective Management: Social Psychological Approach* (Englewood Cliffs, N.J.: Prentice-Hall, Inc., 1972).	Chaps. 1, 19, 20, 21	Chap. 6 (109–117)	Chap. 18	Chaps. 2, 3, 4, 5, 6, 8, 9, 10, 11, 12, 13, 14, 15, 16, 17	Chap. 18	
Sayles, Leonard R. and Strauss, George, *Human Behavior in Organizations* (Englewood Cliffs, N.J.: Prentice-Hall, Inc, 1966).	Chap. 19	Chap. 18	Chaps. 7, 10, 15	Chaps. 1, 2, 3, 4, 6, 8, 9, 12, 16, 17	Chap. 13	
Scott, William G. and Mitchell, Terence R., *Organization Theory* (Homewood, Ill.: Richard D. Irwin, Inc., 1972).	Chaps. 17, 18, 19, 20	Chaps. 1, 2, 3, 4, 14	Chaps. 8, 9	Chaps. 5, 6, 7, 10, 11, 12, 13	Chaps. 15, 16	
Weissenberg, Peter, *Introduction to Organizational Behavior* (Scranton, Pa.: International Textbook Co., 1971).	Chaps. 1, 2, 3, 9, 15, 16	Chaps. 4, 6		Chaps. 5, 7, 11, 12, 13, 14	Chaps. 8, 10	
Whyte, William Foote, *Organizational Behavior* (Homewood, Ill.: Richard D. Irwin, Inc., 1969).	Chaps. 1, 2, 32	Chap. 3	Chaps. 29, 30	Chaps. 4, 5, 6, 7, 8, 9, 10, 11, 12, 13, 14, 15	Chaps. 24, 25, 27	Chaps. 31, 32, 33

Part I

INTRODUCTION

The articles in this section introduce four recurring themes in the management and organization literature. At the highest level of abstraction is the process of theory development, particularly the development of theories which integrate what is known about organizational behavior and which indicate what is not known. A prerequisite for theory is a conceptual framework, that is a catalog system which permits the researcher, student, and manager to classify organizational phenomena. The framework which the editors used to classify the articles in this book recognizes three major organizational variables: *structure, process,* and *behavior.* An integrative theory would describe and explain the relationships among these three major variables, as well as the relationships among subordinate variables. The current literature suggests that general systems theory offers the best likelihood of developing an integrative theory of organization.

A second theme of this book is the contribution that the behavioral sciences can make to our understanding of organizational behavior. The literature of psychology, sociology, social psychology, and anthropology is the source of many of the articles chosen. Other articles from the broader literature of management and business administration which use behavioral science theories, concepts, or methods of inquiry have also been included. Our purpose is to demonstrate that the behavioral sciences are rich sources of understanding about the way people behave in organizational settings.

Our third theme is that managers of organizations must come to know and appreciate the behavioral science contributions. To this end, we have included a selection of articles which deal with the practical problems of

1

modifying organizations. The literature of organizational development and the management of change has increased substantially in the past several years through the efforts of behavioral scientists in particular. The articles in this section speak to a number of issues that managers must confront as they engage in the process of developing the capability of their organizations.

The final theme and the one which is seemingly more concrete is that of organizational effectiveness. This theme pervades the entire book. The authors whose work is represented here are concerned with various aspects of organizational effectiveness. Thus they write about leadership effectiveness, group effectiveness, communication effectiveness, structural effectiveness, and the like. They also are concerned with conceptual and measurement problems of effectiveness. What is effectiveness? How should it be measured? These questions are not easily resolved, as the reader will come to realize.

The four articles which comprise this first section introduce these four themes. We begin with the theme of theory building.

Bernard P. Indik's article, "Toward an Effective Theory of Organizational Behavior" quotes Kurt Lewin's comment that there is nothing so practical as a good theory. Indik then proceeds to show the necessity for a framework which can be used to classify information about organizations. The framework which he proposes is quite compatible with the one which we have used to classify the articles in this reader. Indeed, Indik identifies organization structure, processes, and behavior (group and individual) variables and then further elaborates each of these three major classes. As Indik notes, a conceptual framework is not an integrative theory, but it is the necessary first step in the process of theory building. Whatever one's particular interest in organizations, whether as theoretician, researcher, or manager, a consistent framework for classifying organizational phenomena is essential.

The second and corollary theme is that knowledge of the behavioral sciences makes important contributions to the management of organizations. This theme is introduced and developed by Gordon L. Lippitt in the second article of this section, "Implications of the Behavioral Sciences for Management." Lippitt surveys the findings of selected research on group behavior, intergroup relations, social systems, communications, decision making, leadership, development, and change from the perspective of managerial relevance. From this perspective, he derives implications for management *and* for future research.

A third theme is the emphasis on management. Professor Mintzberg's article, "Managerial Work: Analysis from Observation" reports research on managerial behavior. He argues that earlier descriptions of managerial work behavior in terms of planning, organizing, coordinating, and controlling are not meaningful. The author bases his conclusion on observations of the chief executives of a consulting firm, a school system, a technology firm, a manufacturer, and a hospital. He postulates that managerial work in large organizations is better described in terms of three role behaviors: interpersonal, informational, and decisional roles. In this context, the manager is viewed as a facilitator of organization processes.

The final article in this part, "A System Resource Approach to Organizational Effectiveness," is authored by Ephraim Yuchtman and Stanley Seashore. Their article addresses the issue of organizational effectiveness, thus introducing the fourth major theme of the book. Yuchtman and Seashore propose that organizational effectiveness must be evaluated in systems theory terms. Systems theory focuses attention away from a narrow concern with the organization's goals and toward a broader concern with the organization's relationships with its environment and with its components. A multidimensional set of criteria is offered as an alternative to the single-dimensional goal approach.

The themes of theory, behavioral science, management, and effectiveness appear throughout the next five parts. The final part integrates these themes in the context of actual case studies in three companies.

1

Toward an Effective Theory
of Organization Behavior
BERNARD P. INDIK

Some years ago Kurt Lewin said, "There is nothing so practical as a good theory." By this he was referring to the point that if you had an effective theory that you could operate by, you could make your practical decisions very efficiently. And what's more, they would be more likely correct than if you did not have this kind of theory. All too often, I think, we have forgotten Lewin's dictum, for many times in looking for the answer to a particular problem we have looked only at the very specific nature of that problem. This sort of piecemeal narrow approach has led us down the primrose path. As a result, we know a little bit about a lot of things and have very little perspective on what the whole picture is. This specifically applies to our knowledge of how people behave in groups within organizations.

Many have been dismayed by the way in which the various studies have been done. For example, with relation to productivity, absenteeism and turnover, we have been attempting to predict each of these three dimensions. We sometimes come up with very, very different findings, depending on all sorts of characteristics of the situation and the personnel involved. True, there are general trends; we find some kind of simple relationships, but most often we find that the relationships are not simple.

Source: Reprinted by permission from Bernard P. Indik, "Toward an Effective Theory of Organization Behavior," *Personnel Administration*, July-August 1968, pp. 51–59; copyright 1968, Society for Personnel Administration, Washington, D.C. 20004.

Furthermore, we have not been able, effectively, to combine the pieces of information that have become available to us. Why is this? Fundamentally because we have not faced up to the problems of building an adequate taxonomy or theory, so that we can organize the tremendous fund of fragmented information that we now have available to us. Without some kind of framework for organizing the information now available, we face not only inadequate theory, or inefficient theory, but inability to handle the large number of facts that we have been able to accumulate. Further, one of the extremely useful characteristics of a good theory is that it suggests new hypotheses as well as helps to order present findings. Most of the theories or hypotheses that have been developed up to now are little more than strong hunches. They have not been embedded in any larger framework so that systematic propositions could be developed.

A useful framework for organizing information which is relevant in developing a theory of organizational behavior would recognize the following seven general classes of variables: (1) organization structure; (2) organization process and function; (3) small group structure; (4) small group process and function; (5) organizationally relevant individual attitudes, perceptions, abilities, temperaments and motivations; (6) organizationally relevant individual behaviors; and (7) organizational environment. (See Figure 1.)

Organization structure would include those attributes of organizations that are relatively static over time. These include: (1) organization size; (2) span of control; (3) the number of authority levels in the organization; (4) the authority structure; (5) the communication structure; (6) the degree

FIGURE 1

Organizational Environment

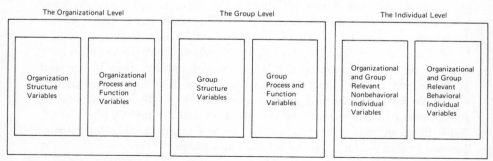

* The three pairs of categories of variables are paired because it is expected that the variables at the same level of analysis are more likely and consistently related to each other. Further we expect that variables in categories to be directly closest to each other will be more likely to be related to each other. Two-way reflexive relationships will be frequently found. Finally, we expect that there will be tendencies for variables to show either positive or negative interrelationships consistently, but the amount of these relationships and sometimes the signs of those relationships will be dependent on the conditions, relations and interactions of other related variables.

of task specification; (7) the degree of task interdependence; (8) the degree of task specialization; (9) the status and prestige structure; (10) the psychological distance between the decision-making and the operating levels in the organization.

Organizational functions and processes would include:

1. Communication
   a) The average amount of communication interaction within the organization
   b) The distribution of that communication interaction.
2. Influence that is developed in the organization
   a) The amount of influence
   b) The distribution of influence
   c) The discrepancy between the actual distribution of influence and the desired distribution of influence in the organization.
3. Coordination, the process by which the parts of the organization are geared and articulated toward the objectives of the whole organization.
4. Organizational socialization processes
   a) The recruitment process
   b) The orientation and adaptation process
   c) The reward process
5. Supervision
   a) Initiating structure
   b) Consideration
   c) Leadership style
   d) Supervisory skill mix
6. Adaptability to change
7. The conflict control process
8. The degree of bureaucracy
9. The amount and distribution of communication interaction by members of the organization with non-organization members for organizational purposes.

The next two sets of variables refer to the small group level of analysis. The first may be called *small group structure variables.* These very closely parallel the organization structure class of variables and include: (1) size of the group; (2) the authority structure of the group; (3) the communication structure of the group; (4) the degree of task specification; (5) the degree of task interdependence; (6) the degree of task specialization; (7) the status and prestige structure of the group; (8) the psychological distance between the leaders of the group and the rest of its members.

The *group function* or *process* category of variables also very closely parallels the organizational function and process class of variables. It includes:

1. Communications
    a) The average amount of communication interaction in the group.
    b) The distribution of communication interaction within the group.
    c) The proportion of socioemotional negative communications.
    d) The proportion of socioemotional positive communications.
    e) The proportion of "asking for information" communication.
    f) The proportion of "giving information" communication.
    g) The amount and distribution of communication with the larger system in the organization.
2. The influence process
    a) The amount of influence exerted by members of the group.
    b) The distribution of influence exerted by members of the group.
    c) The discrepancy between actual distribution of influence and the desired distribution of influence.
    d) The amount of influence which comes from a larger system.
3. Coordination
    a) The extent to which the parts of the group are geared and articulated to the objectives of the group.
    b) The clarity of understanding of the goals by the members.
    c) The extent to which the parts of the group are articulated toward the objectives of the larger organization.
4. The group socialization processes
    a) The recruitment process.
    b) The orientation and adaptation process.
    c) The reward process.
5. The supervision process
    a) Initiating structure.
    b) Consideration.
    c) Leadership style.
    d) Supervisory skill mix.
6. Adaptability to change
7. The conflict control processes
8. The degree of mutual understanding of role relationships
9. The degree of bureaucracy

The fifth general category or class of variables are *individual, non-behavioral variables that are relevant to group and organizational functioning*. These include:

1. Motivational variables
    a) Need for achievement.
    b) Need for affiliation.
    c) Need for power.
    d) Need for ego support.
    e) Need for status and recognition.

   f) Need for affection.
   g) Need for acquisition.
2. Attitudinal variables
   a) The attitude toward the organization.
   b) The attitude toward supervision.
   c) The attitude toward the work group.
   d) Attitude toward the job.
      (i) Intrinsic job satisfaction.
      (ii) Extrinsic job satisfaction.
   e) Attitude toward the local union or union-like organization.
3. The perceptual role relations variables
   a) The discrepancies between perceived expectations in the individual, and his experiences as he sees them.
   b) The job-related stresses that he sees.
   c) The role conflicts, as he views them.
4. The aptitude variables, which differ from the attitude variables and the motivational variables in that the variables in this sub-category reflect the capabilities and capacities of the individuals to perform organizationally relevant behaviors. In this sense they form the upper and lower limits on their behavioral tendencies.
   a) Perceptual variables.
      (i)   Color sensitivity.
      (ii) Attention.
      (iii) Length estimation.
      (iv) Sensitivity to visual movement.
      (v)   Auditory sensitivity, etc.
   b) The psychomotor dimensions.
      (i)   Strength.
      (ii) Impulsion.
      (iii) Motor speed.
      (iv) Static precision.
      (v)   Dynamic precision.
      (vi) Coordination (this is motor coordination).
   c) The intellectual dimensions.
      (i)   Memory.
      (ii) Visual cognition.
      (iii) Auditory cognition.
      (iv) Symbolic cognition.
      (v)   Verbal comprehension.
      (vi) Etc. (as per Guilford, 1959).
   d) Evaluative factors—These abilities have to do with testing information and conclusions as to their suitability.
      (i) Judgments of identity.
      (ii) Judgments of relations.

(iii) Factors for judging in terms of systematic consistency.

(iv) Factors involving judgment of goal satisfaction.

5. The dimensions of temperament—These include those temperamental traits that have to do with the manner in which actions occur.

  a) Factors of general disposition.

  b) Factors of emotional disposition.

  c) Factors of social disposition.

  d) Masculinity versus femininity.

  e) Personal tempo (that is, rate of movement).

  f) Perseveration (which is the mental inertia versus the quickness of originality).

  g) Oscillation.

  h) Suggestibility.

The latter several lists of variables have been very carefully researched in the area of personality measurement and are more clearly distinguishable than have been the variables specified prior to this category.

The sixth general category includes *those organizationally relevant individual behaviors* that we are frequently most concerned with in studying organizational behavior. These include:

1. Member job outputs

  a) The relative number of job cycle units per unit time (this refers to repetitive jobs).

  b) The relative quality of job performance in repetitive type jobs.

  c) The relative amount of job performance of unequal units of job performance in complex jobs.

  d) The relative quality of performance of unequal units of job performance in complex jobs.

2. Member participation—that is, the relative frequency of attendance when attendance is expected by the organization.

  a) The attendance rates.

  b) One minus the turnover rates.

  c) One minus the lateness rates.

3. The strain symptoms that are characteristic of the organization. This category of variables refers to those behavioral forces generated within the system by individuals in response to stress phenomenologically in the individual. They are indicated by discomfort and malfunction.

  a) The rate of inappropriate individual behavior for the individual.

  b) The rate of inappropriate behavior for the organization.

  c) The rate of inappropriate behavior for the group.

The seventh major category of variables that one should consider is the *organizational environment*. These include:

1. The various natural aspects of the environment

    a) Weather.
    b) Gravity.
    c) Terrain.
    d) Natural resources.
2. The availability of resources that are needed by the organization
    a) Personnel resources.
    b) Material resources.
    c) Market resources.
    d) Financial resources.
    e) Technological resources.
3. The structural relations with the social environment
    a) The technological structure.
    b) The amount of contact with non-organizational personnel.
    c) The dependence on the social environment.
    d) Etc. (See Sells, 1963.)

There is a whole roster, of course, of other environmental characteristics that influence the relationships and behavior of system members.

What is the value of all this specification of a large number of variables, with reference to the problems of understanding organizational behavior, or more accurately, individual behavior in groups and organizations? What do we know now that we didn't know before? Furthermore, what promise does the present system have for payoff in the future?

The present system is essentially a set of building blocks, of more or less clear structure—a rudimentary framework that can be built upon, elaborated, simplified, clarified, and tested. Up to this point we have had only a very limited view of the variables that influence behavior of members of organizations. This is not an exhaustive system, just a beginning. It does give some indication of the complexity of the problem that we face in understanding individual behavior in groups and organizations and points out the deficiencies of a more simple approach.

First of all, this systematization helps us organize the information that is presently available about the *adequacy* of measures of each of the variables. (Indik *et al.*, 1968.) Thus we find that many dimensions have not been well measured, a large number are reasonably well measured, and most of the dimensions have only crude measurement techniques available for them. Furthermore, we find that inadequate measurement is most prevalent with respect to group and organizational variables. Much more has been done with respect to providing reliable and valid measures of individual variables. Possibly then, some explanations of the inconsistency of findings may be based on unreliable, invalid, or inappropriate measures.

The systematic classification of variables facilitates the development of a compendium (Indik *et al.*, 1968)—a catalog of measures that are presently available and some estimates as to the adequacy of these measures for the variables that we have been considering here. The literature is very diversely found and very diversely held. Hopefully, over the long run, it should be possible to provide a roster of measures and information on their adequacy with reference to any and all the variables in this scheme. Secondly, it should be possible to specify more clearly what set of mutually exclusive variables should be conceived of within each of the general categories of variables to be considered. Stogdill's recent work is helpful on this problem (Stogdill, 1965). Both Stogdill's efforts and our own seem to indicate that different kinds of organizations generate differentially important descriptive dimensions. (Indik, 1965.)

Such a compendium should be useful in solving the basic question of how a given dimension shall be measured. There are innumerable measures of some specific concepts, and there is no standardized agreement as to how they should be measured. Very frequently it is left up to the predilection of the particular measurer rather than to objective criteria. Hopefully there may be some kind of criteria, generally psychometric criteria, on which to base opinions as to the adequacy of measurement.

Third, the systematic framework will help organize theoretically the research findings as they accumulate. The theory that develops, of course, will be somewhat complex but should enable us to understand organizational behavior much more adequately than we do today.

Fourth, the theory that emerges will enable us to suggest which variables or factors are important to consider when one is attempting to understand what causes variation in, for example, member absenteeism or member job output. Today, we tend to fly by the seat of our pants. Tomorrow maybe we can, on the basis of a practical theory built on supporting evidence and a clear classification scheme, select the appropriate variables; and by this selection indicate the range of possible managerial actions and indicate the relative effectiveness of each of the potential choices of action.

REFERENCES

The research reported in this article was supported by the Group Psychology Branch, Office of Naval Research, under Contract Nonr–404(10) and Nonr–001. (Reproduction, translation, publication, use and disposal in whole or in part by or for the United States Government is permitted.)

Guilford, J. P. *Personality,* New York: McGraw Hill Book Co. Inc., 1959.

Indik, B. P. "The relationship between organization size and supervision ratio." *Administrative Science Quarterly,* 1964, 9, 3, 301–12.

Indik, B. P. *The Study of Organizational and Relevant Small Group and Individual Dimensions,* Technical Report No. 13, Rutgers, The State University, New Brunswick, N.J., 1963.

Indik, B. P. *Three Studies of Organizational and Individual Dimensions of Organizations,* Technical Report No. 15, Rutgers, The State University, New Brunswick, N.J., 1965.

Indik, B. P., and Berrien, F. K. (ed.).   *People, Groups and Organizations,* New York, Teachers College, Columbia Press, 1968.

Indik, B. P., Georgopoulos, B. S. and Seashore, S. E.   "Superior-subordinate relationships and performance," *Personnel Psychology,* 1961, 14, 4, 357–71.

Indik, B. P., Hockmeyer, M. and Castore, C. A.   *Compendium of Measures of Individuals, Groups and Organizations Relevant to the Study of Organizational Behavior,* Technical Report No. 16, Rutgers, The State University, New Brunswick, N.J. 1968 (forthcoming).

Sells, S. B.   *Stimulus Determinants of Behavior,* New York, Ronald Press Co., 1963.

Stogdill, R. M.   *Managers, Employees and Organizations,* Bureau of Business Research, Ohio State University, Columbus, Ohio, 1965.

2

Implications of the Behavioral Sciences for Management

GORDON L. LIPPITT

In the past 20 years the behavioral sciences have made an ever-growing contribution to the field of management. In the textbooks in schools of business and public administration, in the executive development programs of government and industry, we find constant reference to the mounting importance of behavioral sciences to our understanding of organizational management. One reason has been the increased quality and quantity of research in organizational problems; another, and related reason, the increased demand by management for answers to organizational problems that become more and more complex.

Behavioral science and management together cover a vast area. The behavioral sciences are usually thought of as being psychology, sociology, and cultural anthropology. While these may be the three major behavioral sciences, it is well to include the behavioral aspects of political science, economics, educational psychology, and biology. The behavioral sciences are defined in different terms by different scholars. Manek S. Wadia defines it this way in "Management Education and the Behavioral Sciences" *(Advanced Management, XXIV:9)*:

Source: Reprinted by permission of the author and publisher from *Public Personnel Review*, Vol. 27 (1966), pp. 184–91. This article is based on an address presented March 16, 1966, in the Distinguished Lecture Series on Management sponsored by Southeastern University in Washington, D.C.

A behavioral science is a body of systemized knowledge pertaining to how people behave, what is the relationship between human behavior and the total environment, and why people behave as they do.

In a real sense, behavioral science is the study of the problem-solving behavior of man. Using this definition, one can envision readily its importance to the processes, concepts, and practices of management. New findings in the behavioral sciences are relevant to management as well as to systems of the culture.

AREAS OF BASIC RESEARCH

This section of the paper will identify some of the areas of basic research in the behavioral sciences that are contributing to a deeper understanding of the human element in organizational systems.

In the past 25 years, both scholars and practitioners have become increasingly aware that management is influenced by a host of noneconomic factors as well as the traditional economic ones. One reason has been the extensive research in the field of human motivation. Earlier concepts of motivation to the effect that people inherit most of their capability to perform well, and that they are influenced only by reward or punishment, have been shown to be an inadequate basis for the understanding of human behavior.

Management is aware that employees and managers themselves harbor expectations and needs that yearn for satisfaction. We realize that man is often motivated by social needs, and obtains many of his basic satisfactions through relationships with others. In these relationships, man desires ego satisfaction as well as a feeling of accomplishment. As we look at Dr. Maslow's "hierarchy of needs concept," we become aware of the various levels of man's needs which prompt him to search constantly for self-identification and self-realization.

Most management practitioners and theorists today recognize that people in organizations develop a "psychological contract" between themselves and the organization. Dr. H. Levinson of the Menninger Foundation refers to this process as "reciprocation." In other words, the organization enforces its expectation through the use of power and authority, while the employee enforces his expectation by attempting to influence the organization or by withholding his participation and involvement—as when he goes on a strike or alienates himself. Both parties in this psychological contract are guided by assumptions as to what is fair, equitable, and correct. Research into the behavior of the individual has brought new insights and heightened perception to his understanding of others, and of himself. Especially important to management today is research into individual performance in the organizational structure. Personality studies have furthered understanding of the early life of the individual, and of his behavior pattern as an adult in a working situation. Such research not only is providing us with deeper knowledge of the individual, but is prompting us to reassess our previous assumptions about personal motivation.

Examining Dyadic Relationship

Social interaction involves two or more individuals. The relationship between one individual and another is the smallest of groups. As Dr. George C. Homans points out in his book, *The Human Group* (New York: Harcourt, Brace, 1950), the paired relationship represents man's most natural attempt at socialization. Whether one focuses on the influence of one's peer and its effect in a working relationship, or examines the superior-subordinate relationship as another dyad, it is obvious that the two-person relationship is inevitable in organizational behavior and management practice.

Studies tell us much more than we knew formerly about the distribution of power between superior and subordinate, and how its use or abuse affects morale, productivity, and human satisfactions. It is important to note that the more reciprocal the attempts of two individuals to influence one another, the more effective the relationship. This is true even though the degree of reciprocity may vary considerably with the nature of the work and other factors. Trust between the persons in a two-person relationship, of course, is of prime importance. Another less obvious factor important to the growth and development of a relationship is the manner in which the feedback from one to the other in the dyad is conducted. These are only a few of the considerations in two-person relationships that illustrate the importance of this smallest subsystem to the organizational system as a whole.

Research on Group Behavior

Down through the years, the small group has remained the most crucial form of social organization. This is highlighted by Dr. Abraham Zaleznik and Dr. David Moment in *The Dynamics of Interpersonal Behavior* (John Wiley & Sons, Inc., New York, N.Y., 1964), when they comment as follows:

Although the small group lies at the foundation of society and persists despite the rise and fall of institutions in the large social structure, it is also true that the effectiveness of large-scale organizations depends, in large measure, on the development of effective small groups. Not only must groups build their own cohesion and continually resolve their own internal problems, they must also maintain a positive identification with other groups and with a larger organization. The fact that small groups satisfy important human needs assures their survival as a form of organization. But this does not assure the development of effective groups and consequently effective organizations in the larger institutions of society. It is on this point that administrators or applied social scientists face an important challenge.

Research in group dynamics has contributed vitally to the behavioral sciences in the last two decades. Studies of how a group behaves in terms of its communication patterns, norms, cohesion, goals, procedures, leadership, and membership has formed a mosaic of new and useful knowledge. These research results also are furthering our understanding of group relationships which involve working morale and productivity.

Intergroup Relationships

The organization is made up of many groups that develop a complex of relationships to build its processes and substance. These intergroup relationships have been studied by both sociologists and psychologists during the past two decades. To study the effects of cooperation and competition between and among groups is important for the manager in today's organization. The work of Sherif and Blake in Texas on the factors affecting cooperation and competition have contributed to our understanding of this significant area of behavior. This research indicates that competing groups see one another as the enemy. According to R. R. Blake and Jane B. Mouton in "Reactions to Intergroup Competition Under Win-Lose Conditions" (*Management Science*, 1961, VII), distorted views of group value occur, therefore, and behavior becomes stereotyped, with members of one group refusing to listen to the other. Studies and experience indicate that the resolution or reduction of intergroup conflict will contribute greatly to the achievement of organizational goals. Interaction, rotation of members amongst groups, avoidance of win-lose situations, and focus on total group objectives are useful ways to lessen intergroup conflict and develop collaborative relationships—even between labor and management.

Organizations as Social Systems

Sociologists have contributed to the understanding of the organization as a social system. In one way, the organization can be seen as a system of systems. It is helpful for the student and practitioner of management to recognize that the various subsystems that make up the complex organism of the organization have certain elements in common. The fact that the individual, dyad, group, and total organization share goals, perpetuation, communications, norms, roles, and values provides a link to the understanding of these subsystems. The work of such sociologists as Dr. Charles Loomis has contributed a great deal to such understanding which is extremely important to management. In *Organizational Psychology* (Prentice-Hall, Inc., Englewood Cliffs, N. J., 1965), Dr. Edgar Schein states:

> Perhaps the most important argument for a systems conception of organization is that the environment within which organizations exist is becoming increasingly unstable. With the rapid growth of technology, the expansion of economic markets, and rapid social political change, come constant pressures for organizations to change, adapt, and grow to meet the challenges of the environment. And, as one examines this process, one is struck that it is the total organization, not merely some key individuals, who must be studied if this process is to be properly understood.

Seeing the organization as a social system is not the prerogative of only the sociologists. Research at the Tavistock Institute on the concept of the organization as a social-technical system, requiring attention to both production and people, has helped to integrate management sciences with behavioral sciences. Dr. Rensis Likert at the University of Michigan has developed the concept of the overlapping group model of an organization. He sees the organization as a system of interlocking groups connected by individuals who occupy key and dual positions as leaders of one group and members of another.

Research on Larger Systems

In reporting behavioral science research and its implications for management, one should not neglect the extremely important contribution being made in the field of cultural anthropology. As anthropologists study the culture, they uncover systems of beliefs and practices that affect the way organizations work and exist. The cultural views of work, honesty, leadership, and other concepts affect how individuals, groups, and organizations behave. We have seen tremendous effects on the norms of our culture in the last 20 years. Dr. Clyde Kluckhohn has defined culture as "the historically created designs for living, explicit and implicit, rational, irrational, and nonrational which exist at any given time as potential guides for the behavior of man."

It is in these areas that man finds the rationale for definitions of achievement, values, and the successful life. In this modern age, as organizations, both governmental and business, become more international, we must think not only in organizational frames of reference, but also in cultural and cross-cultural terms. The next step in our process of thinking about behavioral science and management will be to look at the implications of some specific areas of research.

RESEARCH INTO MANAGING PROCESS

In addition to the studies of subsystems in the organization, behavioral science has conducted research into some of the processes of managing. Let us take a look at a selective sample of those areas.

Process of Communication

The communication process and how it works in interpersonal dynamics has been evaluated by psychologists and sociologists. The factors that affect communication have been analyzed and organized to make more effective the understanding of the two-way processes involved. Research indicates that a manager devotes considerable time to the listening process. Some of the filters that affect listening have been identified. The work has covered the informal communication system within organizations as well as the formal. Sociologists have explored the concept of the "self-fulfilling prophecy" in communication. These explorations indicate that inputs from the sender come back to him as outputs from the receiver. Thus, confirmation is provided of his original set of intentions and assumptions which began the communication cycle.

Research into the effectiveness of various styles of communication, values of participation in group behavior, and the relationship of information to people's commitment to the task are but a few areas that have implications for management. The correct use of information and its transmission are important dimensions of the management process.

Decision-Making Process

Research in the behavioral sciences has raised some questions about the most effective way to make decisions. It has explored the effect of hierarchy in organizations and the use of that authority. A variety of research studies on decision making have challenged some of the uses of the manager's authority. Some research has focused on the sources and supply of information for decision making, some research has been directed at improving the capability of the skills of the individual administrator, and other studies have been concerned with decision making as a complex process. Decision making is seen as a process in which many persons in the organization exert their influence, not just those at the policy or management level. As Professor McCamy of the University of Wisconsin has pointed out:

> . . . No single individual alone ever makes decisions in administration. He is always influenced by other persons, whether present in person or in spirit, and his conclusions are the result of advice, objection,

hostility, fear, envy, admiration, contempt, or condescension, involving a complex of human relationships that pervade administration.

Today's managers should realize that it is necessary to analyze the background factors that affect decision making—the perception of the decision maker and those affected by the decision, the analytical steps in decision making, and the action and reaction to the process itself. These factors are highlighted in research on decision making by the behavioral sciences.

Research on Leadership

Many studies in the behavioral sciences are bringing new insights and understanding to the practice and theory of leadership. Early studies of leadership focused largely on the personality traits of the leader. Generally, these studies were disappointing, with little agreement about the nature and importance of any particular set of traits. In the late 1930's, several pioneering studies were made of autocratic, democratic, and laissez-faire styles of leadership. More recently, researchers have focused on the functions of leadership that are necessary to get a particular job done. Some of the research has focused on the leadership actions that affect group action.

Neither behavioral sciences nor successful leaders can give a simple, definitive answer to the question of what constitutes effective leadership. Emerging research results indicate that an effective leader is one who is flexible rather than rigid. An effective leader is aware of forces in himself and understands his own motivation. An effective leader is one who builds trust relationships with those he leads. An effective leader is one who takes into account both the short-range and long-range nature of the situation and involves those who are to implement the decision in making the decision. A concept of a leadership continuum has developed in the last few years out of the work of Tannenbaum and Schmidt. They indicate that the forces in the leader, forces in group members, and forces in the situation make it necessary for a leader to respond with a particular style of leadership that is appropriate to that situation.

Developing Others

Research by the behavioral sciences in the learning process is also contributing to the successful practice of management. Recognizing that people come into a learning situation with an image of themselves as self-directing and responsible persons—not as dependent individuals—is one of the important realities to a superior trying to develop his subordinates. Also we know from behavioral science research that there are different levels of change in the development process. We know that people can increase their knowledge, insight, understanding, skills, attitudes, values, and interests; and we know that different methods are involved in developing different levels of these skills or knowledge. Research in the behavioral sciences indicates the following facts about the development process:

1. Self-development is an internal process and is related to the individual's having had an experience with a problem or having recognized a gap in his own skills or knowledge.
2. Learning is more efficient when the goals are clear.
3. Learning involves change in behavior—and change tends to be resisted.
4. Learning is facilitated and strengthened through group experience.
5. Learning is enhanced by evidence of progress.

This is, of course, an abbreviated list, but suggests some of the implications for management in recent research on effective leadership in an organization.

Research on Process of Change

Behavioral scientists have been studying the process of change during the past 10 years. They have found that high-producing work units consistently have foremen whose understanding of the personal needs of workers is superior to that of foremen in low-producing units. Sociologists and psychologists have studied productivity, morale, and change within groups and discovered that it is affected by the degree of cohesiveness. The processes of planned change are also being studied by the behavioral scientists. It has been shown that people tend to resist change when they are not involved in the planning for change, when change is ambiguous, when it does not take into account group norms, when it is made for personal reasons, when there is poor communication, and when the rewards for making the change are inadequate or seen as inadequate by those concerned.

Related Areas of Research

The behavioral scientists have conducted other kinds of studies that are related to the processes of management. One can examine research done in the field of selection, on the evaluation of training, studies made relative to the effects of certain kinds of work and psychosomatic illness, the relationship of different acts of delegation and its effect on the subordinate, research into the role-performance concept and theory of organizations, research on morale and productivity, and many other areas of direct concern and value to management. This paper is not intended to cover all the areas of research, but rather to suggest the pattern of exploration that is rapidly developing in this portion of professional management.

IMPLICATIONS OF RESEARCH STUDIES

The implications of these various research studies are multiple. It is obvious that behavioral science research is causing us to re-examine our assumptions about people and their motivation. It is also giving us a better understanding of the behavior pattern of managers and the effects of their leadership within the organization. The following are implications that seem to be most important:

Implication No. 1: The increased interdependence between the creators and appliers of knowledge. Research coming from behavioral science indicates a need for a closer link between those who do research and create new knowledge, and those who apply knowledge. A manager who graduated from a school of business administration or public administration 10 years ago may be out of date now. Rapid obsolescence of the manager makes it important to be creative about the inter-relationships of organizational researchers and management. This relationship between management and research scientists needs to be developed, and their common concerns more closely interwoven to stimulate further study and mutual benefits.

Implication No. 2: Closer focus on the education of managers. The rapid obsolescence rate of today's managers makes it a prerequisite to develop management through both internal and external (to the organization) training and educational programs. Opportunities for managers to be upgraded in new knowledge and skills is of first priority.

Implication No. 3: A situational focus on the role, skills, and practice of managerial leaders. The research on leadership indicates that there is no one concept or simple set of rules for effective leadership. It is increasingly obvious that the manager must examine each situation and the persons in that situation to determine the appropriate action. More and more managers are coming to realize the relative importance of focusing on the situation, as opposed to proceeding on the assumption that there exists a ready-made set of all-weather techniques which guarantee effective leadership.

Implication No. 4: Need for developing adaptive organizational systems so that organizations can remain viable for the future. Research indicates that the organization of the future must remain adaptive. It will need to remain flexible to cope with consumers, services, production techniques, technical skills, changing marketing conditions, economic forces, and all the other many factors that affect an organization. A particular theory of management suggesting that either scientific management or human relations is the right approach will not be adequate. Management needs to recognize that the organization has to meet the multiple requirements of the various social systems to which it is related. The organization of the future must be adaptive to remain viable.

Implication No. 5: Greater focus on the process or transactional nature of management. Research in the behavioral sciences indicates that the quality of inter-relationships of the human parts of the organization is far more important than their quantity. In searching for quality, the manager of tomorrow needs to recognize the value of confrontation, of search, and of coping.

Implication No. 6: Need for integrating management and behavioral sciences. Research in the behavioral sciences indicates that separation of productive work requirements and human relations is ineffective management. People need a sense of accomplishment and achievement. This is best done through effective work output and production. Relatively heavy emphasis on one or the other will be inadequate. A manager needs to see the importance of both and to become competent in both.

Implication No. 7: The need for a manager to be a diagnostician rather than a treater of symptoms. Research in the behavioral sciences indicates the importance of the manager's ability to diagnose the causes of people's behavior. The treatment of symptoms is not adequate. Absenteeism, turnover, apathy at staff meetings, and similar phenomena are symptoms, not causes. The manager of tomorrow will be required to understand the dynamics of behavior to diagnose its causes and improve skills.

BETTER UTILIZATION NEEDED

It is encouraging to see increased research in behavioral science, but it is discouraging to see findings unused by management. Some of the needs for improving utilization include the following:

1. *Need to focus on behavioral problems facing practitioners.* In many cases research in the behavioral sciences has resulted from the interest of behavioral scientists and not from the practitioners. There is a great need for practitioners to confront the behavioral scientists with the questions that most concern them, and in a collaborative way, develop those research studies helpful to practitioners.

2. *Need for improved communication by those in behavioral science.* There has been considerable criticism by practitioners in management of the language and the esoteric nature of behavioral science writings. Up until 10 years ago, most behavioral science research was found in highly technical research journals. In the past few years, we have seen an increase in the number of books and applied journals that assist managers. Nevertheless, the highly technical knowledge and "gobbledygook" that finds its way into the literature is a "block" to many practitioners in securing the comprehension and understanding they desire. It behooves the behavioral scientists to improve the methods by which they communicate their findings to management and, thereby, to reach a larger audience.

3. *Need for behavioral science to focus more of its research on large*

organizational phenomena. We are living in a society made up of organizations of continually increasing size. Whether we think of large government, large business, large labor, large churches, or large welfare institutions, we can see that this increased size creates greater and greater complexity. Such complexity makes it more difficult to do the research, but makes the challenge all the greater. The problems of large bureaucracy need more attention in the behavioral science research of the future.

4. *Need for replication of research for greater validity of the findings.* Much of the research in behavioral science is reported from individual university research centers where the sample is relatively small. This causes many practitioners to question the applicability of the findings to varied settings. There is a great need for the encouragement of inter-university planning of research so that replication within the same theoretical formulation and conceptual framework might take place in different settings with different samples. The results could then be more widely applied.

5. *A need for cross-cultural comparison studies.* Much of the research in the behavioral sciences has taken place in the United States and northern European countries. There has been too little cross-cultural comparisons of the findings on leadership, human behavior, management, and organizational phenomena. Undoubtedly, cultural values and cultural differences greatly affect the accepted mode of behavior in these different organizational settings. Such comparisons are needed to test the validity of findings as they might apply in the developing countries. This is vital if we are to raise the level of professional management in all continents of the world.

6. *Need for increased emphasis on the multi-disciplinary approach to the complex problems of today's management.* It is a prime necessity that both practitioners and behavioral scientists recognize that the problems of today's organizations require multi-disciplinary efforts. There is still a considerable amount of parochial interest in single disciplines that may be appropriate, but at the same time is limiting when related to the larger problems of organizational management. It is necessary to further the cross-pollenization of the disciplines.

7. *Need for a closer linkage between management science and the behavioral science.* The information and operational systems people who are developing many valuable concepts and methods frequently are not being related to the behavioral scientists and their work. There is an urgent need for greater collaboration and integration of these two major contributors to the field of management.

8. *A need for improved behavioral science methods to study complex phenomena.* In achieving their status in the past quarter of a century, the behavioral sciences frequently have utilized the method of the physical sciences. While this has been valuable, the behavioral scientists have found it necessary to invent new methods of research to fit the conditions of

their endeavor. One of these conditions, of course, is that the behavioral scientists cannot control all the variables as easily as the physical scientists. Thus, it has been a challenge to develop methods that are scientifically respectable and will contribute to sound research. While methods of action research, survey research, field analysis concepts, and other approaches have been developed, it is important that other methods be evolved to conduct sound research on the complex phenomena in the society of tomorrow.

SUMMARY

Behavioral science is making many contributions to our understanding of organizational complexities. The organization is a complex open system that has multiple subsystems and functions. These subsystems have mutual dependence and interdependence. We recognize that the organization exists in a dynamic environment consisting of other systems which affect it. As the behavioral scientists look at the managerial effectiveness of these organizations, they must examine the effectiveness in terms of the complexity indicated above.

Earlier theorists of organization were content to talk of measuring effectiveness in terms of adequate profits, efficient service, good productivity, or effective employee morale. These are not adequate in and of themselves. Managers of an organizational system need to define its effectiveness in terms of its capacity to survive, maintain itself, adapt, and to develop toward its own goals and in the performance of multiple functions that also affect society. Dr. Warren Bennis comments on this matter as follows:

If we view organizations as adaptive, problem solving, organic structures, then inferences about effectiveness have to be made, not from static measures of output, though these may be helpful, but on the basis of the processes through which the organization approaches problems. In other words, no single measurement of organizational efficiency or satisfaction—no single time-slice of organizational performance—can provide indicators of organizational health.

Such criteria for effectiveness brings a challenge to both the behavioral scientists and management to continue their search for understanding of the complexities of today's organizational systems, including the confrontation-search-coping cycle common to all.

REFERENCES

Kluckhohn, C., & Kelby, W. The concept of culture. In R. Linton (ed.), *The Science of Man*. New York: Columbia University Press, 1945.
Loomis, C. *Social Systems*. Princeton, N. J.: D. Van Nostrand, 1960.

3

Managerial Work:
Analysis from Observation

HENRY MINTZBERG

What do managers do? Ask this question and you will likely be told that managers plan, organize, coordinate, and control. Since Henri Fayol [9]* first proposed these words in 1916, they have dominated the vocabulary of management. (See, for example, [8], [12], [17].) How valuable are they in describing managerial work? Consider one morning's work of the president of a large organization:

As he enters his office at 8:23, the manager's secretary motions for him to pick up the telephone. "Jerry, there was a bad fire in the plant last night, about $30,000 damage. We should be back in operation by Wednesday. Thought you should know."

At 8:45, a Mr. Jamison is ushered into the manager's office. They discuss Mr. Jamison's retirement plans and his cottage in New Hampshire. Then the manager presents a plaque to him commemorating his thirty-two years with the organization.

Mail processing follows: An innocent-looking letter, signed by a Detroit lawyer, reads: "A group of us in Detroit has decided not to buy any of your products because you used that anti-flag, anti-

---

Source: Reprinted by permission from Henry Mintzberg, "Managerial Work: Analysis from Observation," *Management Science*, October 1971. B97–B110.

* Numbers refer to References at the end of the article.

American pinko, Bill Lindell, upon your Thursday night TV show."
The manager dictates a restrained reply.

The 10:00 meeting is scheduled by a professional staffer. He
claims that his superior, a high-ranking vice-president of the organization, mistreats his staff, and that if the man is not fired, they will
all walk out. As soon as the meeting ends, the manager rearranges
his schedule to investigate the claim and to react to this crisis.

Which of these activities may be called planning, and which may be
called organizing, coordinating, and controlling? Indeed, what do words
such as "coordinating" and "planning" mean in the context of real activity?
In fact, these four words do not describe the actual work of managers at
all; they describe certain vague objectives of managerial work. ". . . they are
just ways of indicating what we need to explain." [1, p. 537]

Other approaches to the study of managerial work have developed,
one dealing with managerial decision-making and policy-making
processes, another with the manager's interpersonal activities. (See, for
example, [2] and [10].) And some empirical researchers, using the "diary"
method, have studied, what might be called, managerial "media"—by
what means, with whom, how long, and where managers spend their time.[1]
But in no part of this literature is the actual content of managerial work
systematically and meaningfully described.[2] Thus, the question posed at
the start—what do managers do?—remains essentially unanswered in the
literature of management.

This is indeed an odd situation. We claim to teach management in
schools of both business and public administration; we undertake major
research programs in management; we find a growing segment of the management science community concerned with the problems of senior management. Most of these people—the planners, information and control
theorists, systems analysts, etc.—are attempting to analyze and change
working habits that they themselves do not understand. Thus, at a conference called at M.I.T. to assess the impact of the computer on the manager,
and attended by a number of America's foremost management scientists, a
participant found it necessary to comment after lengthy discussion [20, p.
198]:

I'd like to return to an earlier point. It seems to me that until we get
into the question of what the top manager does or what the functions

---

[1] Carlson [6] carried out the classic study just after World War II. He asked nine
Swedish managing directors to record on diary pads details of each activity in which
they engaged. His method was used by a group of other researchers, many of them
working in the U.K. (See [4], [5], [15], [25].)

[2] One major project, involving numerous publications, took place at Ohio State University and spanned three decades. Some of the vocabulary used followed Fayol. The
results have generated little interest in this area. (See, for example, [13].)

are that define the top management job, we're not going to get out of the kind of difficulty that keeps cropping up. What I'm really doing is leading up to my earlier question which no one really answered. And that is: Is it possible to arrive at a specification of what constitutes the job of a top manager?

His question was not answered.

RESEARCH STUDY ON MANAGERIAL WORK

In late 1966, I began research on this question, seeking to replace Fayol's words by a set that would more accurately describe what managers do. In essence, I sought to develop by the process of induction a statement of managerial work that would have empirical validity. Using a method called "structured observation," I observed for one-week periods the chief executives of five medium to large organizations (a consulting firm, a school system, a technology firm, a consumer goods manufacturer, and a hospital).

Structured as well as unstructured (i.e., anecdotal) data were collected in three "records." In the *chronology record,* activity patterns throughout the working day were recorded. In the *mail record,* for each of 890 pieces of mail processed during the five weeks, were recorded its purpose, format and sender, the attention it received and the action it elicited. And, recorded in the *contact record,* for each of 368 verbal interactions, were the purpose, the medium (telephone call, scheduled or unscheduled meeting, tour), the participants, the form of initiation, and the location. It should be noted that all categorizing was done during and after observation so as to ensure that the categories reflected only the work under observation. [19] contains a fuller description of this methodology and a tabulation of the results of the study.

Two sets of conclusions are presented below. The first deals with certain characteristics of managerial work, as they appeared from analysis of the numerical data (e.g., How much time is spent with peers? What is the average duration of meetings? What proportion of contacts are initiated by the manager himself?). The second describes the basic content of managerial work in terms of ten roles. This description derives from an analysis of the data on the recorded *purpose* of each contact and piece of mail.

The liberty is taken of referring to these findings as descriptive of managerial, as opposed to chief executive, work. This is done because many of the findings are supported by studies of other types of managers. Specifically, most of the conclusions on work characteristics are to be found in the combined results of a group of studies of foremen [11], [16], middle managers [4], [5], [15], [25], and chief executives [6]. And although there is little useful material on managerial roles, three studies do provide some evidence of the applicability of the role set. Most important, Sayles' empirical study of production managers [24] suggests that at least five of the ten roles are performed at the lower end of the managerial hierarchy. And some further evidence is provided by comments in Whyte's study of leadership in a street gang [26] and Neustadt's study of three U.S. presidents [21]. (Reference is made to these findings where appropriate.) Thus, although most of the illustrations are drawn from my study of chief executives, there is some justification in asking the reader to consider when he sees the terms "manager" and his "organization" not only "presidents" and their "companies," but also "foremen" and their "shops," "directors" and their "branches," "vice-presidents" and their "divisions." The term *manager* shall be used with reference to all those people in charge of formal organizations or their subunits.

SOME CHARACTERISTICS OF MANAGERIAL WORK

Six sets of characteristics of managerial work derive from analysis of the data of this study. Each has a significant bearing on the manager's ability to administer a complex organization.

Characteristic 1. The Manager Performs a Great Quantity of Work at an Unrelenting Pace

Despite a semblance of normal working hours, in truth managerial work appears to be very taxing. The five men in this study processed an average of thirty-six pieces of mail each day, participated in eight meetings (half of which were scheduled), engaged in five telephone calls, and took one tour. In his study of foremen, Guest [11] found that the number of activities per day averaged 583, with no real break in the pace.

Free time appears to be very rare. If by chance a manager has caught up with the mail, satisfied the callers, dealt with all the disturbances, and avoided scheduled meetings, a subordinate will likely show up to usurp the available time. It seems that the manager cannot expect to have much time for leisurely reflection during office hours. During "off" hours, our chief executives spent much time on work-related reading. High-level managers appear to be able to escape neither from an environment which recognizes the power and status of their positions nor from their own minds which have been trained to search continually for new information.

Characteristic 2. Managerial Activity is Characterized by Variety, Fragmentation, and Brevity

There seems to be no pattern to managerial activity. Rather, variety and fragmentation appear to be characteristic, as successive activities deal with issues that differ greatly both in type and in content. In effect the manager must be prepared to shift moods quickly and frequently.

A typical chief executive day may begin with a telephone call from a director who asks a favor (a "status request"); then a subordinate calls to tell of a strike at one of the facilities (fast movement of information, termed "instant communication"); this is followed by a relaxed scheduled event at which the manager speaks to a group of visiting dignitaries (ceremony); the manager returns to find a message from a major customer who is demanding the renegotiation of a contract (pressure); and so on. Throughout the day, the managers of our study encountered this great variety of activity. Most surprisingly, the significant activities were interspersed with the trivial in no particular pattern.

Furthermore, these managerial activities were characterized by their brevity. Half of all the activities studied lasted less than nine minutes and only ten percent exceeded one hour's duration. Guest's foremen averaged 48 seconds per activity, and Carlson [6] stressed that his chief executives were unable to work without frequent interruption.

In my own study of chief executives, I felt that the managers demonstrated a preference for tasks of short duration and encouraged interruption. Perhaps the manager becomes accustomed to variety, or perhaps the flow of "instant communication" cannot be delayed. A more plausible explanation might be that the manager becomes conditioned by his workload. He develops a sensitive appreciation for the opportunity cost of his own time. Also, he is aware of the ever present assortment of obligations associated with his job—accumulations of mail that cannot be delayed, the callers that must be attended to, the meetings that require his participation. In other words, no matter what he is doing, the manager is plagued by what he must do and what he might do. Thus, the manager is forced to treat issues in an abrupt and superficial way.

Characteristic 3. Managers Prefer Issues That Are Current, Specific, and Ad Hoc

Ad hoc operating reports received more attention than did routine ones; current, uncertain information—gossip, speculation, hearsay—which flows quickly was preferred to historical, certain information; "instant communication" received first consideration; few contacts were held on a routine or "clocked" basis; almost all contacts concerned well-defined issues. The managerial environment is clearly one of stimulus-response. It breeds, not reflective planners, but adaptable information manipulators who prefer the live, concrete situation, men who demonstrate a marked action-orientation.

Characteristic 4. The Manager Sits Between His Organization and a Network of Contacts

In virtually every empirical study of managerial time allocation, it was reported that managers spent a surprisingly large amount of time in horizontal or lateral (nonline) communication. It is clear from this study and from that of Sayles [24] that the manager is surrounded by a diverse and complex web of contacts which serves as his self-designed external information system. Included in this web can be clients, associates and suppliers, outside staff experts, peers (managers of related or similar organizations), trade organizations, government officials, independents (those with no relevant organizational affiliation), and directors or superiors. (Among these, directors in this study and superiors in other studies did *not* stand out as particularly active individuals.)

The managers in this study received far more information than they emitted, much of it coming from contacts, and more from subordinates who acted as filters. Figuratively, the manager appears as the neck of an hourglass, sifting information into his own organization from its environment.

Characteristic 5. The Manager Demonstrates a Strong Preference for the Verbal Media

The manager has five media at his command—mail (documented), telephone (purely verbal), unscheduled meeting (informal face-to-face), scheduled meeting (formal face-to-face), and tour (observational). Along with all the other empirical studies of work characteristics, I found a strong predominance of verbal forms of communication.

Mail. By all indications, managers dislike the documented form of communication. In this study, they gave cursory attention to such items as operating reports and periodicals. It was estimated that only thirteen percent of the input mail was of specific and immediate use to the managers. Much of the rest dealt with formalities and provided general reference data. The managers studied initiated very little mail, only twenty-five pieces in the five weeks. The rest of the outgoing mail was sent in reaction to mail received—a reply to a request, an acknowledgment, some information forwarded to a part of the organization. The managers appeared to dislike this form of communication, perhaps because the mail is a relatively slow and tedious medium to use.

Telephone and Unscheduled Meetings. The less formal means of verbal communication—the telephone, a purely verbal form, and the unscheduled meeting, a face-to-face form—were used frequently (two-thirds of the contacts in the study) but for brief encounters (average duration of six and twelve minutes respectively). They were used primarily to deliver requests and to transmit pressing information to those outsiders and sub-ordinates who had informal relationships with the manager.

Scheduled Meetings. These tended to be of long duration, averaging sixty-eight minutes in this study, and absorbing over half the managers' time. Such meetings provided the managers with their main opportunities to interact with large groups and to leave the confines of their own offices. Scheduled meetings were used when the participants were unfamiliar to the manager (e.g., students who request that he speak at a university), when a large quantity of information had to be transmitted (e.g., presentation of a report), when ceremony had to take place, and when complex strategy-making or negotiation had to be undertaken. An important feature of the scheduled meeting was the incidental, but by no means irrelevant, information that flowed at the start and end of such meetings.

Tours. Although the walking tour would appear to be a powerful tool for gaining information in an informal way, in this study tours accounted for only three percent of the managers' time.

In general, it can be concluded that the manager uses each medium for particular purposes. Nevertheless, where possible, he appears to gravitate to verbal media since these provide greater flexibility, require less effort, and bring faster response. It should be noted here that the manager does not leave the telephone or the meeting to get back to work. Rather, communication is his work, and these media are his tools. The operating work of the organization—producing a product, doing research, purchasing a part—appears to be undertaken infrequently by the senior manager. The manager's productive output must be measured in terms of information, a great part of which is transmitted verbally.

Characteristic 6. Despite the Preponderance of Obligations, the Manager Appears to Be Able to Control His Own Affairs

Carlson suggested in his study of Swedish chief executives that these men were puppets, with little control over their own affairs. A cursory examination of our data indicates that this is true. Our managers were responsible for the initiation of only thirty-two percent of their verbal contacts and a smaller proportion of their mail. Activities were also classified as to the nature of the managers' participation, and the active ones were outnumbered by the passive ones (e.g., making requests vs. receiving requests). On the surface, the manager is indeed a puppet, answering requests in the mail, returning telephone calls, attending meetings initiated by others, yielding to subordinates' requests for time, reacting to crises.

However, such a view is misleading. There is evidence that the senior manager can exert control over his own affairs in two significant ways: (1) It is he who defines many of his own long-term commitments, by developing appropriate information channels which later feed him information, by initiating projects which later demand his time, by joining committees or outside boards which provide contacts in return for his services, and so on. (2) The manager can exploit situations that appear as obligations. He can lobby at ceremonial speeches; he can impose his values on his organization when his authorization is requested; he can motivate his subordinates whenever he interacts with them; he can use the crisis situation as an opportunity to innovate.

Perhaps these are two points that help distinguish successful and unsuccessful managers. All managers appear to be puppets. Some decide who will pull the strings and how, and they then take advantage of each move that they are forced to make. Others, unable to exploit this high-tension environment, are swallowed up by this most demanding of jobs.

THE MANAGER'S WORK ROLES

In describing the essential content of managerial work, one should aim to model managerial activity, that is, to describe it as a set of programs. But an undertaking as complex as this must be preceded by the development of a useful typological description of managerial work. In other words, we must first understand the distinct components of managerial work. At the present time we do not.

In this study, 890 pieces of mail and 368 verbal contacts were categorized as to purpose. The incoming mail was found to carry acknowledgements, requests and solicitations of various kinds, reference data, news, analytical reports, reports on events and on operations, advice on various situations, and statements of problems, pressures, and ideas. In reacting to mail, the managers acknowledged some, replied to the requests (e.g., by sending information), and forwarded much to subordinates (usually for their information). Verbal contacts involved a variety of purposes. In 15% of them activities were scheduled, in 6% ceremonial events took place, and a few involved external board work. About 34% involved requests of various kinds, some insignificant, some for information, some for authorization of proposed actions. Another 36% essentially involved the flow of information to and from the manager, while the remainder dealt specifically with issues of strategy and with negotiations. (For details, see [19].)

In this study, each piece of mail and verbal contact categorized in this way was subjected to one question: Why did the manager do this? The answers were collected and grouped and regrouped in various ways (over the course of three years) until a typology emerged that was felt to be satisfactory. While an example,, presented below, will partially explain this process to the reader, it must be remembered that (in the words of Bronowski [3, p. 62]): "Every induction is a speculation and it guesses at a unity which the facts present but do not strictly imply."

Consider the following sequence of two episodes: A chief executive attends a meeting of an external board on which he sits. Upon his return to his organization, he immediately goes to the office of a subordinate, tells of a conversation he had with a fellow board member, and concludes with the statement: "It looks like we shall get the contract."

The purposes of these two contacts are clear—to attend an external board meeting, and to give current information (instant communication) to a subordinate. But why did the manager attend the meeting? Indeed, why does he belong to the board? And why did he give this particular information to his subordinate?

Basing analysis on this incident, one can argue as follows: The manager belongs to the board in part so that he can be exposed to special information which is of use to his organization. The subordinate needs the information but has not the status which would give him access to it. The chief executive does. Board memberships bring chief executives in contact with one another for the purpose of trading information.

Two aspects of managerial work emerge from this brief analysis. The manager serves in a "liaison" capacity because of the status of his office, and what he learns here enables him to act as "disseminator" of information into his organization. We refer to these as *roles*—organized sets of behaviors belonging to identifiable offices or positions [23]. Ten roles were chosen to capture all the activities observed during this study.

All activities were found to involve one or more of three basic behaviors —interpersonal contact, the processing of information, and the making of decisions. As a result, our ten roles are divided into three corresponding groups. Three roles—labelled *figurehead, liaison,* and *leader*—deal with behavior that is essentially interpersonal in nature. Three others—*nerve center, disseminator,* and *spokesman*—deal with information-processing activities performed by the manager. And the remaining four—*entrepreneur, disturbance handler, resource allocator,* and *negotiator*—cover the decision-making activities of the manager. We describe each of these roles in turn, asking the reader to note that they form a *gestalt,* a unified whole whose parts cannot be considered in isolation.

The Interpersonal Roles

Three roles relate to the manager's behavior that focuses on interpersonal contact. These roles derive directly from the authority and status associated with holding managerial office.

Figurehead. As legal authority in his organization, the manager is a symbol, obliged to perform a number of duties. He must preside at ceremonial events, sign legal documents, receive visitors, make himself available to many of those who feel, in the words of one of the men studied, "that the only way to get something done is to get to the top." There is evidence that this role applies at other levels as well. Davis [7, pp. 43–44] cites the case of the field sales manager who must deal with those customers who believe that their accounts deserve his attention.

Leader. Leadership is the most widely recognized of managerial roles. It describes the manager's relationship with his subordinates—his attempts to motivate them and his development of the milieu in which they work. Leadership actions pervade all activity—in contrast to most roles, it is possible to designate only a few activities as dealing exclusively with leadership (these mostly related to staffing duties). Each time a manager encourages a subordinate, or meddles in his affairs, or replies to one of his requests, he is playing the *leader* role. Subordinates seek out and react to these leadership clues, and, as a result, they impart significant power to the manager.

Liaison. As noted earlier, the empirical studies have emphasized the importance of lateral or horizontal communication in the work of managers at all levels. It is clear from our study that this is explained largely in terms of the *liaison* role. The manager establishes his network of contacts essentially to bring information and favors to his organization. As Sayles notes in his study of production supervisors [24, p. 258], "The one enduring objective [of the manager] is the effort to build and maintain a predictable, reciprocating system of relationships. . . ."

Making use of his status, the manager interacts with a variety of peers and other people outside his organization. He provides time, information, and favors in return for the same from others. Foremen deal with staff groups and other foremen; chief executives join boards of directors, and maintain extensive networks of individual relationships. Neustadt notes this behavior in analyzing the work of President Roosevelt [21, p. 150]:

> His personal sources were the product of a sociability and curiosity that reached back to the other Roosevelt's time. He had an enormous acquaintance in various phases of national life and at various levels of government; he also had his wife and her variety of contacts. He extended his acquaintanceships abroad; in the war years Winston Churchill, among others, became a "personal source." Roosevelt quite deliberately exploited these relationships and mixed them up to widen his own range of information. He changed his sources as his interests changed, but no one who had ever interested him was quite forgotten or immune to sudden use.

The Informational Roles

A second set of managerial activities relates primarily to the processing of information. Together they suggest three significant managerial roles, one describing the manager as a focal point for a certain kind of organizational information, the other two describing relatively simple transmission of this information.

Nerve Center. There is indication, both from this study and from those by Neustadt and Whyte, that the manager serves as the focal point in his organization for the movement of nonroutine information. Homans, who analyzed Whyte's study, draws the following conclusions [26, p. 187]:

> Since interaction flowed toward [the leaders], they were better informed about the problems and desires of group members than were any of the followers and therefore better able to decide on an appropriate course of action. Since they were in close touch with other gang leaders, they were also better informed than their followers about conditions in Cornerville at large. Moreover, in their positions at the focus of the chains of interaction, they were better able than any follower to pass on to the group decisions that had been reached.

The term *nerve center* is chosen to encompass those many activities in which the manager receives information.

Within his own organization, the manager has legal authority that formally connects him—and only him—to *every* member. Hence, the manager emerges as *nerve center* of internal information. He may not know as much about any one function as the subordinate who specializes in it, but he comes to know more about his total organization than any other member. He is the information generalist. Furthermore, because of the manager's status and its manifestation in the *liaison* role, the manager gains unique access to a variety of knowledgeable outsiders including peers who are themselves *nerve centers* of their own organizations. Hence, the manager emerges as his organization's *nerve center* of external information as well.

As noted earlier, the manager's nerve center information is of a special kind. He appears to find it most important to get his information quickly and informally. As a result, he will not hesitate to bypass formal information channels to get it, and he is prepared to deal with a large amount of gossip, hearsay, and opinion which has not yet become substantiated fact.

Disseminator. Much of the manager's information must be transmitted to subordinates. Some of this is of a *factual* nature, received from outside the organization or from other subordinates. And some is of a *value* nature. Here, the manager acts as the mechanism by which organizational influencers (owners, governments, employee groups, the general public, etc., or simply the "boss") make their preferences known to the organization. It is the manager's duty to integrate these value positions, and to express general organizational preferences as a guide to decisions made by subordinates. One of the men studied commented: "One of the principal functions of this position is to integrate the hospital interests with the public interests." Papandreou describes his duty in a paper published in 1952, referring to management as the "peak coordinator" [22].

Spokesman. In his *spokesman* role, the manager is obliged to transmit his information to outsiders. He informs influencers and other interested parties about his organization's performance, its policies, and its plans. Furthermore, he is expected to serve outside his organization as an expert in its industry. Hospital administrators are expected to spend some time serving outside as public experts on health, and corporation presidents, perhaps as chamber of commerce executives.

The Decisional Roles

The manager's legal authority requires that he assume responsibility for all of his organization's important actions. The *nerve center* role suggests that only he can fully understand complex decisions, particularly those involving difficult value tradeoffs. As a result, the manager emerges as the key figure in the making and interrelating of all significant decisions in his organization, a process that can be referred to as *strategy-making*. Four roles describe the manager's control over the strategy-making system in his organization.

Entrepreneur. The *entrepreneur* role describes the manager as initiator and designer of much of the controlled change in his organization. The manager looks for opportunities and potential problems which may cause him to initiate action. Action takes the form of *improvement projects*—the marketing of a new product, the strengthening of a weak department, the purchasing of new equipment, the reorganization of formal structure, and so on.

The manager can involve himself in each improvement project in one of three ways: (1) He may *delegate* all responsibility for its design and approval, implicitly retaining the right to replace that subordinate who takes charge of it. (2) He may delegate the design work to a subordinate, but retain the right to *approve* it before implementation. (3) He may actively *supervise* the design work himself.

Improvement projects exhibit a number of interesting characteristics. They appear to involve a number of subdecisions, consciously sequenced over long periods of time and separated by delays of various kinds. Furthermore, the manager appears to supervise a great many of these at any one time—perhaps fifty to one hundred in the case of chief executives. In fact, in his handling of improvement projects, the manager may be likened to a juggler. At any one point, he maintains a number of balls in the air. Periodically, one comes down, receives a short burst of energy, and goes up again. Meanwhile, an inventory of new balls waits on the sidelines and, at random intervals, old balls are discarded and new ones added. Both Lindblom [2] and Marples [18] touch on these aspects of strategy-making, the former stressing the disjointed and incremental nature of the decisions, and the latter depicting the sequential episodes in terms of a stranded rope made up of fibres of different lengths each of which surfaces periodically.

Disturbance Handler. While the *entrepreneur* role focuses on voluntary change, the *disturbance handler* role deals with corrections which the manager is forced to make. We may describe this role as follows: The organization consists basically of specialist operating programs. From time to time, it experiences a stimulus that cannot be handled routinely, either because an operating program has broken down or because the stimulus is new and it is not clear which operating program should handle it. These situations constitute disturbances. As generalist, the manager is obliged to assume responsibility for dealing with the stimulus. Thus, the handling of disturbances is an essential duty of the manager.

There is clear evidence for this role both in our study of chief executives and in Sayles' study of production supervisors [24, p. 162]:

> The achievement of this stability, which is the manager's objective, is a never-to-be-attained ideal. He is like a symphony orchestra conductor, endeavoring to maintain a melodious performance in which contributions of the various instruments are coordinated and sequenced, patterned and paced, while the orchestra members are having various personal difficulties, stage hands are moving music stands, alternating excessive heat and cold are creating audience and instrument problems, and the sponsor of the concert is insisting on irrational changes in the program.

Sayles goes further to point out the very important balance that the manager must maintain between change and stability. To Sayles, the manager seeks "a dynamic type of stability" (p. 162). Most disturbances elicit short-term adjustments which bring back equilibrium; persistent ones require the introduction of long-term structural change.

Resource Allocator. The manager maintains ultimate authority over his organization's strategy-making system by controlling the allocation of its resources. By deciding who will get what (and who will do what), the manager directs the course of his organization. He does this in three ways:

(1) *In scheduling his own time,* the manager allocates his most precious resource and thereby determines organizational priorities. Issues that receive low priority do not reach the *nerve center* of the organization and are blocked for want of resources.

(2) In designing the organizational structure and in carrying out many improvement projects, the manager *programs the work of his subordinates.* In other words, he allocates their time by deciding what will be done and who will do it.

(3) Most significantly, the manager maintains control over resource allocation by the requirement that he *authorize all significant decisions* before they are implemented. By retaining this power, the manager ensures that different decisions are interrelated—that conflicts are avoided, that resource constraints are respected, and that decisions complement one another.

Decisions appear to be authorized in one of two ways. Where the costs and benefits of a proposal can be quantified, where it is competing for specified resources with other known proposals, and where it can wait for a certain time of year, approval for a proposal is sought in the context of a formal *budgeting* procedure. But these conditions are most often not met—timing may be crucial, nonmonetary costs may predominate, and so on. In these cases, approval is sought in terms of an *ad hoc request for authorization.* Subordinate and manager meet (perhaps informally) to discuss one proposal alone.

Authorization choices are enormously complex ones for the manager. A myriad of factors must be considered (resource constraints, influencer preferences, consistency with other decisions, feasibility, payoff, timing, subordinate feelings, etc.). But the fact that the manager is authorizing the decision rather than supervising its design suggests that he has little time to give to it. To alleviate this difficulty, it appears that managers use special kinds of *models* and *plans* in their decision-making. These exist only in their minds and are loose, but they serve to guide behavior. Models may answer questions such as, "Does this proposal make sense in terms of the trends that I see in tariff legislation?" or "Will the EDP department be able to get along with marketing on this?" Plans exist in the sense that, on questioning, managers reveal images (in terms of proposed improvement projects) of where they would like their organizations to go: "Well, once I get these foreign operations fully developed, I would like to begin to look into a reorganization," said one subject of this study.

Negotiator. The final role describes the manager as participant in negotiation activity. To some students of the management process [8, p. 343], this is not truly part of the job of managing. But such distinctions are arbitrary. Negotiation is an integral part of managerial work, as this study notes for chief executives and as that of Sayles made very clear for production supervisors [24, p. 131]: "Sophisticated managers place great stress on negotiations as a way of life. They negotiate with groups who are setting standards for their work, who are performing support activity for them, and to whom they wish to 'sell' their services."

The manager must participate in important negotiation sessions because he is his organization's legal authority, its *spokesman* and its *resource allocator.* Negotiation is resource trading in real time. If the resource commitments are to be large, the legal authority must be present.

These ten roles suggest that the manager of an organization bears a great burden of responsibility. He must oversee his organization's status system; he must serve as a crucial informational link between it and its environment; he must interpret and reflect its basic values; he must maintain the stability of its operations; and he must adapt it in a controlled and balanced way to a changing environment.

MANAGEMENT AS A PROFESSION AND AS A SCIENCE

Is management a profession? To the extent that different managers perform one set of basic roles, management satisfies one criterion for becoming a profession. But a profession must require, in the words of the *Random House Dictionary,* "knowledge of some department of learning or science." Which of the ten roles now requires specialized learning? Indeed, what school of business or public administration teaches its students how to disseminate information, allocate resources, perform as figurehead, make contacts, or handle disturbances? We simply know very little about teaching these things. The reason is that we have never tried to document and describe in a meaningful way the procedures (or programs) that managers use.

The evidence of this research suggests that there is as yet no science in managerial work—that managers do not work according to procedures that have been prescribed by scientific analysis. Indeed, except for his use of the telephone, the airplane, and the dictating machine, it would appear that the manager of today is indistinguishable from his predecessors. He may seek different information, but he gets much of it in the same way—from word-of-mouth. He may make decisions dealing with modern technology but he uses the same intuitive (that is, nonexplicit) procedures in making them. Even the computer, which has had such a great impact on other kinds of organizational work, has apparently done little to alter the working methods of the general manager.

How do we develop a scientific base to understand the work of the manager? The description of roles is a first and necessary step. But tighter forms of research are necessary. Specifically, we must attempt to model managerial work—to describe it as a system of programs. First, it will be necessary to decide what programs managers actually use. Among a great number of programs in the manager's repertoire, we might expect to find a time-scheduling program, an information-disseminating program, and a disturbance-handling program. Then, researchers will have to devote a considerable amount of effort to studying and accurately describing the content of each of these programs—the information and heuristics used. Finally, it will be necessary to describe the interrelationships among all of these programs so that they may be combined into an integrated descriptive model of managerial work.

When the management scientist begins to understand the programs that managers use, he can begin to design meaningful systems and provide help for the manager. He may ask: Which managerial activities can be fully reprogrammed (i.e., automated)? Which cannot be reprogrammed because they require human responses? Which can be partially reprogrammed to operate in a man-machine system? Perhaps scheduling, information collecting, and resource-allocating activities lead themselves to varying degrees of reprogramming. Management will emerge as a science to the extent that such efforts are successful.

IMPROVING THE MANAGER'S EFFECTIVENESS

Fayol's fifty-year-old description of managerial work is no longer of use to us. And we shall not disentangle the complexity of managerial work if we insist on viewing the manager simply as a decision-maker or simply as a motivator of subordinates. In fact, we are unlikely to overestimate the complexity of the manager's work, and we shall make little headway if we take overly simple or narrow points of view in our research.

A major problem faces today's manager. Despite the growing size of modern organizations and the growing complexity of their problems (particularly those in the public sector), the manager can expect little help. He must design his own information system, and he must take full charge of his organization's strategy-making system. Furthermore, the manager faces what might be called the *dilemma of delegation.* He has unique access to much important information but he lacks a formal means of disseminating it. As much of it is verbal, he cannot spread it around in an efficient manner. How can he delegate a task with confidence when he has neither the time nor the means to send the necessary information along with it?

Thus, the manager is usually forced to carry a great burden of responsibility in his organization. As organizations become increasingly large and complex, this burden increases. Unfortunately, the man cannot significantly increase his available time or significantly improve his abilities to manage. Hence, in the large, complex bureaucracy, the top manager's time assumes an enormous opportunity cost and he faces the real danger of becoming a major obstruction in the flow of decisions and information.

Because of this, as we have seen, managerial work assumes a number of distinctive characteristics. The quantity of work is great; the pace is unrelenting; there is great variety, fragmentation, and brevity in the work activities; the manager must concentrate on issues that are current, specific, and ad hoc, and to do so, he finds that he must rely on verbal forms of communications. Yet it is on this man that the burden lies for designing and operating strategy-making and information-processing systems that are to solve his organization's (and society's) problems.

The manager can do something to alleviate these problems. He can learn more about his own roles in his organization, and he can use this information to schedule his time in a more efficient manner. He can recognize that only he has much of the information needed by his organization. Then, he can seek to find better means of disseminating it into the organization. Finally, he can turn to the skills of his management scientists to help reduce his workload and to improve his ability to make decisions.

The management scientist can learn to help the manager to the extent he can develop an understanding of the manager's work and the manager's information. To date, strategic planners, operations researchers, and information system designers have provided little help for the senior manager. They simply have had no framework available by which to understand the work of the men who employed them, and they have had poor access to the information which has never been documented. It is folly to believe that a man with poor access to the organization's true *nerve center* can design a formal management information system. Similarly, how can the long-range planner, a man usually uninformed about many of the *current* events that take place in and around his organization, design meaningful strategic plans? For good reason, the literature documents many manager complaints of naïve planning and many planner complaints of disinterested managers. In my view, our lack of understanding of managerial work has been the greatest block to the progress of management science.

The ultimate solution to the problem—to the overburdened manager seeking meaningful help—must derive from research. We must observe, describe, and understand the real work of managing; then and only then shall we significantly improve it.

REFERENCES

1. Braybrooke, David. "The Mystery of Executive Success Re-examined," *Administrative Science Quarterly,* Vol. 8 (1964), pp. 533–60.
2. ——— and Lindblom, Charles E. *A Strategy of Decision,* Free Press, New York, 1963.
3. Bronowski, J. "The Creative Process," *Scientific American,* Vol. 199 (September 1958), pp. 59–65.
4. Burns, Tom. "The Directions of Activity and Communications in a Departmental Executive Group," *Human Relations,* Vol. 7 (1954), pp. 73–97.
5. ———. "Management in Action," *Operational Research Quarterly,* Vol. 8 (1957), pp. 45–60.
6. Carlson, Sune. *Executive Behavior,* Strömbergs, Stockholm, 1951.
7. Davis, Robert T. *Performance and Development of Field Sales Managers,* Division of Research, Graduate School of Business Administration, Harvard University, Boston, 1957.
8. Drucker, Peter F. *The Practice of Management,* Harper and Row, New York, 1954.
9. Fayol, Henri. *Administration industrielle et générale,* Dunods, Paris, 1950 (first published 1916).
10. Gibb, Cecil A. "Leadership," Chapter 31 in Gardner Lindzey and Elliot A. Aronson (editors), *The Handbook of Social Psychology,* Vol. 4, Second edition, Addison-Wesley, Reading, Mass., 1969.

11. Guest, Robert H. "Of Time and the Foreman," *Personnel,* Vol. 32 (1955–56) pp. 478–86.
12. Gulick, Luther H. "Notes on the Theory of Organization," in Luther Gulick and Lyndall Urwick (editors), *Papers on the Science of Administration,* Columbia University Press, New York, 1937.
13. Hemphill, John K. *Dimensions of Executive Positions,* Bureau of Business Research Monograph Number 98, The Ohio State University, Columbus, 1960.
14. Homans, George C. *The Human Group,* Harcourt, Brace, New York, 1950.
15. Horne, J. H. and Lupton, Tom. "The Work Activities of Middle Managers—An Exploratory Study," *The Journal of Management Studies,* Vol. 2 (February 1965), pp. 14–33.
16. Kelly, Joe. "The Study of Executive Behavior by Activity Sampling," *Human Relations,* Vol. 17 (August 1964), pp. 277–87.
17. Mackenzie, R. Alex. "The Management Process in 3D," *Harvard Business Review* (November–December 1969), pp. 80–87.
18. Marples, D. L. "Studies of Managers—A Fresh Start?," *The Journal of Management Studies,* Vol. 4 (October 1967), pp. 282–99.
19. Mintzberg, Henry. "Structured Observation as a Method to Study Managerial Work," *The Journal of Management Studies,* Vol. 7 (February 1970), pp. 87–104.
20. Myers, Charles A. (Ed.). *The Impact of Computers on Management,* The M.I.T. Press, Cambridge, Mass., 1967.
21. Neustadt, Richard E. *Presidential Power: The Politics of Leadership,* The New American Library, New York, 1964.
22. Papandreou, Andreas G. "Some Basic Problems in the Theory of the Firm," in Bernard F. Haley (ed.), *A Survey of Contemporary Economics,* Vol. II, Irwin, Homewood, Illinois, 1952, pp. 183–219.
23. Sarbin, T. R. and Allen, V. L. "Role Theory," in Gardner Lindzey and Elliot A. Aronson (eds.), *The Handbook of Social Psychology,* Vol. I, Second edition, Addison-Wesley, Reading, Mass., 1968, pp. 488–567.
24. Sayles, Leonard R. *Managerial Behavior: Administration in Complex Enterprises,* McGraw-Hill, New York, 1964.
25. Stewart, Rosemary. *Managers and Their Jobs,* Macmillan, London, 1967.
26. Whyte, William F. *Street Corner Society,* second edition, University of Chicago Press, Chicago, 1955.

4

A System Resource Approach
to Organizational Effectiveness

EPHRAIM YUCHTMAN and STANLEY E. SEASHORE

We are badly in need of an improved conceptual framework for the description and assessment of organizational effectiveness. Nearly all studies of formal organizations make some reference to effectiveness; the growing field of comparative organizational study depends in part upon having some conceptual scheme that allows comparability among organizations with respect to effectiveness and guides the empirical steps of operationalization and quantification.

Aside from these needs of social scientists, consideration should also be given to the esthetic and applied requirements of organization managers. They experience high emotional involvement, pleasurable or otherwise, in the assessment of the relative success of their organizations; they are, of course, intensively and professionally engaged, informally, in the formulation and testing of hypotheses concerning the nature of decisions and actions that alter organizational effectiveness. They need a workable conception of "effectiveness" to sustain their egos and their work.

The social scientist designing or interpreting an organizational study is presently in a quandary. Most of the research concerned with the problem has been devoted to the study of the *conditions* under which organizations are more or less effective. The classic paradigm consists of some measure-

Source: Reprinted by permission of the authors and publisher from *American Sociological Review,* Vol. 32 (December 1967), pp. 891–902.

ment of effectiveness—productivity or profit, for example—as the dependent variable, and of various sociological and social-psychological measures as the independent variables. The independent variables are usually treated in a relatively sophisticated manner; little attention, however, has been given to the concept of effectiveness itself. The latter remains conceptually a vague construct; in consequence there is available a large amount of empirical data with little understanding of these data. As stated recently by Katz and Kahn:

> There is no lack of material on criteria of organizational success. The literature is studded with references to efficiency, productivity, absence, turnover, and profitability—all of these offered implicitly or explicitly, separately or in combination, as definitions of organizational effectiveness. Most of what has been written on the meaning of these criteria and on their interrelatedness, however, is judgmental and open to question. What is worse, it is filled with advice that seems sagacious but is tautological and contradictory.[1]

Similar conclusions, on the same or on different grounds, have been reached by other students of organizations.[2] While emphasizing different aspects of the problem, all agree that results from studies of organizational effectiveness show numerous inconsistencies and are difficult to evaluate and interpret, let alone compare. The inconsistencies arise, often, from discrepant conceptions of "organizational effectiveness." In the present paper an attempt is made, first, to show some of the limitations inherent in traditional approaches to organizational effectiveness and, second, to provide an improved conceptual framework for dealing with that problem.

TRADITIONAL APPROACHES TO ORGANIZATIONAL EFFECTIVENESS

In spite of the variety of terms, concepts, and operational definitions that have been employed with regard to organizational effectiveness, it is hardly difficult to arrive at the generalization that this concept has been traditionally defined in terms of goal attainment. More specifically, most investigators tend implicitly or explicitly to make the following two assump-

---

[1] Daniel Katz and Robert L. Kahn, *The Social Psychology of Organizations* (New York: John Wiley & Sons, 1966), p. 149.

[2] Basil S. Georgopoulos and Arnold S. Tannenbaum, "A Study of Organizational Effectiveness," *Amer. Sociol. Rev.* 22 (Oct. 1957): 534–40; Mason Haire, "Biological Models and Empirical Histories of the Growth of Organizations," in *Modern Organization Theory*, Mason Haire, ed. (New York: John Wiley & Sons, 1959), pp. 272–306; Amitai W. Etzioni, "Two Approaches to Organizational Analysis: A Critique and a Suggestion," *Admin. Sci. Quart.* 5 (Sept. 1960): 257–78; Robert M. Guion, "Criterion Measurement and Personnel Judgments," *Personnel Psychol.* (Summer 1961): 141–49; Charles Perrow, "Organizational Goals," in *International Encyclopedia of Social Sciences* (New York: Macmillan Co., 1968), pp. 854–66; Stanley E. Seashore, "Criteria of Organizational Effectiveness," *Michigan Bus. Rev.* 17 (July 1965): 26–30.

tions: (1) that complex organizations have an ultimate goal ("mission," "function") toward which they are striving and (2) that the ultimate goal can be identified empirically and progress toward it measured. In fact, the orientation to a specific goal is taken by many as the defining characteristic of complex organizations. A few organizational theorists[3] avoid making these assumptions, but they represent the exception rather than the rule.

Beyond these two common assumptions, however, one may discern different treatments of the matter, especially with regard to the rationale and operations for identifying the goals of organizations. It is useful to distinguish between two major doctrines in this respect. The first may be called the "prescribed goal approach." It is characterized by a focus on the formal charter of the organization, or on some category of its personnel (usually its top management) as the most valid source of information concerning organizational goals. The second may be referred to as the "derived goal approach." In it the investigator derives the ultimate goal of the organization from his (functional) theory, thus arriving at goals which may be independent of the intentions and awareness of the members. The prescribed and derived doctrines will be referred to as the *goal approach* and the *functional approach,* respectively.

THE GOAL APPROACH TO ORGANIZATIONAL EFFECTIVENESS

The goal approach, which itself has taken many forms, is the most widely used by students of organizations. Some have adopted it only as part of a broader perspective on organizations.[4] Others have employed it as a major tool in their study of organizations.[5] The goal approach has been attacked recently on various grounds. Katz and Kahn, while noting that ". . . the primary mission of an organization as perceived by its leaders furnishes a highly informative set of clues," go on to point out that:

Nevertheless, the stated purpose of an organization as given by its by-laws or in the reports of its leaders can be misleading. Such

---

[3] James G. March and Herbert A. Simon, *Organizations* (New York: John Wiley & Sons, 1958); Etzioni, op cit.; Perrow, op. cit.; Katz and Kahn, op. cit.

[4] Chester I. Barnard, *The Functions of the Executive* (Cambridge, Mass.: Harvard University Press, 1938); Peter F. Drucker, *The Practice of Management* (New York: Harper & Row, Publishers, 1954).

[5] Robert Michels, *Political Parties* (New York: Free Press, 1949); William J. Baumol, *Business Behavior, Value and Growth* (New York: Macmillan Co., 1959); James K. Dent, "Organizational Correlates of the Goals of Business Management," *Person. Psychol.* 12 (Autumn 1959): 365–93; Carl M. White, "Multiple Goals in the Theory of the Firm," in *Linear Programming and the Theory of the Firm,* ed. Kenneth E. Boulding and W. Allen Spivey (New York: Macmillan Co., 1960) pp. 181–201; Bertram M. Gross, "What Are Your Organization's Objectives? A General-Systems Approach to Planning," *Human Relations* 18 (August 1965): 195–216.

statements of objectives may idealize, rationalize, distort, omit, or even conceal some essential aspects of the functioning of the organization.[6]

The goal approach is often adopted by researchers because it seems to safeguard them against their own subjective biases. But Etzioni attacks precisely this assumption:

> The (goal) model is considered an objective and reliable analytical tool because it omits the values of the explorer and applies the values of the subject under study as the criteria of judgment. We suggest, however, that this model has some methodological shortcomings, and it is not as objective as it seems to be.[7]

Furthermore, argues Etzioni, the assessment of organizational effectiveness in terms of goal attainment should be rejected on theoretical considerations as well:

> Goals, as norms, as sets of meanings depicting target states, are cultural entities. Organizations, as systems of coordinated activities of more than one actor, are social systems.[8]

We understand this statement as rejecting the application of the goal approach in the study of organizational effectiveness for two reasons: first, goals as ideal states do not offer the possibility of realistic assessment; second, goals as cultural entities arise outside of the organization as a social system and cannot arbitrarily be attributed as properties of the organization itself. A similar criticism is offered by Starbuck, who calls attention to a hazard in the inferring of organizational goals from the behavior of organizational members:

> To distinguish goal from effect is all but impossible. The relation between goals and results is polluted by environmental effects, and people learn to pursue realistic goals. If growth is difficult, the organization will tend to pursue goals which are not growth oriented; if growth is easy, the organization will learn to pursue goals which are growth oriented. What one observes are the learned goals. Do these goals produce growth, or does growth produce these goals?[9]

It should be noted that the authors cited above tend to treat the problem as a methodological one even though, as we will show, theoretical differences and uncertainties are present as well. In order to escape some of these methodological shortcomings, several investigators have attempted

---

[6] Katz and Kahn, op. cit., p. 15.

[7] Etzioni, op cit., p. 258.

[8] Etzioni, op. cit., p. 258.

[9] William H. Starbuck, "Organizational Growth and Development," in *Handbook of Organizations*, James G. March, ed. (Chicago: Rand McNally & Co., 1965), p. 465.

to rely upon inferential or impressionistic methods of goal identification. Haberstroh, for example, makes the distinction between the formal objectives and the "common purpose" of the organization, the latter serving as the "unifying factor in human organizations."[10] But how, one may wonder, can that factor be empirically identified? Haberstroh maintains that it can be discovered through a systematic inquiry into the communication processes of the organization and by knowledge of the interests of its leadership, especially those in key positions. An empirical investigation conducted in accordance with that advice resulted in a list of operational (task) goals that, according to the investigator's own acknowledgment, do not adequately represent his notion of the "common purpose" of the organization. The latter remains therefore a rather vague concept and, it may be added, not surprisingly so. If one assumes that Haberstroh's "common purpose" stands for those objectives that are shared by the organization's members, he is reminded by several students of organizations[11] that such objectives are generally highly ambiguous, if not controversial, and therefore difficult to identify and measure.

The same kind of criticism can be applied to those who rely on the organization's charter, whether formal or informal, as containing the main identifying features of the organization, including its goals. Such an approach is represented by Bakke; he refers to the organization's charter, in the broad sense of the term, as expressing ". . . the image of the organization's unique wholeness." Such an image is created by ". . . selecting, highlighting, and combining those elements which represent the *unique* whole character of the organization and to which uniqueness and wholeness all features of the organization and its operations tend to be oriented."[12] The reader is left puzzled about how to discover the goals of the organization even after knowing that they are contained somewhere in the "image of the organization's unique wholeness."

The difficulty of identifying the ultimate goals of an organization is illustrated by some of the research on mental hospitals and other "total" institutions, as discussed by Vinter and Janowitz and, particularly, by Perrow and Etzioni.[13] Many of these institutions have been judged to be

---

[10] Chadwick J. Haberstroh, "Organization Design and Systems Analysis," in *Handbook of Organizations*, James G. March, ed. (Chicago: Rand McNally & Co., 1965), pp. 1171–1211.

[11] Abraham D. H. Kaplan, Joel B. Dirlam, and Robert F. Lanzillotti, *Pricing in Big Business* (Washington: Brookings Institution, 1958); Richard M. Cyert and James G. March, "A Behavioral Theory of Organizational Objectives," in *Modern Organization Theory*, Mason Haire, ed. (New York: John Wiley & Sons, 1959), pp. 76–90.

[12] E. Wight Bakke, "Concept of the Social Organization," in *Modern Organization Theory*, Mason Haire, ed. (New York: John Wiley & Sons, 1959), pp. 16–75.

[13] Robert Vinter and Morris Janowitz, "Effective Institutions for Juvenile Delinquents: A Research Statement," *Soc. Serv. Rev.* 33 (June 1959): pp. 118–30; Charles Perrow, "The Analysis of Goals in Complex Organizations," *Amer. Sociol. Rev.* 26 (Dec. 1961): 854–66.

ineffective since they fail to achieve their presumed therapeutic goals. Vinter and Janowitz demonstrate, however, that the goal of therapy is held only by a limited segment of the public, and that the institutions themselves are oriented mainly to custody, not therapy.

Etzioni elaborates upon this issue as follows:

> When the relative power of the various elements in the environment are carefully examined, it becomes clear that, in general, the sub-publics (e.g., professionals, universities, well-educated people, some health institutions) which support therapeutic goals are less powerful than those which support the custodial or segregating activities of these organizations. Under such conditions, most mental hospitals and prisons must be more or less custodial.[14]

This observation, like Starbuck's argument quoted above, amounts to saying that organizational goals are essentially nothing more than courses of action imposed on the organization by various forces in its environment, rather than preferred end-states toward which the organization is "striving." Such a perspective on the nature of organizational goals seems to undermine the rationale behind the use of goals as a yardstick for assessing organizational effectiveness. How, we may ask, can a given social unit be regarded as "effective" if it cannot even determine its goals for itself, i.e., if the reference is wholly to the needs of entities other than itself? It would seem that the capacity of an organization to attain its own goals is a consideration of higher priority than that of success in attainment of imposed goals. An adequate conceptualization of organizational effectiveness cannot therefore be formulated unless factors of organization-environment relationships are incorporated into its framework.

Finally, it is not only in its external environment that the organization is faced with a variety of forces exerting influence on its behavior. The organization itself is composed of a large variety of individuals and groups, each having its own conceptions about any claims on the organization. The managers of an organization do not wholly agree among themselves about the organizational goals; in addition it is not certain that these goals, even if agreed upon, would prevail. This complicated reality is highlighted by the analysis of Cyert and March. They warn against the confusion in understanding organizational behavior whenever any one individual or group, such as the top management, is selected to represent the organization as a whole:

> The confusion arises because ultimately it makes only slightly more sense to say that the goal of the business organization is to

---

[14] Etzioni, op. cit., p. 264.

maximize profit than it does to say that its goal is to maximize the salary of Sam Smith, Assistant to the Janitor.[15]

These considerations, taken together, seem to cast a serious doubt on the fruitfulness of the goal approach to organizational effectiveness. This is not to suggest that the concept of organizational goals should be rejected *in toto*. For certain analytical purposes it is useful to abstract some goal as an organizational property. In the study of persons in organizational settings, the concept of goal is useful and perhaps essential.[16] In the study of organizational effectiveness, however, the goal approach has appeared as a hindrance rather than as a help.

THE FUNCTIONAL APPROACH TO ORGANIZATIONAL EFFECTIVENESS

The functional approach to organizational effectiveness can be characterized as "normative" in the sense that the investor reports what the goals of an organization are, or should be, as dictated by the logical consistency of his theory about the relationship among parts of larger social systems. From this point of view, the functional, or derived goal, approach has an important advantage over the prescribed goal doctrine since it appears to solve the problem of identifying the ultimate goals of complex organizations: Given the postulates and premises of the functional model about the nature of organizations and their interconnectedness with the total social structure one can derive from it the specific goals of an organization, or of a class of organizations. This is evident mainly in the work of Parsons, one of the outspoken advocates of functional analysis, in his suggestions for a theory of organizations.[17] The Parsonian scheme also illustrates, however, a major weakness inherent in the functional approach. This weakness can be usefully discussed in terms of "frames of reference."

Organizations, or other social units, can be evaluated and compared from the perspective of different groups or individuals. We may judge the effectiveness of an organization in relation to its own welfare, or we may assess how successful the organization is in contributing to the well-being of some other entities. While the selection of a given frame of reference is a question of one's values and interests, the distinction among them must be clearly made and consistently adhered to. Vital as this requirement appears to be, one encounters various treatments of effectiveness that im-

---

[15] Cyert and March, op. cit., p. 80.

[16] Alvin F. Zander and Herman M. Medow, "Individual and Group Levels of Aspiration," *Human Relations* 16 (Winter 1963): 89–105; Alvin F. Zander and Herman M. Medow, "Strength of Group and Desire for Attainable Group Aspirations," *J. Personality* 33 (Jan. 1965): 122–39.

[17] Talcott Parsons, "Suggestions for a Sociological Approach to a Theory of Organizations—I," *Admin. Sci. Quart.* 1 (June 1956): 63–85; Talcott Parsons, *Structure and Processes in Modern Societies* (New York: Free Press, 1960), pp. 16–96.

plicitly or explicitly refer to different frames of reference interchangeably, as if effectiveness from the point of view of the organization itself is identical with, or corresponds to, effectiveness viewed from the vantage point of some other entity, such as a member, or owner, or the community, or the total society.

The point of departure for Parsons' analysis of complex organizations is the "cultural-institutional" level of analysis. Accordingly, "The main point of reference for analyzing the structure of any social system is its value pattern. This defines the basic orientation of the system (in the present case, the organization) to the situation in which it operates; hence, it guides the activities of participant individuals."[18] The impact of the value pattern, furthermore, is felt through institutional processes which ". . . spell out these values in the more concrete functional contexts of goal attainment itself, adaptation to the situation, and integration of the system."[19] These functional prerequisites, including the value pattern, are universally present in every social system. Their specific manifestations and their relative importance, however, vary according to the defining characteristic of the system and its place in the superordinate system. In the case of complex organizations, their defining characteristic is the primacy of orientation to the attainment of a specific goal. This goal, like all other organizational phenomena, must be legitimated by the value pattern of the organization. The nature of this legitimation is a crucial element in Parsons' analysis; the following quotation shows its relevance for the present discussion as well:

> Since it has been assumed that an organization is defined by the primacy of a type of a goal, the focus of its value-system must be the legitimation of this goal in terms of the functional significance of its attainment for the superordinate system, and secondly, the legitimation of the primacy of this goal over other possible interests and values of the organization and its members.[20]

In terms of our analysis, this states explicitly that the focal frame of reference for the assessment of organizational effectiveness is not the organization itself but rather the superordinate system. Not only must the ultimate goal of the organization be functionally significant in general for that system but, in the case of a conflict of interests between it and the organization, the conflict is always resolved in favor of the superordinate system—since the value pattern of the organization legitimates only those goals that serve that system. In other words, the *raison d'être* of complex organizations according to this analysis, is mainly to benefit the society to

---

18 Parsons, op. cit., 1956, p. 67.

19 Parsons, op. cit., 1956, p. 67.

20 Parsons, op. cit., 1956, p. 68.

which they belong, and that society is, therefore, the appropriate frame of reference for the evaluation of organizational effectiveness. In order to avoid misunderstanding in this respect the following illustration is provided by Parsons:

> For the business firm, money return is a primary measure and symbol of success and is thus part of the goal structure of the organization. But it cannot be the primary organizational goal because profit-making is not by itself a function on behalf of the society as a system.[21]

Now there is no argument that the organization, as a system, must produce some important output for the total system in order to receive in return some vital input. However, taking the organization itself as the frame of reference, its contribution to the larger system must be regarded as an unavoidable and costly requirement rather than as a sign of success. While for Parsons the crucial question is "How well is the organization doing for the superordinate system?", from the organizational point of view the question must be "How well is the organization doing for itself?"

It was suggested earlier that a major weakness of the goal approach has been its failure to treat the issue of organizational autonomy in relation to organizational effectiveness. This seems to be the Achilles heel of the functional approach as well. In Parsons' conception of organizations, and of social systems in general, there exists the tendency to overemphasize the interdependence among the parts of a system and thus, as argued by Gouldner, fail ". . . to explore systematically the significance of variations in the degree of interdependence," ignoring the possibility that ". . . some parts may vary in their dependence upon one another, and that their interdependence is not necessarily symmetrical."[22]

Gouldner's proposition of "functional autonomy" may be examined on several different levels. For example, one may regard the organization itself as the total system, looking for variations in the degree of autonomy among its own parts; this has been the focus of Gouldner's analysis. But the same line of analysis can be attempted at a different level, where society is taken as the total system. Here the investigator may be exploring variations in the degree of autonomy of various parts and sub-systems, an instance of which are complex organizations. Such an analysis underlies the typology offered by Thompson and McEwen, in which the relations between organizations and their environments are conceived in terms of

21 Parsons, op. cit., 1956, p. 68.

22 Alvin W. Gouldner, "Organizational Dynamics," in Sociology Today, ed. Robert K. Merton et al. (New York: Basic Books, 1959), p. 419.

the relative autonomy, or dominance, of the organization vis-à-vis its environment.[23]

The proposition of functional autonomy implies that organizations are capable of gearing their activities into relatively independent courses of action, rather than orienting themselves necessarily toward the needs of society as the superordinate system. Under such assumptions it is difficult to accept as a working model of organizations the proposition that the ultimate goal of organizations must always be of functional significance for the larger system.

Comparing the goal and the functional approaches, it can be concluded that both contain serious methodological and theoretical shortcomings. The goal approach, while theoretically adhering to an organizational frame of reference, has failed to provide a rationale for the empirical identification of goals as an organizational property. The functional approach, on the other hand, has no difficulty in identifying the ultimate goal of the organization, since the latter is implied by the internal logic of the model, but the functional model does not take the organization as the frame of reference. Furthermore, neither of the two approaches gives adequate consideration to the conceptual problem of the relations between the organization and its environment.

A SYSTEM RESOURCE APPROACH TO
ORGANIZATIONAL EFFECTIVENESS

The present need, to which we address our attention, is for a conception of organizational effectiveness that: (1) takes the organization itself as the focal frame of reference, rather than some external entity or some particular set of people; (2) explicitly treats the relations between the organization and its environment as a central ingredient in the definition of effectiveness; (3) provides a theoretically general framework capable of encompassing different kinds of complex organizations; (4) provides some latitude for uniqueness, variability, and change, with respect to the specific operations for assessing effectiveness applicable to any one organization, while at the same time maintaining the unity of the underlying framework for comparative evaluation; (5) provides some guide to the identification of performance and action variables relevant to organizational effectiveness and to the choice for empirical use.

A promising theoretical solution to the foregoing problems can be derived from the open system model as it is applied to formal social organiza-

[23] James D. Thompson and William J. McEwen, "Organizational Goals and Environment: Goal-Setting as an Interaction Process," *Amer. Sociol. Rev.*, 23 (Feb. 1958): 23–31.

tions. This model emphasizes the distinctiveness of the organization as an identifiable social structure or entity, and it emphasizes the interdependency processes that relate the organization to its environment. The first theme supports the idea of treating formal organizations not as phenomena incidental to individual behavior or societal functioning but as entities appropriate for analysis at their own level. The second theme points to the nature of interrelatedness between the organization and its environment as the key source of information concerning organizational effectiveness. In fact, most existing definitions of organizational effectiveness have been formulated, implicitly or explicitly, in terms of a *relation* between the organization and its environment, since the attainment of a goal or the fulfillment of a social function imply always some change in the state of the organization vis-à-vis its environment. The crucial task, then, is the conceptualization of that relation. The system model, with its view of the nature of the interaction processes between the organization and its environment, provides a useful basis for such a conceptualization.

According to that model, especially as applied to the study of organization by Katz and Kahn,[24] the interdependence between the organization and its environment takes the form of input-output transactions of various kinds relating to various things; furthermore, much of the stuff that is the object of these transactions falls into the category of *scarce and valued resources*. We shall have more to say about "resources" below. For the moment it will suffice to indicate that the value of such resources is to be derived from their utility as (more or less) generalized means for organizational activity rather than from their attachment to some specific goal. This value may or may not correspond to the personal values of the members of the organization, including their conception of its goals. It should be noted also that scarce and valued resources are, for the most part, the focus of competition between organizations. This competition, which may occur under different social settings and which may take different forms, is a continuous process underlying the emergence of a universal hierarchical differentiation among social organizations. Such a hierarchy is an excellent yardstick against which to assess organizational effectiveness. It reflects what may be referred to as the "bargaining position" of the organization in relation to resources and in relation to competing social entities that share all or part of the organization's environment.[25]

---

[24] Katz and Kahn, op. cit.

[25] The differential amounts of success of organizations with regard to their bargaining positions implies the possibility of exploitation of one organization by another, a possibility which may endanger the stability of social order. This asymmetry in interorganizational transactions and its consequences for the problem of social order underlie the sociological interest in exchange processes and their normative regulation. As pointed out recently by Blau:

"Without social norms prohibiting force and fraud, the trust required for social exchange could not serve as a self-regulating mechanism within the limits of these

We propose, accordingly, to define the effectiveness of an organization in terms of its bargaining position, as reflected in the ability of the organization, in either absolute or relative terms, to exploit its environment in the acquisition of scarce and valued resources.

The concept of "bargaining position" implies the exclusion of any specific goal (or function) as the ultimate criterion of organizational effectiveness. Instead it points to the more general capability of the organization as a resource-getting system. Specific "goals" however can be incorporated in this conceptualization in two ways: (1) as a specification of the means or strategies employed by members toward enhancing the bargaining position of the organization; and (2) as a specification of the personal goals of certain members or classes of member within the organizational system. The better the bargaining position of an organization, the more capable it is of attaining its varied and often transcient goals, and the more capable it is of allowing the attainment of the personal goals of members. Processes of "goal formation" and "goal displacement" in organizations are thus seen not as defining ultimate criteria of effectiveness, but as strategies adopted by members for enhancing the bargaining position of their organizations.

The emphasis upon the resource-getting capability of the organization is not intended to obscure other vital aspects of organizational performance. The input of resources is only one of three major cyclic phases in the system model of organizational behavior, the other two being the throughput and the output. From this viewpoint the mobilization of resources is a necessary but not a sufficient condition for organizational effectiveness. Our definition, however, points not to the availability of scarce and valued resources as such, but rather to the bargaining position with regard to the acquisition of such resources as the criterion of organizational effectiveness. Such a position at a given point of time is, so far as the organization's own behavior is concerned, a function of all the three phases of organizational behavior—the importation of resources, their use (including allocation and processing), and their exportation in some output form that aids further input.

By focusing on the ability of the organization to exploit its environment

---

norms. Moreover, superior power and resources, which often are the results of competitive advantages gained in exchange transactions, make it possible to exploit others." [*Exchange and Power in Social Life* (New York: John Wiley & Sons, 1964), p. 255.]

Blau's discussion is concerned mainly with the more limited case of exchange between individuals as social actors. Nevertheless, it points to the potential asymmetry involved in exchange processes in general and the consequences of such asymmetry namely, the emergence of a hierarchical differentiation among the interacting units with regard to their exploitative ability. For the purposes of the present discussion it is important to note that such an advantageous bargaining position, which may be dysfunctional for the system as a whole, is from the organization's point of view a sign of its success.

in the acquisition of resources we are directed by the basic yet often neglected fact that it is only in the arena of competition over scarce and valued resources that the performance of both like and unlike organizations can be assessed and evaluated comparatively. To put it somewhat differently, any change in the relation between the organization and its environment is affected by and results in a better or worse bargaining position vis-à-vis that environment or parts thereof.

It should be noticed that the proposed definition of effectiveness does not imply any specific goal toward which an organization is striving, nor does it impute some societal function as a property of the organization itself. Our definition focuses attention on *behavior*, conceived as continuous and never-ending processes of exchange and competition over scarce and valued resources.[26] We shall now discuss some of the concepts central to our definition of organizational effectiveness.

COMPETITION AND EXCHANGE

Our emphasis upon the competitive aspects of interorganizational relations implies that an assessment of organizational effectiveness is possible only where some form of competition takes place. This raises the question of how general or limited is the scope of applicability of our definition, since interorganizational transactions take forms other than competition. An old and useful distinction in this respect has recently been formulated by Blau:

> A basic distinction can be made between two major types of processes that characterize the transactions of organized collectivities—as well as those of individuals, for that matter—competitive processes reflecting endeavors to maximize scarce resources and exchange processes reflecting some form of interdependence. Competition occurs only among like social units that have the same objectives and not among unlike units. . . . Competition promotes hierarchical differentiation between more or less successful organizations, and exchange promotes horizontal differentiation between specialized organizations of diverse sort.[27]

Blau's assessment that ". . . competition promotes hierarchical differentiation between more or less *successful* organizations" is, of course, in

---

26 One reader of an early draft of this paper, Dr. Martin Patchen, inquired about the sources of directive energy in goal-less organizations. The answer is that persons who are members of the organization, and acting both within their role prescriptions and in idiosyncratic deviation from role prescriptions, impart personal values and goals which may modify the system in a directed way.

27 Peter Blau, *Exchange and Power in Social Life* (New York: John Wiley & Sons, 1964), p. 255.

line with our definition of organizational effectiveness; furthermore, there is no question about the mainly competitive character of relations among "like" social units.

However, Blau's contention that competition occurs *only* among like organizations is an oversimplification. Indeed, it is difficult to point to any interrelated organizations that are not in competition with respect to some kinds of resources, and it is easy to point to organizations that are dominantly competitive, yet have some complementarity and interdependence in their relations. A university and a business firm, for example, may be involved in an exchange of knowhow and money, and still compete with respect to such resources as manpower and prestige. The type of pure complementarity of exchange is very limited indeed. We suggest, accordingly, that exchange and competition are the extremes of a continuum along which interorganizational transactions can be described. The proposed definition of effectiveness allows then for the comparative evaluation of any two or more organizations that have some elements of rivalry in their relations. Such a comparative evaluation becomes more meaningful—in the sense of encompassing the crucial dimensions of organizational behavior—as the variety and number of competitive elements in these relations increase. The clearest and most meaningful comparison obtains when the evaluated organizations compete directly for the same resources. This condition implies that the compared organizations are engaged in like activities and share to a large degree the same temporal and physical life space. In such cases the comparison is facilitated by the fact that the competition refers to the same kinds of resources and that the assessment variables—both of input and output—are measured in like units. Comparisons are also possible, however, in the case of organizations that do not compete directly, but that compete in environments that are judged to be similar in some relevant respects.

As the characteristic transactions between organizations come closer to the exchange pole of the continuum the problem of comparison becomes more complex: first, the elements of competition may be very few in number and peripheral in importance, thus making the comparison trivial; second, the more unlike the organizations, the more difficult it is to measure their performance units on common scales. In any case, the identification of the competitive dimensions in interorganizational transactions is the key problem in the assessment of organizational effectiveness. Some clarification and possible ways of solution for this problem can be achieved through an examination of the concept of "resources."

RESOURCES

A key element in this definition is the term *resources*. Broadly defined, resources are (more or less) generalized means, or facilities, that are potentially controllable by social organizations and that are potentially usable —however indirectly—in relationships between the organization and its environment. This definition, it should be noted, does not attribute directionality as an inherent quality of a resource, nor does it limit the concept of resources to physical or economic objects or states even though a physical base must lie behind any named resource. A similar approach to "resources" is taken, for example, by Gamson. He argues that the "reputation" of individuals or groups as "influentials" in their community political affairs is itself a resource rather than simply ". . . the manifestation of the possession of large amounts of resources. . . ."[28]

One important kind of resource that is universally required by organizations, that is scarce and valued, and that is the focus for sharp competition, is energy in the form of human activity. The effectiveness of many organizations cannot be realistically assessed without some accounting for the organization's bargaining position with respect to the engagement of people in the service of the organization. One thinks, of course, of competition in the industrial or managerial labor market, but the idea is equally applicable to the competition, say, between the local church and the local political party, for the evening time of persons who are potentially active in both organizations.

Since human activity is such a crucial class of organizational resource, we elaborate on the meaning that is intended and one of the implications. We view members of an organization as an integral part of the organization with respect to their organizational role-defining and role-carrying activities, but as part of the environment of the organization with respect to their abilities, motives, other memberships, and other characteristics that are potentially useful but not utilized by the organization in role performance. An "effective" organization competes successfully for a relatively large share of the member's personality, engaging more of the personality in organizationally relevant ways, thus acquiring additional resources from its environment.

A number of other distinctions may usefully be made with respect to the resources that are involved in the effectiveness of organizations:

Liquidity. Some resources are relatively "liquid" in the traditional economic sense of that term and are readily exchangeable by an organization for resources of other kinds. Money and credit are highly liquid, being exchangeable for many other (but not all) kinds of resources. By contrast, the resource represented by high morale (among members) is relatively low in liquidity; under some conditions it is not directly exchangeable at full value in transactions with other organizations but must be internally transformed, e.g., into products or services, before exchange. Some organiza-

---

[28] William A. Gamson, "Reputation and Resources in Community Politics," *Amer. J. Sociol.* 72 (Sept. 1966): 121–31.

tions are characterized by having a large proportion of their resources in relatively non-liquid forms.

Stability. Some resources are transient in the sense that they must be acquired and utilized continuously by an organization, while other resources have the property of being stored or accumulated without significant depreciation. An organization that acquires a rapidly depreciating resource and fails to utilize this resource within an acceptable period will suffer loss of part of the value. The current high turnover among technical staff in some industrial firms is an example of loss of effectiveness through failure to utilize transient resources. By contrast, money is a highly stable resource that can be stored indefinitely at small loss and can be accumulated against future exchange requirements. Political influence is a resource of notorious instability.

Relevance. In principle, all resources are relevant to all organizations to the extent that they are capable of transformation and exchange. The degree of relevance, however, is of considerable interest, since identification of resources of high relevance offers a guide to a useful classification of organizations and serves to direct priority in comparative analyses to those kinds of resources that most clearly reflect the relative bargaining power of organizations. Degree of relevance also has a bearing upon the analysis of symbiotic relationships among organizations (high rates of exchange with relatively little bargaining and high mutual benefit) and upon the analysis of monopolistic forces (dominance of a given resource "market" and consequent enhancement of bargaining power). The degree of relevance of a given resource can be estimated on an *a priori* basis from a knowledge of the typical outputs of an organization and a knowledge of its characteristic throughout activities. Critical resources might be discerned from an analysis of changes in the pattern of internal organizational activity, for such changes can be interpreted to be a response to an enhanced requirement or a threatened deficit with respect to a given type of resource. Organizations are frequently observed to mobilize activities in a way that enhances their power to acquire certain resources. A judgment of future organizational effectiveness might accordingly be improved by information concerning the organization's ease of adaptation to shifts among classes of resources in their degree of relevance.

Universality. Some resources are of universal relevance in the sense that all organizations must be capable of acquiring such resources. The universally required classes include: (1) personnel; (2) physical facilities for the organization's activities; (3) a technology for these activities; and (4) some relatively liquid resource, such as money, that can be exchanged for other resources. The amount required of each class may in some cases be very modest, but all organizations must have, and must be able to replenish, resources of these kinds. The non-universal resources are, in general, those for which competition is limited, either because of irrelevance to many organizations or because the particular resource is ordinarily obtained amply through symbiotic exchange.

Substitution. Organizations with similar typical outputs competing in a common environment do not necessarily share the same roster of relevant and critical resources. One reason for this is that the internal processes of organizational life may be adapted to exploit certain readily available resources rather than to acquire alternative scarce resources in hard competition. An example of this is seen in the case of a small, ill-equipped guerrilla army facing a force of superior size and equipment. While exploiting rather different resources, they may compete equally for the acquisition of territorial and political control.

A crucial problem in this context is the determination of the relevant and critical resources to be used as a basis for absolute or comparative assessment of organizational effectiveness. In stable, freely competitive environments with respect to relatively liquid resources, this determination may be rather easy to make, but under other conditions the determination may be problematic indeed. The difficulties arise primarily in cases in which the competing organizations have differential access to relatively rich or relatively poor environments, where symbiotic exchange relationships may develop, where the resources are not universal, and where the possibilities of substitution are great. In such situations, the analytic approach must employ not a static conception of the relationships between an organization and its environment but rather, a conception that emphasizes adaptation and change in the organizational patterns of resource-getting.

OPTIMIZATION VS. MAXIMIZATION

In their recent analysis of complex organizations, Katz and Kahn proposed defining organizational effectiveness as "the maximization of return to the organization by all means."[29] This definition shares with the one we propose an emphasis on resource procurement as the sign of organizational success; it differs, however, in invoking the notion of maximization, a concept we have avoided. The position taken here is that maximization of return, even if possible, is destructive from the viewpoint of the organization. To understand this statement it should be remembered that the bargaining position of the organization is equated here with the ability to exploit the organization's environment—not with the maximum use of this ability. An organization that fully actualizes its exploitative potential may risk its own survival, since the exploited environment may become so depleted as to be unable to produce further resources. Furthermore, an organization that ruthlessly exploits its environment is more likely to incite a strong orga-

---

[29] Katz and Kahn, op. cit., p. 170.

nized opposition that may weaken or even destroy the organization's bargaining position. Thus, the short-run gains associated with overexploitation are likely to be outweighed by greater long-run losses. Also, the resource itself may lose value if over-exploited; for example, an effective voluntary community organization may enjoy extraordinary bargaining power in the engagement of prestigeful people, but this power may not safely be used to the maximum, because excessive recruitment risks the diminishing of the value of membership when membership ceases to be exclusive.

These considerations lead to the proposition that the highest level of organizational effectiveness is reached when the organization maximizes its bargaining position and optimizes its resource procurement. "Optimum" is the point beyond which the organization endangers itself, because of a depletion of its resource-producing environment or the devaluation of the resource, or because of the stimulation of countervailing forces within that environment. As stated by Thompson and McEwen:

> It is possible to conceive of a continuum of organizational power in environmental relations, ranging from the organization that dominates its environmental relations to one completely dominated by its environment. Few organizations approach either extreme. Certain gigantic enterprises, such as the Zaibatsu in Japan or the old Standard Oil Trust in America, have approached the dominance-over-environment position at one time; most complex organizations, falling somewhere between the extremes of the power continuum, must adopt strategies for coming to terms with their environments.[30]

We may add, however, that the need "for coming to terms with their environments" applies to organizations that approximate the dominance-over-environment extreme as well. A powerful enterprise like General Motors must exercise its potential power with much restraint in order to avoid the crystallization of an opposition which may weaken its bargaining power considerably, through legislation or some other means.

It is of course very difficult, if possible at all, to determine in absolute terms the organization's maximum bargaining position and the optimal point of resource procurement that is associated with that position. Since most organizations, however, fall short of maximizing their bargaining position, the optimization problem, though theoretically important, is only of limited empirical relevance. In practice, organizational effectiveness must be assessed in relative terms, by comparing organizations with one another. The above discussion on the nature of "resources" provides at best a general outline for carrying out such a task. A more detailed discussion and a preliminary effort to apply empirically the conceptual scheme presented here

---

[30] Thompson and McEwen, op. cit., p. 25.

is reported elsewhere.[31] Briefly, the following steps seem necessary for a meaningful comparative assessment of organizational effectiveness: (1) to provide an inclusive taxonomy of resources; (2) to identify the different types of resources that are mutually relevant for the organizations under study; and (3) to determine the relative positions of the compared organizations on the basis of information concerning the amount and kinds of resources that are available for the organization and its efficiency in using these resources to get further resources.

SOME IMPLICATIONS

We end this discussion with a few speculations about the impacts that might arise from a general acceptance and use of the conception of organizational effectiveness that we have proposed. These may affect theorists, empirical researchers and managers in various ways:

1. The rejection of the concept of an ultimate goal, and the replacement of this singular concept with one emphasizing an open-ended multidimensional set of criteria, will encourage a broadening of the scope of search for relevant criterion variables. Past studies have tended to focus too narrowly upon variables derived from traditional accounting practice or from functional social theory, or on narrowly partisan "goals" attributed to organizations. A conception of organizational effectiveness based upon organizational characteristics and upon resource-acquisition in the most general sense will encourage the treatment as criteria of many variables previously regarded as by-products or incidental phenomena in organizational functioning.

2. Past comparative studies of organizations have, in general, been of two kinds: (a) Comparison of organizations differing markedly in their characteristics, e.g. prisons and factories, so that issues of relative effectiveness were deemed irrelevant and uninteresting as well as impractical; and (b) comparisons among organizations of a similar type, so that they could be compared on like variables and measurement units. The conception we offer provides the possibility of making accessible for study the large middle range of comparisons involving organizations that have only limited similarities such that they compete with respect to some but not all of their relevant and crucial resources.

3. Case studies of single organizations will be aided by the provision of a conceptual basis for treating a more inclusive and more realistic range of variables that bear on the effectiveness of the organization.

---

[31] Stanley E. Seashore and Ephraim Yuchtman, "The Elements of Organizational Performance," a paper prepared for a symposium on People, Groups and Organizations: An Effective Integration of Knowledge, Rutgers University, November 1966. (This paper appears in *Admin. Sci. Quart.*, 1967); Ephraim Yuchtman, "A Study of Organizational Effectiveness," Ph.D. diss., University of Michigan, 1966.

4. The meaning of some familiar variables will need to be reassessed and in some cases changed. For example, distributed profit, a favorite variable for the comparative assessment of business organizations, will be more widely recognized as a cost of organizational activity and not as an unequivocal sign of success or goal achievement. Some managers have already adopted this view. Similarly, growth in size, usually interpreted as a sign of organizational achievement, can now be better seen as a variable whose meaning is tied closely to environmental factors and to the position of the organization with respect to certain other variables; the conception we have presented highlights the idea that growth in size is not in itself an unmitigated good, even though it may mean greater effectiveness under some conditions. In a similar fashion, it will be seen as necessary that the judgment of the meaning of each criterion variable rests not upon an absolute value judgment or a universal conceptual meaning, but rather upon the joint consideration of an extensive integrated set of organizational performance and activity variables.

Part II

STRUCTURE OF
ORGANIZATIONS

The structure of an organization consists of relatively fixed relationships among jobs and groups of jobs. The formal structure is created by managerial decisions which (1) *define* jobs, (2) *group* jobs into departments, (3) *determine* size of groups reporting to a single manager, and (4) *delegate* authority to the manager. The resultant structure of jobs and authority determines to a considerable degree the activities and behaviors of people who perform the jobs.

The decisions which managers must make in designing the structure relate to each of the four steps. The job definition subdecision must determine the extent to which jobs are highly specialized or highly generalized; the departmentalization subdecision determines the extent to which departments are highly homogenous or highly heterogenous; the size of the group must define whether a small or large number of subordinates reports to a manager; and the delegation subdecision must determine the extent to which authority is centralized or decentralized. If the range of alternatives for each of the four subdecisions is viewed as a continuum, then one can visualize an infinite variety of alternative organization structures.

A number of general theories of organization structure appear in the literature. Important in this regard are the concepts of bureaucracy and System 4 organization. The bureaucratic theory argues that effective organization structures tend to be at one extreme of the continua—specialized jobs, homogenous departments, narrow spans of managerial control, and centralized authority. System 4 organization proposes the opposite case— organizations characterized by generalized jobs, heterogenous departments, wide spans, and decentralized authority are more effective. Contemporary theory is now making the case for a situational, or contingency, point of view. According to situational theory, the most effective organization structure must be related to the situational factors such as environmental demands and technological parameters.

Yet even with some generalized theory to guide the organizational design decision, management must still deal with specific problems of specialization, departmentalization, span of control, and delegation. Each of the five articles in this part discuss one or more of these problems. Moreover we shall see that these problems have their counterparts in academic departments and hospitals as well as in business firms.

The first article, "Order and Innovation: A New Look at Bureaucracy," by Duncan describes an approach which combines the advantages of bureaucratic organization and laissez-faire organization. The result is an organizational structure which facilitates orderly progress toward objectives and, at the same time, innovative adaptation. This synergistic model recognizes the necessity for both the rigidity of the hierarchy *and* the adaptability of humans and argues that the two can be combined through emphasis on organizational and individual objectives.

The article by Walker and Lorsch, "Organizational Choice: Product vs. Function" examines the problem of departmentalization. They studied two firms operating in the same industry; one firm organized by product and the other organized by function. The product-based organization was characterized by heterogenous grouping of jobs; whereas, the function-based organization had more homogenous groupings of jobs. The question that the researchers posed was whether the bases for departmentalization made any difference in the effectiveness of the organization. They concluded that either product *or* function can be the appropriate basis, depending upon the environmental demands and the nature of the task performed by the organization.

The appropriate span of control has long been a key managerial issue. Wide spans are related to fewer managerial levels, indirect supervision, and decentralized authority. Narrow spans are related to numerous managerial levels, direct supervision, and centralized authority. The optimum span of control can be specified if one can measure the important variables, according to C. W. Barkdull in his article "Span of Control—A Method of Evaluation." This author reports an approach which one organization used to obtain measures of the variables which determine the optimum span. The variables, or span factors, are measured and weighted to determine an index which, in turn, determines the optimum span of control.

The fourth article in this part, "The Operation of Academic Departments" examines the manner in which university academic departments are structured. Of special interest is the way different structures are created to deal with different decisions. Some decisions are made in a democratic structure, others are made by oligarchies, while yet others are made through simple division of labor. The authors, Hobbs and Anderson, are particularly interested in the conflicts which arise among these three coexistent structures.

The last article in this part, "The Rationale for Decentralization in Large Hospitals" is authored by David B. Starkweather. He focuses attention on the organization of large hospitals and reviews the concepts of structure in relation to them. He proposes that the fundamental criterion for structural decisions should be patient service, rather than hospital operations. From this criterion he advances the argument for decentralization.

5

Order and Innovation: A New Look at Bureaucracy

W. JACK DUNCAN

In every age there is a strain toward the organizational form that will encompass and exploit the technology of the time and express its spirit.

—Warren G. Bennis

Formal organizations are complex social systems composed of individuals who participate in order to accomplish personal and collective objectives. In this sense they are simply the methods employed by man as the means of realizing subjectively determined ends.

To the individual, organizations represent the possibility of a higher standard of living and at times a degree of self-realization. To society, they are an efficient means of resource allocation. In other words, organizations are created and perpetuated to assist in the satisfaction of human and social needs.

The bureaucracy is the most common form of organizing found in the business environment. Among other things, it is characterized by the division of labor through functional specialization, a well-defined hierarchy, and a complex set of procedures and rules.

All these elements combine to make the bureaucracy a rational and efficient form of organization. This "inherent logic" prompted Max Weber to observe that "the fully developed bureaucratic mechanism compares with other organizational forms as does the machine with nonmechanical means of production." Such an observation raises a valid practical question as to why this "structure" offers so many advantages with respect to efficiency.

Source: Reprinted by permission from *Personnel Journal* (July 1972), pp. 518–22.

THE BUREAUCRATIC IDEOLOGY

The logic of the bureaucracy is founded upon the principles of specialization, standardization, and centralization. It is, for all practical purposes, a monocratic system because there is only one point of legitimacy on its elaborate hierarchy.[1] The result is often a rigid and static structure that provides for little flexibility.

No doubt this structure has evolved from the technological requirements of the day which make tremendous investments in human and capital resources an absolute necessity. For similar reasons, social and economic factors dictate the existence of bureaucracy. Group insurance programs and economies of large scale operation are hardly possible in small business establishments. In reality, every organization, large and small, must exist in an environment which imposes upon it behavioral characteristics which persist over time.[2] However, environments change faster than organizations so that lags develop as organizations attempt to adjust to changing situations. It is precisely with respect to this period of adjustment that the greatest problems develop with respect to the bureaucratic structure.

DIMENSIONS OF ORGANIZATIONAL CHANGE

Man, in order to function effectively must be able to diagnose situations, possess the ability to act, and remain flexible to change so as to improve situations in the interest of a more meaningful participation.[3] Organizations, too, must be concerned with the factors that engender buoyancy and fearlessness of revision.[4]

J. Robert Oppenheimer illustrates the inevitability of change in the following statement:

> . . . the world alters as we walk in it so that the years of a man's life measure not some small growth or rearrangement of what he learned in childhood but a great upheaval.[5]

Unfortunately, within the organizational framework there are various types of change, some of which are more troublesome to deal with than others. One can classify this phenomenon under the headings of sociological and technological modifications.

---

[1] Victor A. Thompson, "Bureaucracy and Innovation," *Administrative Science Quarterly,* Vol. X, No. 1 (June, 1965), p. 2.

[2] Paul R. Lawrence, *The Changing of Organizational Behavior,* Harvard University Graduate School of Business, Research Division, Boston, 1958, p. 6.

[3] H. E. Frank, "An Indirect Approach to Organizational Improvement," *Management International Review,* No. 4 (1966), p. 35.

[4] Warren G. Bennis, *Changing Organizations,* McGraw-Hill Book Company, Inc., New York, 1966, p. 258.

[5] *Ibid,* p. 19.

Technological change relates to any measurable alteration in the product being produced or the physical routines of the job. Sociological change, on the other hand, describes the way those affected by technological fluctuations think it will alter their established relationships within the organizations.[6] Administratively, the latter is often more difficult to deal with if for no other reason than a tendency on the part of management to neglect its existence.[7]

Bureaucracies experience little difficulty with technological change. In fact, their ability to take advantage of developing technology is one of their greatest virtues. The same cannot be said with respect to sociological change. The very same rationality which is receptive to technology requires an attitude that is not sympathetic with the consequences of social variations.

The future can only intensify these complications because reactionary changes are becoming less and less sufficient. To the contrary, progressive organizations cannot enjoy the luxury of reaction in our modern society, but must initiate alterations and by their very actions create the social pressures they will be called upon to reduce. Thus, the manager must become an administrator of conflict as well as an agent of change.

With this in mind, the basic problem becomes evident. How can organizations be structured so as to maintain order, while simultaneously providing a climate conducive to innovation?

TOWARD THE CREATIVE BUREAUCRACY

Tomorrow's organization must be an adaptive yet dynamic system capable of changing as well as co-existing with its external and internal environment. This will obviously require an understanding of the forces regulating innovation and change and increase the pressure for a science of organizational behavior.[8] But this will require a fundamental alteration in our traditional philosophy of organization. Specifically, it will require changes in the following areas:[9]

1. A new concept of man based on increased knowledge of his complex and shifting needs.
2. A new concept of power based on collaboration and reason.
3. A new concept of organizational values based on humanistic-demo-

---

[6] Paul R. Lawrence and John A. Seiler, *Organizational Behavior and Administration,* Revised edition, Richard D. Irwin, Homewood, Ill. 1965, pp. 929–30.

[7] Maurice J. Warnock, "Adapting to Change," *Advanced Management Journal,* Vol. XXXI, No. 2 (April, 1966), p. 30.

[8] M. A. Robinson, "The Science of Organizations," *Management International Review,* No. 4, 1966, p. 5.

[9] Warren G. Bennis, "Organizational Revitalization," *California Management Review,* Vol. IX, No. 1 (Fall, 1966), p. 55.

cratic ideas to replace the depersonalized mechanistic value system typical of pure bureaucracy.

To be sure, the bureaucratic mechanism, so capable of coordinating men and power in a stable environment of routine tasks, is not necessarily successful in a society typified by flux.[10]

THE BASIC PROBLEM

Healthy organizational climates require a supportive relationship between employee and employer. This, in turn, requires at least some degree of compatibility between individual needs and organizational objectives. If this does not exist, problems develop.

Bureaucracies emphasize conformity. This is their means of providing order. Difference and flux become the enemy, not the friend of the organizational man.[11] Organizational conformity, however, results in the reduction of individual freedom. This conflict becomes accentuated as more university-trained employees enter the work force. These individuals are, in general, more inclined to become intellectually committed to their work and require more involvement, participation, and autonomy in their jobs. Structured and rigorous hierarchies are rarely capable of accomplishing such a relationship. The structure capable of this will likely be a temporary system of diverse specialists linked together by the tasks at hand.[12]

A PROPOSED SOLUTION

The elaborations to follow are an outgrowth of Mary Parker Follet's concepts of cross-functioning, group responsibility, and cumulative responsibility.[13] It is impossible for any individual to operate in isolation, because each function must be viewed in terms of its interdependence with and its contribution to other tasks. Obviously, this is hinting at the idea of a system where an environment exists which encourages cross-functioning rather than excursions up and down the hierarchy.

It must be noted at this point that the system envisioned does not question the legitimacy of managerial authority—this issue was settled decades

---

[10] Alexander Winn, "Social Change in Industry: From Insight to Implementation," *The Journal of Applied Behavioral Science,* Vol. II, No. 2 (April-May-June, 1966), p. 170.

[11] David Ewing, *The Managerial Mind,* Collier-McMillian, Limited, London, 1964, pp. 33–34.

[12] Warren G. Bennis, "Changing Organizations," *The Journal of Applied Behavioral Science,* Vol. II, No. 3 (July, August, September, 1966), p. 249.

[13] Joel M. Rosenfeld and Matthew J. Smith, "Mary Parker Follet: The Transition to Modern Management Thought," *Advanced Management Journal,* Vol. XXXI, No. 4 (Oct., 1966), p. 36.

ago. Any time there is more than one way to accomplish a specific objective, authority must be exercised. The proposed system does, however, question the absolute nature of organizational authority and its method of usage. Specifically, it attempts to distinguish between essential and substitutional authority and show how the two can be properly combined to acquire a quasi-creative bureaucracy.[14]

Essential authority provides some agency with enough authority to provide stability and see to it that differences between various levels are corrected. Substitutional authority is different in that it displays two general characteristics.[15]

1. It is aimed at the proper good of the organization and the individual.
2. It is self-destructive in that it attempts to develop the skill of an individual to the point where competency no longer requires authority.

Graphically this condition can be illustrated with the aid of Figure 1. The horizontal axis measures the degree of individual development, while the vertical axis measures authority. Essential authority is represented by a straight horizontal line which is at all points equidistant from the x-axis because it is constant over time. The line illustrating substantial authority is downward sloping and approaches the horizontal axis at high levels of individual development.

Therefore, total authority (T_A) present in an organization at a given time is the sum of the essential (E_A) and substitutional (S_A) counterparts, so that:

$$T_A = E_A + S_A$$

In all cases E_A is constant since it is the minimum amount necessary to provide the organization with operational stability. It is, in other words, the absolute minimum required to establish and define orderly relationships.

Unlike E_A, S_A is a decreasing function of the degree of development. It is a gradual reduction which provides authority only when it is needed, not just for the sake of its application. Authority does not decay but as the individual develops, his objectives become more compatible with the organization's. If not, he will likely disassociate himself from it. Likewise, the necessity for control diminishes because the individual and the organization begin to mutually reinforce each other.

Of course, some will not develop yet retain their membership. This confronts practicing management with the dilemma "Shall the structure be designed to control the few who seek to destroy the system or to benefit the

[14] Robert Albanese, "Substantial and Essential Authority," *Academy of Management Journal*, Vol. IX, No. 2 (June, 1966), pp. 140–41.

[15] *Ibid.*, p. 142.

FIGURE 1
Essential and Substitutional Authority

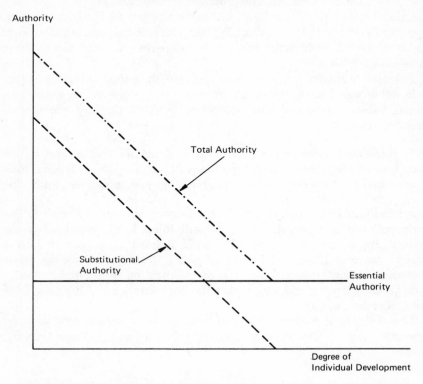

Source: Adopted from some basic concepts developed in Robert Albanese, "Substitutional and Essential Authority," *Academy of Management Journal,* Vol. IX, No. 2 (June 1966).

many who can and will operate within and improve it?"[16] If they select the latter, the solution must be a combination of several structures.

A SYNERGISTIC MODEL

Whereas the bureaucracy is typified by a hierarchy and impersonality, the essentials of a laissez-faire system are personality and incentive.[17] Bureaucracies are formal and orderly, while laissez-faire structures adapt easily to change. The weakness of the former is power anxiety, while the latter may result in excessively random actions. Therefore, what is needed

---

[16] Raymond E. Miles, "The Affluent Organization," *Harvard Business Review,* Vol. XL, No. 3 (May-June, 1966), p. 113.

[17] Marshall E. Dimock, *Administrative Vitality,* Harper and Brothers, New York, 1959, pp. 1–2.

is a philosophy which will maximize the advantages and minimize the disadvantages of the respective systems and provide meaningful directions in
the rational quest for individual and organizational goals.

Figure 2 presents a visual representation of a model proposing to combine the two philosophies in a synergistic fashion, that is, via a consolidation of the two something better than the sum of the parts is obtained.
Reading from the bottom to the top, it may be observed that the orderliness
and technological adaptability of bureaucracy is provided through the
exercise of essential authority. Personality and innovation are obtained by
the reductive nature of the substitutive element. Thus, the hierarchy is
retained but its rigidity is reduced.

It should be recognized that this combination, by its very nature, will
complicate rather than simplify the manager's job. Only the most talented
administrator could accomplish the type of "fine-tuning" that will be required. Above all it will require the exercise of expert judgment and a
sense of devotion to the objective. Only after this is accomplished is it
possible for the individual and the organization to reinforce each other's
objectives.

FIGURE 2
The Creative Bureaucracy

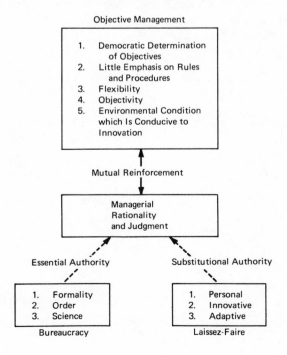

At this point, administration takes on its most meaningful dimension, which is the management of objectives (the coordinating of individual and organizational goals), not the rigid control of individuals. It places upon the manager the proper function of providing direction and coordinating accomplishments toward desired ends. The results would be an increased dignity and importance to the functions of management, as well as a sense of participation and meaning to the individual. The creative bureaucracy is the creation of an innovative atmosphere within an orderly climate. It is the management of objectives through the administration of men.

In conclusion, it must be noted that this model is not proposed as a universal solution to the problem of organization. Its applicability is restricted almost completely to firms whose employees are technically and professionally trained individuals. It is not likely to provide satisfactory results where low-skilled and immature individuals are involved. But it is not the lower-skilled workers who are seriously damaged, professionally and occupationally, from the traditional bureaucracy. The real problem exists with the highly trained.

Since managerial judgment determines the relative "mix" of bureaucracy and laissez-faire, fluctuating circumstances can be provided for with very little difficulty. Since both alternatives are available, order can be provided where it is needed while free-reigns can be given where the situation dictates. It is in this fashion that the constraints placed upon organizations by the scarcities of the human resource can be converted into dynamic interactions and provide the ability not only to adapt but to create and direct change in the best interest of all concerned.

6

Organizational Choice:
Product vs. Function

ARTHUR H. WALKER and JAY W. LORSCH

Of all the issues facing a manager as he thinks about the form of his
organization, one of the thorniest is the question of whether to group activities primarily by product or by function. Should all specialists in a
given function be grouped under a common boss, regardless of differences
in products they are involved in, or should the various functional specialists
working on a single product be grouped together under the same superior?

In talks with managers we have repeatedly heard them anguishing over
this choice. For example, recently a divisional vice president of a major
U.S. corporation was contemplating a major organizational change. After
long study, he made this revealing observation to his subordinate managers:

> We still don't know which choice will be the best one. Should the
> research, engineering, marketing, and production people be grouped
> separately in departments for each function? Or would it be better
> to have them grouped together in product departments, each depart-
> ment dealing with a particular product group?
>
> We were organized by product up until a few years ago. Then we
> consolidated our organization into specialized functional departments,
> each dealing with all of our products. Now I'm wondering if we

Source: Reprinted by permission from *Harvard Business Review* (November-December 1968) 129–38. © 1968 by the Presidents and Fellows of Harvard College; all
rights reserved.

wouldn't be better off to divide our operations again into product units. Either way I can see advantages and disadvantages, trade-offs. What criteria should I use? How can we predict what the outcomes will be if we change?

Companies that have made a choice often feel confident that they have resolved this dilemma. Consider the case of a large advertising agency that consolidated its copy, art, and television personnel into a "total creative department." Previously they had reported to group heads in their areas of specialization. In a memo to employees the company explained the move:

> Formation of the "total creative" department completely tears down the walls between art, copy, and television people. Behind this move is the realization that for best results all creative people, regardless of their particular specialty, must work together under the most intimate relationship as total advertising people, trying to solve creative problems together from start to finish.
>
> The new department will be broken into five groups reporting to the senior vice president and creative director, each under the direction of an associative creative director. Each group will be responsible for art, television, and copy in their accounts.

But our experience is that such reorganizations often are only temporary. The issues involved are so complex that many managements oscillate between these two choices or try to effect some compromise between them.

In this article we shall explore—from the viewpoint of the behavioral scientist—some of the criteria that have been used in the past to make these choices, and present ideas from recent studies that suggest more relevant criteria for making the decision. We hope to provide a way of thinking about these problems that will lead to the most sensible decisions for the accomplishment of organizational goals.

The dilemma of product versus function is by no means new; managers have been facing the same basic question for decades. As large corporations like Du Pont and General Motors grew, they found it necessary to divide their activities among product divisions.[1] Following World War II, as companies expanded their sales of existing products and added new products and businesses, many of them implemented a transition from functional organizations handling a number of different products to independently managed product divisions. These changes raised problems concerning divisionalization, decentralization, corporate staff activities, and the like.

As the product divisions grew and prospered, many companies ex-

---

[1] For a historical study of the organizational structure of U.S. corporations, see Alfred D. Chandler, Jr., *Strategy and Structure* (Cambridge, The M.I.T. Press, 1962).

tended the idea of product organization further down in their organizations under such labels as "the unit management concept." Today most of the attention is still being directed to these changes and innovations *within* product or market areas below the divisional level.

We are focusing therefore on these organizational issues at the middle and lower echelons of management, particularly on the crucial questions being faced by managers today within product divisions. The reader should note, however, that a discussion of these issues is immensely complicated by the fact that a choice at one level of the corporate structure affects the choices and criteria for choice at other levels. Nonetheless, the ideas we suggest in this article are directly relevant to organizational choice at any level.

ELEMENTS TO CONSIDER

To understand more fully the factors that make these issues so difficult, it is useful to review the criteria often relied on in making this decision. Typically, managers have used technical and economic criteria. They ask themselves, for instance, "Which choice will minimize payroll costs?" Or, "Which will best utilize equipment and specialists?" This approach not only makes real sense in the traditional logic of management, but it has strong support from the classical school of organization theorists. Luther Gulick, for example, used it in arguing for organization by function:

> It guarantees the maximum utilization of up-to-date technical skill and . . . makes it possible in each case to make use of the most effective divisions of work and specialization. . . . [It] makes possible also the economies of the maximum use of labor-saving machinery and mass production. . . . [It] encourages coordination in all of the technical and skilled work of the enterprise. . . . [It] furnishes an excellent approach to the development of central coordination and control.[2]

In pointing to the advantages of the product basis of organization, two other classical theorists used the same approach:

> Product or product line is an important basis for departmentalizing, because it permits the maximum use of personal skills and specialized knowledge, facilitates the employment of specialized capital and makes easier a certain type of coordination.[3]

In sum, these writers on organization suggested that the manager should make the choice based on three criteria:

[2] Luther Gulick, "Notes on the Theory of Organization," in *Papers on the Science of Administration*, edited by Luther Gulick and Lyndall F. Urwick (New York, New York Institute of Public Administration, 1937), pp. 23–24.

[3] Harold D. Koontz and C. J. O'Donnell, *Principles of Management* (New York, McGraw-Hill Book Company, Inc., 2nd edition, 1959), p. 111.

1. Which approach permits the maximum use of special technical knowledge?
2. Which provides the most efficient utilization of machinery and equipment?
3. Which provides the best hope of obtaining the required control and coordination?

There is nothing fundamentally wrong with these criteria as far as they go, and, of course, managers have been using them. But they fail to recognize the complex set of trade-offs involved in these decisions. As a consequence, managers make changes that produce unanticipated results and may even reduce the effectiveness of their organization. For example:

A major manufacturer of corrugated containers a few years ago shifted from a product basis to a functional basis. The rationale for the decision was that it would lead to improved control of production costs and efficiencies in production and marketing. While the organization did accomplish these aims, it found itself less able to obtain coordination among its local sales and production units. The functional specialists now reported to the top officers in charge of production and sales, and there was no mechanism for one person to coordinate their work below the level of division management. As a result, the company encountered numerous problems and unresolved conflicts among functions and later returned to the product form.

This example pinpoints the major trade-off that the traditional criteria omit. Developing highly specialized functional units makes it difficult to achieve coordination or integration among these units. On the other hand, having product units as the basis for organization promotes collaboration between specialists, but the functional specialists feel less identification with functional goals.

Behaviorists' Findings

We now turn to some new behavioral science approaches to designing organization structure. Recent studies[4] have highlighted three other important factors about specialization and coordination:

As we have suggested, the classical theorists saw specialization in terms of grouping similar activities, skills, or even equipment. They did not look at its psychological and social consequences. Recently, behavioral scientists (including the authors) have found that there is an important relationship between a unit's or individual's assigned activities and the unit members' patterns of thought and behavior. Functional specialists tend to

---

[4] See Paul R. Lawrence and Jay W. Lorsch, *Organization and Environment* (Boston, Division of Research, Harvard Business School, 1967); and Eric J. Miller and A. K. Rice, *Systems of Organization* (London, Tavistock Publications, 1967).

develop patterns of behavior and thought that are in tune with the demands of their jobs and their prior training, and as a result these specialists (e.g., industrial engineers and production supervisors) have different ideas and orientation about what is important in getting the job done. This is called *differentiation*, which simply means the differences in behavior and thought patterns that develop among different specialists in relation to their respective tasks. Differentiation is necessary for functional specialists to perform their jobs effectively.

Differentiation is closely related to achievement of coordination, or what behavioral scientists call *integration*. This means collaboration between specialized units or individuals. Recent studies have demonstrated that there is an inverse relationship between differentiation and integration: the more two functional specialists (or their units) differ in their patterns of behavior and thought, the more difficult it is to bring about integration between them. Nevertheless, this research has indicated, achievement of both differentiation and integration is essential if organizations are to perform effectively.

While achievement of both differentiation and integration is possible, it can occur only when well-developed means of communication among specialists exist in the organization and when the specialists are effective in resolving the inevitable cross-functional conflicts.

These recent studies, then, point to certain related questions that managers must consider when they choose between a product or functional basis of organization:

1. How will the choice affect differentiation among specialists? Will it allow the necessary differences in viewpoint to develop so that specialized tasks can be performed effectively?

2. How does the decision affect the prospects of accomplishing integration? Will it lead, for instance, to greater differentiation, which will increase the problems of achieving integration?

3. How will the decision affect the ability of organization members to communicate with each other, resolve conflicts, and reach the necessary joint decisions?

There appears to be a connection between the appropriate extent of differentiation and integration and the organization's effectiveness in accomplishing its economic goals. What the appropriate pattern is depends on the nature of external factors—markets, technology, and so on—facing the organization, as well as the goals themselves. The question of how the organizational pattern will affect individual members is equally complex. Management must consider how much stress will be associated with a certain pattern and whether such stress should be a serious concern.

To explore in more detail the significance of modern approaches to organizational structuring, we shall describe one recent study conducted in two manufacturing plants—one organized by *product,* the other on a *functional* basis.[5]

PLANT F AND PLANT P

The two plants where this study was conducted were selected because they were closely matched in several ways. They were making the same product; their markets, technology, and even raw materials were identical. The parent companies were also similar: both were large, national corporations that developed, manufactured, and marketed many consumer products. In each case divisional and corporate headquarters were located more than 100 miles from the facilities studied. The plants were separated from other structures at the same site, where other company products were made.

Both plants had very similar management styles. They stressed their desire to foster employees' initiative and autonomy and placed great reliance on selection of well-qualified department heads. They also identified explicitly the same two objectives. The first was to formulate, package, and ship the products in minimum time at specified levels of quality and at minimum cost—that is, within existing capabilities. The second was to improve the capabilities of the plant.

In each plant there were identical functional specialists involved with the manufacturing units and packing unit, as well as quality control, planning and scheduling, warehousing, industrial engineering, and plant engineering. In Plant F (with the *functional* basis of organization), only the manufacturing departments and the planning and scheduling function reported to the plant manager responsible for the product (see *Exhibit 1*). All other functional specialists reported to the staff of the divisional manufacturing manager, who was also responsible for plants manufacturing other products. At Plant P (with the *product* basis of organization), all functional specialists with the exception of plant engineering reported to the plant manager (see *Exhibit 2*).

State of Differentiation

In studying differentiation, it is useful to focus on the functional specialists' differences in outlook in terms of:

1. Orientation toward goals.
2. Orientation toward time.
3. Perception of the formality of organization.

---

[5] Arthur H. Walker, *Behavioral Consequences of Contrasting Patterns of Organization* (Boston, Harvard Business School, unpublished doctoral dissertation, 1967).

EXHIBIT 1

Organizational Chart at Plant F

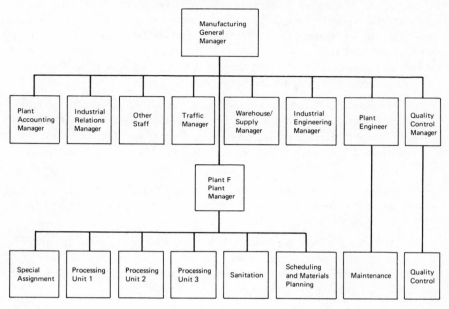

EXHIBIT 2

Organizational Chart at Plant P

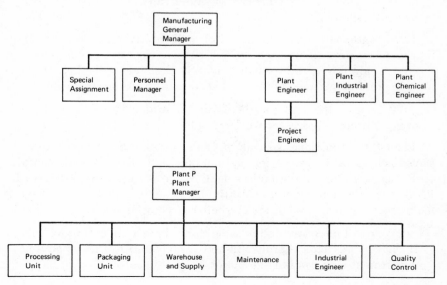

Goal Orientation.   The bases of organization in the two plants had a marked effect on the specialists' differentiated goal orientations. In Plant F they focused sharply on their specialized goals and objectives. For example, quality control specialists were concerned almost exclusively with meeting quality standards, industrial engineers with methods improvements and cost reduction, and scheduling specialists with how to meet schedule requirements. An industrial engineer in Plant F indicated this intensive interest in his own activity:

> "We have 150 projects worth close to a million dollars in annual savings. I guess I've completed some that save as much as $90,000 a year. Right now I'm working on cutting departmental costs. You need a hard shell in this work. No one likes to have his costs cut, but that is my job."

That these intense concerns with specialized objectives were expected is illustrated by the apologetic tone of a comment on product goals by an engineering supervisor at Plant F:

> "At times we become too much involved in production. It causes a change in heart. We are interested in production, but not at the expense of our own standards of performance. If we get too much involved, then we may become compromised."

A final illustration is when production employees stood watching while members of the maintenance department worked to start a new production line, and a production supervisor remarked:

> "I hope that they get that line going soon. Right now, however, my hands are tied. Maintenance has the job. I can only wait. My people have to wait, too."

This intense concern with one set of goals is analogous to a rifle shot; in a manner of speaking, each specialist took aim at one set of goals and fired at it. Moreover, the specialists identified closely with their counterparts in other plants and at divisional headquarters. As one engineer put it:

> "We carry the ball for them (the central office). We carry a project through and get it working right."

At Plant P the functional specialists' goals were more diffuse—like buckshot. Each specialist was concerned not only with his own goals, but also with the operation of the entire plant. For example, in contrast to the Plant F production supervisor's attitude about maintenance, a Plant P maintenance manager said, under similar circumstances:

> "We're all interested in the same thing. If I can help, I'm willing. If I have a mechanical problem, there is no member of the operating department who wouldn't go out of his way to solve it."

Additional evidence of this more diffuse orientation toward goals is provided by comments such as these which came from Plant P engineers and managers:

> "We are here for a reason—to run this place the best way we know how. There is no reluctance to be open and frank despite various backgrounds and ages."
>
> "The changeovers tell the story. Everyone shows willingness to dig in. The whole plant turns out to do cleaning up."

Because the functional specialists at Plant F focused on their individual goals, they had relatively wide differences in goals and objectives. Plant P's structure, on the other hand, seemed to make functional specialists more aware of common product goals and reduced differences in goal orientation. Yet, as we shall see, this lesser differentiation did not hamper their performance.

Time Orientation.   The two organizational bases had the opposite effect, however, on the time orientation of functional managers. At Plant F, the specialists shared a concern with short-term issues (mostly daily problems). The time orientation of specialists at Plant P was more differentiated. For example, its production managers concentrated on routine matters, while planning and industrial engineering focused on issues that needed solution within a week, and quality control specialists worried about even longer-term problems.

The reason is not difficult to find. Since Plant P's organization led its managers to identify with product goals, those who could contribute to the solution of longer-term problems became involved in these activities. In Plant F, where each unit focused on its own goals, there was more of a tendency to worry about getting daily progress. On the average, employees of Plant P reported devoting 30% of their time to daily problems, while at Plant F this figure was 49%. We shall have more to say shortly about how these factors influenced the results achieved in the two plants.

Organizational Formality.   In the study, the formality of organizational structure in each functional activity was measured by three criteria:

1. Clarity of definition of job responsibilities.
2. Clarity of dividing lines between jobs.
3. Importance of rules and procedures.

It was found that at Plant F there were fewer differences among functional activities in the formality of organization structure than at Plant P. Plant F employees reported that a uniform degree of structure existed across functional specialties; job responsibilities were well defined, and the distinctions between jobs were clear. Similarly, rules and procedures were extensively relied on. At Plant P, on the other hand, substantial differences in the formality of organization existed. Plant engineers and industrial engineers, for example, were rather vague about their responsibilities and about the dividing line between their jobs and other jobs. Similarly, they reported relatively low reliance on rules and procedures. Production managers, on the other hand, noted that their jobs were well defined and that rules and procedures were more important to them.

The effects of these two bases of organization on differentiation along these three dimensions are summarized in *Exhibit 3*. Overall, differentiation was greater between functional specialists at Plant P than at Plant F.

EXHIBIT 3

Differentiation in Plants F and P

Dimensions of differentiation	Plant F	Plant P
Goal orientation	More differentiated and focused	Less differentiated and more diffuse
Time orientation	Less differentiated and shorter term	More differentiated and longer term
Formality of structure	Less differentiated, with more formality	More differentiated, with less formality

Integration Achieved

While the study found that both plants experienced some problems in accomplishing integration, these difficulties were more noticeable at Plant F. Collaboration between maintenance and production personnel and between production and scheduling was a problem there. In Plant P the only relationship where integration was unsatisfactory was that between production and quality control specialists. Thus Plant P seemed to be getting slightly better integration in spite of the greater differentiation among specialists in that organization. Since differentiation and integration are basically antagonistic, the only way managers at Plant P could get both was by being effective at communication and conflict resolution. They were better at this than were managers at Plant F.

Communication Patterns. In Plant P, communication among employees was more frequent, less formal, and more often of a face-to-face nature than was the case with Plant F personnel. One Plant P employee volunteered: "Communications are no problem around here. You can say it. You can get an answer."

Members of Plant F did not reflect such positive feelings. They were heard to say:

"Why didn't they tell me this was going to happen? Now they've shut down the line."

"When we get the information, it is usually too late to do any real planning. We just do our best."

The formal boundaries outlining positions that were more prevalent at Plant F appeared to act as a damper on communication. The encounters observed were often a succession of two-man conversations, even though more than two may have been involved in a problem. The telephone and written memoranda were more often employed than at Plant P, where spontaneous meetings involving several persons were frequent, usually in the cafeteria.

Dealing with Conflict. In both plants, *confrontation* of conflict was reported to be more typical than either the use of power to *force* one's own position or an attempt to *smooth* conflict by "agreeing to disagree." There was strong evidence, nevertheless, that in Plant P managers were coming to grips with conflicts more directly than in Plant F. Managers at Plant F reported that more conflicts were being smoothed over. They worried that issues were often not getting settled. As they put it:

"We have too many nice guys here."

"If you can't resolve an issue, you go to the plant manager. But we don't like to bother him often with small matters. We should be able to settle them ourselves. The trouble is we don't. So it dies."

Thus, by ignoring conflict in the hope it would go away, or by passing it to a higher level, managers at Plant F often tried to smooth over their differences. While use of the management hierarchy is one acceptable way to resolve conflict, so many disagreements at Plant F were pushed upstairs that the hierarchy became overloaded and could not handle all the problems facing it. So it responded by dealing with only the more immediate and pressing ones.

At Plant P the managers uniformly reported that they resolved conflicts themselves. There was no evidence that conflicts were being avoided or smoothed over. As one manager said:

"We don't let problems wait very long. There's no sense to it. And besides, we get together frequently and have plenty of chances to discuss differences over a cup of coffee."

As this remark suggests, the quicker resolution of conflict was closely related to the open and informal communication pattern prevailing at Plant P. In spite of greater differentiation in time orientation and structure, then, Plant P managers were able to achieve more satisfactory integration because they could communicate and resolve conflict effectively.

Performance and Attitudes

Before drawing some conclusions from the study of these two plants, it is important to make two more relevant comparisons between them—their effectiveness in terms of the goals set for them and the attitudes of employees.

Plant Performance. As we noted before, the managements of the two plants were aiming at the same two objectives:

1. Maximizing current output within existing capabilities.
2. Improving the capabilities of the plant.

Of the two facilities, Plant F met the first objective more effectively; it was achieving a higher production rate with greater efficiency and at less cost than was Plant P. In terms of the second objective, however, Plant P was clearly superior to Plant F; the former's productivity had increased by 23% from 1963 to 1966 compared with the latter's increment of only 3%. One key manager at Plant F commented:

"There has been a three- or four-year effort to improve our capability. Our expectations have simply not been achieved. The improvement in performance is just not there. We are still where we were three years ago. But our targets for improvements are realistic."

By contrast, a key manager at Plant P observed: "Our crews have held steady, yet our volume is up. Our quality is consistently better, too."

Another said: "We are continuing to look for and find ways to improve and consolidate jobs."

Employee Attitudes. Here, too, the two organizations offer a contrast, but the contrast presents a paradoxical situation. Key personnel at Plant P appeared to be more deeply involved in their work than did managers at Plant F, and they admitted more often to feeling stress and pressure than did their opposite numbers at Plant F. But Plant F managers expressed more satisfaction with their work than did those at Plant P; they liked the company and their jobs more than did managers at Plant P.

Why Plant P managers felt more involved and had a higher level of stress, but were less satisfied than Plant F managers, can best be explained by linking these findings with the others we have reported.

Study Summary

The characteristics of these two organizations are summarized in *Exhibit 4.* The nature of the organization at Plant F seemed to suit its stable but high rate of efficiency. Its specialists concentrated on their own goals and performed well, on the whole. The jobs were well defined and managers worked within procedures and rules. The managers were concerned primarily with short-term matters. They were not particularly effective in communicating with each other and in resolving conflict. But this was not very important to achieve steady, good performance, since the coordination necessary to meet this objective could be achieved

EXHIBIT 4

Observed Characteristics of the Two Organizations

Characteristics	Plant F	Plant P
Differentiation	Less differentiation except in goal orientation	Greater differentiation in structure and time orientation
Integration	Somewhat less effective	More effective
Conflict management	Confrontation, but also "smoothing over" and avoidance; rather restricted communication pattern	Confrontation of conflict; open, face-to-face communication
Effectiveness	Efficient, stable production; but less successful in improving plant capabilities	Successful in improving plant capabilities, but less effective in stable production
Employee attitudes	Prevalent feeling of satisfaction, but less feeling of stress and involvement	Prevalent feeling of stress and involvement, but less satisfaction

through plans and procedures and through the manufacturing technology itself.

As long as top management did not exert much pressure to improve performance dramatically, the plant's managerial hierarchy was able to resolve the few conflicts arising from daily operations. And as long as the organization avoided extensive problem solving, a great deal of personal contact was not very important. It is not surprising therefore that the managers were satisfied and felt relatively little pressure. They attended strictly to their own duties, remained uninvolved, and got the job done. For them, this combination was satisfying. And higher management was pleased with the facility's production efficiency.

The atmosphere at Plant P, in contrast, was well suited to the goal of improving plant capabilities, which it did very well. There was less differentiation between goals, since the functional specialists to a degree shared the product goals. Obviously, one danger in this form of organization is the potential attraction of specialist managers to total goals to the extent that they lose sight of their particular goals and become less effective in their jobs. But this was not a serious problem at Plant P.

Moreover, there was considerable differentiation in time orientation and structure; some specialists worked at the routine and programmed tasks in operating the plant, while others concentrated on longer-term problems to improve manufacturing capability. The latter group was less constrained by formal procedures and job definitions, and this atmosphere was conducive to problem solving. The longer time orientation of some specialists, however, appeared to divert their attention from maintaining schedules and productivity. This was a contributing factor to Plant P's less effective current performance.

In spite of the higher degree of differentiation in these dimensions, Plant P managers were able to achieve the integration necessary to solve problems that hindered plant capability. Their shared goals and a common boss encouraged them to deal directly with each other and confront their conflicts. Given this pattern, it is not surprising that they felt very involved in their jobs. Also they were under stress because of their great involvement in their jobs. This stress could lead to dissatisfaction with their situation. Satisfaction for its own sake, however, may not be very important; there was no evidence of higher turnover of managers at Plant P.

Obviously, in comparing the performance of these two plants operating with similar technologies and in the same market, we might predict that, because of its greater ability to improve plant capabilities, Plant P eventually will reach a performance level at least as high as Plant F's. While this might occur in time, it should not obscure one important point: the functional organization seems to lead to better results in a situation where stable performance of a routine task is desired, while the product organization leads to better results in situations where the task is less predictable and requires innovative problem solving.

CLUES FOR MANAGERS

How can the manager concerned with the function versus product decision use these ideas to guide him in making the appropriate choice? The essential step is identifying the demands of the task confronting the organization.

Is it a routine, repetitive task? Is it one where integration can be achieved by plan and conflict managed through the hierarchy? This was the way the task was implicitly defined at Plant F. If this is the nature of the task, or, to put it another way, if management is satisfied with this definition of the task, then the functional organization is quite appropriate. While it allows less differentiation in time orientation and structure, it does encourage differentiation in goal orientation. This combination is important for specialists to work effectively in their jobs.

Perhaps even more important, the functional structure also seems to permit a degree of integration sufficient to get the organization's work done. Much of this can be accomplished through paper systems and through the hardware of the production line itself. Conflict that comes up can more safely be dealt with through the management hierarchy, since the difficulties of resolving conflict are less acute. This is so because the tasks provide less opportunity for conflict and because the specialists have less differentiated viewpoints to overcome. This form of organization is less psychologically demanding for the individuals involved.

On the other hand, if the task is of a problem-solving nature, or if management defines it this way, the product organization seems to be more appropriate. This is especially true where there is a need for tight integration among specialists. As illustrated at Plant P, the product organization form allows the greater differentiation in time orientation and structure that specialists need to attack problems. While encouraging identification with superordinate goals, this organizational form does allow enough differentiation in goals for specialists to make their contributions.

Even more important, to identify with product ends and have a common boss encourages employees to deal constructively with conflict, communicate directly and openly with each other, and confront their differences, so they can collaborate effectively. Greater stress and less satisfaction for the individual may be unavoidable, but it is a small price to pay for the involvement that accompanies it.

The manager's problem in choosing between product and functional forms is complicated by the fact that in each organization there are routine tasks and tasks requiring problem solving, jobs requiring little interdependence among specialists and jobs requiring a great deal. Faced with these mixtures, many companies have adopted various compromises between product and functional bases. They include (in ascending order of structural complexity):

1. *The use of cross-functional teams to facilitate integration.* These teams provide some opportunity for communication and conflict resolution and also a degree of the common identification with product goals that characterizes the product organization. At the same time, they retain the differentiation provided by the functional organization.

2. *The appointment of full-time integrators or coordinators around a product.* These product managers or project managers encourage the functional specialists to become committed to product goals and help resolve conflicts between them. The specialists still retain their primary identification with their functions.[6]

3. *The "matrix" or grid organization, which combines the product and functional forms by overlaying them.* Some managers wear functional hats and are involved in the day-to-day, more routine activities. Naturally, they identify with functional goals. Others, wearing product or project hats, identify with total product goals and are more involved in the problem-solving activity required to cope with long-range issues and to achieve cross-functional coordination.

These compromises are becoming popular because they enable companies to deal with multiple tasks simultaneously. But we do not propose them as a panacea, because they make sense only for those situations where the differentiation and integration required by the sum of all the

---

[6] See Paul R. Lawrence and Jay W. Lorsch, "New Management Job: The Integrator," *Harvard Business Review*, November-December 1967, p. 142.

tasks make a middle approach necessary. Further, the complexity of inter-personal plus organizational relationships in these forms and the am-biguity associated with them make them difficult to administer effectively and psychologically demanding on the persons involved.

In our view, the only solution to the product versus function dilemma lies in analysis of the multiple tasks that must be performed, the differ-ences between specialists, the integration that must be achieved, and the mechanisms and behavior required to resolve conflict and arrive at these states of differentiation and integration. This analysis provides the best hope of making a correct product or function choice or of arriving at some appropriate compromise solution.

7

Span of Control—
A Method of Evaluation

C. W. BARKDULL

Since the original popularization of the term "Span of Control" as an organizational principle, there has been a great amount of thinking and writing on the subject, but unfortunately there has not evolved a common agreement as to what the proper span of control should be, i.e., how many persons should report to a given manager. Graicunas has suggested that a limited span is desirable because of the great increases in interrelationships as the number of persons supervised increases.[1] Considering all levels of supervision in the several companies with which I have had personal experience, limited spans of fewer than 5 or 6 appear to be the general rule. This is confirmed by Healey in his study of 620 firms.[2] In contrast, as one reviews the spans toward the top of many organizations, it is not unusual to find 8, 10, 12, and even more persons reporting to an executive, apparently without undue strain. Dale found great variances in his study of the Presidents' spans in 100 large organizations, with a significant number ex-

Source: Reprinted by permission from *Michigan Business Review*, Vol. 15 (1963), pp. 25–32. Published by the Graduate School of Business Administration, The University of Michigan.

[1] V. A. Graicunas, "Relationship in Organization," *Papers on the Science of Administration*, ed. L. Gullick and L. Urwick, New York, Columbia University, 1947.

[2] James H. Healey, "Coordination and Control of Executive Functions," *Personnel*, Sept. 1956, pp. 106–17.

ceeding 10.[3] Entwisle and Walton found this same phenomenon to a lesser degree in their study of college and smaller company presidents.[4] Broad spans are also sometimes found at lower levels, and the subject managers have not appeared to be significantly more overworked or harried than other managers with limited spans.

Why such a divergence of practice and opinion? Suojanen has concluded that span of control is no longer an applicable principle in modern organizations.[5] But it would seem that from the standpoint of logic there must be a *limit* to the number of persons who can be effectively supervised by another. From the standpoint of business administration, there must be an *optimum number* under a given set of circumstances. That optimum number, I would like to suggest, is affected by a number of factors which vary between positions, and perhaps vary in time.

One factor which appears quite obviously to affect span of control is the degree to which an executive is assisted in the execution of his duties by staff departments and assistants. This perhaps accounts for the greater spans of some of the presidents studied by Dale, Entwisle, and Walton. Another somewhat obvious factor is that some managers, because of their education, experience, and general competence, just do not require a great amount of supervision.

It was these observations which led to the exploration of the possibility that there was a finite number of factors affecting span, and that these factors might be measured in some way. The objective was to find a means of evaluating logically a given managerial position and of arriving at a fair and supportable conclusion as to what the proper span of control should be.

The rest of this article will describe the case history of the development of an evaluation method of determining proper spans of control.

Description of the Problem

A description of the specific organizational problems is significant to an understanding of why the problem of span was undertaken in the first place. The company in question, a division of a larger corporation, had experienced a very rapid growth over a period of five years—from a small handful of scientific personnel to a sizable enterprise of 25,000 employees, consisting of three divisions, each under a general manager, together with several staff and service activities reporting to the president and executive vice president.

---

[3] Ernest Dale, *Planning and Developing the Company Organization Structure*, New York, American Management Association, 1952.

[4] Doris R. Entwisle, and John Walton, "Observations on the Span of Control," *Administrative Science Quarterly*, March 1961, p. 522.

[5] W. W. Suojanen "The Span of Control—Fact or Fable," *Advanced Management*, Nov. 1955, pp. 5–13.

Technically, the company had done an outstanding job, but problems were beginning to emerge from various sources. Employees and supervisors were finding it increasingly difficult to get a job done. Costs were climbing to a point where the management was somewhat alarmed.

In reviewing the organizational structure prior to writing a set of organizational policies, two things became particularly predominant—the frequency with which very limited spans of control occurred, (i.e., two and three), and the great many levels of supervision which existed throughout the major components of the company.

The company was to a degree aware that there was a problem, but had attempted to resolve it by establishing certain criteria on supervisory ratios (which is the result of dividing the total non-supervisory personnel by total supervision in a given organizational component). It appeared that these objectives were being met by increasing the number of non-supervisory persons reporting to supervisors at the lowest level.

The span at the director level (the level just below a general manager) ranged from 5 to 10. This was considered to be quite satisfactory. The lowest level of supervision, i.e., the level having only non-supervisory personnel reporting to them, averaged 15 to 18, in the major components. This, too, appeared to be satisfactory. However, the spans of supervision between the directors and first-line supervision (which for this purpose will be termed "middle management") averaged only 3.2 for the company as a whole with little variation between major components.

Great pressure had been exerted by executives and managers all through the development of the company for additional levels of supervision, until in quite a number of cases in the larger of the company's components there were seven levels of supervision up to the directors. This excluded direct line assistants, which if included would have increased the levels in some instances to as many as eleven. The General Managers and the President made two additional levels.

Importance of Span of Control and Levels of Supervision

Why is the problem of spans of control and levels of supervision important to management?[6] There are several undesirable ramifications of a situation where there are limited spans and too many levels. First, it creates over-supervision. Supervisors tend to spend time reviewing and directing subordinates in much greater detail than necessary. Second, it impedes and lengthens communication. Multiple levels of supervision tend to slow down the flow of information, suggestions, instructions, etc., up and down

---

[6] For an outstanding discussion of a concept of managing and the relation of span of control to managing, see Richard C. Anderson, *Management Practices*, New York, McGraw-Hill, 1960, pp. 5–9 and 79–80.

the chain of command. In many cases, the information may lose its original meaning, intent, and impact. Third, it delays decisions and action because of the many levels of review. Fourth, it decreases initiative and morale. Too many levels often limit delegation of any real authority to the lower levels which in turn interferes with the accomplishment of assigned tasks, and makes the subordinates overly dependent on the superiors. This lack of a sense of accomplishment can lead to low morale. Fifth, it decreases opportunity for responsibility and development. Narrow spans limit the supervision to a few activities and deprive them of the benefit to be derived from supervising a number of related activities. Sixth, it increases costs. Narrow spans and added levels increase the number of supervisors and the attendant extra expenses of secretaries, space, facilities, supplies and services.

The correction of this kind of a situation, then, should improve communication, produce a more responsive organization, stimulate greater initiative, and provide greater opportunity for personnel and supervisory development.

The close relationship between levels of supervision and spans of control is illustrated in Exhibit 1 which shows the effect of varying spans on

EXHIBIT 1

Required Supervision and Levels at Varying Spans in a Branch of
3800–4000 Employees

	Six Levels at Average Span of Three* (302 Supervisory Employees)	Five Levels at Average Span of Four* (268 Supervisory Employees)	Four Levels at Average Span of Six* (241 Supervisory Employees)
Supervisory	1	1	1
Employees	3	4	6
Required at	8	13	none
Each Level	23	none	none
	67	50	34
	200	200	200
Nonsupervisory Employees	3600	3600	3600

* Applied to middle-management and director levels.

the number of levels required. In a hypothetical organization having approximately 3600 non-supervisory employees and 200 first-line supervisors, six levels and 302 supervisory employees would be required under an average span of three; five levels and 268 supervisory employees under average spans of four; and only four levels and 241 supervisory employees under average spans of six. (The fact that most organizations do not build up quite this evenly from one level to another because of variations in the sizes of the components, would change the figures somewhat but would not change the effects substantially.)

A vigorous program of increasing spans and decreasing levels was called for, but such a program would have to be based on a logical criteria for determining what the proper spans and levels should be.

The Factors Affecting Spans

The first step was to determine the most significant factors which had a bearing on spans. Literature on the subject contained a number of leads. Experience provided a few more. From these, seven factors were selected and defined:

1. Similarity of functions supervised
2. Geographic contiguity of functions supervised
3. Complexity of functions supervised
4. Direction and control required by the personnel supervised
5. Coordination required of the supervisor
6. Planning required of the supervisor
7. Organizational assistance received by the supervisor

Another analyst and student of organization principles might very well have selected different factors. It is recognized that other factors have bearing on individual cases. For example, the incumbent of a given supervisory position himself has a bearing on the span. His personal ability, background, experience, and personality may have an important bearing on how many he can supervise effectively. But, as in the establishing of any other standard of measurement, differences in individual abilities should not be worked into the standard.

The definitions of the seven factors were established as follows.

Similarity of Functions. This refers to the degree to which functions performed by the various components or personnel reporting to the supervisor are alike or different—whether they are the same functions, (perhaps organized on a geographic basis) or whether they differ in *nature* (perhaps grouped because of their relation to one another). Its importance is that as the functions increase in the degree of variability the more interrelations to be kept in mind and the fewer number of persons that the supervisor can effectively handle.

Geographic Contiguity. This factor refers to the physical locations of the components and personnel reporting to a supervisor. Geographic separation of functions makes for greater difficulty in supervision because of necessity for more formal means of communication, time to get together for necessary discussions, and time to personally visit the separated activities.

Complexity of Functions. This factor refers to the nature of the duties being performed by the majority of non-supervisory personnel, and involves a determination of the degree of difficulty in performing satisfactorily. It is generally considered that the salary and hourly ratings are a reasonably fair reflection of complexity. Hence this factor was related to the job classifications of the more important of the non-supervisory positions in the component. Generally the greater the complexity of the function supervised the smaller the number of persons a supervisor should be expected to handle.

Direction and Control. This factor refers to the nature of the personnel reporting directly to the supervisor and reflects the degree of attention which they require for proper supervision of their actions. High-level competent managers with years of background and experience, or highly qualified scientists with Ph.D.'s will require minimum attention except for general administrative and planning matters; while other personnel might require closer supervision, direction, guidance, and training. This also reflects the extent to which responsibility can be delegated to subordinates; the extent to which problems and decisions can be resolved at subordinate levels; the amount of training they require; and the degree to which objective standards can be applied. The greater the degree to which subordinates require direction and control, the smaller the span should be of the subject supervisor. (This factor may appear to measure the same thing as complexity, and to some extent they are counter-acting. However, while complexity measures the *work* of the non-supervisory personnel, direction and control measures the degree to which subordinates *require supervision.*)

Coordination. As opposed to the previous factors which mainly relate to the duties and personnel supervised, the factor of coordination (and the next one—planning) reflect the nature of the supervisory position itself. It measures the extent to which the supervisor must exert time and effort (1) in keeping the functions, actions and output of his components properly correlated, balanced and going in the same direction to accomplish the goals of the activity, and (2) in keeping his components keyed in with other activities of the division to accomplish divisional plans and programs. Again, the greater the complexity of the coordination functions and the greater the amount of time required to perform them, the fewer number of people who should report to him.

Planning. This factor refers to the importance, complexity, and time requirements of one of the primary functions of a manager or supervisor— that of reviewing the objectives and the output requirements in the future, and programming the actions, organization, staff, and budgets necessary to accomplish them. Some distinction must be made in the evaluation of a given position as to how much of these functions are actually performed by others for him, and where planning must be done on a continuing basis or might essentially be accomplished once a year when budgets and programs are proposed and approved. As the importance, complexity, and time required of the supervisor increases, the more prudent it will be to reduce the numbers of persons reporting to him.

Organizational Assistance. This factor considers the assistance received within the organizational component from direct line assistants, assistants to, staff activities or personnel having administrative, planning and control responsibilities, and (at the first-line supervisory level) leadmen.

Evaluation of the Factors

An experienced organization analyst could take these factors as identified and develop a "feel" for the numbers of persons who could be supervised effectively in a given situation, based on his experience and on general comparisons. But his thinking process might not be uniform in all cases, thereby leading to some inequities between positions; and probably there would not be uniformity of application between analysts.

Most important, however, it would be difficult to convince an operating manager who was trying to build up his organization unnecessarily the how and why of the answer the analyst came up with, and that he was being evaluated on the same basis as other managers.

This, then, led to the reduction of a thinking process to mathematical weightings and the development of a "Supervisory Index" which represents the relative difficulty of the supervisory job. The approach is similar to job evaluation. Many of the same techniques are used.

Finding the right weightings was not a simple task. A number of different weightings were tried and compared with actual situations before arriving at the final weights described in summary in Exhibit 2. (Detailed descriptions were prepared for each of these weightings in order to provide a basis for uniform applications. They are not included here because of the length.)

Each of the supervisory factors was applied to each supervisory position studied, and the degrees of supervisory burden determined. The sum total of the values represented a comparative measurement of the supervisory burden. This total point value, modified for assistants (described below), was called the "Supervisory Index."

Equating for organizational assistance in the supervisory index represented a different kind of problem. It was not really a separate factor, such as Similarity of Functions, Planning, etc., and it did not make sense to apply weights in the same manner. Its effect was to *reduce* the supervisory burden rather than increase it. Therefore, it was decided to apply fractional multiplier values which would reduce the total supervisory index.

This sounded reasonable too from the standpoint that organizational

EXHIBIT 2

Degrees of Supervisory Burden within Span Factors

Span Factor	Degree of Supervisory Burden				
Similarity of Functions	Identical 1	Essentially Alike 2	Similar 3	Inherently Different 4	Fundamentally Distinct 5
Geographic Contiguity	All Together 1	All in One Building 2	Separate Buildings, One Plant Location 3	Separate Locations, One Geographic Area 4	Dispersed Geographic Areas 5
Complexity of Functions	Simple Repetitive 2	Routine 4	Some Complexity 6	Complex, Varied 8	Highly Complex, Varied 10
Direction and Control	Minimum Supervision and Training 3	Limited Supervision 6	Moderate Periodic Supervision 9	Frequent Continuing Supervision 12	Constant Close Supervision 15
Coordination	Minimum Relationships with Others 2	Relationships Limited to Defined Courses 4	Moderate Relationships, Easily Controlled 6	Considerable Close Relationship 8	Extensive Mutual Non-recurring Relationships 10
Planning	Minimum Scope and Complexity 2	Limited Scope and Complexity 4	Moderate Scope and Complexity 6	Considerable Effort Required, Guided Only by Broad Policies 8	Extensive Effort Required, Areas and Policies Not Charted 10

assistance tended to decrease the supervisor's burden in several if not all of the other areas considered. Again, finding the right set of multipliers was somewhat of a trial-and-error process, until a set of factors was determined which seemed to properly fit the actual circumstances.

Adjustment for Assistance

The multiplier factors for positions with subordinate supervision are as follows:

Organizational Assistance Provided	Multiplier Factor
Direct line assistant *and* staff activities	.60
Direct line assistant (only)	.70
Staff activities (administrative, planning *and* control functions)	.75
Staff activities (administrative, planning, *or* control functions)	.85
Assistant to (limited duties)	.95

Leaders working for first-line supervision were adjusted for as follows:

Number of Leaders	Multiplier
1	.85
2	.70
3	.55
4	.40
5	.25

Determination of Standard Spans

A number of positions were evaluated using the weightings developed. Exhibit 3 shows a tabulation of the results of the evaluation in the middle management and director areas. Most of the cases, of course, had actual spans of 2, 3, and 4, and these showed no relationship to the supervisory indices. However, much to our delight, those cases having spans of five and over tended to have a very definite relationship to the index, that is, as the supervisory index decreased (indicating lesser supervisory burden) the spans increased. This was strong indication that there was validity to our supervisory index, and, since these represented actual cases within the company, it was felt that they could be used effectively and justifiably as standards of performance for the rest of the organization.

The actual standards were developed in the case of middle management and directors by plotting the supervisory index against the actual spans of those five and over, and calculating the regression line (or line of relationship) to fit the sample. A range was then provided to allow for varying

EXHIBIT 3

Conversion of Supervisory Index into Span of Management

Supervisory Index	Range of Actual Spans (Number of Cases*)										Suggested Standard Spans
	2	3	4	5	6	7	8	9	10	11	
40–42		1	1	1							4–5
37–39	1	1	4	5	4						4–6
34–36	10	9	13		3						4–7
31–33	10	6	12	7	3	1	1				5–8
28–30	12	17	7	3	2	1					6–9
25–27	3	3					1	1			7–10
22–24	1	1	1			1		1	1	1	8–11
Total Cases	37	38	38	16	12	3	2	2	1	1	

* Total of 150 cases taken from PMS, SS, Operations, QATS, Research, Finance, and Industrial Relations.

circumstances. A number of cases were also evaluated at the first-line supervisory level. A similar relationship developed here, but with broader spans (see Exhibit 4).

EXHIBIT 4
Proposed Standard Span of Management

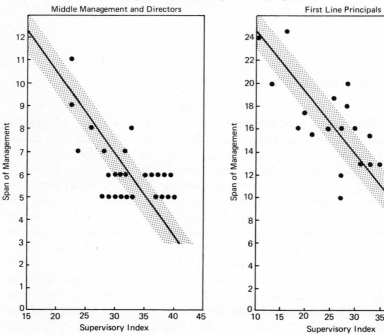

EXHIBIT 5
Examples of Reorganization to Effect Fewer Levels and Greater Spans

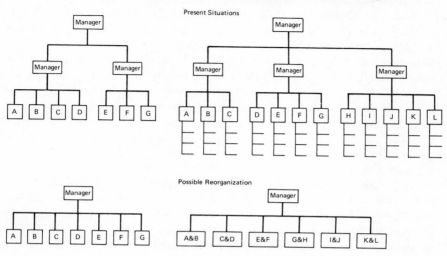

The question might be asked why should there have to be different scales for first-line supervision and for supervisors who have other supervisors reporting to them. One might argue that the same factors and weights should apply. Unfortunately, this study did not arrive at an answer to that question. Perhaps there is a greater difference in the amount of planning, co-ordinating and directing performed between the first-line supervision and higher levels than is reflected in the point values applied. Instead of a straight line relationship, perhaps the line of relationship should be an S curve which would equate for the greater spans of the first-line supervisors. This will have to be a further refinement. The actual situation was that the span for first-line supervision at a given supervisory index was approximately double that of higher supervision with the same index. It appeared proper that the standards should reflect this.

The Plan of Implementation

The feasibility of the end result was readily recognized by management, but getting there was another problem, since it would mean a considerably less requirement for supervision in the middle management areas. To accomplish the job in a short time through a series of rather sweeping reorganizations, would demoralize the organization and negate the improvements in organizational atmosphere for which we are striving. Hence, goals were set to which the various components were to work over a period of time—an average span of six, with a minimum of five; four levels of supervision in the larger components and three in the others. Provision, of course, was made for exceptions.

Each component was then introduced to the program and its background, and requested to prepare a long-range organization plan, including a program for accomplishing it over a period of time. Various means were to be taken to arrive at the goals. Attrition of supervisory personnel (getting jobs outside the company, retirement, etc.) would take care of quite a number of situations. Further expansion of the company would create demands for supervision which would be filled from present supervisory personnel. Careful scrutiny of the supervisory requirements of the other corporate divisions would be made in order to transfer qualified supervisory personnel to open positions there. Some would have to be taken care of through reclassification.

An illustration of how the criteria were used is shown in Exhibit 5. An evaluation of the supervisory burden might indicate that the spans of the managers in the two cases shown could be 5–8. In the case on the left, the possibility of eliminating the middle level of managers would clearly be indicated. In the case on the right, it would indicate that the twelve components on the lower level might be combined into six (or perhaps 5, 7, or 8) which in turn would permit the elimination of the three managers on the second level.

Results of the Program

As of the writing of the article, a number of reorganizations had been effected in several of the company's organizational units. The results were quite gratifying. Although the goals were not yet fully reached, the accomplishment, even in its four months of operation, was significant. Some of the organizations, as was expected, had situations where components just could not be reorganized into logical groupings of more than three or four. In other cases, other important considerations (such as the organization of activities serviced, management emphasis, etc.) dictated something less than the desirable spans.

Many components, however, were able to reach the objectives, in some cases even exceeding the standards; most made significant advances toward the desired goals. Probably the most dramatic of the changes succeeded in cutting out two full levels of supervision (from 7 to 5), increased the average span of middle management from 3.9 to 5.9, reduced supervisory personnel by 7 (mostly in transfers to other expanding activities) and cut supervisory payroll by the rate of over $70,000 per year.

Although not designed as a cost reduction program, total results in those activities in which the program had been installed amounted to a rate of over $280,000 per year in supervisory payroll. To this saving could be added the cost of the secretarial assistance, fringe benefits, office space, and supplies required by the supervision eliminated.

Conclusion

The development of the supervisory indices and the establishment of standard ranges for spans of control were designed as another of the several tools of management and the organization analyst. It was not intended that it be used to the exclusion of the other sound principles of organization. It was not intended to force an organization structure into the standard spans, but rather to use the span-of-control evaluations in cases where span was a real factor in the determination of the optimum organization.

A study of this nature can point up that, in many areas of an organization, limited spans and many levels have been built up where it has been entirely unnecessary and with an unwarranted build-up of supervisory costs. It can be used to re-establish the organization structure on a sounder basis, and thus contribute importantly not only to reduced costs but to a healthier organizational climate.

8

The Operation of
Academic Departments

WALTER C. HOBBS and G. LESTER ANDERSON

Colleges, universities and "multiversities" are the organizational structures in which higher education generally is pursued. Academic departments, in turn, constitute the fundamental elements of those structures: it is primarily within departments and quasi-departmental groupings such as interdisciplinary programs that faculty locate themselves institutionally, that curricula are offered, and that students identify and give expression to their substantive academic objectives.

Despite the fundamental nature of these organizational units, however, academic departments appear to be more diverse than similar. The literature of college and university administration is rich with analyses which depict departments as autocracies, fiefdoms, oligarchies, bureaucracies, democracies, laissez-faire congeries of scholars, and a multitude of combinations of such forms ([1],* [3], [4], [6], [9], [12], [13], [15], [16], [18], [20], [24], [25], [26], [28]). In addition, some departments defy description in conventional terminology. There are "one-man-carries-the-load" organizations in which the "one man" is distinctive not for his power and authority (which are sparse indeed) but rather solely for his function: he

Source: Reprinted by permission from Walter C. Hobbs and G. Lester Anderson, "The Operation of Academic Departments," *Management Science* (October 1971), pp. B134–B144.

* Numbers refer to items in Reference list at end of Reading.

serves, he does not command. Other departments are best described in terms of "decentralized responsibility": necessary tasks are widely distributed among the department's members. And still other departments engage in "symbiotic administrative processes, with one man doing the rest"; that is, a School or College or some other superstructure provides most of the organizational framework and performs most of the necessary administrative tasks, while one departmental member, or a few, accomplishes the remainder.

There is an explanation, however, of the plethora of analytic descriptions of academic departments which goes beyond the simple assertion of diversity: that explanation is the absence to date of a comprehensive theory of academic organization [2], [12]. Although general organizational theory provides at a gross level bench-marks for inquiry into specific academic structures—for example, one might expect on the basis of organizational theory that the tension which obtains between hierarchy and professional autonomy in industrial research laboratories will be seen in university departmental life as well—there is a scarcity of data-based conceptual material with which to construct a theoretical framework for academic organization per se. Uninformed by such a framework, the analysis of specific elements of academic organization, such as departments, understandably proceeds willy-nilly.

The research which is reported in the following pages was designed to contribute to a correction of this state of affairs in which the analysis of organization enjoys little or no benefit of theory. The approach that was used, however, turned the issue around: the focal research question was, "Who runs academic departments, and how?" On the basis of data concerning the organizational behavior of departmental personnel, a theoretical model of the academic department was developed. Glaser and Strauss's [10, pp. 101–115] "constant comparative method" for generating theory from data was employed: categories of topics which constituted departmental concerns were constructed from the data gathered in initial interviews; additional data then were collected to permit amendment—including occasional deletion—and the integration of those categories. Finally, the refined categories were embellished by explanatory categories, also grounded in the data, until the model of the organization of academic departments emerged.

Members of thirty-four departments in five colleges and universities were interviewed by means of loosely structured interview schedules. For a study conducted by Paul Dressel and two associates at Michigan State University, one of the authors of this paper spoke with chairmen and faculty members in fourteen departments of two state universities in the South. The remaining data were collected by both authors from chairmen of departments in three other institutions in the North: a state university, a state college and a church-related college. Departments were selected from the social sciences, humanities, natural sciences, life sciences and the professions.

The model which developed of academic departmental organization involves several coexistent organizational structures: departments vary not only *among* themselves organizationally but, of equal or perhaps greater importance, they vary *within* themselves as well.[1] Different structures of authority, accountability and power obtain with respect to different type tasks and problems which the department confronts. Two departmental processes are of fundamental significance and together they constitute the basis upon which the model is built: (1) governance, the process by which decisions are made; and (2) administration, the process by which tasks necessary to the implementation of programs and policies are accomplished.

The distinction between governance and administration may be clear enough to individuals familiar with the terms, but it may well be opaque to others. However, counterparts (*not* synonyms) are to be found in (*a*) the political-legal distinction between substantive and procedural law, in (*b*) the ethical distinction between categorical and hypothetical imperatives, and in (*c*) the managerial distinction between policy and program; the last, of course, is the most closely related to the distinction between governance and administration as the terms are used in this analysis. In the development of the academic departmental model, the processes by which value-laden departmental decisions were reached (called *governance*), and the processes by which those decisions were implemented (called *administration*), assumed analytic importance. The two processes, to be sure, are endemic to all organization, but they are differently manifested and differently related within different systems [8]. The task in this research became that of identifying the nature of those manifestations and relationships within academic departments.

Anyone who has had anything at all to do with academic departments will recognize it is naïve to suggest that departmental governance and administration are separable. However, as indicated above, the two are conceptually distinct. In the discussions which follow, we shall first consider each process and its correlative structure as if it were an island unto itself: various statements therefore may initially seem quite rash. But before we close, we shall address ourselves to commonalities and points of contact between the processes, thereby including the necessary qualifications.

ORGANIZATION FOR DEPARTMENTAL ADMINISTRATION

One organizational mode for administration was common to every academic department whether in the natural sciences, the social sciences, the

---

[1] Coexisting structures within organizations are by no means unique to academic departments; cf., e.g., Goss [11].

humanitiés or the professions. That mode was simply a "division of labor among peers" (by peers is meant precisely that: "persons of equal standing"; but recall immediately the caution concerning rash statements and qualifications to follow). In each department, various faculty members accepted responsibility for the accomplishment of certain tasks. Department members who were unwilling to comply with the administrative actions of their colleagues would try to modify those actions by making known to the administrator their preferences and advice—an informal but very real procedure which both they and the individual they approached recognized to be their right to exercise. The observation by Julian [14, p. 389] that there is in complex organizations a relationship between "a free flow of communication, the use of normative sanctions and low degrees of control" is applicable to academic departments as well. No one who was interviewed stated, or even implied, that faculty members serving in administrative capacities either gave orders to other faculty or received orders from "superiors;"[2] *consultation* and *coordination* were the strongest terms used to describe the interactions of departmental administrators with other departmental members. Administrative activities per se were consistently spoken of as services rendered the department by faculty, not jobs for which "administrators" were hired.

Administrative titles were quite varied. There were department chairmen; associate chairmen; assistant chairmen; vice-chairmen; department heads; assistant department heads; executive officers; coordinators of . . . ; liaison officers for . . . ; and directors of. . . . Areas of administrative responsibility were as diverse as were administrative titles, including student advisement; the coordination and integration of evening division activities; supervision of departmental nonfaculty employees (which was delegated in some instances to nonfaculty "administrative assistants" or "assistants to . . ."); the conduct of experimental programs; direction of research projects; management of facilities, e.g., laboratories, special libraries; and publication of both serial and occasional, disciplinary and institutional, material.

Why faculty are willing to assume responsibilities which to the outsider would seem to be onerous, thankless "lesser" tasks is a topic which goes beyond the scope of this paper. But a few suggestions can be offered, such

---

[2] The rhetoric with which academic departmental administration is commonly described abounds with "bureaucracy" and related terms. But such descriptions play fast and loose with a construct that deserves better treatment. A close look at departmental administrative behavior, followed by a reading of Weber's descriptive definition of bureaucracy [27, pp. 329–41] will reveal discrepancies between the two which are more than sufficient to cast doubt on the applicability of the concept *bureaucracy* to academic departments. By way of brief example, departmental administrative offices are not hierarchically organized, such offices are not the primary occupations of the faculty members who fill them, and there is no "promotion" from one departmental administrative office to another.

as greater access to clerical assistance, an expectation that one will be "in the know"; a salary increase; a sense of power (no matter how realistic or naïve) in being close to the inner circle; a decrease of load in respect to some less appealing activity; an interest in academic administration as a career; ego satisfaction deriving from recognition by one's associates; or—not least of all—an awareness of an academic need coupled with a concern born of professionalism or of genuine goodwill that departmental responsibilities be met.

The extent to which departmental labor was distributed among the department's faculty varied with the degree to which the department was engaged in research, teaching and service activities requiring coordination of personnel.[3] The chemistry departments, for example, which faced a wide variety of tasks necessary to the conduct of extensive laboratory-based instruction and research, each maintained elaborate distributions of responsibility among their faculty. History departments, on the other hand, left their administrative responsibilities to one or two individuals—except for one such department, which was engaged in the publication of a journal, where several faculty members served in various administrative capacities related primarily with the special enterprise. Similarly, departments whose higher echelon units (e.g., Schools, Colleges) undertook responsibility for major services such as continuing education or the maintenance of student personnel records, sustained minimal divisions of departmental labor. But exceptions occurred even among these: departments which hosted sponsored research projects also developed more extensive distributions of labor among their faculty than did counterpart departments.

The model which emerged, then, is this: administrative labor in academic departments is distributed among the faculty, who conduct themselves in their administrative roles as equals, not superiors, of their colleagues. The distribution is minimal in some departments and extensive in others, varying with the degree to which departmental activity requires coordination of personnel.

ORGANIZATION FOR DEPARTMENTAL GOVERNANCE

Unlike the singular division-of-labor-among-peers model of organization which describes administrative structures in academic departments, the models of organization for governance are multiple. Two, however, predominate: collegium in curricular concerns and oligarchy in professional matters.

In the area of professional affairs the faculty addresses itself to issues of scholarly and occupational significance, the most weighty of which are

---

[3] This observation derived in part from a reading of Parsons and Platt [19].

promotion and appointment to tenure. Here faculty *rank* has its greatest relevance and power. For purposes of such decision-making, departments commonly organize as formal oligarchies: respondents consistently reported that "rank votes on rank, and tenure on tenure." Occasionally departments organized along lines of laissez-faire, e.g., superstar scholars negotiating independently with extradepartmental administrators such as deans or academic vice-presidents concerning the terms of their appointments and activities. But in no instance in the data did any department organize as a radical democracy to make decisions about professional concerns.

The term *oligarchy* is used in this context in a purely nonpejorative sense (despite Michels [17, p. 390]). By it is meant simply the rule of the group by a subgroup, specifically in this case by tenured personnel or the senior ranks. To some persons, *collegium* might be a preferable term, i.e., a "body consisting of 'elders.' Their collegial function is primarily to guarantee that the law which is applied is really authentically traditional," or in this context, professional (Weber [27, p. 395]). But *collegium* does own another meaning which is more widely used in academic circles and is exceptionally appropriate to the organizational structure generally employed by departments for curricular decision-making.

In curricular matters, e.g., the proposed addition of new courses or the nature of requirements to be met by students majoring in the discipline, faculty democracy is the rule. Members, regardless of rank or administrative title, share equal voice in the decisions which are made. Such departmental organizations are collegiums in the meaning most commonly assigned the word: all actions are "subject to the rule that a plurality of individuals must cooperate for their act to be valid. This cooperation may follow the principle of unanimity or of decision by majority" (Weber [27, p. 393]).

With but two exceptions, in every department investigated, curricular matters were determined by the department faculty *in toto* either by vote or by informally expressed consensus. Action was initiated by various sources such as the department chairman, by departmental administrators such as Coordinators of Undergraduate Curriculum, or by an interested faculty member who might raise a given matter by presentation in a department meeting.

In one of the two departments which differed, a clique of certain tenured full professors (an oligarchy in both the technical and the pejorative sense of the term) made all significant decisions in all areas. The genesis of the group is unknown, but their continued power seems solely to be a matter of precedent and custom: new members are accepted in the group only when they protest so vigorously that it is less disruptive to coopt them than to exclude them further. In the other differing department, a clinical department in a professional school whose chairman was seeking to renovate the curriculum, curricular decisions were made by committees appointed by the chairman from among full-time full professors only, constituting a hybrid autocracy-oligarchy structure. These two exceptions, the clique and the hybrid structure, signify the possibility that in any given department any one of a number of structures for governance may be found. But the exceptions do accentuate the rule: departments organize as collegia for purposes of deciding curricular matters and as oligarchies for professional concerns.

QUALIFICATIONS: DISTORTIONS AND OVERLAPS

Given the foregoing conceptualization of academic departmental organization which suggests there is one structure for administrative tasks, namely, a division-of-labor-among-peers, and a different one or more for governance, commonly an oligarchy and a collegium, two qualifications warrant consideration.

The first concerns "distortions" that occur in the manner in which various department faculty play their roles within the respective organizational structures. The issue here is neither deviance nor idiosyncrasy. It is rather that persons who play roles in several different contexts occasionally find their behavior in one context affected by their susceptibility to, or their capacity for, the exercise of power in another. For example, a nontenured assistant professor may be considerably influenced in the performance of some administrative chore by a tenured "peer" who the former is well aware will participate in a decision concerning his professional status. The professional concern may be wholly irrelevant to the administrative task in question. But that by no means suggests the tenure matter will therefore be ignored.[4] Similarly, a department member who can be of assistance to colleagues in furthering their careers, e.g., a person whose reputation and visibility in the field place him in contact with many people in many places, may enjoy considerable support from those colleagues when he is arguing within the collegium or the oligarchy for a given course of departmental action, however valid or invalid his argument may be. And of course, department faculty who hold appointment to important university-wide committees or administrative offices have a singular capacity for influence in the department which others may not share.

Similar role distortions may occur when conflict arises. Faculty do not see themselves as subordinates in a hierarchy who are obligated either by duty or by sanction to respond affirmatively to every administrative action of other faculty in the department. Consequently, they take their conflicts

---

[4] Such susceptibility may also be another reason why a faculty member might accept a given administrative responsibility in the department, especially an onerous task which no tenured member will take. (See above.)

with departmental administrators not "up" a hierarchical ladder but to the applicable organizational structure in which governance concerning the issue in conflict is pursued. But again, such conflict may be precluded, or if it arises it may be resolved without recourse to the department's governance processes, by the fact that one of the disputants may enjoy opportunity for exercising power over the other in a context not related to that in which the conflict arose.

The most obvious potential for applications of power that was indicated in the data, namely, the chairman's budgetary discretion in matters of salary, was "built into the departmental system." In part, therefore, such budgetary activity can not be considered a role "distortion." With one exception, every chairman alone decided the distribution of merit increases among the departmental faculty's salaries[5] and, in addition, all such actions were taken in confidence.[6] Some chairmen spoke of their role in this matter straightforwardly and without comment. Others, however, apparently felt constrained to explain or to justify their power in salary affairs, and their remarks all were phrased in terms of the utility of such a procedure for maintaining departmental peace and morale. There is no question that peace and morale are significant departmental concerns; but another chairman, not part of our sample, also said of this salary issue, "It's the only real power I have." Hill and French [13] concluded that, essentially, faculty share that view.

The second qualification involves the matter of intersect, or overlap, among administrative issues and the two types of governance issues, curricular and professional concerns. Certain departmental issues fall jointly in more than one area.[7]

Curricular concerns, for example, are the rationales underlying certain decisions having obvious *professional* implications, e.g., the appointment of new faculty: when necessity dictates that certain courses be offered, faculty who can offer them must be recruited. Similarly, curricular concerns also intersect administrative affairs in the matter of course and class scheduling: curricular offerings clearly require coordination, but who-teaches-what-and-when is arranged in consultation with individual faculty, not established by administrative *fiat*. Professional concerns and administrative concerns likewise overlap: The endorsement of research proposals, for example, frequently requires administrative review in order that the avail-

---

[5] Such decisions were officially recommendations, subject to approval or disapproval by senior institutional administrators.

[6] The chairman who was the exception decided salary increases for the only other full professor on that faculty, but he discussed with that colleague all increases for the two associate and three assistant professors.

[7] It may plausibly be argued that all do, that though each may be spoken of as conceptually distinct yet they are very much related. Nonetheless, it is not unreasonable—and it is quite useful—to describe certain activities and decisions as falling within a specific dimension and others as falling within areas of intersect.

ability of institutional resources such as space be insured. And certain issues such as the determination of normal teaching loads for each faculty rank intersect all three areas, professional, curricular and administrative. By contrast, issues such as (a) appointment to tenure, (b) whether or not to offer a service course for nonmajors and (c) the maintenance of student records, are treated by departments as virtually solely professional, curricular and administrative, respectively, in nature.

The persons who were interviewed were at best vague in their descriptions of how matters which fell in areas of intersect were handled by the faculty. But their ambiguity did not seem to be evasiveness. One received the impression rather that the respondents were simply unable to describe a general pattern in how outcomes in these areas were achieved.

Such uncertainty is not mysterious, for the "intersect" phenomenon reflects the confluence of three distinct traditions which have informed American higher education for most of its brief history. When colonial institutions were first established their model was the English college of that day. Although these institutions were frequently puritanical and parietal extensions of the prep school [22], they placed great emphasis upon the curriculum and the norm of faculty collegiality. In the early 1800's the Germanic scholarly influence was introduced, and by mid-century the age of the graduate school had dawned; the new emphasis upon scholarly performance provided a basis for making distinctions, both rational and invidious, among academic ranks. But although academic professionalism had a new foundation, it did not have an entirely new home. The curriculum continued to be the core component of the educational enterprise, and its corollary, the collegial determination of curricular decisions by all faculty regardless of rank, was simply reinforced by the insistence in the Germanic system upon the academic integrity of all faculty regardless of rank, the *sine qua non* of scholarship. The Germanic-scholarly tradition had joined, it did not supplant, the English-collegial tradition.

The third tradition, less widely discussed but no less operative in earlier American higher education, was that of simplistic systems for administration: "The administration of colleges and universities in this country was always a model of simplicity. . . . Apart from the faculty members themselves there were few people at an academic institution in earlier days to whom a president might delegate administrative duties" [21, p. 4]. For two decades that norm has been in jeopardy at the institutional level, but at the departmental level it is still robust; contemporary departments are operated in much the same manner as were the early colleges: peers, one of whom is designated *primus inter pares*, attend to the necessary details of everyday activity.[8]

---

[8] Ten large departments in our sample, however, did include in their organization nonfaculty administrative assistants.

But the tradition of administrative simplicity is of little influence when routine everyday tasks take on profound curricular and/or professional implications. And the observation can be generalized. Although problems which are solely curricular, professional or administrative may be handled in terms respectively prescribed by the English-collegial tradition, the Germanic-scholarly tradition and the simplistic-administrative tradition, there is no comprehensive supratradition to provide a reconciliation of any intersection of the three when needed.

DISCUSSION

In human affairs, the likelihood of the threat of the use of power by any-one who has it is high at all times. And the actual exercise of power is vir-tually certain if feelings run deep or if stimuli to other forms of interaction fail. There is little reason to suppose that in these regards academic men are fundamentally different from others. Without leadership, therefore, complex academic organizations are as susceptible to ineffectiveness or to insensitive utilizations of power as are any other complex organizations.

Selznick [23] speaks of leadership as "the infusion of an organization with value." For the academic department with its several structures, with the potential within those structures for role distortions, and with a likeli-hood among structures of a common interest in various issues yet differing traditions for resolving them, we would submit that value infusion would consist at least in part of encouraging the development of a local "supra-tradition." Priorities and interests may vary from department to depart-ment. But in any given department those priorities are more likely of realization if there is some rubric established within which to respond to problematic situations, rather than if the only possible response is a harried attempt to react impulsively with any useful means at hand. Some intuitive people can do the latter well, but most can not.

For example, in many departments lately students have used first per-suasion and then disruptive power to gain for themselves both a role in the collegium addressed to curricular concerns and an opportunity to affect departmental administration. Whether or not they will also prove success-ful in gaining entree to the oligarchies which commonly pass on profes-sional matters remains to be seen. But well they might, especially if having once consolidated their gains in curricular and administrative participation they begin to focus their attention on issues such as new appointments or the allocation of resources within the department, issues which lie in areas of overlap between various dimensions. This organization analysis is not the place for an essay on the merits or lack thereof in such student par-ticipation. But whatever the empirical outcomes may be, the point is that those outcomes will very likely be a function of the extent to which aca-demic leaders (departmental and otherwise) do or do not infuse among their colleagues supratraditional values in terms of which to respond to the possibilities.

These observations, together with other recent research, suggest that selection of the chairman may be a significant element in departmental governance. Dressel and his colleagues [7] found that the influence of "competent" chairmen can be considerable. In departments which are dependent upon institutional resources due to the nature of their disciplines (history, for example, or philosophy), department members "cast about for the most articulate and powerful personality among their group and expect him to represent their interests. . . . The chairman who succeeded in getting resources could run the show" [7, pp. 275–276]. And in departments which could attract resources from outside the university (such as physics or physiology), the effective chairman was one who "maintained the confidence of his colleagues by virtue of his strong national credentials and his ability to guide younger faculty members into prominence on the national scene" [7, p. 276].

The selection of the chairman, it would seem, is important not simply for structural reasons but for reasons of leadership.[9] The competence of the chairman in commanding resources, and the visibility of the chairman within his discipline, have implications for his capacity to infuse supratraditional values which are the *sine qua non* of rational governance and administration in "overlapping" issues. An effective chairman, that is, commands respect and influence among his colleagues by virtue of his capacity to assist them professionally, which influence he then may use to enhance the reconciliation of conflicting positions which may not be easily treated by means of the well-received traditions. The attitude expressed in many quarters that the chairmanship is a responsibility of modest significance, a necessary chore (if not a trial) to be assumed by someone under nominal conditions of *noblesse oblige*, may be a luxury which many departments in contemporary academe can not afford, any more than can an industrial research laboratory afford a division chief who is utterly innocent of either scientific or organizational skills.

SUMMARY

Faculty within academic departments organize in different structures for different purposes. To accomplish the ordinary everyday tasks of implementing their programs they effect a division of labor among themselves as peers: individual members accept responsibility for the performance of necessary chores, but such individuals are amenable to advice and information, including preferences, from their fellow faculty members whose co-

---

[9] Robert A. Dahl [5] reached precisely the same conclusion with respect to mayors of American cities.

operation and compliance they solicit and can even reasonably expect, but which they can not command. The extent to which administrative labor is divided among the faculty is a function of the extent to which research, teaching and service activities requiring interaction and coordination are conducted by departmental members.

For purposes of decision-making, a number of *possible* organizational modes obtain, e.g., autocracy, oligarchy or democracy. However, two major types of departmental decisions are distinguishable, and for each type a particular organizational structure is common. Decisions having to do with professional concerns such as tenure are frequently determined by an oligarchy consisting of the senior professional ranks. And decisions having to do with curricular affairs such as degree requirements are determined most frequently by the collegium (i.e., by democratic process).

Certain departmental matters lie in areas of intersection between curricular decisions, professional decisions and administrative tasks. Such matters create ambiguity in departmental activities because there is no traditional, logical or indeed any other basis for referring the matter to any given organizational structure for action. In such situations the presence or absence of leadership will vitally influence the character of the department's corporate behavior.

Even when issues fall clearly in a given area, not every problem is necessarily treated solely in terms of the structure most logically appropriate to it. Role "distortions" can occur in the behavior of members who enjoy certain advantages over others in the department by virtue of positions they occupy elsewhere, either in another of the department's organizational structures, in the university at large or in a separate context such as the discipline. Such individuals may exploit their advantages for purposes of affecting outcomes in particular departmental activities over which they would ordinarily have less control.

The most widely applicable model of academic departmental organization is a composite of (1) a division of labor among peers for administrative activities, (2) an oligarchy of the senior professional ranks for decision-making with respect to professional concerns, and (3) a collegium, i.e., a democracy, for decision-making with respect to curricular affairs. But given (a) departments with varying degrees of activities requiring coordination, and hence varying extents of division of administrative labor, (b) several *possible* structures for governance, whether in professional or curricular concerns, (c) numerous departmental matters which fall in areas of intersect between administration and governance, and (d) the inclination of many, if not most, individuals to exploit whatever power they may enjoy in one context when participating in another—the combinational possibilities of organizational models with which to describe any given academic department are legion.

This analysis, however, does not purport to describe (let alone to prescribe) organizational forms of given specific departments. It is designed instead to delineate the major categories of academic departmental realities, to note the general traditions which inspire much of the activity pursued within those categories, and to draw attention to the acute absence of an overarching tradition within which to reconcile conflicting interests arising among those categories. With such conceptual supplies, the probability of more adequate analysis and theory construction in academic organization is increased.

REFERENCES

1. Baum, Werner A. "University Organization for Geophysics Education," *Science,* Vol. 146 (1964), pp. 619–21.
2. Bennis, Warren. "Organizations of the Future," *Personnel Administration* (September-October 1967), pp. 6–19.
3. Bowles, Ned W. "Who Should Be in Charge of the Department— Head or Chairman?" *Journal of Higher Education,* Vol. 33 (1962), pp. 315–18.
4. Corson, John J. *Governance of Colleges and Universities,* McGraw-Hill, New York, 1960.
5. Dahl, Robert A. *Who Governs?* Yale University Press, New Haven, 1961.
6. Demerath, Nicholas J. *et al. Power, Presidents and Professors,* Basic Books, New York, 1967.
7. Dressel, Paul L. *et al.* "Departmental Operations: The Confidence Game," *Educational Record,* Vol. 50 (1969), pp. 274–78.
8. Etzioni, Amitai. *A Comparative Analysis of Complex Organizations,* Free Press, New York, 1961.
9. Euwema, Ben. "The Organization of the Department," *Educational Record,* Vol. 34 (1953), pp. 38–43.
10. Glaser, Barney G. and Strauss, Anselm L. *The Discovery of Grounded Theory,* Aldine, Chicago, 1967.
11. Goss, Mary E. W. "Influence and Authority among Physicians in an Outpatient Clinic," *American Sociological Review,* Vol. 26 (1961), pp. 39–50.
12. Gross, Edward. "Review of Bureaucracy in Higher Education, by Herbert Stroup," *American Review,* Vol. 31 (1966), p. 873.
13. Hill, Winston W. and French, Wendell L. "Perception of the Power of Department Chairmen by Professors," *Administrative Science Quarterly,* Vol. 11 (1967), pp. 548–74.
14. Julian, Joseph. "Compliance Patterns and Communication Blocks in Complex Organizations," *American Sociological Review,* Vol. 31 (1966), pp. 382–89.
15. Lovett, Robert E. "Essential Factors and Considerations in the Ad-

ministration of a College Music Department," unpublished doctoral dissertation, Washington State University, Department of Education (1964).

16. Marcson, Simon. "Decision-Making in a University Physics Department," *American Behavioral Scientist*, Vol. 6 (1962), pp. 37–39.

17. Michels, Robert. *Political Parties: A Sociological Study of the Oligarchical Tendencies of Modern Democracy*, Free Press, Glencoe, 1949.

18. Murray, Robert K. "On Departmental Development: A Theory," *Journal of General Education*, Vol. 16 (1964), pp. 227–36.

19. Parsons, Talcott and Platt, Gerald M., *The American Academic Profession: A Pilot Study*, National Science Foundation, 1968.

20. Porter, Kirk H. "Department Head or Chairman?" *AAUP Bulletin*, Vol. 47 (1961), pp. 339–42.

21. Rourke, Francis E. and Brooks, Glenn E. *The Managerial Revolution in Higher Education*, Johns Hopkins, Baltimore, 1966.

22. Schmidt, George P. *The Liberal Arts College*, Rutgers, New Brunswick, 1957.

23. Selznick, Philip. *Leadership in Administration*, Harper & Row, New York, 1957.

24. Strong, Edward W. "Shared Responsibility," *AAUP Bulletin*, Vol. 49 (1963), pp. 109–13.

25. Twaddell, William F. "Departmental Organization at the University of Wisconsin," *AAUP Bulletin*, Vol. 26 (1940), pp. 196–200.

26. Walker, Donald E. and Holmes, Darrell C. "The University Professor and His Department," *Educational Record*, Vol. 41 (1960), pp. 34–36.

27. Weber, Max. *The Theory of Social and Economic Organization*, Hodge, London, 1947.

28. Williams, Lloyd P. "Democracy and Hierarchy: A Profile of Faculty Meetings in Department 'x'," *Journal of Educational Sociology*, Vol. 30 (1956), pp. 168–72.

9

The Rationale for
Decentralization
in Large Hospitals

DAVID B. STARKWEATHER

As hospitals grow, they become more specialized and thus more complex. The proliferation of services has clear advantages for patients, in terms of scientific care, but it also has organizational drawbacks. Organizational performance, defined here as the ability of the hospital to properly articulate and coordinate the components necessary for the delivery of effective hospital care to patients, is significantly lower in large hospitals.

This can be demonstrated on theoretical as well as empirical grounds. In theoretical terms, the medical economist H. E. Klarman has stated: "In other words, there are limits to the advantages of division of labor. One of them is when strict scheduling cannot occur . . . Another is when tasks require coordination of a delicate or complicated variety. In the latter case the loss arising from non-specialization is offset by the gains achieved through coordination [1]." And the medical sociologist, H. E. Wooden, has stated: "The more all-inclusive in purpose the institution becomes, the more strained and complex the institutional setting becomes—with resulting less achievement in terms of its original objectives. . . . There tends to be some critical point, yet undefined, beyond which the extent of achieving the original care objective varies inversely with the degree of complexity of operation—a point of diminishing return [2]."

Source: Reprinted with permission from the quarterly journal of the American College of Hospital Administrators, *Hospital Administration,* Vol. 15 (Spring 1970), pp. 27–45.

Empirical evidence of this fact comes from a study of six carefully selected hospitals which were alike in virtually all respects except for size [3]. Three tests of organizational performance were developed which, in combination, assessed the degree of coordination between most direct patient-service departments of a hospital. Two of the tests concerned time-lag in patient service and one test concerned accuracy. The first test, admitting-time lag, measured the time a patient first presented himself to the hospital for inpatient admission to the time he received his first hospital clinical (as compared to administrative) service. The second test, bed-turnaround time, revealed the total time an inpatient was out of his hospital bed for purposes of obtaining a test or treatment at a remote location. This total time was reduced by the actual time-in-service, producing net transportation and waiting time. This time is of considerable inconvenience to the patient, often resulting in missed meals and delays in the rendering of other services. During this time, the patient is beyond the observation and supervision of ward doctors and nurses—those who know most of his medical condition. The third test, accuracy in diet service, measured the coordination between nursing and dietary departments in meal service to patients with special diets. Observations were made at the point of actual delivery of food to patients, and only specific dietary errors were recorded (as compared to matters of food preference, temperature, etc.)

Results are shown in Table 1. The relationship between hospital performance and size is highly apparent: larger hospitals are poorer performers. This is shown in two ways: (1) the mean values (of 540 observations

TABLE 1

Means and Standard Deviations of Three Measures of Hospital
Performance, by Hospital Size, Six Hospitals, 1967

Measure	Small		Medium		Large	
	Hospital A 141 Beds	Hospital B 152 Beds	Hospital C 270 Beds	Hospital D 300 Beds	Hospital E 400 Beds	Hospital F 462 Beds
Means						
Admission time lag (in minutes)	58.4	59.6	78.8	99.0	125.9	109.8
Bed turnaround time (in minutes)	20.2	22.9	38.4	66.6	87.9	66.5
Accuracy of diet services (percent error)	8.0	0.8	4.7	5.2	19.8	25.1
Standard Deviations						
Admission time lag (in minutes)	8.5	7.9	10.0	10.9	11.0	11.6
Bed turnaround time (in minutes)	4.3	5.2	4.6	6.7	5.6	6.4
Accuracy of diet services (percent error)	.07	.03	.14	.05	.08	.10

for admitting-time lag, 420 for bed-turnaround time, and 96 for diet accuracy) for all three tests are significantly related to size, and (2) the
standard deviations (a statistic which reveals variability in the observed
times and percents) suggest that, regardless of average times and relative
accuracy, larger hospitals simply are not in as great *control* of their operations. They cannot predict and regulate the flow of their routines as well
as smaller hospitals, even if they were to consider it desirable to have their
patients experience substantial delays and inaccuracies in the services they
receive.

The theory that increased size reduces the hospital's organizational performance in rendering patient services is thus supported. This lower performance of large hospitals is a function of organization and administration, not a function of the quality of the individual service components
which comprise the hospital system. The problem should thus be amenable
to organizational innovation and solution.

The reorganization proposed herein would preserve for patients the
technical advantages of large hospitals and would reduce the disadvantages stemming from their lowered operating performance. In broad terms,
the proposal calls for new departmentation of the hospital organization,
accompanied by broad delegation of a special type of authority.

DEPARTMENTATION

Departmentation refers to the structural framework of an organization,
as compared to delegation, which is the assignment of authority.[1] Four
types have been identified by management theorists: functional, process,
territorial, and product.

Functional departmentation is the grouping of activities according to
an enterprise's major tasks, such as engineering, manufacturing, sales, and
finance, in an industrial firm; or institutional, financial, patient care, and
professional groupings in hospitals. For small organizations this type of
departmentation has the advantage of economy, since it captures the gains
available from specialization. Its disadvantages include a tendency towards
sub-optimization (the strengthening of individual functions at the expense
of the overall), and a pattern of authority in which operating responsibility
is diffuse. It is difficult to pinpoint responsibility if the organization is not
performing well. Also, a functionally departmented organization is a poor
training ground for top managers, since no single department offers the
breadth of activity which is characteristic of a chief executive's responsibilities.

Departmentation according to process is the grouping of activities

---

[1] Although conceptually distinct, in practice the two are complementary. Certain
forms of departmentation make delegation both easier and more effective.

around equipment and machinery, in order to carry out a particular operation. It is similar to functional departmentation, the major difference being the emphasis on man-machine relationships. This type of departmentation takes advantage of the economies of automation. Its disadvantages are similar to those of organization by function.

Territorial departmentation is the grouping of activities on the basis of geography. It has the advantage of placing decision-making close to operations, but in so doing the economies of functionalism may be sacrificed. Territorially departmented organizations provide good opportunities for the development of managers.

Product departmentation is the grouping of activities on the basis of output. It has the advantage of improved coordination. Organizational responsibility for end results can be readily identified and assigned. Its major disadvantage is the possible loss of central control.

Functional and process types of departmentation are similar and comprise a "composite-component" organizational pattern. Territorial and product types of departmentation are similar and make up a "federated-unitary" pattern. These distinctions, originally offered by J. March and H. Simon [4],[2] are shown in matrix form as follows:

Organizational Level	*Organizational Type*	
	Functional or Process	*Territorial or Product*
Organization (chief executive level)	Composite*	Federated
Departments (primary level)	Component	Unitary*
Divisions (derivative level)	Component	Component

* Level of integration.

The "level of integration," the lowest level at which all activities relating to a particular enterprise can be formally coordinated, is different for the two patterns of departmentation; it is one level lower in the second (territorial or product) organizational type.

FUNCTIONAL AUTHORITY

A fairly recent contribution to management theory has to do with concepts of managerial authority. Two forms of authority are widely recognized: line and staff. Line authority is the authority of office. It represents the direct "chain of command." Line officers of an organization are usually

---

[2] See also the excellent discussion of functional and parallel decentralization by S. W. Becker and G. Gordon [5].

generalists. They bear full responsibility for the operation of the organization. Staff authority is the authority of knowledge and operates purely in an advisory capacity. Staff personnel are usually specialists. They bear no direct responsibility for the conduct of the organization.

Two generalizations concerning line and staff are pertinent to this discussion. First, the use of staff persons is increasing as additional special talents are needed to manage the complex tasks undertaken by modern organizations. Second, the distinctions between line and staff are not as obvious in practice as they are in theory. For a variety of reasons, most organizations are unable to clearly maintain these distinctions, leading to misunderstanding, confusion, and open conflicts [6].

In response to both of these conditions, some firms, notably in the defense, space, aircraft, electronics, and research industries, have evolved a third type of authority, "functional authority," which is a purposeful blending of elements of both line and staff. When a manager delegates functional authority, he in effect identifies a "slice of his authority" and grants it to a staff specialist. The staff specialist acquires line authority in the specific realms designated, rather than mere advisory or informational power. This delegation is usually limited to the area of the staff person's special competence.

A subordinate in this arrangement in effect acquires two superiors: one concerned with general operational matters and one concerned with technical or specialized matters. The relationship between the three parties is seen in Figure 1. In the industries noted above, the organizational pattern which results from the use of functional authority is known as "project" or "matrix" management. An example in hospitals is the dual responsibility of a hospital nurse: to a nursing or administrative superior for matters of general hospital and patient care operations and to a physician for specialized medical matters.[3]

EXISTING STRUCTURE OF LARGE HOSPITALS

The administration of most large hospitals is functionally organized. Primary departmentation is created by the delegation of responsibilities to assistants or associates. Although there is variation among institutions, one assistant typically will be in charge of financial matters, one of plant services, one of ancillary professional services, one of patient-care services such as nursing, and one of staff-organized activities such as personnel, public relations, and hospital volunteers.

The nursing services of a large hospital are typically a mixture of process,

---

[3] As a practical matter it is stretching a point to state that the hospital management assigns the job of medical practice to a doctor in the manner of delegated functional authority. In fact, however, this is true, since the ultimate authority for the doctor's practice in the hospital rests with the hospital board.

FIGURE 1
Line, Staff, and Functional Authority Relationships

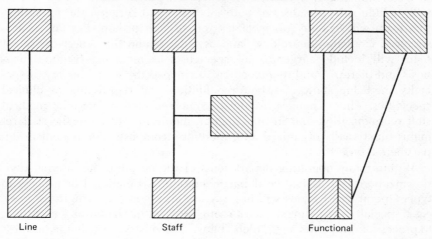

Line   Staff   Functional

territorial, and product organization. Three nursing activities have strong elements of process departmentation: surgery, delivery and emergency care. The "nursing stations" of the hospital, where patients receive their 24-hour care, are grouped primarily along territorial lines ("second floor," "west wing," etc.), with some specialization included (i.e., the second floor may house obstetric patients as compared to surgical or medical patients). There are a number of variations in this pattern. For instance, the post-partum unit may fall under the supervision of the head of the department of delivery rooms rather than under the appropriate "nursing station" supervisor. Or the process-type activities of surgery, delivery, and emergency care may be removed completely from the director of nurses' jurisdiction and be made the responsibility of one of the chief executive's assistants. In short there is a mix of process, territorial, and functional departmentation,[4] with some features of a federated-unitary type organization with respect to the 24-hour-care nursing station, but also strong elements of composite-component organization. The level of integration in the composite-component organization is no lower than the director of nurses, and may be higher.

The medical staff is a functionally-organized unit, with primary as well as derivative departmentation by clinical specialization (internal medicine, pediatrics, surgery, etc.). Derivative divisions contain sub-specialties (or super-specialties) such as orthopedics and ophthalmology under surgery, and cardiology and dermatology under internal medicine. However, these

---

[4] There is also departmentation by time: day shift, evening shift, night shift.

distinctions are becoming increasingly difficult to maintain. For instance, in major and highly specialized medical centers the heart surgery team will include sub-specialists of both medicine and surgery, the rehabilitation team will include sub-specialists of surgery (orthopedics and neurosurgery), medicine (neurology), and psychiatry, and the cancer-treatment team will include surgeons, sub-specialists of medicine (isotope diagnosis and therapy), and roentgenologists. Indeed the whole history of specialty medicine shows constant redefinition and regrouping of clinical specialties. These changes usually become reflected in periodic medical staff reorganization, but in fundamental hierarchic structure the staff remains functionally organized and, therefore, composite-component in departmental type.

Within many operating departments of the hospital, the internal divisionalization, i.e., derivative departmentation, is functional or process in type. Operating divisions within x-ray are arranged according to process, e.g., "specialty procedures," "dark room," etc., within laboratory according to process and function, e.g., "blood bank," "chemistry," within the business office according to function, e.g., "accounting," "collections," and within central supply according to process and product, e.g., "gloves," "needles." A few activities are territorially organized. For instance, the housekeeping department has supervisors assigned according to area. Some departments, like nursing, offer a mix. For instance, the dietary department has its food production activities organized along process and product lines ("regular meals," "special meals," "cafeteria") and its therapeutic activities organized along territorial and perhaps functional lines, i.e., therapeutic dietician for second floor, or therapeutic dietitian for medical patients.

In summary, functional and process departmentation are the predominant modes. Both the professional and administrative activities of large hospitals are organized predominantly in the composite-component pattern. Not only *within* each of these two hierarchies does this lead to difficulties of coordination, but the same problems exist *between* hierarchies. The level of integration is at the top of both hierarchies, and therefore only the top officials of each have the capacity to integrate the two semi-autonomous groupings. This places enormous pressure at the few points of contact between the two hierarchies—pressure with which the principals are often ill-qualified to deal, i.e., medical staff officials often do not comprehend administration, and the administrator, particularly if lay, may not understand the fundamental motivations of professionals. Participants in both organizations, namely patients and their attending physicians, are required to make difficult adjustments for the fact that the two hierarchies of which they are simultaneously a part do not coincide. For instance, a maternity patient may fail to see the rationale for her delivery and post-partum services being under separate jurisdictions. Or a physician attending a diabetic patient may find it difficult to coordinate two of the service units which are important for this patient: nursing and dietary.

A PROPOSED REORGANIZATION

A solution to problems of operational coordination in the large hospital lies in shifting the organization away from the widely accepted pattern of component-type departmentation within a composite organization to a pattern of unitary departmentation within a federated organization. This would be accomplished by transforming activities currently organized along functional and process lines to activities grouped by product or territory and by making wider use of the concept of functional authority. Such a reorganization would make possible the decentralization of hospital operations and delegation of authority to sub-units—both of which would go well beyond that which currently prevails in most large hospitals.[5] The key advantage of the proposed reorganization is that it places the "level of integration" at a lower point in the organization, thus reducing the organizational barriers and operating inflexibilities which are characteristic of large hospitals. This is necessary because the relative efficiency and effectiveness of these two types vary with organization size. In general, small organizations can obtain marginal economies by functional or process type departmentation. But a point is reached where increased costs are incurred due to poor coordination. The "point of crossover" will obviously vary from organization to organization,[6] depending in large part on the broad characteristics of the industry in which the organization operates. As shown in Figure 2, it is likely that this point is at a larger size for hospitals than for many other organizations, due to the dual-power nature of the hospital organizational hierarchy. Each of two authority structures, medical and administrative, must operate in partnership with the other, thus prohibiting either from adapting the structure which it might choose, were it a monolithic organization. The findings reported in Table 1 suggest

---

[5] A number of large teaching hospitals have made extremely worthwhile approaches in the direction suggested herein, although none, to the knowledge of the author, have done so on the basis of the above theory and evidence, or to the same full extent. Reports from these institutions, including Ohio State University Hospital [7], Presbyterian St. Luke's Hospital, Chicago [8, 9], University of Florida Teaching Hospital [101], Evanston Hospital, Illinois [11], Temple University Hospital, Philadelphia [12], and Salt Lake County General Hospital [13] are uniformly enthusiastic. The evidence is that the reorganization must be accomplished on something of an all-or-nothing basis in order to obtain desired and expected results.

The proposed reorganization would make hospitals more like traditional European "pavilion" hospitals: strong clinical service chiefs in charge of autonomous and relatively self-sufficient sub-units, occupying defined hospital territories or separate pavilion buildings. This has often led to extremes of sub-optimization. The organization proposed here is different in important detail from the pavilion system, and would in general not go as far in delegation (i.e., beyond the point of control). Also it is important to distinguish between departmentation which results from a federation of previously "feudal" units, and departmentation which evolves by way of "controlled decentralization" from a previously centralized authority.

[6] In the size range of 250 to 1,000 employees, according to the American Management Association [14].

FIGURE 2

Size and Unit Cost, Two Principal Types of Departmentation, Hospitals and Other Institutions

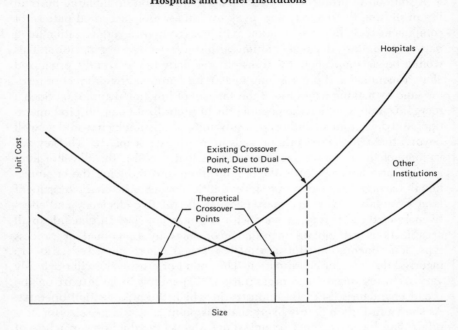

that hospitals in the middle size range (approximately 300 beds) are candidates for this type of reorganization, and larger hospitals have in most cases passed beyond the hypothetical "crossover" point without adapting organization patterns more appropriate to their size.

The administrative, nursing, and medical staff aspects of the proposed "mini-hospitals" will first be discussed, followed by suggestions for reorganization of several operating and supporting activities.

Assistant administrators would be deployed on a territorial basis, with one assistant for approximately every 100 beds.[7] These officials would be directly responsible to the chief executive officer, would be well-trained and well-paid and would enjoy substantial organization status.[8] Each assistant would be held fully accountable for all hospital administrative activities insofar as these activities related to his assigned 100-bed unit. These would include program and financial planning for the unit, development of appropriate organization and staffing patterns, and personnel,

---

[7] Rationale for this number is discussed. R. E. Adams [15].

[8] The position is thus distinguished from the "ward manager" job which some hospitals have created. The training of such persons has obvious implications for formal hospital administration education.

budgetary, and fiscal control. These assistants would be the management specialists for their 100-bed units.

NEW ROLE FOR NURSES

The nursing service would strengthen its territorially-patterned organization through delegation of greater authority to head nurses (typically two or three for each 100 beds), and particularly through the development of a highly qualified chief clinical nurse to serve each 100-bed unit. This chief clinical nurse and the two or three head nurses would be selected, recognized, and promoted for their nursing skills rather than their administrative skills (thus signaling a shift away from the emphasis which prevails in most hospital nursing services). The chief clinical nurse and the head nurses would be specialized in the branches of medicine most appropriate for the patients hospitalized on the unit.[9] They would hold associate membership in the hospital's medical staff, and would generally be recognized as professional colleagues of the physicians with whom they worked.[10]

The hospital's director of nurses would hold no line authority over the chief clinical nurse or other nurses of each 100-bed unit.[11] The director's job would instead emphasize the recruitment and training of clinical nursing talent, the evaluation of patient care in the hospital, and the development of new hospital clinical services. She would be an active participant in important medical staff discussions and decisions, would hold full medical staff membership, and would sit on the medical staff executive committee. The director of nurses position would thus move from the level of operations to the level of overall policy and decision-making.

The major change in medical staff organization would be the creation of a new position to provide linkage between physicians and the hospital at the operating (as compared to policy) level. A "medical advisor" position would be created for each 100-bed unit. This position would typically be part-time. The person would be on contract with the hospital for provision of the following duties:

a) professional advice to the nursing staff on specialty-related clinical matters;

b) coordination between the 100-bed unit and physicians admitting patients to the unit;

---

[9] The proper matching or nurse specialization, medical staff specialty departmentation, and geographic assignment of patients to hospital areas would require a series of imaginative regroupings.

[10] See [16] for full discussion by Hans Mauksch of the organizational content of nursing practice, with comments in support of the above scheme.

[11] Thus mitigating the dependence on hierarchy which commonly prevails in the hospital nursing organization.

c) participation in the management of the unit, working with the chief clinical nurse and the assistant administrator.

The unit medical advisor would typically be a younger physician whose experience in hospital-based practice had been relatively recent (residency training) and who would have time to devote to such duties.[12] He would be responsible to the hospital for the performance of specific functions for which he would be properly paid and held accountable.[13] He would be appointed to the position upon the consent of the appropriate department(s) of the medical staff, but would not be popularly elected to office in the traditional manner of medical staff department chiefs and officers of non-teaching hospitals. (These latter officials would continue to operate primarily at the hospital-wide policy level.)

HOSPITAL MANAGEMENT TROIKA

These three officials—specialists in administration, nursing, and medicine—would function as a management "troika." Important decisions would require the consent of all three.[14] They would be forced to develop patterns of communication, coordination, and cooperation which would improve services to patients on each 100-bed unit and would be an example for other components of the hospital to follow. The relationships of these three officials to each other and to the over-all hospital organization are shown in Figure 3. The proposed organization reflects the use of functional authority, as well as the more common staff and line relationships. This organizational pattern would require clear definition of both type and scope of authority. Otherwise potential gains in organizational performance could be lost in confusion over the limits of authority held by the various members of the mini-hospital management teams.[15]

The concept of functional authority would be used in reorganization of a number of hospital support departments. Personnel from departments

---

[12] In teaching hospitals a senior or chief resident would partially fulfill these duties, and in some medical school hospitals a junior member of the faculty could function in the capacity described. "Full-time chiefs of service" would also operate partially in this capacity. For the many large non-teaching hospitals, however, the proposed contractual relationship would need to be undertaken.

[13] For an example involving financial responsibility, see "MD's at Temple to Fix Budgets for Specialists" [17].

[14] Imaginative rules for decision-making have been developed at the Evanston Hospital, Evanston, Ill. [18].

[15] As stated by R. E. Adams, "It would also seem that one of the reasons there has been less than optimal cooperation traditionally between professional and administrative personnel has been that they have not essentially worked side-by-side on patient care problems. . . . It is a major breakthrough in making hospital administration relevant to the care enterprise. Management personnel are direct partners in care, truly associates of the physician and the nurse [19]."

FIGURE 3

Proposed Large-Hospital Organization Authority and Relationships

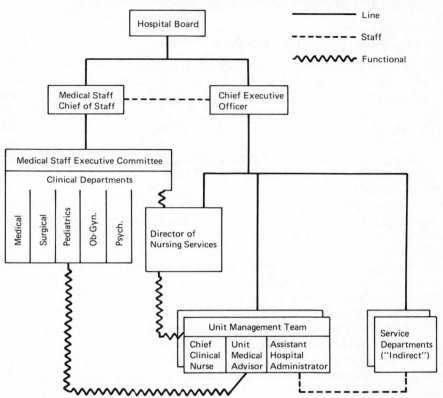

which usually operate along process lines would be reassigned to the 100-bed mini-hospitals. This would permit the level of integration to move to a lower plane in the organization, through a shift from composite-component to federated-unity structure. Thus, persons who typically receive *both* operating and technical supervision from one source, a staff or support department, would instead be accountable for operating matters to the 100-bed medical-nursing-administrative unit, and for technical matters to the appropriate staff department. This would give the mini-hospitals the organizational capacity to accomplish the type of coordination which the research findings reported in Table 1 show is deficient in large hospitals.

There are clearly some disadvantages to the assignment of personnel in such a way that additional positions of "multiple-subordination" are created. Yet it is probably better to have such conflicts centered within individual positions than to leave them operative at the organizational level. Problems of personnel adjustment and morale might arise, but the strengthened managerial component at the 100-bed unit level could presumably deal effectively with such problems.

DEPARTMENTAL REORGANIZATION

In general, reorganization of support departments which deal *directly* with patients would be most useful, leaving those departments which support patient care *indirectly* to continue operation on a functional or process basis, where economies of scale in operation may still exist. Suggested reorganizations of *direct* patient-care departments are as follows:

Admitting: Bed reservations and control would continue to be centralized, but patient admission clerks would be assigned to the several 100-bed units. Hospital admission routine would thus be decentralized from the "front lobby" to patients' rooms.

Dietary: Therapeutic dietitians would be staffed as part of the 100-bed unit organization. Final food preparation and tray assembly would be accomplished on the 100-bed units, in pantry areas designed for the preparation of pre-processed foods.

Pharmacy: Pharmacists would be assigned to and function as a part of each 100-bed unit, for pharmacological advice to physicians and nurses, monitoring of medications, ordering, and safety routines [20].

Physical therapy: Physical therapists would be assigned to selected 100-bed units, for closer integration of physical therapy and general medical and nursing therapy, earlier use of "modalities," etc.

Housekeeping: Maids and janitors would be staffed as part of each 100-bed unit organization, with recruitment and functional supervision continuing from the housekeeping department.

Radiology: X-ray procedures can be classified into two groups: (1) specialty procedures of low volume, high complexity, and long duration, and (2) routine procedures of high volume, low complexity, and short duration. Through redesign, physical renovation, and equipment location, procedures of the second category could be performed in the 100-bed unit locations [20]. A radiology technician would be assigned to each unit[16] and perform tests of the second type on location. This would reduce considerably the problems of patient transportation and peak-load scheduling. Films would be processed and interpreted either at the central department location or in the several dispersed areas, depending on available technology. If possible, radiologists should be available for consultation at the 100-bed unit locations.

Laboratory services: The collection and processing of lab specimens could be organized in a fashion analogous to radiology. Since professional

---

[16] Or share two units.

interpretations are required for only a few specimens, rapid technological advances will undoubtedly make possible an electronically linked network of partially centralized and partially decentralized processing and reporting stations.

Social work: Psychiatric and medical social workers would be assigned [22] in the manner of dietitians, pharmacists, and physical therapists. This deployment would be particularly useful for assistance to physicians in discharge planning, brought on by the requirements for utilization review.

Several support departments which serve patients *indirectly* could also be reorganized, although not as much would be gained from these reorganizations as from those involving direct services.

Centrally purchased, sterilized, and stocked products: The several departments which serve these functions would be merged, and, in addition to their internal functional-process divisions, there would be a "user-expediter" assigned to each 100-bed unit. These persons would assure the proper flow of materials to patient units. These expediters would be located within the 100-bed unit areas, and would be responsible for carefully controlled inventories of products stocked specifically to serve each unit's needs.

Medical records: No change in central filing system would be necessary, except for the assignment of file clerks to serve each of the 100-bed units instead of assignment by "terminal digit number." Transcriptionists would be assigned to (but not located in) each 100-bed unit. Assistant medical records librarians would be assigned to each 100-bed unit, for assistance in medical record problems, improvements in the system of transmitting and recording orders and clinical data (i.e., computer technology), participation in utilization committee affairs, etc.

Budget, cost accounting, and financial management: Primary budget, report, expense, and income centers would be by mini-hospitals.

ADVANTAGES OF SUGGESTED REORGANIZATION

The technical and professional advantages of large hospitals would be preserved, while the disadvantages of "bureaucracy" would be reduced. High costs of coordination, inherent in large organizations structured on a functional basis, would be reduced. This applies to the speed and appropriateness of decision-making as well as the efficiency of operational and logistical coordination. Organization of hospital services would be more responsive to patients, particularly in respect to variations in clinical requirements of groups of patients and in respect to the capacity of the organization to flexibly adjust and respond to individual patient needs. Administrative and clerical burdens placed on registered nurses would be drastically reduced, permitting better deployment of this scarce resource and great job satisfaction. Formation of relatively complete operating teams serving each mini-hospital would provide the opportunity for heightened individual and group motivation.[17] A variety of paramedical persons would for the first time be in positions to observe end-results of their efforts, and to experience the satisfactions of direct patient service rather than the dissatisfactions of indirect and impersonal mechanical processing.[18] Concerning group behavior, opportunities would be opened for collective motivation, constructive competition, and productivity incentives —all of which have been used in for-profit industry but seldom applied to hospitals. Finally, reorganization would enhance the ability of the hospital to measure true output through performance standards and accounting techniques which properly group the wide range of activities and costs associated with care of given types of patients. The opportunity to perform program budgeting in the hospital setting would be enhanced.

DISADVANTAGES

Adjustments in hospital design and physical layout would be necessary, with moderately higher capital costs a likely result. Uniformity among all operating units would be lost, as each 100-bed unit would acquire organizational and procedural differences which reflected the special needs and characteristics of its constituents. The use of float staffs and the transfer of personnel from one unit to another would be made more difficult. Central administrative control might be reduced, due to reorganization of the nursing hierarchy, formation of the three-man management teams instead of the traditional pyramidal hierarchy, and the generally increased organizational strength and capacity of the mini-hospitals. Finally, in an effort to gain operating efficiency at the patient-care level the possibility of operating inefficiencies within some support departments would be introduced. For instance, a pharmacist within a central pharmacy might be able to fill more subscriptions than the pharmacist of a 100-bed unit, simply because the demand for prescriptions from the 100-bed unit would not exactly match his prescription-filling capacity.

BASIC JUSTIFICATION

To this last point, probably the crucial argument against the new organization, a certain rebuttal is in order—one which summarizes the entire

---

[17] Including, possibly group-based productivity incentive plans, as developed by Scanlon and colleagues [23].

[18] As described by R. Holloway and W. Lonergan as follows: "The increased isolation produced by multiple hierarchies of authority, increased departmentation, and rapid growth creates a situation in which work group conflict runs rampant. Strawbossism, contradictory orders, and unfriendly relations between groups make cooperation difficult [21]."

rationale and meaning of the proposal. Standard measures of hospital "efficiency" are incomplete. By these measures overall efficiency is simply the sum of functional department efficiencies. This measures overlooks the *inefficiency* produced in one component by the "efficiency" in another. Thus in the operating interplay of sub-units there develops in large hospitals some serious inefficiencies which are simply overlooked by traditional techniques of measurement. Some activities become efficient, and in so doing create inefficiencies for other activities, and in the overall system.

This proposal implies that it is worth decreased efficiency in some components to obtain greater overall efficiency—a type of efficiency which recognizes patient service rather than hospital operation as the fundamental criterion.

REFERENCES

1. Klarman, H. E. *The Economics of Health.* New York: Columbia University Press, 1965, p. 24.
2. Wooden, H. E. "The System May Come Ahead of the Patient," *Modern Hospital,* 92:99–104, September, 1958, p. 99.
3. Starkweather, D. B. "Hospital Size and Organizational Performance," Dr. P.H. dissertation, unpublished, University of California, Los Angeles, 1968.
4. March, J. G., and Simon, H. A. *Organizations.* New York: Wiley & Sons, 1958, pp. 194–96.
5. Becker, S. W. and Gordon, G. "An Entrepreneurial Theory of Formal Organizations, Part I: Patterns of Formal Organizations," *Administrative Science Quarterly,* December, 1966, pp. 315–44.
6. Dalton, M. *Men Who Manage,* New York: John Wiley and Sons, 1959.
7. Howe, E. "Decentralization Aids Coordination of Patient Care Services," *Hospitals,* 43:53–55, March 1, 1966.
8. Adams, R. E. "Unit Management: Growing Care Needs, A Shrinking Skilled People Pool, and an Obvious Answer," in *The Hospital Medical Staff Conference,* October 2–6, 1967, Office of Postgraduate Medical Education, University of Colorado School of Medicine.
9. Brady, H. A., et al. "The Unit Manager," *Hospital Management,* 101: 6:30–36, June, 1966.
10. Taylor, C. "How Unit Manager System Works for Us"; Mercadente, L. T., "Unit Manager Plan Gives Nurses Time to Care for Patients"; Houtz, D. B., "The Unit Manager Plan Provides Administrative Control of Wards"; Martin, S. P., "Medical Staff Agrees: Unit Plan Is Good for Patients," *The Modern Hospital,* 99:2:69–76, 140.
11. Danielson, J. "Patient Care Administration: A New Management," unpublished manuscript, Circa 1967.

12. Durbin, R. L. and Springall, H. W. *Organization and Administration of Health Care*, St. Louis; C. V. Mosby, 1969, pp. 23–110.

13. McBeth, M., Carpenter, Jr., D. "Seven Year Appraisal of Ward Manager System: Salt Lake County (Utah) General Hospital," *Hospitals*, 40:79, March 16, 1966.

14. American Management Association. *Problems and Policies of Decentralization Management.* General Management Series, No. 154. New York: The Association, 1952.

15. Adams, R. E. *op. cit.*

16. Mauksch, H. O. "The Organizational Context of Nursing Practice," *The Nursing Profession,* F. Davis, Editor, New York: John Wiley, 1966.

17. Nichols, Sallie. "MD's at Temple to Fix Budgets for Specialties," *The Evening Bulletin,* Philadelphia, November 28, 1968.

18. Danielson, J. *op. cit.*, pp. 7, 8.

19. Adams, R. E. *op. cit.*

20. Oliver, J. M. "Improved Concept for Hospital Pharmacy Service: Patient Care Environment (Pace)," *Hospital Management,* 103:78, June, 1967.

21. Wallace, McHaig, Roberts, and Todd, in conjunction with Bolt, Beranek and Newman, Inc. *Temple University Health Sciences Center: Interim Report on Long Range Development Plan,* 1967, p. 111.

22. Howe, G. E. *op. cit.*, p. 54.

23. Lessieur, F. (ed.). *The Scanlon Plan,* New York: Technology Press, for M.I.T., 1958.

24. Holloway, R. G., Lonergan, W. G. "A Survey Program for Management and Organizational Development." *Hospitals,* 42:59–65, August 16, 1968, p. 63.

Part III

PROCESSES WITHIN ORGANIZATIONS

Introduction

This section of the book contains articles related to the *processes* within organizations: communication and decision making. These are processes which are common to all organizations.

COMMUNICATION

The manager in any organization—business, hospital, governmental, educational—must have accurate information that he communicates if the most effective decisions are to be made. The process of communication serves as a vital link between the manager, his subordinates, his peers, and the external environment. A careful analysis of these linkages points up the fact that communication involves decision making, organization structure, motivation, group dynamics, leadership, organizational climate and organizational development.

In the first article in this section "Communication Networks in the Business Organization Structure," A. K. Wickesberg reports the results of a study undertaken at the University of Minnesota to investigate the composition and nature of several communication networks, and the breadth of individual contacts throughout the firm as the individual builds his total communications net to carry out his task assignment. Ninety-one businessmen in the school's Executive Master of Business Administration program recorded all communications, oral as well as written, issued or received over a sample five-day period. In all, 35 different organizations were represented from a wide range of industrial, transportation, retailing, financial and educational organizations. The principal functional areas of marketing, production, finance, engineering, and research and development were represented in about equal proportions.

In the final article on communications, "Communication and Productivity," Jack R. Gibb examines the problem of communications from the standpoint of managerial decision making, i.e., what does top management or the individual manager do? The article is organized around nine fundamental communication issues that confront a manager. These issues are drawn from theory, research, and experience. The author distinguishes two clusters of related managerial behaviors for each of the nine fundamental issues. These are described as the "persuasion manager" and the "problem-solving manager." Each has different views on the role of communication.

DECISION MAKING

Various kinds of information are transmitted up, down, and across organizations. This information serves as a necessary starting point in the decision-making process which occurs daily in any organization. For example, in a business organization the information that a manager has about suppliers, buyers, competitors, government agencies, and other individuals and groups allow him to make price, quality, and distribution decisions. Thus, the actual growth, stability, and survival of an organization depends largely upon the transmittal of information to managers who must make *decisions*.

In the first article on decision making, "The Management of Decision Making within the Firm: Three Strategies for Three Types of Decision-Making," André L. Delbecq sets forth three decision-making strategies, each of which is tailored to a different type of problem-solving situations encountered within the firm. He examines each strategy to determine the degree to which it differs from the logic of classical organization models.

In his article "Decision Making by Consensus," Jack J. Holder, Jr., assistant vice president and director of management development at Yellow Freight System, Inc. describes his organization's experience with decision making by consensus. This article supports this approach to decision making; the advantages of group decision making by consensus are cited and specific examples are provided of the application of this management philosophy at Yellow Freight.

In the final article in this section, "Organizational Joint Problem-Solving," Robert L. Swinth approaches joint problem solving from a normative point of view. He examines the organization or some portion of it as a system for solving complex problems. He formulates propositions to describe how authority and responsibility should be distributed, how the processes of search and coordination should be carried out and how the major components of the organization—participants, environment, and task—should be linked together to perform effectively as a problem-solving system.

10

Communication Networks in the Business Organization Structure*

A. K. WICKESBERG

In recent years there has been an increasing interest in the detailed workings of organization structure with particular reference to communications patterns. Harold J. Leavitt[1] and more recently Guetzkow and Dill[2] and others have constructed laboratory experiments in which communications patterns such as the "wheel," the "chain," and the "star" are artificially imposed to restrict communications ability and the effect on task performance noted. Another group of researchers, Burns,[3] Sayles,[4] Ponder,[5] and Walker, Guest, and Turner,[6] have sought to record communications as they occur in actual business conditions. A principal contribution stemming from these latter studies is the indication of the sub-

* Source: Reprinted by permission from *Academy of Management Journal* (July 1968), 253–62.

[1] Harold J. Leavitt, "Some Effects of Certain Communication Patterns on Group Performance," *Journal of Abnormal and Social Psychology* (1951), pp. 38–50.

[2] H. Guetzkow and W. R. Dill, "Facets in Organizational Development of Task-Oriented Groups," *Sociometry*, XX (1957), 175–204.

[3] Tom Burns, "The Direction of Activity and Communications in a Departmental Executive Group," *Human Relations*, VII (1954), 73–97.

[4] Leonard R. Sayles, *Managerial Behavior* (New York: McGraw-Hill, 1964).

[5] Quentin Ponder, "Supervisory Practices of Effective and Ineffective Foremen" (unpublished Ph.D. dissertation, Columbia University, 1958).

[6] Charles R. Walker, Robert H. Guest, and Arthur N. Turner, *The Foreman on the Assembly Line* (Cambridge: Harvard University Press, 1956).

stantial amount of time individuals spend in communicating with others in the organization.[7]

The bulk of the studies outside the laboratory setting, however, deal with factory (assembly) environments and record single firm experience. Data are lacking on what communications nets occur for what purposes, how many persons comprise any one individual's own communications network, and what differences there are between such networks for managers and for nonmanagers.

To secure some preliminary insights into the dimensions of individual network membership, a study was undertaken at the University of Minnesota to investigate the composition and nature of the several subnets, and the breadth of individual contacts throughout the firm as the individual builds his total communications net to carry out his task assignment. Ninety-one businessmen in Minnesota's Executive Master of Business Administration program recorded all communications, oral and written, issued or received, over a sample five-day period which consisted of Monday from Week I, Tuesday from Week II, Wednesday from Week III, Thursday from Week IV, and Friday from Week V. In all, 35 organizations in the Twin Cities were represented from a wide range of industrial, transportation, educational, retailing, and financial organizations. Participants were almost equally divided between managerial (those with subordinates formally assigned to them) and nonmanagerial positions. While occupational titles ranged widely, the principal functional areas of marketing, production, finance, engineering, and research and development were represented in about equal proportions.

No superior-subordinate pairs were present, nor were there any communications pairs among the participants. To include communications pairs (both issuer and receiver of a given communication) creates problems in analyzing the data to avoid double counting of a communication as received by one individual and reported as issued by another. Absence of communications pairs also serves to in effect double the size of the reporting group.

Each participant maintained a daily log of his communications including information on the nature or purpose of the communication, whether written or oral, the amount of time taken for each entry, and to whom or from whom the communication was issued or received. The log contained a brief description of the subject matter as well as a purpose code. In addition to the log, each participant provided the researcher with an organization chart and a brief statement pointing out any unusual features in his communications patterns for the period studied plus any other information

---

[7] Robert Dubin, "Business Behavior *Behaviorally* Viewed," *Social Science Approaches to Business Behavior,* ed. George Strother (Homewood, Ill.: Richard D. Irwin, 1962), pp. 11–55.

he felt would contribute to better understanding of that individual's communications behavior.

DIMENSIONS OF THE COMMUNICATIONS NETWORK

Examination of the data suggests the following as major categories for classifying the different purposes of the reported communications:

1. information received or disseminated,
2. instructions given or received,
3. approval given or received,
4. problem-solving activities, and
5. nonbusiness related communications or scuttlebutt.

General Purposes for Which Communications Take Place

The five categories into which data are grouped to study the purposes for which communications occur indicate several general conclusions (see Table 1). First, communications separate into four frequency levels with

TABLE 1

Communications Frequency Classified by Purpose and Position

Purpose	*Position*	*Per Cent of Total Communications*	*Frequency Level*
Information	Manager	53.5	Level I
	Nonmanager	54.2	
Instruction	Manager	22.4	Level II
	Nonmanager	21.3	
Problem-solving	Manager	11.1	Level III
	Nonmanager	12.5	
Scuttlebutt	Manager	6.6	Level IV
	Nonmanager	8.2	
Approval	Manager	6.2	
	Nonmanager	3.8	

transmission of information by far the highest, followed by instruction and problem-solving in middle position, and with scuttlebutt and approval showing lowest frequency levels. In addition, there is little variation between manager and nonmanager in the frequency composition of his communications subject matter. While one might expect such frequencies to be identical where the participants consist of communications pairs, where such pairs are lacking and where the respondents range widely over both position and industry categories, closeness of the data for each category is indeed of interest. It should also be noted that the findings showing the high frequency of information over other categories of communications are consistent with other research reports and with intuitive reflections on organization practice.

Direction of Communications Flow

In an organizational context, communications may be transmitted vertically up or down the scalar chain, horizontally to one's peers either within or outside one's own organizational unit, or diagonally to or from an organizational unit and hierarchical level outside the reporter's own formal organizational location. The data suggest very little difference between managers and nonmanagers in terms of the direction of communications flow analyzed by purpose with the exception of scuttlebutt or nonbusiness related communications. Nonmanagers restrict nonbusiness communications to horizontal organizational relationships to a far greater extent than do managers (see Table 2).

TABLE 2

Direction of Communications Flow as Per Cent of Total
Entries for Each Purpose and for All Communications

Direction	Informa-tion	Instruc-tion	Approval	Problem-solving	Scuttle-butt	All Communi-cations
Horizontal:						
Manager	31.0	25.1	21.5	33.3	43.1	30.2
Nonmanager	41.3	43.7	33.4	45.6	67.9	44.7
Vertical:						
Manager	29.7	38.7	42.2	31.3	23.5	32.8
Nonmanager	22.8	23.2	34.5	22.8	19.1	23.1
Diagonal:						
Manager	39.4	36.1	35.8	35.4	33.3	36.9
Nonmanager	35.9	33.0	32.2	31.5	13.1	31.7

Of particular interest is the proportion of communications for all five purposes which utilizes *diagonal* relationships. Considerable contact between individuals regardless of position and unit takes place in the performance of the day-to-day activities related to their task assignment.

Managers and nonmanagers alike seek out contributors to their task effectiveness and in so doing direct approximately one-third of their communications to persons in units and organizational levels other than their own. To the superior-subordinate and peer contacts reported in the literature, one must add and not overlook the presence and significance of the diagonal component.

Data on initiation of communications were submitted by 47 of the 48 managers and by 39 of the 43 nonmanagers. While perceptions undoubtedly differ on who is the initiator and who is the receiver, the data provided in the reporter logs clearly demonstrate that nonmanagers as well as managers initiate not only information and scuttlebutt but also play a sizeable role in the managerial communications activities of instruction, approval, and problem-solving. These nonmanagers, as their communications networks indicate, are engaged in managing the accomplishments of those duties and tasks assigned to them regardless of where in the organization such activities may take them.

Of course, managers differ from nonmanagers in that nonmanagers have no opportunity for downward communications, for they are by definition the lowest members of the organizational hierarchy. In those organizational levels to which both managers and nonmanagers communicate, however, the bulk of these communications contacts occur at their own organizational level and at the level immediately above them. At these two levels, there are seldom any significant differences between managers and nonmanagers in the proportion of individuals in each category initiating communications for all five purposes. And the communications so initiated are directed by both managers and nonmanagers vertically, horizontally, and diagonally to every major segment of the organization at those two levels (see Table 3).

TABLE 3

Acceptance or Rejection of the Hypothesis That Significant Differences
Exist between Managers and Nonmanagers in the Proportion
of Individuals Initiating Communications for All Purposes
to Selected Organizational Unit-level Cells*

Organization Level Initiated to:	Organizational Unit Initiated to:			
	To Own Unit	Outside Unit, To Own Department	Outside Department, To Own Division	Outside Division, To Own Firm
To One Level Up	Reject	Reject	Reject	Accept
At Own Level	Reject	Reject	Reject	Reject

* Using chi square test with acceptance at .05 level.

Questioning of respondents indicates that few horizontal or diagonal relationships are prescribed in the formal authority statements or procedures. This may be a function of the kinds of positions and the nature of the industries represented by the reporters. That such movement is so widespread, however, suggests that individuals move wherever in the organization information, advice, counsel, and expertise may be found to assist in gaining satisfactory accomplishment of the goals assigned. Managers and nonmanagers are alike in this behavior. Formal organization boundaries and levels yield to the demands of the task and situation.

Network Membership

The composition of a communications network for a given individual may be considered in terms of (1) the total number of individuals with whom he communicates and their unit location in the organization, (2) the organizational level of these individuals in terms of communicating vertically, horizontally, or diagonally, and (3) the nature or purpose of the communication.

The data indicate that both managers and nonmanagers have communications network members who total far more than traditional spans of management or control would indicate and which are in excess of what one would conclude from examination of the organization charts and prescribed procedures alone (see Table 4). Furthermore, the scope of these

TABLE 4

Number of Members in Average Individual Network (by Organization Unit)

	Within Own Unit	Outside Unit, in Own Dept.	Outside Dept., in Own Div.	Outside Div., in Own Firm	Outside Firm	Total Net Members
Manager	7	9	9	9	2	36
Nonmanager	4	6	10	6	2	28

networks varies only slightly between manager and nonmanager. The very large proportion of members outside one's own immediate organizational unit should be noted. This amounts to 80 per cent for managers and 85 per cent for nonmanagers and confirms Leonard Sayles' experience.[8]

This sizeable component of net membership occurring outside one's own organizational unit and the substantial amount of communications movement regardless of formal organization and hierarchy boundaries are further supported in Table 5. Relatively few persons are present from the scalar chain, the vertical structure. The bulk of the network membership is to be found among one's peers in other units (the horizontal structure) and in persons at higher or lower levels in units other than the reporter's home base (diagonal structure). Taking into consideration the fact that nonmanagers have no subordinates and are at the lowest level in the hierarchy so they can have no "vertical down" or "diagonal down" communi-

---

[8] Sayles, *op. cit.*, p. 39.

TABLE 5

Number of Members in Average Individual Network (by Direction of Communication)

	Vertical Up	Vertical Down	Diagonal Up	Diagonal Down	Hori- zontal	Total
Manager	2	5	5	10	14[a]	36
Nonmanager	2	—	10	—	16[b]	28

[a] in own unit—1; outside unit—13.
[b] in own unit—2; outside unit—14.

cation, there is again close correspondence between managers and non-managers both in the total network size and in the network composition classified by direction of communication.

In addition to network membership examined in terms of organization location of the members and the direction of flow of communications issued or received, membership may be analyzed according to the function or purpose served by the individual network member (see Table 6). As in

TABLE 6

Number of Members in Average Individual Network[*] (by Type of Communication)

Communication Type	Position	Number of Members
Information	Manager	25
	Nonmanager	19
Instruction	Manager	11
	Nonmanager	9
Problem-solving	Manager	10
	Nonmanager	7
Approval	Manager	4
	Nonmanager	2
Scuttlebutt	Manager	4
	Nonmanager	4

[*] Any one individual may be a member of more than one subnet.

the case of communications frequency (see Table 1), network membership shows a predominance of individuals who serve the information function. The next highest number of members is less than one-half the number engaging in the information function. At this second level, the number of individuals in a network for instructional purposes is similar to those present for the problem-solving activity. The similar number of individuals for these latter two purposes departs from their volume characteristics as displayed in Table 1 where the number of instructional communications exceeds substantially the frequency of problem-solving items. As in Table 1, however, the approval and scuttlebutt purposes show the fewest number of subnet members. The magnitude for these two purposes is again less than one-half the number at the next higher level. Thus, with the exception of problem-solving and instruction, there is close correspondence between the functional frequency of communications and the number of net members participating in the performance of that function.

While some network members are present for multiple communications purposes, it is of interest to note that a substantial proportion of a given network membership is present to service but a single function (see Table 7). In the average managerial network, 22 individuals (approximately 60

TABLE 7

Number of Members Serving Single Purpose Only in Average Net

	Information		Instruction		Approval		Problem-Solving		Scuttle-butt		Total Members
	This Only	Total	This Only	Total	This Only	Total	This Only	Total	This Only	Total	
Manager	13	25	3	11	.7	4	4	10	1	4	36
Nonmanager	11	19	3	9	.3	2	1	7	1	4	28

per cent) participate in one function alone while for nonmanagers 16 persons (approximately 58 per cent) are single-function participants. Once again, the information category has the highest proportion of persons present for a single activity.

QUALITATIVE OBSERVATIONS FROM REPORTER LOGS

The large number of instances where communications take place outside the scalar chain indicates a substantial task orientation in the companies represented in the study. Such communications across organizational boundaries and in directions other than vertical suggest the existence of procedures regulating the flow of such communications. Little evidence, however, exists in the comments of participants to support the presence of formally prescribed procedures governing communications channels in the day-to-day activities. For the most part, reporting individuals were left to seek out and establish those network relationships which they believed to be useful or essential in the performance of their tasks.

The predominance of inter-unit and inter-level network membership and the substantial role of the nonmanager in initiating communications in all five purpose categories may well be a reflection of the high component among the reporters of professional or technical competence, of a sample bias toward aggressive, ambitious, younger individuals, and of a large component of so-called staff positions. At the same time, regardless of one's position title, his organization unit, his location in the hierarchy, and the presence or absence of formal structure, the qualitative as well as the quantitative data reflect the day-to-day emphasis on effective and economical task performance unrestricted by formal limits.

While one might feel that "staff" individuals would of course range widely through the organization, attempts at identification of "line" versus "staff" positions and relationships prove of little value. Position titles are of minor help in such classifications and give few clues as to the actual relationships existing between individuals in a network. As one might suspect, examination of the communication itself provides the best indicator of the character of such relationships. And the data fail to provide any clear-cut distinction between "line" and "staff" or between "manager" and "non-manager" based on the communications themselves. Any individual regardless of position title or organization location could be a member of either group depending on the time and the situation.

CONCLUSIONS

Several conclusions stem from the quantitative and qualitative data. First, the extent of the total communications network and therefore the range of individual contacts in an organization are far wider for both manager and nonmanager than one would gather from such traditional concepts as formal structure, span of management, and superior-subordinate relationships. This is illustrated in the large proportion of horizontal and diagonal contacts which exist outside the formal prescriptions of structure and procedure.

Second, on a day-to-day basis, the concept of manager should be expanded to include all individuals performing managerial functions whether or not these persons have subordinates assigned in the formal organizational hierarchy. Both managers and nonmanagers perform activities which are essentially managerial in planning for, implementing, and controlling those tasks assigned to them. Without recognition of the managerial characteristics of those traditionally classified as nonmanagerial individuals, these persons often are denied the official resources to perform satisfactorily and must rely primarily on their expertise and persuasive abilities to obtain from others those contributions necessary for effective goal attainment.

Performance of managerial functions by persons historically considered as nonmanagerial coupled with the substantial crossing of organizational boundaries and surmounting of hierarchical levels by both managers and nonmanagers suggest the growing contribution of informal relationships developed by individuals to further task accomplishment. This is a phenomenon which increases as complexity and sophistication of organizational requirements increase. Greater efforts must be made in the assignment or resources better to serve the activities and contributions of these informal relationships. More effective resource allocation is essential if informal relationships are to be relied upon to an ever-larger degree in solving complex tasks and in drawing to the maximum on the expertise present wherever it may be found in the organization.

That these are observations based on data from highly qualified professional reporters does not reduce their relevance for the nontechnical or less professionally dominated organization membership. These are observations drawn from individuals in organizations many of which are at the forefront of technological advance and therefore are indicators of structural changes and relationships likely to develop in any organization as its level of technology and the general expertise of its membership advance.

It is therefore suggested that management scholars and practitioners alike give greater attention to achieving organization balance by more carefully identifying the resource needs and structural relationships arising *de facto* from task requirements, project objectives, and individual expertise and initiative. Resource allocation based on formal power structures embedded in traditional concepts of superior-subordinate relationships, unit boundaries, and organizational hierarchy is no longer sufficient in meeting the demands produced by increasing levels of technology and higher levels of member competence.

11

Communication
and Productivity*

JACK R. GIBB

Communication is a process of people relating to other people. As people relate to each other in doing work and in solving problems they communicate ideas, feelings and attitudes. If this communication is effective the work gets done better and the problems are solved more efficiently. Thus, in one sense, at this level of abstraction, there is an obvious relationship between communication and productivity.

Work and problem solving can each be viewed as the taking of appropriate roles at appropriate times as the task or problem evolves. Role taking *is* communication. This apparent and real relationship has caused management to take an increasing interest in all phases of communication. Books are written, training courses are devised, and communications specialists are created and demanded. The rapid growth of literature and programs has far out-distanced the relevant research and the clear knowledge that management can use in making decisions about communications programs. The literature is confusing, contradictory and voluminous.

Although in the most global sense it is fairly obvious that communication is related to productivity, it is very difficult to find satisfying evidence of clear relationships between specific communicative programs or acts,

* Source: Reprinted by permission from *Personnel Administration* (January-February 1964), pp. 485–87. Copyright 1964, Society for Personnel Administration, Washington, D.C. 20004.

on the one hand, and measures of productivity, profit or corporate vitality on the other. Most studies of communication are short term in nature and relate aspects of communication to various personal and group variables that are perhaps assumed to be related to productivity in the long run, but whose relationships are tenuous at best.

It is the purpose of this paper to look at the overall problem from the standpoint of managerial decision making. What does top management or the individual manager do? The paper is organized around nine fundamental communication issues that confront management in today's corporate world. These issues grow out of research, theory and management experience. While it is true that in both practice and theory there are many and varied legitimate positions on each issue, it is possible to distinguish two clusters of related managerial behaviors that are fairly consistently antithetical on each of the fundamental issues. In Table One are sum-

TABLE 1

Two Alternative Views of the Communication Processes

A Persuasion Approach— The Focus Is on:	A Problem-Solving Approach— The Focus Is on:
1. Remedial programs	1. Diagnosis and etiology
2. Staff responsibility	2. Line responsibility
3. Morale and hygiene	3. Work product and job requirements
4. Persuasion	4. Problem solving
5. Control of communication flow	5. Trust and openness
6. Verbal communication	6. Management action
7. One-way messages	7. Interaction and climate
8. Knowledge and logic	8. Attitudes and feelings
9. Output and telling	9. Input and listening

marized the extreme positions of the conflicting views—the views of the "persuasion manager" and of the "problem-solving manager"—on each of the nine issues. Each issue is stated in more detail at the beginning of each of the nine sections of the paper. The issues are practical, overlapping and in general are worded in the language of management rather than in the language of the specialist.

In general, the *persuasion approach* to communication tends to assume that it is the responsibility of management to regulate the flow of fact and feeling through the organization, to use such regulation as a convenient managerial tool, to build staff roles to work on communication problems, to spend a great deal of time and energy building "communications" programs, and to show a high concern about the information flow in the organization, particularly about verbal and written messages downward.

An alternative approach, designated for convenience as the *problem-*

solving approach, is to assume that effective communication is an intrinsic component of effective work and efficient problem solving, that if communications problems exist they are symptoms of aberrant organization or poor line management, that communication is improved by more adequate line management action and problem solving rather than by staff action, and that by creating a managerial climate in which trust and openness is a norm, appropriate facts, attitudes and feelings tend to be spontaneously fed into the process of getting the job done.

In each of the following sections a focus or viewpoint consistent with each of the two above approaches is discussed.

1. SYMPTOM OR CAUSE

Is communication seen primarily as a symptom of more basic organizational processes or as itself a fundamental factor to be manipulated by management in the quest for greater productivity and organizational vitality? Is communication best viewed as a symptom or as a cause?

A manager with what might be termed a persuasion approach to management sees communication primarily as a management tool to be used in getting people to get the job done. When he sees some defect in the work pattern that must be remedied he tends to attempt to manipulate the flow of communications as a remedial action. Communicative distortion is seen as a basic cause of poor work or problem solving and is worked on directly by altering managerial communications.

A manager with what might be termed a problem-solving approach to management tends to see communication primarily as a symptom or indicator of more basic organizational or managerial inadequacy. Information about communicative distortion is used as diagnostic data which will guide the manager in taking new managerial actions, reorganizing work patterns, or achieving new attitudes toward the organization or the people in it.

The evidence is fairly clear that when people are in an effective problem-solving or work relationship with each other they tend to communicate relevant feelings, ideas and perceptions with each other. When there is goal ambiguity, poor supervision or role inadequacy, then communicative distortion occurs as a symptom of these more basic problems.

An analogy occurs in the concurrently flowering field of human relations. Human relations can be viewed as a symptom or as a cause. The growing awareness of human relations and communications problems is symptomatic of growing feelings of inadequacy on the part of management, and of a growing awareness of basic inadequacies in both management and organization theory and practice. When people have trouble getting along with each other and understanding each other, it is probably an indication that somehow they have been unable to create satisfactory jobs or a satisfying and effective work organization. The way to improve human relations and communications is to evolve new job prescriptions and more adequate work organizations—to change managerial actions. It may be a temporary solution to build human relations training programs and communications workshops—but this is at best a *temporary* or intermediate solution, a step that is getting at symptoms rather than more basic causes, and that is working on the shadow of the problem rather than on the problem itself.

2. STAFF OR LINE

Who is primarily responsible for effective communication—staff or line? The persuasion manager tends to emphasize the staff role in improvement of communications. The problem-solving manager tends to build responsibility for communications and human relations directly into the line functions.

A differentiating characteristic between the persuasion manager and the problem-solving manager is his emphasis upon one of two paths. The persuasion manager tends to build a communications staff with many responsibilities for studying communications, instituting programs, managing information and data flow within the organization, training people to communicate, and using various media to *persuade* people to change behavior or to communicate more adequately.

The problem-solving manager makes the assumption that communication is a direct line responsibility, that communication *must* occur in the process of doing work, solving problems, controlling distribution, or getting the job done. He works directly on the line causes of communicative errors. He works with others towards recomposing work groups, changing organizational patterns, reorganizing work space, or creating more adequate man-job relationships. He tends to change his behavior rather than his speech. He tends to control actions rather than to control talk.

It seems well at this point to call attention to the fact that we are describing two extreme typologies of management. In one sense the two types of managers being considered are hypothetical or "ideal" cases. The pure cases do not exist in the natural state. However, anyone with wide experience on the industrial scene can recognize the *genre*. The intent is to sharpen assumptions and to focus attention upon the implications of communications research for management practices. In practice, individual managers tend to show mixtures of the above patterns.

3. HYGIENE OR PRODUCTION

If there is a "communications program" is it primarily centered upon the requirements of the job and the product or is it primarily remedial in nature? Is it directed toward morale, hygiene and human relations or is it directed toward work and productivity?

The persuasion manager tends to direct the communication program toward improvement of morale and hygiene around the plant. He fights fires, drops verbal bombs where they are presumed to do the most good, centers upon remedial aspects of the situation, and directs plant and company campaigns toward curing ills such as absenteeism and waste.

The problem-solving manager tends to have no special communications program as such. When he does create such a program he tends to deal with analyses of job requirements, production schedules, goals of the enterprise, information storage and retrieval, efficiency of work flow, and other aspects of communication flow that are directly relevant to job performance and problem solving.

Hygiene-centered communication programs tend to send out information that is irrelevant, distorted to fit management goals, camouflaged to cover management errors, sent in too great a quantity, irrelevant to the concerns of the moment that *grow out of* task and problem demands or out of spontaneous group maintenance demands. Such programs are often met with suspicion and apathy, and may be seen as propaganda or as attempts to meet management needs rather than work needs or worker needs.

There is some evidence that communication is best when it is in response to natural interaction on the job between people who are learning appropriate trust, when it is in small groups or face-to-face situations, when it is asked for, and when it is between members who do not have too great psychological or hierarchical distance. The most effective communication thus tends to arise spontaneously out of situational demands.

Effective communication tends to be best in work units, where line managers and co-workers are learning a degree of trust appropriate to their relationship, and are learning to send and receive attitudes, feelings and information that are necessary for appropriate job performance. The interrelated assumptions here are that people like to do meaningful work, feel good when they have satisfactory job relationships, have good morale when they do challenging work that is related to their own choices, goals, and abilities, and that effective communication is a residual property of effective work and problem solving.

4. PERSUASION OR PROBLEM-SOLVING

Is the communication program focussed upon persuasion of people or upon indivudial and team problem solving?

The persuasion manager tends to see communication as primarily an influence process through which people can be changed, controlled, guided or influenced. Communication becomes education, propaganda, leadership, or guidance. Managers try to sell ideas, or to motivate others to work harder, feel better, have higher morale, and be more loyal.

If one were to believe the public statements and writings of leading administrators, one could believe that most of them are genuinely

anchored in the democratic style. Few will openly admit being autocratic of bureaucratic. After all, this is the age of the enlightened executive who assumes his social responsibility. However, upon close
inspection they show a tendency to cling to the democratic theme out
of feelings of inadequacy and uncertainty. They are democrats out of
fear of public opinion rather than because they genuinely understand
the needs and problems of people. [—Eugene E. Jennings in *The
Executive—Autocrat, Bureaucrat, Democrat,* 1962]

The problem-solving manager sees communication primarily as a necessary adjunct of the process of doing work or solving problems. In order to
solve the problem or get the job done certain information must be obtained,
certain feelings must be expressed, and a certain amount of interpersonal
perceptions must be exchanged in order for a team to be a healthy work
or problem-solving unit. Job demands or team maintenance demands
determine the amount and kind of communication that is necessary. Communication *is* problem solving.

The difference in the two approaches is one of *focus.* Communication is
both influence and problem solving. The emphasis and the approach are
the significant things. Persuasive communication tends to produce resistance, distrust, circumvention, or counter-persuasion. It is seen by the
worker or subordinate as "news management," as propaganda, or as an
effort to get him to do what he may not want to do. Research has shown
persuasion-centered communications programs to be discouragingly ineffective in accomplishing management goals.

Problem-solving communication is subordinate to the demands of the
job or the problem. The nature of the job or the problem calls forth certain
bits of information, feelings or preceptions that are relevant to job accomplishment or problem solution. In general, the research shows that when
conditions are created which produce relevant emergent communications
out of the work situation, that communications problems are reduced.
Thus, face-to-face communications in small groups tend to be superior to
other forms of communication because there is a greater likelihood that
communications will emerge from interactive job and problem demands.

5. REGULATION OR TRUST

Does one trust the manager and the worker or does one regulate the
communication flow?

An increasingly clear body of evidence indicates that communication is
related to the trust level in the relationship or in the organization. People
who trust each other tend to be more open with each other. With high trust
people are free to give information and feelings and to respond spontaneously to questions, are less apt to devise control strategies to manipulate
others, are less apt to be closed and devious, are less apt to manufacture

rumors or distortions, perhaps have less need to engage in extra communication, and thus they lay the groundwork for higher productivity. With low trust, people use more strategy, filter information, build interpersonal facades, camouflage attitudes, deliberately or unconsciously hold back relevant feelings and information in the process of interpersonal in-fighting, distort feedback upward in the direction of personal motivations, engage in extra communication, and thus indirectly sabotage productivity.

Managers tend to regulate the communication flow when distrust is high and tend to be more spontaneous and open with feelings and information when distrust is low. The persuasion manager tends to regulate communication flow—both in his personal actions and in his managerial policies. The problem-solving manager tends to create trust by allowing communications to follow the demands of the work situation. The openness-trusting stance is antithetical to the persuasion stance. Experimentation indicates that work and problem-solving efficiency is dependent upon the spontaneous flow of information and feelings through the system. Trust and openness are related to productivity.

6. TALK OR ACTION

Does a manager talk or act? Given a choice of where to focus effort, does management spend energies getting the problems solved and the jobs done or deciding what kinds of communications to send to the subordinate and the worker?

With articulate people words can become a fetish. What shall we say to the worker? What can I tell my subordinate? How shall I word the message? Part of this word-focus habit arises from a naïve confidence that people will take the words at face value, part of it perhaps from an unconscious protest to one's intuitive understanding that talk will make little difference and that people won't listen at all. Interviews with managers indicate bimodal reactions of naïve trust or equally naïve cynicism about the effectiveness of words in communication.

Experimental and field studies can be interpreted to show that actions are more significant than words in communication. Gestures, bodily attitudes, empathic postures, and management actions communicate a great deal more than words do. A manager who says verbally that he trusts a subordinate and then proceeds to require detailed and frequent reports, or to make frequent checks on the subordinate's work, usually is *perceived* as distrusting the subordinate. Actions take priority over words in the communication channels.

7. TRAFFIC OR CLIMATE

Is the "communication problem" basically a climate problem or a traffic problem? Do we focus attention upon refining the messages we send or upon creating a climate in which "messages" are decreasingly necessary? Is communication primarily directional or is it an interaction among people doing a job? Is the management problem one of creating a climate for interaction or one of regulating the message traffic?

The persuasion manager tends to be a traffic man, usually centering attention upon the one-way channels down the hierarchy or command channel. Great attention is paid to the mass media, refinement of the message, timing of the presentation, organizing the campaign, hitting at the psychological moment, and devising an appropriate propaganda strategy. Public relations, advertising and visual aids are in great demand. The problem is control of the traffic patterns of communication. Communication is often one-way.

The problem solving alternative to such action is to focus upon the interactive climate of work, to rely upon face-to-face interaction in line units who are working or solving problems together, to give all relevant information to line managers with maximum openness, to arrange the geography of work in such a way as to optimize relevant interaction, and to encourage questions, criticisms and all forms of informal interaction. Group discussions, small, flexible and overlapping work teams, and open channels are seen as communication tools. The problem is seen as one of creating a climate for work and problem solving. Communication is seen as flowing in a field of interaction, rather than as occurring on a one-way street—or even on a two-way street. Communication is a relationship.

8. KNOWLEDGE OR ATTITUDE

Which is more central in determining effective communication—information and logic or attitudes and feelings? If communication is seen as poor does the manager direct his energies toward refining the flow of information or toward changing the attitudes of persons engaged in communicating? Which is a more critical "leverage point" in adequate communication—knowledge and logic or attitudes and feelings?

The persuasion technologist tends to place an emphasis upon information and upon getting the "facts" to the right people. He tends to assume that information will change attitudes and behavior, and that information can be transmitted with acceptably high reliability through formal channels.

The evidence seems to point to the relative importance of attitudinal and motivational factors over informational factors in management and in behavior change. Campaigns to increase information usually accomplish considerably less than management would hope. Information does not necessarily change attitudes, value systems, or even perceptions. People tend to perceive information or reinterpret data in the direction of their motivations and wishes. People hear what they want to hear. They forget what they want to forget. There are various motivational reasons why people select from available information, ignore posters and pamphlets, overperceive or underperceive the "facts," and in general add their own distortions to the information that they receive.

The communication of intangibles like warmth, acceptance, respect, and trust are complex processes which are poorly correlated with the words people use and the information that is conveyed. The problem-solving manager tends to place emphasis upon feelings and perceptions of people, and to focus upon the work climate which will determine the way information is received and which may make special ccommunication decreasingly necessary.

9. OUTPUT OR INPUT

If something goes wrong does the manager start telling or listening? If a manager wishes to take a diagnostic stance toward the communication problem in his company does he accomplish more by refining the outputs or the inputs? Supposing we knew no other information about the alternatives than the titles of the courses, which management development course would we keep going: "Management Public Speaking" or "Management Listening?"

The persuasion manager tends to think in terms of output. He tends to talk of getting the message across, telling subordinates about the goals of the company, motivating people to work, seeing that people understand what management is trying to do, and putting out the message efficiently and quickly with a minimum of effort.

The problem-solving manager tends to think more in terms of input. He may ask himself such questions as the following. What information is needed? How do others look at the problem? What other solutions are there to problems that face us? How can we get more data? How can we interpret what information is available? What cues are we failing to process?

In examining the above clusters of management behavior we find that tradition and precedent are on the side of the persuasion manager. Most of the scientific evidence where it is available is on the side of the problem-solving approach. The skills and habits of persuasion are readily available. The skills, habits, and attitudes appropriate to the problem-solving approach are less easily acquired. The paths to creative problem solving are unclear. The managerial rewards are presumably very great.

BIBLIOGRAPHY

1. Gibb, Jack R. "Defensive Communication." *J. Commun.*, 11 (1961) 141–48.
2. Gibb, Jack R. "Climate for Trust Formation," in Bradford, Leland P.,

Gibb, Jack R., and Benne, Kenneth, eds., *T-group Theory and Laboratory Method.* New York: John Wiley & Sons, 1963.

3. Jackson, Jay M. "The Organization and Its Communication Problems." *J. Commun.,* 9 (1959): 158–67, 189).

4. Johannsen, James R., and Edmunds, Carolyn Y. *Annotated Bibliography on Communication in Organizations.* La Jolla, California: Western Behavioral Sciences Institute, 1962.

5. Mellinger, G. D. "Interpersonal Trust As a Factor In Communication." *J. Abnorm. Soc. Psychol.,* 52 (1956): 304–9.

6. Schutz, William C. Interpersonal Underworld. *Har. Bus. Rev.,* 36 (1958) 123–35.

12

The Management of Decision Making within the Firm: Three Strategies for Three Types of Decision Making*

ANDRÉ L. DELBECQ

Recent theory concerned with group problem-solving suggests that different types of decision making require different group structures and processes. The administrator who "manages" the decision-making process must, therefore, organize the executive team in different ways as he deals with the variety of decision-making situations within the firm.

Every practicing administrator is well aware of these qualitative differences in the problem-solving situations which he and his management team face. Further, even without conscious effort on his part, the management group will often change its pattern of communication and individual managers will adjust their roles, as the management team faces different tasks. Research evidence shows that over time, problem-solving groups tend to adjust their behavior in keeping with changes in the nature of group problem-solving.[1]

On the other hand, the process of adjustment to new decision-making situations is often slow, usually incomplete, and occasionally nonexistent. Managers develop expectations about appropriate behavior in decision-

---

* Source: Reprinted by permission from *Academy of Management Journal* (December 1967), pp. 329–39.

[1] Harold Guetzkow and Herbert A. Simon, "The Impact of Certain Communication Nets upon Organization and Performance in Task-Oriented Groups," *Management Science*, 1 (1955), 233–50; Rocco Carzo, Jr., "Organization Structure and Group Effectiveness," *Administrative Science Quarterly* (March 1963), pp. 393–425.

making meetings with their superiors, so that their behavior falls into a pattern with limited variability which may be appropriate for some types of decision making, but highly inappropriate for other decision-making situations.[2] However, if the manager is highly sensitive to differences in the decision-making tasks faced by the management team, and can verbally redefine both his own and his subordinates' roles in a fashion congruent with the new decision-making situation, research indicates that the management group can much more readily change its behavior as the result of such role redefinition in order to adjust to a new decision-making situation.[3]

The purpose of this article is to set forth three decision-making strategies, each of which is tailored to a different type of problem-solving situation encountered within the firm. Further, each strategy will be examined to determine the degree to which it differs from the logic of classical organization models. It is hoped that this examination of the three different strategies will fulfill the following purposes:

1. The administrator will become more sensitive to the kind of group structure and process which each of the three problem-solving tasks demand,
2. The problems of implementing the strategies within a traditional formal organization culture will be clearer, and
3. The implications for the redesign of traditional formal organization models to facilitate greater flexibility for problem-solving can be suggested.

THE RELEVANCE OF "TASK" FOR GROUP STRUCTURE

Since the body of this article proposes that managers should reorganize group structure and process as they face different types of decision tasks, a word about the relevance of task as a variable around which to construct "organization" is appropriate. It is axiomatic to say that individual behavior is goal directed,[4] and that group behavior is purposeful or goal directed as well.[5] The task of a group is normally thought of, however, only in terms of the stated goal of the group's activity. Thus, there are familiar typologies

---

[2] Leonard Berkowitz, "Sharing Leadership in Small, Decision-Making Groups," *Journal of Abnormal and Social Psychology* (1953), pp. 231–38; André L. Delbecq, "Managerial Leadership Styles in Problem-Solving Conferences," *Academy of Management Journal*, VII, No. 4 (Dec. 1964), 255–68.

[3] André L. Delbecq, "Managerial Leadership Styles in Problem-Solving Conferences: Research Findings on Role Flexibility," *Academy of Management Journal*, (March 1965), 32–43.

[4] Harold J. Leavitt and Ronald A. H. Mueller, *Managerial Psychology* (Chicago: University of Chicago Press, 1964), pp. 8–9.

[5] Robert T. Golembiewski, *The Small Group* (Chicago: University of Chicago Press, 1962), p. 181.

of groups based on stated goals. For example, Wolman classifies groups as being Instrumental Groups (which individuals join for the satisfaction of "to take" needs, e.g., business associations), Mutual Acceptance Groups (in which "give" and "take" motives are important, e.g., friendship relations), and Vectorial Groups (which people join for the purpose of serving a lofty goal).[6]

Another typology dealing with organizations as macro-groups is that of Scott and Blau who speak of Mutual Benefit Associations (where the prime beneficiary is the membership), Business Concerns (where the owner is the prime beneficiary), Service Organizations (where the client group is the prime beneficiary), and Commonweal Organizations (where the prime beneficiary is the public at large).[7]

What is not immediately apparent in each of these descriptive typologies is that task, as a variable, affects several dimensions of the system (regardless of whether one is referring to a small group or a large organization) including:

1. *Group Structure:* In terms of the relationship between the individual members.
2. *Group Roles:* In terms of the behavior required of individual group members which are necessary to facilitate task accomplishment.
3. *Group Process:* In terms of the manner of proceeding toward goal accomplishment.
4. *Group Style:* In terms of the social-emotional tone of interpersonal relationships (e.g., the amount of stress on individual members, the congeniality of interpersonal relations, the perceived consequences of individual and group success or failure.
5. *Group Norms:* Relative to each of the preceeding four dimensions.

Thus, in treating task as merely the end goal, many of the theoretical as well as the practical implications of the group's or organization's tasks are not made explicit. For example, when mutual benefit organizations are compared with business concerns, one would expect the former to be characterized by greater dispersion of power (structure), broader membership participation in goal setting (roles and process), greater emotional support of individual members (style), and stronger egalitarianism (norms).

In a similar fashion, the problem-solving "task" faced by a particular managerial team, within a particular organization, at a particular point of time, likewise must affect the structure, roles, process, style, and norms

[6] Benjamin Wolman, "Instrumental, Mutual Acceptance and Vectorial Groups," Paper read at the Annual Meeting of the American Sociological Association, August 1953.

[7] Peter M. Blau and W. Richard Scott, *Organizations, A Comparative Approach* (San Francisco: Chandler Publishing Co., 1962).

of the management team if the group is to optimally organize itself to deal with its task.[8]

STRATEGIES FOR GROUP PROBLEM SOLVING

Against this background, we can now proceed directly to classify decision situations as found in groups and organizations and to specify group strategies implied in behaviorally oriented group and organization studies appropriate for dealing with each of the situations.[9]

Strategy One: Routine Decision Making

The first decision situation with which we will deal is the routine decision-making situation. In Simon's terminology, this is the "programmed" decision-situation; in Thompson's terminology, the "computational" decision.[10] Here, the organization or group agrees upon the desired goal, and technologies exist to achieve the goal. In such a situation, the following strategy can be specified as consistent with behavioral models:

1. *Group Structure:* The group is composed of specialists, with a coordinator (leader).
2. *Group Roles:* Behavior is characterized by independent effort, with each specialist contributing expertise relative to his own specialty, including the coordinator (leader) who specializes in coordination across task phases.
3. *Group Process:* At the beginning of the planning period, specialists, with the coordinator, specify the productivity objectives. Subsequently, excepting occasional joint meetings to review progress, coordination of specialist endeavors is generally obtained by means of dyadic (two-person) communication between individual specialists and their coordinator, or through horizontal communication between specialists.
4. *Group Style:* Relatively high stress is characteristic. Stress is achieved through quality and quantity commitments and time constraints, agreed

---

[8] W. C. Schutz, "Some Theoretical Considerations for Group Behavior," *Symposium on Techniques for the Measurement of Group Performance* (Washington, D.C.: U.S. Government Research and Development Board, 1952), pp. 27–36.

[9] The reader should be clearly forewarned that each of the strategies is the author's own conceptualization. While an extensive review of the literature, both theoretical and empirical, underlies each strategy, it is not meant to be implied that the strategy represents a model about which scholars universally agree. Rather, the strategies represent the theoretical position of the author which is consistent with much of the literature, but is admittedly open to question and refinement.

[10] J. Thompson and Arthur Tuden, "Strategies, Structures and Processes of Organizational Decision," *Comparative Studies in Administration*, ed. Thompson et al. (Pittsburgh, Pa.: University of Pittsburgh Press, 1959), pp. 198–99; H. Simon, *The New Science of Management Decisions* (New York: Harper Bros., 1960), Chapters 2, 3.

upon in joint consultation at the beginning of the planning period. Responsibility is decentralized within areas of specialization, but coordination is centralized in the coordinator.

5. *Group Norms:* Norms are characterized by professionalism (high sense of individual responsibility and craftsmanship); commitment to shared team objectives relative to quantity and quality of output; economy and efficiency.

The above strategy evidences both similarity and dissimilarity when compared with classical organizational models. It is similar in that there is a clear division of labor, functional and structural specialization (specialization in work, and between work and coordination), and centralized coordination.

On the other hand, this "optimal" model is dissimilar in several significant ways. To begin with, responsibility is obtained primarily through team commitments to group objectives, dealing with both the quantity and quality of the output. This commitment, elicited through joint discussion between the specialists and the coordinator at the beginning of the planning period, places responsibility on both the team members and the coordinator, rather than locating responsibility solely in the coordinator.

Control is obtained in two ways. First, the coordinator provides the feedback mechanism for the team by monitoring the progress of individual specialists to assure conformity to shared productivity and time objectives. Situations where actual performance deviated from prior commitments are brought to the shared attention of the team, which institutes appropriate correction measures. Thus, discipline rests upon joint commitments rather than upon superordinate sanctions.[11] Second, because motivation is task-intrinsic, specialists are "normatively" expected to be "self-controlled" through professional, reference-group standards. Authority is likewise decentralized, based upon specialist expertise and shared norms.

Since responsibility, authority, and discipline are shared within the management team, there is less status disparity between the coordinator and the specialist than is the case between supervisor and subordinates in traditional organization models. Indeed, coordination is seen as a type of specialization, rather than as a function of superior personal attributes, or positional status. As a consequence, there is a propensity for fluid changes in group personnel; different task experts bring to bear their differentiated competences at different points of time as the group encounters various phases of decision making in the completion of a project. Further, the role

---

[11] For a treatment of the manner in which group norms control individual behavior, see André L. Delbecq and Fremont A. Shull, "Norms, A Feature of Symbolic Culture: A Major Linkage Between the Individual, the Small Group and Administrative Organization," *The Making of Decisions,* ed. W. J. Gore and J. W. Dyson (N.Y.: The Free Press of Glencoe, 1964), pp. 213–42.

of the coordinator may shift between the specialists on occasions, as the coordination requirements demand different admixtures of skills at various phases of project management.

Admittedly, the strategy assumes high-quality personnel in terms of both task skills and interpersonal skills. Further, it requires a degree of autonomy for both individual specialists and each specialist team, an autonomy which must be predicated on personal and organizational maturity. It also assumes that the objectives of the organization and each group can be integrated into a meaningful, internally consistent ends-means chain, where, at each level and between each area, objectives can be translated in terms of appropriate technologies.

Nonetheless, although a "pure" strategy (best approximated in project management, matrix management, or task-force groups), movement towards such a model for structuring groups dealing with "routine" tasks appears capable of avoiding many of the dysfunctions of classical organizational models, while captivating the advantages of division of labor, specialization, centralized coordination, and task-intrinsic motivation.

Strategy Two: Creative Decision Making

The second decision situation with which we will deal is the creative decision-making situation. Here we are talking about decision making which in Simon's terminology is "heuristic" and in Thompson's terminology is "judgmental."[12] The central element in the decision making is the lack of an agreed-upon method of dealing with the problem; this lack of certitude may relate to incomplete knowledge of causation, or lack of an appropriate solution strategy. In such a situation, the following strategy can be specified as consistent with behavioral models:[13]

1. *Group Structure:* The group is composed of heterogeneous, generally competent personnel, who bring to bear on the problem diverse frames of reference, representing channels to each relevant body of knowledge (including contact with outside resource personnel who offer expertise not encompassed by the organization), with a leader who facilitates creative (heuristic) processes.

---

[12] Herbert A. Simon and Allen Newell, "Heuristic Problem Solving: The Next Advance in Operations Research," *Operations Research Journal* (Jan.-Feb. 1958); Thompson and Tuden, *op. cit.*

[13] Particularly useful models dealing with individual and group creativity can be found in William E. Scott, "The Creative Individual," *Journal of Management* (Sept. 1965); Larry Cummings, "Organizational Climates for Creativity," *Journal of the Academy of Management* (Sept., 1965); Victor A. Thompson, "Bureaucracy and Innovation," *Administrative Science Quarterly* (June 1965); Gary Steiner, *The Creative Organization* (Chicago: University of Chicago Press, 1965); and Norman R. F. Maier, *Problem-Solving Discussions and Conferences* (New York: McGraw-Hill, 1963).

2. *Group Roles:* Behavior is characterized by each individual, exploring with the entire group all ideas (no matter how intuitively and roughly formed) which bear on the problem.
3. *Group Processes:* The problem-solving process is characterized by:
   a) spontaneous communication between members (not focused in the leader)
   b) full participation from each member
   c) separation of idea generation from idea evaluation
   d) separation of problem definition from generation of solution strategies
   e) shifting of roles, so that interaction which mediates problem solving (particularly search activities and clarification by means of constant questioning directed both to individual members and the whole group) is not the sole responsibility of the leader
   f) suspension of judgment and avoidance of early concern with solutions, so that emphasis is on analysis and exploration, rather than on early solution commitment.
4. *Group Style:* The social-emotional tone of the group is characterized by:
   a) a relaxed, nonstressful environment
   b) ego-supportive interaction, where open give-and-take between members is at the same time courteous
   c) behavior which is motivated by interest in the problem, rather than concern with short-run payoff
   d) absence of penalities attached to any espoused idea or position.
5. *Group Norms:*
   a) are supportive of originality, and unusual ideas, and allow for eccentricity
   b) seek behavior which separates source from content in evaluating information and ideas
   c) stress a nonauthoritarian view, with a relativistic view of life and independence of judgment
   d) support humor and undisciplined exploration of viewpoints
   e) seek openness in communication, where mature, self-confident individuals offer "crude" ideas to the group for mutual exploration without threat to the individual for "exposing" himself
   f) deliberately avoid credence to short-run results, or short-run decisiveness
   g) seek consensus, but accept majority rule when consensus is unobtainable.[14]

---

[14] In development of the above model, we have consciously avoided the issue of "nominal" groups (where members work without verbal interaction in generating solution strategies) vs. "interacting" groups. While preliminary evidence favors "nominal" groups in generating ideas, the question as to the appropriateness of the nominal

Obviously, the above prescription for a strategy to deal with creativity does not easily compliment classical organization theory. Structural differentiation and status inequality (other than achieved status within the group) are deemphasized. The decisive, energetic, action-oriented executive is a normative misfit. Decisions evolve quite outside the expected frame of reference of the "pure" task specialist. Communication is dispersed, rather than focused in a superior or even a coordinator. Motivation is totally task-intrinsic, the pleasure being much more in the exploration than in an immediately useful outcome. Indeed, the very personnel who thrive by excellent application and execution of complex technologies in the first strategy, find the optimal decision rules for the second strategy unnatural, unrealistic, idealistic, and slow.

Nonetheless, although all members of any organization will not find both of the strategies equally comfortable, it can be expected that most organizational members can approximate the strategy given appropriate role definitions. The point, here, is that the group structure and process which is called for to facilitate creativity is intrinsically different from our first strategy. While the first strategy called for an internally consistent team of complementary specialists who are "action" oriented, the second strategy calls for a heterogeneous collection of generalists (or at least generically wise specialists not restricted to the boundaries of their own specialized frame of reference, and even, not necessarily of the immediate group or organization) who are deliberately and diagnostically patient in remaining problem-centered. The membership, roles, processes, style, and norms of strategy two are more natural to the scientific community (or a small subset thereof) than to the practicing executive. The general implications, however, must await the exposition of the third strategy.

Strategy Three: Negotiated Decision Making

The third decision situation with which we will deal is the negotiated decision-making strategy. In this instance, we are concerned with a strategy for dealing with opposing factions which, because of differences in norms, values, or vested interests, stand in opposition to each other, concerning

---

group strategy for the total decision process (i.e., evaluation as well as idea generation) remains in question.

Further, the experimental tasks used in the studies may be different in kind from organizational decision making. In any event, the above model seems quite adaptable to separation into nominal and interacting processes at various phases, using modifications which do not vitiate the general tenor of the model. For a discussion of nominal vs. interacting groups, see Alan H. Leader, "Creativity in Management," Paper read at the Midwest Division of the Academy of Management, April 8, 1967; P. W. Taylor, P. C. Berry, and C. H. Block, "Does Group Participation When Using Brainstorming Facilitate or Inhibit Creative Thinking?" *Administrative Science Quarterly*, III (1958), 23–47.

either ends or means, or both.[15] Organization theory has never given much attention to groups in conflict, since several elements of classical models precluded such open conflict. One element was, of course, the existence of monocratic authority. At some level in the hierarchical system, authority to "decide" was to be found. Parties representing various opinions might be given a hearing, but ultimately Manager X was to make the decision. Another element in classical thought which precluded open conflict was the conviction, however utopian, that conflict was merely symptomatic of inadequate analysis. Adequate problem solving would surely show that the conflict was artificial and that an integrative decision could be reached. Thus, the study of mechanisms for negotiation between groups in conflict was left to the student of political science and social conflict and was excluded from organizational models.

Nonetheless, the realities of conflict have been ubiquitous. Present models encourage the sublimation of conflict, veiling it in portended rationality. As one wag expressed the matter, "If people don't agree with me, it isn't that I am wrong, or that they are right, but merely that I haven't been clear." In spite of Trojan efforts at "clear communication," the elimination of all conflict through analysis is, indeed, a utopian desire. There have been, and will be, instances where the organization finds itself encompassing two "camps," each supported by acceptable values and logic, and each committed to a different course of action, relative to either means, ends, or both. The question remains, then, as to what would be an appropriate strategy in those cases where "analysis" cannot provide an acceptable solution to both parties since the disparate opinion or positions are based on assumptions and premises not subject to total decision integration.

The following strategy can be specified:

1. *Group Structure:* The group is composed of proportional representation of each faction (but with the minority never represented by less than two persons), with an impartial formal chairman.[16]
2. *Group Roles:* Each individual sees himself as a representative of his faction, seeking to articulate and protect dominant concerns of the group he represents, while at the same time negotiating for an acceptable compromise solution.
3. *Group Processes:* The problem-solving process is characterized by:
    a) orderly communication mediated by the chairman, providing oppor-

---

[15] In this respect, we assume a position different from that of Thompson and Tuden in their earlier model who posit that "compromise" decision making is predicated on disagreement about ends. Thompson and Tuden, *op. cit.*

[16] The justification for the minority never being represented by less than two persons is that it is difficult for one person to represent his group across the boundary and that a minority of one is easy prey for a majority coalition of two members, let alone more than two.

tunity for each faction to speak, but avoidance of factional domination

 b) formalized procedures providing for an orderly handling of disputation
 c) formalized voting procedure
 d) possession of veto power by each faction
 e) analytical approaches to seeking compromise, rather than mere reliance on power attempts.
4. *Group Style:* Group style is characterized by:
 a) frankness and candor in presenting opposing viewpoints
 b) acceptance of due process in seeking resolution to conflicts
 c) openness to rethinking, and to mediation attempts
 d) avoidance of emotional hostility and aggression.
5. *Group Norms:* Group norms are characterized by:
 a) desire on the part of all factions to reach agreement
 b) the perception of conflict and disagreement as healthy and natural, rather than pathological
 c) acceptance of individual freedom and group freedom to disagree
 d) openness to new analytical approaches in seeking acceptable compromise
 e) acceptance of the necessity of partial agreement as an acceptable, legitimate, and realistic basis for decision making.

There is, obviously, no parallel in either structure or norms to the above strategy in classical organizational models. The acceptance of open conflict; provision for due process between conflicting groups; openness to compromise; evolution of policy and objectives through negotiation; and "representative groups" while found in the "underworld" in most organizations, are outside the general organizational model. Indeed, managers involved in "negotiations," either in the personnel (labor relations) or marketing (customer relations) areas, find it difficult to articulate the legitimacy of many of their decisions except through rationalizations.

CONCLUSIONS AND IMPLICATIONS

Both the propensities for groups to change the nature of their interaction as they change task, and/or task phases, and the prescriptions for group strategies dealing with differentiated decision situations as set forth above, indicate that the structure and processes of groups must be related to changes in the characteristics of the decision-making tasks. Whether one agrees with each proposition in each of the decision strategy models set forth in this article or not, the fact that each of the decision-making situations is endemically different is difficult to refute.

On the other hand, formal organizations as conceived in present organizational models are presumably structured in terms of the predominant type of task encountered by the system. (Thus, the "bureaucratic" model is based on facilitating "routine" decision making; the labor union council is structured to deal with negotiated decision making; etc.). Since task is, in the most pertinent sense, what members of the organization subjectively define it to be as they respond to the situation in which they find themselves, the internal features of a decision group within the organization will generally be conditioned by the predominant structured roles created to deal with the "typical" decisions encountered in day-to-day organizational tasks. As a result, role expectations and behaviors conditioned in the central organizational system (the formal organization) may inhibit the decision task performance in the subsystem (the decision-making committee, conference, or task force).

Since there are several types of decisions to be made within complex organizations, with each general type calling for a different group structure and process, a major role of the manager in such a system is the evoking of appropriate changes in behaviors on the part of the managerial team as it moves across the task types by means of role redefinition. This assumes that the manager can classify decision tasks according to the models presented here, or some other conceptual scheme, and that the managerial team can respond with congruent role flexibility. Earlier pilot research by the author indicates that such flexibility seems to be within the capacities of a large portion of the population, given appropriate role redefinition by the superior.[17]

In a real sense, then, management of the decision-making process is management of the structure and functioning of decision groups, so that these decision-making processes become congruent with changes in the nature of the decision-making task being undertaken at a particular point of time within the organization.

Finally, we spent considerable time delineating the "task-force," "systems management" or "matrix organizational" approach (strategy one)[18] as

---

[17] André L. Delbecq (March 1965). We agree that some individuals will find it impossible to assume flexible roles due to their particular developmental history which results in a fixated behavior pattern. We also agree that some roles will be more natural than others for individuals due to their developmental history. We disagree, however, with the notion that the normal population cannot assume at least functionally relevant roles in accordance with the various strategies, a point which appears to be the position of some theorists. A more conservative viewpoint than ours is assumed by Abraham Zaleznic in *Human Dilemmas of Leadership* (New York: Harper & Row, 1965).

[18] For an elaborated treatment of "Matrix Organization" see Fremont A. Shull, *Matrix Structure and Project Authority for Optimizing Organizational Capacity* (Monograph, Business Research Bureau, Southern Illinois University, Carbondale, Illinois, 1965); Warren Bennis, "Beyond Bureaucracy," *Transactions* (Summer 1965); John F. Mee, "Ideational Items: Matrix Organization," *Business Horizons* (Summer 1964), pp. 70–72; and Carl R. Praktish, "Evolution of Project Management," Paper read at Midwest Academy of Management, April 1967.

the appropriate strategy for routine decision making purposefully, since it seems to provide a mechanism for integrating various types of decision making at various phases of project management within a flexible structure. It is felt that strategy one avoids the structural rigidity of formal organization models such as "bureaucracy." There is no reason, for instance, why "creative" or "negotiated" strategies cannot be incorporated into the objectives and standards-setting decision sessions at the beginning of the planning period. Further, there is no reason why personnel other than the "task specialists" cannot mediate the decision making by participation in these early decision phases. Thus, by dropping the assumption of "agreed-upon technologies" and "agreed-upon objectives," and incorporating strategies two and three into these early planning sessions, or intermittently juxtaposing these strategies with strategy one, the possibility for incorporating decision-making flexibility into the "project management" context of strategy one seems not only feasible, but a desirable movement in the direction of fluid group structures and processes. Such a movement toward organizational fluidness is more congruent with the need for role flexibility as the management team moves across decision strategies at various phases of project planning and implementation.

13

Decision Making by Consensus*
JACK J. HOLDER, JR.

Consensus is defined basically as agreement by all parties involved in some group decision or action; it occurs only after deliberation and discussion of pros and cons of the issues, and when all (not a majority) of the managers are in agreement. Each member of the group must be satisfied as to the ultimate course of action to be taken.

Decision making by consensus has been a common practice at Yellow Freight System, Inc. since the early 1950s, especially among the top management group of the company. The process is not a simple one. Some of the more important variables include the leader, the followers, the organizational structure, communications, leadership styles, motivation of group members, and the group itself. Many additional factors could be listed. This article will attempt to provide academic support for the present company policy of management decision making by consensus. An attempt will be made to cover the necessary supplemental information and studies one must understand in order to fully comprehend the process.

PARTICIPATIVE MANAGEMENT

Likert has reported in detail on his research into participative management, which is basically the process of involving people in decisions that

* Source: Reprinted by permission from *Business Horizons* (April 1972), pp. 47–54.

affect them. In one experiment, two groups were established and closely observed. One group was involved in a hierarchically controlled program, where the management relied on authority to get the work done.

Although both programs achieved increases in productivity, they yielded significantly different results in other respects. The productivity increases in the hierarchically controlled program were accompanied by shifts in an *adverse* direction in such factors as loyalty, attitudes, interest, and involvement in the work. Just the opposite was true in the participative program. For example, when more general supervision and increased participation were provided, the employee's feeling of responsibility to see that the work got done increased. Observations showed that when the supervisor was away, the employees kept on working. In the hierarchically controlled program, however, the feeling of responsibility decreased and when the supervisor was absent the work tended to stop.[1]

Likert emphasized most of the ingredients involved in decision making by consensus:

[He] has focused on the problem of interdepartmental communications and group relationships; his thesis is that factors promoting internalization of objectives can be realized by involving all subgroups of the organization in group decision making of a task-oriented character. Separate organizational groups with overlapping common members (linking pins) serve to provide vertical and horizontal communications as well as a task orientation toward common organizational goals. The linking pin concept will be covered in detail at a later point in this article. Specific responsibility for decision making is delegated to each organizational group.[2]

Decision making by consensus requires knowledgeable and well-oriented managers as well as a strong leader.

The most effective leaders are those who best meet and fulfill the needs of their organizations. The use of management committees and other necessary integrating mechanisms does not mitigate the need for a strong executive presence. A strong leader will produce a strong organization. Conceptually, the problem has been that power equalization techniques, such as participative management and management teams, have implied that those who use them must abdicate their leadership role.

Operationally, nothing can be further from reality. What is needed

---

[1] Rensis Likert, *New Patterns of Management* (New York: McGraw-Hill Book Co., 1971), p. 65.

[2] George H. Labovitz, "Organizing for Adaptation: the Case for a Behavioral View," *Business Horizons* (June 1971), p. 21.

is a different team of strong leadership calling for presence rather than prominence. By presence, we mean that state of leadership which permits a manager to achieve a close relationship with his people. He does this by building a climate in which people are free to reach their potential and to grow along with the organization. Two-way communication, participation techniques, and the tools of an "environmental creator" require strong leadership presence, primarily because in a dynamic organization the emphasis is on lack of structure.

In operational matters, the participative approach presupposes that the chief executive cannot run the organization alone, and that those on whom he depends must have free access to information and decisions if they are to personally develop and the organization is to maximize its growth potential.[3]

In addition, the participative program produced more favorable attitudes, a closer relationship between supervisors and employees, greater upwards communications, and greater employee satisfaction with supervisors as their representatives.

Effects on Productivity

Both Likert and Odiorne have commented on the effect of participative management on productivity:

Research findings do not support the conclusion that every organization in which there are high levels of confidence and trust, favorable attitudes, and high levels of job satisfaction will be highly productive. Even though a manager may have built his department into an organization with these qualities his department will not achieve high productivity unless his leadership and the decision-making process used by the organization result in the establishment of high performance goals by the members for themselves. High performance goals as well as favorable attitudes must be present if an organization is to achieve a high degree of productivity.

The conclusion to be reached is that neither tightness of supervision nor looseness is a sole controlling variable, and that participation of itself has no claim to being the core of a new pattern of managing that will guarantee high productivity if universally adopted by managers. There is some evidence, however, that a strong orientation toward goals, coupled with leader enthusiasm, ample rewards for achieving them, and the uniting of people in moving toward them does have a beneficial effect.[4]

---

[3] George H. Labovitz, "Organizing for Adaptation," p. 25, p. 26.

[4] First paragraph from Likert, op. cit., p. 59; second paragraph from George S. Odiorne, Management by Objectives (New York: Pitman Publishing Corp., 1970), p. 145.

Research findings indicate that the general pattern of operations of the highest producing managers tends to differ from that of the managers of mediocre and low-producing units by more often showing certain characteristics. *First,* according to Likert, favorable attitudes tend to prevail on the part of each member of the organization toward all the other members, toward supervisors, toward the work, toward the organization—toward all aspects of the job. These attitudes reflect a high level of mutual confidence and trust, as well as identification with the organization and its objectives and a high sense of involvement in achieving them.

Second, this highly motivated, cooperative orientation toward the organization and its objectives is achieved by harnessing effectively such major forces as motives related to the ego and security, and economic motives.

Third, the organization consists of a tightly knit, effectively functioning social system. This system is made up of interlocking work groups with a high degree of group loyalty, participation, and communication. *Finally,* the leadership acts habitually to tap the motives that produce cooperative and favorable attitudes, participation, and involvement in decisions.[5]

Management Perceptions

Participative management requires a leader who is interested in listening to ideas and suggestions from others in order to reach the best possible decision. Some guides to help the action-oriented manager determine when to listen to others include:

Listening is cheap. The best rule to guide decision making is that listening won't hurt anybody. Even when the aurally received material goes in one ear and out the other, it doesn't harm anything, and helps the person talking. It always opens the possibility that something useful might be said.

When listening makes the program stronger. There are some decisions that will depend upon support and teamwork for the execution. If listening to others' suggestions adds impetus to the execution and gains acceptance for the final decision, it's worthwhile.

When it wins over hostile forces. One of the best ways of gaining an ally is to ask an enemy for assistance and advice. He'll say things that make him part of the decision as it's finally made and will be identified with it.

When the decision to be made is already decided. During the Korean War one firm had decided to go into defense work up to 20 per cent of its sales volume. Numerous suggestions were made and

---

5 Likert, *op. cit.,* pp. 98–99.

arguments given for and against going into defense work for several weeks after the decision was made. . . . 'It didn't hurt us to listen, and we got a lot of our people involved in what was going to happen. . . . they almost all recommended that we do what we were going to do anyhow.'

When the person talking is an expert. At many stages in the decision making process, careful listening to all ideas and especially from people who know some special facet can improve the decision considerably.[6]

Widespread participation is one of the most important approaches employed by the high-producing managers in their efforts to get full benefit from the technical resources and knowledgeability of other managers. Participation also applies to all aspects of the job including decision making in setting goals, controlling costs, organizing the work, personnel changes, and general policy matters.

Manager and Employee Reaction

Research studies show that employees react favorably to experiences that they feel support and contribute to their sense of importance and personal worth. Similarly, persons react unfavorably to experiences that are threatening and decrease or minimize their sense of dignity and personal worth.

With this thought in mind, our management leadership

. . . and other processes of the organization must be such as to insure a maximum probability that in all interactions and all relationships with the organization each member will, in the light of his background, values, and expectations, view the experiences as supportive and one which builds and maintains his sense of personal worth and importance. . . . each member of the organization must feel that the organization's objectives are of significance and that his own particular task contributes in an indispensable manner to the organization's achievement of its objectives. He should see his role as difficult, important and meaningful.[7]

Participation in decision making fosters greater commitment on the part of the individual to the company's goals and objectives, as well as to his own goals and objectives.

Commitment is more than participation. It is not unlike a personal bond—a bond between the individual and his own goals, and/or be-

---

[6] George S. Odiorne, *How People Make Things Happen* (Englewood Cliffs, N.J.: Prentice-Hall, Inc., 1969), pp. 202–3.

[7] Likert, *op. cit.,* p. 103.

tween the individual and the company goals. A definite quid pro quo relationship must exist. Commitment is specifically a personal nature between the individual's own feelings and his attitude or concern for company goals and objectives.

Ideally, the individual goal and the company goal should be the same, or one is achieved by the achievement of the other. Company goals of long run growth and profitability are achieved only on the basis of a number of individual goals and objectives being achieved.[8]

Management By Objectives

The process of management by objectives is basically one whereby:

> . . . the superior and the subordinate managers of an enterprise jointly, identify its common goals, define each individual's major areas of responsibility in terms of the results expected of him and use these measures as guides for operating the unit and assessing the contribution of each of its members.
>
> We realize that it is not an easy task to integrate the goals and objectives of all individuals with the goals of the organization. Yet it is not an impossible task. An approach to this problem which has been used successfully in some organizations in our culture is a process called management by objectives.[9]

Management by objectives should be employed throughout a company, from the top to the lower management levels. Corporate officers and operations division vice-presidents meet each year to formulate the goals and objectives for Yellow Freight. By the same token, branch managers should meet with their operating and sales supervisors to map out the branch goals in a management by objectives fashion.

THE WORK GROUP

The various work groups at Yellow Freight extend from the top company officers to the dock foreman and his crew of dock workers. Our work groups are important to us, and as a result we are highly motivated to behave in ways consistent with the goals and values of the group in order to obtain recognition, support, security, and favorable reactions. We can conclude that Management will make full use of the potential capacities

---

[8] Jack J. Holder, Jr., "Achieving Goals and Objectives in the Motor Carrier Industry," *Transportation Journal* (Spring 1971), pp. 51–59.

[9] Paul Hersey and Kenneth H. Blanchard, *Management of Organizational Behavior* (Englewood Cliffs, N.J.: Prentice-Hall, Inc., 1969), p. 118.

of its human resources only when each person in an organization is a member of one or more effective functioning work groups that have a high degree of group loyalty, effective skills of interaction, and high performance goals.[10]

As managers we should strive to build strong work groups that merit attention and loyalty from their members. The individual who has a strong loyalty is motivated to:

Accept the goals and decisions of the group

Attempt to influence the group's goals and decisions

Communicate fully to other members

Welcome communication and attempts to persuade from other members

Help implement the goals and decisions that are seen as most important

Behave in ways calculated to receive support and favorable recognition from members.

The Linking-Pin Function

The capacity to exert influence upward is essential if a manager is to perform his supervisory functions well. Work groups will provide this capacity if they are linked into an over-all organization through overlapping group memberships. The supervisor in one group is a subordinate in the next, and so on throughout the organization. This process is known as the linking-pin function. Its application to the operations function in Yellow Freight is shown in the accompanying figure.

In order to be effective the linking-pin function requires effective group processes. The following characteristics should be present:

If an organization is to derive the full benefit from its highly effective groups they must be linked to the total organization by means of overlapping groups.

The potential power of the overlapping group form of organization will not be approached until all of the groups of the organization are functioning reasonably well.

The higher an ineffective group in the hierarchy, the greater the adverse effect of its failure on the performance of the organization.

To help maintain an effective organization, it is desirable for superiors not only to hold group meetings of their own subordinates, but also to have occasional meetings over two hierarchical levels.

An organization takes a serious risk when it relies on a single linking pin or single linking process to tie the organization together.[11]

---

[10] Likert, *op. cit.*, p. 104.

[11] Likert, *op. cit.*, pp. 114–15.

Company Organization—Linking Pin Concept

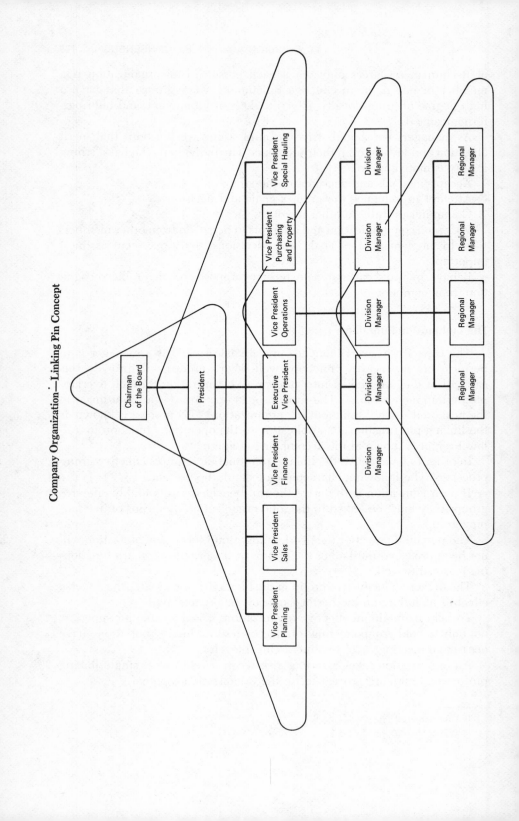

Man-to-Man Organization Structure

The effective group organization structure is highly superior to the typical man-to-man organizational structure. The man-to-man arrangement is structured as in the accompanying chart.

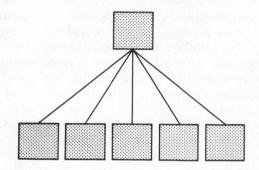

Several inadequacies can be noted in the man-to-man organizing structure. For example, meetings are primarily held for sharing of information and not decision making. Communication is quite difficult and usually filtered or inaccurate; in fact, individuals benefit by keeping as much information as possible to themselves.

In addition, problems are solved from a departmental point of view and not always in the company's best interest, and each manager attempts to enlarge his area of responsibility. Finally, hostilities increase as decisions are made at the top and flow downward.

CONSENSUS DECISION MAKING

Now that we have covered the basic ingredients of participative management, effects on productivity, work groups, the linking-pin concept, and management by objectives, we are ready to examine decision making by consensus. Such a background is necessary to obtain more than a token understanding of the subject.

Decisions can be made on a consensus basis in effective work groups that have the characteristics previously discussed. Consensus, again, means 100 percent agreement to a course of action by members of the group.

The work group provides several advantages in the decision-making process. For example, technical knowledge and expertise may be shared; in fact, in an effective group the motivation is high to communicate accurately all relevant and important information. In addition, individual contributions make the group do a rigorous job of sifting ideas; members become experienced in effective group functioning and leadership; and group regulation of individual members can be exercised. Finally, each member is highly motivated to do his best to implement decisions and to achieve group goals. There are indications that an organization operating in a group fashion can be staffed for less than peak loads at each point.

One can realize the importance of group decision making when observing the basic steps in making a decision. These steps include determination of goals and objectives; proper diagnosis of the problem; conception of one or more good solutions; projection and comparison of the consequences of such alternatives; and selection of a course of action.

The most important advantage of group decision making by consensus, in addition to the opportunity for knowledgeable managers to combine all their efforts to reach a decision, is that the members of the group have an ego identification with the goals. A manager's involvement in decision making in this manner makes him work hard to follow through with the decision; because he helped to make the decision he will help make it succeed.

Decision making by consensus may take more time than decision making by majority. However, in the long run, as has been proven by Yellow Freight's past operations, the best decisions are made by consensus of all parties involved.

Examples at Yellow Freight

Decision making by consensus has been practiced at Yellow Freight since the present management assumed control of the company in the early 1950s. On important matters, the chairman of the board never took action without first discussing the decision with the president; the reverse was also true. Complete agreement was necessary before any action was taken. In later years, and after organizational changes, a new president and executive vice-president joined the chairman and honorary chairman of the board to form a decision-making group for major decisions.

The proper implementation of participative management for consensus decisions can be illustrated in some examples. In these examples, attempts have been made to point out how a manager should formulate a decision-making group and then reach a consensus decision.

First, company officers and division managers decide jointly each year, and on a consensus basis, the goals and objectives for the company during the coming year. In a management-by-objectives process, the division managers have a voice in establishing the goals against which they will be judged.

Second, when a consensus decision is being sought regarding the opening of a new terminal, the division manager should utilize the ability of a number of people. Through his own expert ability, and with a regional and branch manager, sufficient data can be generated indicating whether customer potential is present. Since the opening of a new terminal affects the entire system, the division manager would necessarily have to work with a number of people before a decision could be made. Other managers who should be involved in this decision would include the vice-president of sales, the vice-president of operations, and president of the company, and the chairman of the board.

Third, personnel promotions and shifts at all levels of the company should definitely involve consensus decisions by the appropriate management. When a new branch manager is being selected, a regional manager should work with his division manager, who may involve the vice-presidents of sales and operations, and the president of the company. The regional manager should also look to other branch managers for their opinions and reactions to his suggestion regarding the vacancy.

Fourth, if a branch manager is making a decision to establish or terminate an agreement with an interline carrier, he should involve a number of people in this decision-making group because of their various levels of expertise. The regional manager, the salesman, and, possibly, the office manager (because of accounts receivable) should be involved. It would also be appropriate for the city dispatcher to be included.

When a new account is obtained, the branch manager should involve several people in the terminal in a participative management process. In deciding how this account is to be handled, he should involve the salesman, the operations manager, and the city dispatcher in all aspects of the new account and the procedures necessary to handle that account properly.

Any personnel shift in the terminal should involve several people related to the departments involved. For example, suppose the branch manager wants to move a dock foreman into the position of city dispatcher. The dock foreman's immediate supervisor, the present city dispatcher, the regional manager, the division manager, and other relevant individuals should be a part of the decision-making group. In case a branch manager wants to promote a shift supervisor to operations manager, the group should include city dispatch, line dispatch, office manager, regional manager, division manager, and others in the terminal.

When dock foremen and dispatchers are working with nonmanagement groups, it is not always possible or practical to strive for decision making by consensus. However, they can allow union employees to participate in the implementation measures relating to the decision. For example, a dock foreman can utilize participative management. If a terminal wants to increase its load average by 500 pounds, the foreman can involve his crew; since the dock workers will actually be loading the trailers, they probably will have a number of suggestions about how to increase the load average.

If a terminal is spending too much money in overtime for the city drivers, and their pick-ups have not been at a satisfactory level, their dispatcher could join in participative management with his drivers. He could call them together and discuss possible alternatives regarding work procedures that would be more efficient.

Failure to Reach a Consensus

If a consensus cannot be reached by the group they should forego a decision at that time. Time as a prime consideration for a decision should be minimized. The group's decision not to make a specific decision on an important question may, or may not, be a consensus decision. Yellow Freight's experience has proven that when a decision cannot be reached, action should be deferred. Subsequent events will make a consensus decision easier to achieve because the action requiring a decision will have changed one way or the other.

Hasty decisions, made without a consensus, have proven unprofitable. This is true in many areas, but is especially true in matters relating to operating changes, terminal openings or closings, personnel changes and promotions, and general policy matters.

The Japanese Experience

In Japan most institutions, including governmental agencies and businesses, make decisions on a consensus basis after extensive debate within their organization. This approach is not too practical in the United States because of the likelihood of indecision, lost time, compromise or politicking.

In a recent article, Drucker focused on Japanese management procedures and made some interesting observations about decision by consensus:

> . . . the Westerner and the Japanese mean something different when they talk of "making a decision." With us in the West, all the emphasis is on the answer to the question. Indeed, our books on decision making try to develop systematic approaches to giving an answer. To the Japanese, however, the important element in decision making is defining the question. The important and crucial steps are to decide whether there is a need for a decision and what the decision is about. And it is in this step that the Japanese aim at attaining 'consensus.' Indeed, it is this step that, to the Japanese, is the essence of the decision. . . .
>
> During this process that precedes the decision, no mention is made of what the answer might be. This is done so that people will not be forced to take sides; once they have taken sides, a decision would be a victory for one side and a defeat for the other. Thus, the whole process is focused on finding out what the decision is really about, not what the decision should be.

In this country, we spend a great deal of time "selling" decisions. For the Japanese, this is not necessary.

Everybody has been presold. Also, their process makes it clear where in the organization a certain answer to a question will be welcomed and where it will be resisted. Therefore, there is plenty of time to work on persuading the dissenters, or on making small concessions to them which will win them over without destroying the integrity of the decision.

In this country we are continually spending a great deal of time making small decisions. In contrast, the Japanese system forces them to make the big decisions, and they may simply neglect many small ones.

The following paragraph summarizes Drucker's analysis of the Japanese approach to consensus decision making:

The Japanese process is focused on understanding the problem. The desired end result is certain action and behavior on the part of people. This almost guarantees that all the alternatives will be considered. It rivets management attention to essentials. It does not permit commitment until management has decided what the decision is all about. Japanese managers may come up with the wrong answer to the problem (as was the decision to go to war against the United States in 1941), but they rarely come up with the right answer to the wrong problem.[12]

Effective work groups of supervisors and subordinates, structured in a linking-pin fashion throughout the organization, should be able to make good decisions through participation and to reach decisions on a consensus basis. Managers and employees are committed to decisions when they have helped make decisions. Managers must make every effort to establish effective work groups at the top organizational levels; once these groups have been established, others can be set up throughout the organization, all the way to dock foremen and dispatchers working with dock workers and drivers.

Naturally, a consensus decision cannot be reached on every administrative and day-to-day decision. The make-up of the decision-making group will vary, but should involve all those individuals immediately related to the problem area. Once the group is formed, all must have a voice in the decision, and all must agree on the course of action to be taken. With most companies experiencing high rates of change and increased growth, it is important that we continue to make decisions by consensus. Our management groups throughout the company must remain cohesive.

---

[12] This and preceding quotations from Peter F. Drucker, "What We Can Learn from Japanese Management," *U.S./Japan Outlook, a Digest of American View of Japan,* I (Fall 1971).

14

Organizational Joint Problem-Solving*

ROBERT L. SWINTH

1. INTRODUCTION

The activities of the participants in any organization can be grouped into two broad classes: (1) planning and problem-solving and (2) performing and decision execution [3]. Organizational and systems theorists [8, p. 349], [9] generally agree that the way to carry out the latter activity is to set up what could be called an "organizational servo-mechanism" (OSM). Here the policy center gives a control center a performance standard to meet. The latter then decides what programs must be carried out to reach the standard. These programs are given to operations centers, who execute them, and the results are fed back to the control centers. The control centers compare desired performances with actual; and if the performance standards are not met, they adjust their program instructions.

If the external and internal environments were stable and deterministic, the control and operations aspects of this mechanism would suffice as the totality of organizations. But since they are not, organizations must continually problem-solve, that is, they must set policy and objectives, formulate strategy, search for alternatives, and choose courses of action to make major resource commitments. This suggests a need for an effective organi-

* Source: Reprinted by permission from *Management Science* (October 1971), B68–B79.

zational design for planning and problem-solving. That is the subject of this paper. In particular the focus is on how organizations should and in some cases already do deal with complex novel problems such as the creation and development of a new component or product, or the creation of a regional plan for a metropolitan area.

Several factors define the complex novel problem:

(1) Usually the solution must serve a variety of organizational objectives, and satisfy the goals of a number of participants.

(2) There is typically a high degree of interdependence between parts. The decisions of any one center frequently have consequences for other centers in the system.

(3) Such tasks are too complex to be readily understood and solved by one person or group. It is necessary to put together knowledge, information, and action from several sources.

(4) The cause of the novelty is typically a changing world: change in external environment, or change in the goals of the system. Or the novelty is in the unknowns at the frontier of knowledge or at the interfaces arising from combining existing ideas and techniques in a new way. The best illustration of the latter is in urban planning where architects, economists, etc. must jointly apply their skills to a new kind of problem.

The complex novel problem can be found in a wide variety of environmental settings. In general, it includes situations in which: (1) several centers have a common interest in a problem, and possibly local interests as well, (2) each of these centers commands responsibility for some of the variables used to reach the final solution. This responsibility may range from expertise, such as the opinions of a lawyer which are nearly always respected, to veto, such as the ability of a center to sabotage a project by lack of cooperation. For example, the finding and implementation of new plant facilities or equipment, the design and implementation of a new service, or the development of a new product or a new production or distribution setup typically are complex novel problems. Consider the purchase of a new piece of equipment that is to be used by several departments in an organization. It might be anything from a copy machine to a computer. Here there is both the common interest in the overall success of the organization and in the effectiveness of the equipment for each department. Each department is likely to be responsible for a different use of the equipment, and each has an input to make, variables it controls in the solution to the problem.

In this paper the organization (more typically, some portion of it) is considered as a system for solving complex novel problems. Propositions are formulated to describe how authority and responsibility should be distributed, how the processes of search and coordination should be carried out and how the major components of the organization—the participants, the environment, and the task—should be linked together to perform effectively as a problem-solving system. While the orientation here is normative, one should recognize that many organizations can be found which use some or all of the propositions to be described in §3 of the paper.

2. EXISTING THEORIES

First, consider how such situations are dealt with in existing theories, let us call these the authority approach and the group incremental approach.

The Authority Approach

Problem-solving has long been thought of as a highly individualistic activity. A person is assigned a problem, and he either does it himself or turns parts of it over to subordinates who are responsible to him. Any difficulties (such as two parts not meshing) are the responsibility of the leader. In using this approach with large problems the task is divided into subtasks and a corresponding authority-responsibility structure is superimposed. The top level, i.e., the policy-making center, has the final responsibility for the overall task, and has the authority to impose its wishes on the lower levels. The lower level centers are responsible for various subtasks.

Where there are novel interdependencies, as in the complex problem, this arrangement is dysfunctional. March and Simon [12, p. 191] note that the use of this organizing technique is based on the assumption that the nature of the task is such that the means employed to perform any one subtask will not affect the means employed in other subtasks. Swinth [15] has shown in a laboratory setting that numerous difficulties arise when novel interdependencies *do* exist in organizations so structured. The interdependencies often go untreated or incorrectly handled because either the narrow goals of the participants limit their ability to appreciate the existence of interdependencies or the distance of any superior from his subordinates limits the ability of the former to get the necessary information to make a good decision or provide adequate instruction. Blau and Scott [6, p. 242] have called this the organizational dilemma between the need to coordinate and the need to problem-solve. The hierarchical organizational form, which is best for coordination (of routinized tasks), inhibits the communication needed for problem-solving.[1]

---

[1] Furthermore, hierarchical authority systems in themselves tend to have a suppressing effect on the motivation of subordinates. The authority structure creates social and physical barriers to communication that often make it difficult for upper management to understand how their decisions affect the attainment of their subordinates' personal needs and goals. This lack of sensitivity alienates the subordinates from the organization [13].

The Incremental Approach

To overcome the dysfunctional aspect of the authority approach, problem-solving responsibility is often assigned to groups. Sometimes a leader is appointed to provide final say and to give the group direction as well as be responsible for its housekeeping functions. Such groups, whether they be top level planning committees or project teams, are subject to the undesirable consequence identified by Lindblom [11, p. 156]. First, they cannot successfully optimize. As the author says, the rational comprehensive method requires that the group generate and evaluate all alternatives. This is typically beyond their powers of comprehension and computation. Instead it is suggested that in actual practice both groups and individual planners make incremental changes. Policy is formulated by a series of successive limited comparisons in which the group or planner . . . "builds out from the current situation step-by-step and by small degrees." The criticism has been made that the solutions resulting from using this approach are usually at too low a level. They tend to not encompass enough change or face the full set of consequences for the system. Using the method does not reliably get one close enough to a good solution.

Another serious difficulty with such groups working on large problems is that they function with all participants thinking together, on one wave length so to speak. Only one person speaks at a time and all speak to "the" problem before the group. With little, if any, simultaneous consideration of several issues the rate at which the group can proceed through the problem is significantly inhibited. In addition when the members work together in single focus everyone must know about every area, that is, everyone must be a generalist, or the group must limit itself to the most general level of the problem and leave the "details" to be worked out later within the various centers. This creates difficulties if there are many interdependencies across centers, because unless they all have been resolved in advance —and this is unlikely because of the level at which they occur and their possible novelty—there are no very satisfactory ways for them to be dealt with once the group has finished its work. The only possibilities are direct bargaining between the involved centers or fiat from a central authority.

The group approach also often results in a large portion of the interested centers being excluded from the deliberations because they would make the group too large to function effectively if they were included. The usual technique is to appoint the smaller, hopefully representative, committee which develops the solution, and brings the finished plan to the larger body. If the problem is complex, and the interested centers are dispersed both physically and in their interests, the chances of the solution being satisfactory are small. Yet the whole set of parties can do little: they can only accept, reject, or make small changes, because to deal with major disagreements would require a complete reworking of the problem. Once a solution is reached all the parts become locked together, and it is much more difficult to handle a complaint or proposal than it would have been if it had been raised early in the discussion.

3. ORGANIZATIONAL JOINT PROBLEM-SOLVING

Recognizing that the authority and group incremental approaches have dysfunctional consequences, a way is proposed here to overcome these. Let us call it organizational joint problem-solving (OJPS). Briefly, in OJPS a set of centers are linked together to deal with a problem. Search is initially conducted at the highest problem level to establish goals for the second level. The centers then search within their own components to meet these goals, ignoring for the moment between-component interdependencies. The plan of action developed by any center and the rationale for it is then broadcast to other centers in the system. This permits inconsistencies between components to be resolved. The centers are also able to search coordinatively in new directions. The process of within-component search, broadcasting of actions, and between-component search and coordination is iterated upon until an overall solution is found which is as close to the objectives of the task as the centers can come and is likewise internally consistent between components and across levels. With this method of search it is not necessary for any one center or all centers to understand the whole problem, rather each need only interact with the others at the interfaces between them.

OJPS is applicable to many different multi-center contexts. It is appropriate to the committee appointed to deal with some issue or made responsible for planning. The participants can be made jointly responsible for the success of the mission as a whole, and the leader is then more the manager of the housekeeping functions (maintaining order at meetings, making sure the group has adequate resources, etc.) than he is the guardian of the overall goals of the organizational system. Even where the participants ar not made jointly responsible for the mission as a whole, they can relate to each other more as peers who are each responsible for certain objectives than as subordinates who are obliged to do as they are told.

Organizational joint problem-solving need not be limited to committees. The team project [2] and even the large multi-center project group can operate within this framework. Here, even though each center is responsible for or has expertise in a different area, all can be oriented towards the problem as a whole, or at least all can be relatively equal and have a significant voice in the final outcome. For example, a regional planning group may be composed of city planners, economists, lawyers, psychologists, etc. —each an expert in a different area. Yet none would regard the plan as complete, or permit the plan to be implemented, until the issues of each of the various areas have been dealt with.

In organizational joint problem-solving the entire group of concerned centers need never (or but seldom) meet face to face.[2] Rather, they can interact largely by memorandum, telephone, or subgroup meeting in which two or more centers with a common difficulty jointly pursue it. In other words, OJPS is not simply small-group behavior, rather it is a pattern of problem-solving that extends over a large segment of the organization.

The organizational processes constituting OJPS are described in propositional form below. The first explains the linkage of the centers into a problem-solving system. The subsequent propositions characterize the processes of joint problem-solving.

(1) Link Centers

A set of centers are linked together to deal with a problem. They are given a mission assignment which specifies their objectives, and a system head is appointed to administratively keep the group together. Both within and between centers the participants relate to each other primarily as peers as far as task issues are concerned. Each center has a certain area of responsibility or competence, and is in control of actions within its area. One center may be given responsibility for the top level of the task, or it may be the joint responsibility of the second level (or all) centers. The former will typically be done when the top level of the task is, itself, extensive. The latter will be done when all centers can readily obtain and handle the information relating the overall objectives to the intermediate objectives. This point is discussed further in Proposition 2.

The organizational relationships between centers are much like that described in the organic model of Burns and Stalker [7], low centralization, low formalization, and low stratification. This system of relationships is not intended to replace the existing organizational structure but rather to supplement it. The regular organizational hierarchy continues to hold for the day-to-day problems, and the positions of the participants in that hierarchy may or may not correspond to their relationships in this system. In fact some may belong outside the hierarchy. Furthermore, the portion of one's time spent on the task may vary from person to person. For example, a lawyer in a regional planning group may need to be involved less frequently than other participants. This system exists to deal with the unique

---

[2] They may be separated by distance. For example, R & D in one location, engineering in another, marketing in a third, and production in a fourth, all need to work together to start up a new product. There may simply be too many participants that should be involved for them to meet face to face, or the problem-solving process may extend over such a long period that the center would have to spend an inordinately large amount of time in a group meeting or series of group meetings to solve it.

task assigned to it, and is disbanded when the problem is solved, unless solving such tasks is the primary purpose of this portion of the organization.

To invoke the proper motivational mechanisms towards joint behavior, rewards to the participants, such as pay increases and promotion, are given for seeking overall task goals rather than for seeking subtask or component goals. If a separate reward structure were to be set up for each level in the task, say one reward for the overall mission and another for a piece of equipment for that mission, there would be little joint problem-solving between centers responsible for different levels [15]. For example, there would be relatively little interaction between the government group responsible for a mission and the industrial group designing a piece of equipment for that mission, if the industrial group is simply being paid in accordance with how closely it meets equipment performance specifications.

(2) Search Initially at the Overall Task Level

Find a temporary course of action that satisfies the goals of the highest problem level in the task. Any complex problem will be divided into a hierarchical set of levels, and each level will be composed of one or more components. Naturally, there will be relationships between variables within a component, but there will also be relationships which extend between components. These relationships may occur not only between two components at the same level, but may also extend across two or more levels. Therefore, since the lower of any two levels is an input to the upper, the order in which they are dealt with is important. Search must begin at the upper level so that the lower will have an indication of what direction to pursue.

Incidentally, the various problem levels and centers do not necessarily correspond to any organizational structure. For example, within the same problem level the electrical engineer responsible for the amplifier center and the sound engineer responsible for the speaker center may both be from the same department in the company. Or one contractor may be responsible at the overall level of the problem and another at the level of one of its components, yet they are both bona fide corporations.

In some tasks, the desired overall goals readily translate into goals for each of the main components. The goals for these components then essentially constitute the upper boundary to the task, obviating the need for any center to be made responsible solely for the upper problem level. If, on the other hand, there is extensive complexity at the overall goal level a center must be responsible for it so that search may extend through it also. Suppose the upper boundary for a group designing a tape recorder is drawn at the set of characteristics which describes the performance features of the machine. This is a one-level problem made up of several components, amplifier, speaker, etc., and the main problem relationships are those within and between these centers. If the task boundaries include the market for which this tape recorder is being made, there would be two levels. The upper level would deal with the relationships between consumer demand for music and the possible kinds of equipment to meet that demand. Here there is need for interaction between the two levels as well as between centers at the main component level.

(3) Search within Components

Any center with primary responsibility for a component develops a plan of action (a stable but temporary subplan) that comes moderately close to satisfying the current subgoals for that component. In the first round at least, these goals are generated by the search at the overall task level (Proposition 2). During this period each center is searching in parallel with other centers. Each center assumes that all variables can be varied if necessary. Previous decisions and variables outside of the range of control of any such center are not taken as constraints. Rather, an effort is made to attain closure and develop a subplan even if the result is not close to the current subgoals.

Since by definition the problem is too complex to be solved as a whole through a single thrust, the various parts should be worked on concurrently, each by a different center. This relatively independent development of subplans serves two purposes. If the centers were to work in series, that is, if they were to accept the inputs from other parts of the task as constraints, they would most likely unnecessarily limit the range of possibilities that should be considered [10]. Secondly, by pursuing the problem this far the centers are better able to understand where they will have difficulty. They learn which components are the hardest to develop, and how far away their initial efforts leave them from their goals. They also learn what direction to go to attain their goals or where to revise them. This kind of information is much easier to obtain when one has a "completed" subplan as a baseline, however divergent it may be from the assigned goal. Furthermore, if closure is achieved it is easier to return later to make modifications because the solution does not have to be completely reconstructed [14].

(4) Broadcast Plans and Laws

Whenever a center produces a plan of action or a change in plan for some portion of the task, it is broadcast to the other centers in the system that might be affected by the action. In addition, the supporting laws of the task are broadcast to demonstrate that the plan does indeed lead to the anticipated consequences. As was noted earlier, all the centers are interdependent. Some of the variables in a relationship are in the domain of one center, and some are in the domain of others. Since this is a novel problem, it is likely that the centers do not know the nature of many of the laws relating variables or perhaps they are even unaware of the existence of certain laws. By broadcasting this information they are able to discover where they are interdependent.

A task law is a truth about a relationship between two or more variables in the problem space. Thus to substantiate a set of actions one broadcasts the relational statements that demonstrate the plan's veracity. One purpose of transmitting these statements is to make those affected by the choice more free to change their actions. They are not constrained to the named choice of inputs, because the explanation of relationships gives them a basis for suggesting alternative courses of action. They do not have to accept the plan of another as a constraint because they can use the laws themselves to work out modifications. Also, in a novel problem many of the laws of the task are not understood or known by anyone, and therefore it is necessary to gather data on the nature of the problem situation. With these plans of action and law as cues, the centers are better able to judge where to do additional search.

It is necessary to have some facility by which information can be broadcast. The degree to which everyone is reached by any broadcast network varies from organization to organization, but ideally it includes all centers that can be given the message without overloading them. In such a facility information is broadcast directly among the centers so that any center can quickly receive incoming messages and can quickly react to them. If a center knows who will affect it and who will be affected by its actions it need only send to them. Otherwise, every center in the system receives the information. The introduction of a communication system is important to OJPS because it permits many more centers to be included in the deliberations than is possible in the traditional group approach. In at least one field experiment [17] this type of device was used in a neighborhood to facilitate problem-solving.

(5) Search Between Components

Analyze plans for interdependencies between components, find points of inconsistency (conflict), and note the pattern of relationship between variables in the region of interdependence. Search to find states for the variables that make them consistent across parts of the task.

The problem is too complex for one of the centers in an interdependency to simply pass all of its data to the other center and let the latter find a solution that merges the two components. Both centers must work on the subproblem, yet typically, neither will be able to understand the whole problem in the area of the interdependence. The only way they can effectively search under these conditions is to first note the plans and laws each has broadcast so that they can understand where they are interdependent, and then to search for ways to change the values of variables in this region. Consider an example from electronic equipment design. A tape recorder is being designed through the joint problem-solving approach. The amplifier center develops a subplan in which a transistor of a certain type is to be used, but an input of a certain characteristic is presumed from the center responsible for the speaker. Yet the center designing the speaker has decided upon a component which has a different output characteristic. By using the communication technique they find this inconsistency, and then work together to reconcile it. This approach differs from traditional group search techniques in that *neither* center to an interdependency necessarily understands the whole problem or even the proportion that encompasses both of them. Whereas traditionally one of the centers would have enough information and understanding to decide on all the questions for both, here each is only aware of the other's portion of the task in the immediate vicinity of the interdependence. Once they coordinate on the interdependence each must work out the consequences for his own component. If these consequences turn out to be unsatisfactory, then they must get together again to find still a different way to resolve their interdependence.

Beer [5, p. 140] speaks of this as the "intelligence amplifier." Instead of one person trying to understand the whole and finding the solution which for all parts meets his criteria, each part proposes actions which from its perspective meet the criteria, and the two (or more) parts interact until the actions of each are suitable to the others. No one part understands the whole, yet together they have come as close as possible to the overall criteria.

There are four kinds of between component search.

(*a*) There is search for points of interdependence in which action is taken that improves the level of achievement for one component without affecting the current status of some other component. Here the centers find where they can make a change in some variables that will help some center, but will have little impact on the center making the modifications.

(*b*) There is search for patterns of mutual, or what may be called symbiotic, interdependencies in which changes in components can be made that improve performance for both components [18, p. 54].

(*c*) There is search for points of interdependence in which a center takes an action which for the moment limits the performance of its component but benefits the component of some other center.

(*d*) There is search in which several centers coordinate in the testing of hypotheses.

The existence of symbiotic interdependencies is very important to joint problem-solving because it makes it possible to take actions which improve the task as a whole or a fairly large segment of it rather than just any one component. In other words, each of two centers can take steps which help the other. In labor management bargaining this "integrative" approach [19] leads to both parties being better off.

In problem-solving it is often necessary to propose an action which is not optimum for one component of the task in order to be able to find a solution for another component. Yet quite frequently not enough will be known at the outset to say what the overall impact of the proposal will be. It may turn out that a symbiotic interdependence will be found or a new alternative will be discovered with the result that the center which had to make the local sacrifice will also benefit. Bavelas [4] describes such behavior as "absorbing the uncertainty."[3] A center proposes or goes along with an action without the certainty that the plan will work, but if it does work, both it and the rest of the system benefit.

The centers also coordinate in the formulating of hypotheses and the conducting of experiments that require their joint effort. First, if a center knows how other parts of the task will function, it can use this knowledge to formulate hypotheses whose consequences extend beyond its immediate area. Secondly, it can propose experiments (plans) for several centers to follow which will generate information useful to the system as a whole or a large part of it. Without any one center having to understand the whole problem it is possible to search in totally new directions. If a center discovers a radically new way to approach the problem through picking up cues and inquiries into other areas of the task, it is able to get these ideas tested. The centers jointly expand upon hypotheses, and provide feedback to one another about the consequences of experiments. This is, in fact, the way progress is made in the sciences. Models are proposed via journals and books, and these are used as the basis for experiments and the further development of models. The communication process is very similar to that described here, although much slower. Each contributor transmits to "all," and each subsequent contribution is an iteration from the previous state, that is, it is built from the previous communication.

(6) Iterate on This Search Process

That is, repeatedly recycle through the problem and portions of it to group subplans into ever larger consistent plans. On each iteration mesh a manageable additional portion of the problem until finally the problem solution is consistent over all levels and components. The joint problem-solving system continually iterates through the activities described by Propositions 3, 4 and 5. By this process the plan is gradually refined until

---

[3] March and Simon [12, p. 165] define this term somewhat differently. "Uncertainty absorption takes place when inferences are drawn from a body of evidence and the inferences, instead of the evidence itself, are then communicated."

all inconsistencies are eliminated and a solution is found that will achieve the overall goals for the problem. In the early passes through the problem both the within and between component decisions will be unacceptable in many ways. But by a series of revisions and changes, each built upon the previous steps, it is possible to obtain an acceptable closure.

A center proposes a plan for achieving an objective, and substantiates this with the supporting laws. There is no requirement that this plan constitute a full solution to the problem or that it lead to the achievement of all objectives. The plan and laws are broadcast. Some center extends the factors considered or points out the inconsistencies between plans and perhaps offers a modification. The sequence of plans, modified plans, etc., is continued until the centers have searched sufficiently deeply into the problem to feel that they have found a plan which comes close to their objectives. This iterative mechanism is a very powerful problem-solving tool.

4. PROMOTING THE OJPS CONDITIONS

In the preceding propositions several conditions are implied: (1) the participants accept the overall goals, (2) they each have sufficient expertise in their own areas to be able to do within-component search, and (3) they are able to communicate with each other fairly efficiently. This last point means that they know the language and framework of the task as a whole well enough to (a) understand each other. (b) They are able to reduce the number of centers in any broadcast to those who most likely need to know. (c) Finally there are various communication and information processing aids ranging from telephone, videophone and written reproduction to actual information storage, retrieval, and processing devices.

Even where these conditions are not fully met, there are steps that can be taken to promote organizational joint problem-solving. In regard to point two, if the expertise of a center is limited, additional training can be provided. Of course, OJPS itself includes provision for a center to call on other centers for assistance. On point three, the achievement of good communication between centers always requires maintenance and continual development. Various aids are mentioned above, and can be implemented when not already in use. A recent example of the sophistication one can go to is provided by Boeing in its development of the 747. All major subcontractors were linked to a central computer at the Boeing plant on a time sharing arrangement. Whenever any changes were made in the plans, these were entered into the computer and promptly relayed to the appropriate contractors.

The first condition, acceptance of overall goals, presents the issues that are hardest to handle. Frequently, the centers will have their own goals as well as the system having its overall set of goals. Participants have career goals, areas within a metropolitan region have their local neighborhood goals, etc. These typically cannot be completely subsumed into the superordinate goals of the problem-solving system. For a problem-solving system to fulfill both the local goals of the various centers and the superordinate goals of the system it must not only provide for search and coordination but for the resolution and productive focusing of conflict as well.

Sometimes conflict stems from differences in perceived risk and from differences in acceptable uncertainty. One center judges that the consequences of an action will be X another believes it will be Y. If the former is undesirable, i.e., risky, then the centers will be in conflict over what action to take, particularly if the consequence would be more adverse for one of the centers than the other. Of course, even assuming agreement on the level of risk, there may be conflict. The centers may differ in their preference for risk (tolerance for ambiguity). A high level of uncertainty contributes to conflict because reasonable people can easily reach different conclusions from the same data when it is heavily laden with assumptions and ambiguity. Thus the conflict is not necessarily basic between centers, rather it may be a consequence of the data. If the uncertainty can be reduced through additional data gathering, then the differences in opinion between centers can be reduced.

In the following section several steps are proposed to cope with the conflict in a systematic way. The discussion of these has been divided into two parts. The first is a set of procedures to follow, the second is more a matter of attitude and posture, how the centers should relate to each other. Neither is guaranteed to produce successful integrative problem-solving. The conflict may be too deep; one center may dominate the others and force its will on them, or the task structure may not lend itself to integrative solution, no matter how lengthy and careful the search.

Procedures

(1) Every effort should be made to resolve uncertainties. Whenever possible additional data should be gathered, and experiments that resolve alternative hypotheses should be conducted. (2) As noted in the main propositions, search across centers should be conducted. Often the conflict between centers is never really dealt with because the centers never get together to search for an overall solution. There is little or no problem-solving done. (3) There should be procedures to insure fair consideration of the views of all centers. Each center should feel assured that its views will be heard. Similarly, the solution, whatever it is, should be a fair one, with no undeserved advantage to any center. Such assurance is not common, but increasingly such mechanisms as due process are entering into systems. The resultant feeling of security helps incline one towards exposing himself to risk, taking an overall outlook, etc. (4) Where feasible each center should

have responsibility over its own area, so that it is the one to implement decisions that affect it. (5) Finally, requiring that the centers share information and broadcast their actions (Proposition 4) enables each center to better identify and cope with possible conflict because the true views and position of each center are made clear.

Attitudes

Attitudes are difficult to deal with and difficult to change, but they can make a difference in problem-solving. (1) Attitudes can be modified through appropriate education. One acquires a wider perspective towards problems. One's expanded world view allows him to see more sides to a problem, and allows his goals to rise to a higher level in the process. Participants can be educated and trained to see the value in these goals and the gain in total performance from adopting them (and therefore more for each). (2) Being integrative and trusting contributes to still more integrative and trusting behavior [16]. (3) To encourage experimentation proposals should be viewed and accepted by all as tentative. No center should be forced to finally accept a position it initially took. A center can suggest an alternative and see what the consequences will be, without being concerned that it will be held to what it initially said. (4) Finally, it is generally accepted that the centers are more likely to adopt the overall goals if they can participate in formulating them [1].

5. SUMMARY

To carry out the organization's day-to-day activities an organizational servomechanism is established, with its policy, control and operations centers and with its performance standards, programs and feedback. If the external and internal environments were stable and deterministic, the control and operations aspects of this mechanism would suffice as the totality of organizations. But since they are not, organizations must continually problem-solve. In this paper the organization has been viewed as a system for solving complex problems, and a set of propositions, called organizational joint problem-solving, has been given to describe how authority and responsibility are distributed and how the processes of search and coordination are carried out. Using these propositions the participants, the environment, and the task are linked together to perform effectively as a problem-solving system.

The limits to two existing organizational problem-solving methods have been identified. The authority approach, with its presumption of one person responsible and the others subordinate is limited by the difficulty it has in identifying and treating novel interdependencies and complexities centered at the lower levels. In the group incremental approach, problems are assigned to groups to overcome the difficulties of the first approach, but participants using this method typically lack the overall capability to get much beyond low-level improvements in present practices. Secondly, the use of a single focus by which everyone is kept together on "the" problem seriously reduces the system's computing power. The use of a group also often means that some of the interested centers must be excluded from the deliberations.

In OJPS these limits are overcome as follows: A set of centers is linked together to deal with a problem. Search is initially conducted at the highest problem level to establish goals for the second level. The centers then search within their own components to meet these goals, ignoring for the moment between-component interdependencies. The plan of action developed by any center and the rationale for it is then broadcast to other centers in the system. This permits inconsistencies between components to be resolved. The centers are also able to search coordinatively in new directions. The processes of within-component search, broadcasting of actions and between-component search and coordination is iterated upon until an overall solution is found which is as close to the objectives of the task as the centers can come and is likewise internally consistent between components and across levels. This permits a solution to be reached without any one center or all centers necessarily having to know the whole problem. Provided the conditions can be met that the participants accept the overall goals, are capable in their own areas of responsibility, and are able to communicate efficiently, this is the better design. Even where these conditions are not initially met, steps can be taken to promote them and thereby still use the OJPS approach.

REFERENCES

1. Argyris, C. *Personality and Organization,* Harper & Row, New York, 1957.
2. Bass, B. M. *Organizational Psychology,* Allyn & Bacon, Boston, 1965.
3. ———— and Leavitt, H. "Some Experiments in Planning and Operating," *Management Science,* Vol. 9 (1963), pp. 574–85.
4. Bavelas, A. "Leadership: Man and Function," *Administrative Science Quarterly,* Vol. 4 (1960), pp. 491–98.
5. Beer, S. *Cybernetics and Management,* John Wiley & Sons, Inc., New York, 1959.
6. Blau, P. and Scott, W. R. *Formal Organizations: A Comparative Approach,* Chandler, San Francisco, 1961.
7. Burns, T. and Stalker, G. M. *The Management of Innovation,* Tavistock, London, 1961.
8. Carzo, R., Jr. and Yanouzas, J. N. *Formal Organization: A Systems Approach,* Irwin-Dorsey, Homewood, Ill., 1967.

9. Clough, D. J. *Concepts in Management Science,* Prentice-Hall, Englewood Cliffs, N. J., 1963.

10. Hirschman, A. O. and Lindblom, C. E. "Economic Development, Research and Development, Policy Making: Some Converging Views," *Behavioral Science,* Vol. 7 (1962), pp. 211–22.

11. Lindblom, C. E. "The Science of Muddling Through," *Public Administration Review,* Vol. 19, No. 2 (Spring 1959).

12. March, J. G. and Simon, H. A. *Organizations,* John Wiley & Sons, New York, 1958.

13. Nisbet, R. A. *The Quest for Community,* Oxford University Press, New York, 1953.

14. Simon, H. A. *The Sciences of the Artificial,* MIT Press, Cambridge, 1969.

15. Swinth, R. L. "Organization Planning; Goal Setting in Interdependent Systems," *Industrial Management Review,* Vol. 7 (1966), pp. 57–70.

16. ———, "Establishing the Trust Relationship," *Journal of Conflict Resolution,* Vol. 11 (1967), pp. 335–44.

17. ———, "A Mass Communication System to Facilitate Problem Solving: A Field Experiment," Working Paper 1970, University of Kansas.

18. Thompson, J. D. *Organizations in Action,* McGraw Hill, New York, 1967.

19. Walton, R. E. and McKersie, R. B. *A Behavioral Theory of Labor Negotiations,* McGraw Hill, New York, 1965.

Part IV

BEHAVIOR WITHIN
ORGANIZATIONS

Attempts are continually being made by psychologists, social psychologists, sociologists, and anthropologists to understand human behavior. Administrators and enterpreneurs want to know what caused or made a person behave in a particular way. Theory and research have provided managers with some general knowledge about behavior that can be used in real-world situations.

It is generally agreed that behavior is the product of two things: the nature of the individual that behaves and the nature of the situation in which the individual finds himself. The nature of an individual depends on his heredity, his group affiliations, his culture, and the situations which a person has faced throughout life. These different background factors cause differences in perceptions, attitudes, motivations, and personalities.

The psychologist advances the premise that there is a causal sequence of behavior which a manager should understand. This sequence is briefly presented in Figure 4–1.

The double-headed arrows in Figure 4–1 indicates that the individual interacts with his environment and interprets the various stimuli. Thus, in order to explain behavior, one must be concerned with the stimuli as well as the individual.

This section concentrates upon the stimulus-individual interaction, as well as the behavior and goal achievement which results from this interaction. Specifically, three major organizational concepts are analyzed in

FIGURE 4-1

Psychological View of a Causal Sequence of Behavior

Stimulus ←――――――→	Individual ――――――→	Behavioral ――――→ Pattern	Goal Achievement
Includes:	Includes:	Includes:	Includes:
A. Action of managers or informal leaders	A. Heredity	A. Talking	A. Productivity
B. Climate of the unit	B. Cultural background	B. Expressions	B. Absenteeism
C. Group pressures	C. Situation	C. Thinking	C. Quitting
D. Working conditions	D. Group membership		

the selected readings—motivation, groups, and leadership. These three facets of organizational life in business firms, hospitals, schools, and government agencies are definitely stimuli which interact with individuals and result in various levels of goal achievement.

The first article examines motivation theory. In the article "The New Look in Motivational Theory For Organizational Research," J. G. Hunt and H. W. Hill examine the Maslow, Herzberg, and Vroom models of motivation. They discuss these models separately and then compare them. They examine the empirical research dealing with the Vroom model. Based upon their analysis of these three theories they conclude that the Vroom model holds great promise for predicting behavior in organizations.

A behavioral area which has been discussed and analyzed for over 40 years is job satisfaction. Louis E. Davis in "Job Satisfaction Research: The Post-Industrial View" examines in a historical fashion job satisfaction research and the cultural values of the industrial era. Such concepts as technology, job enlargement, the individual versus the organization, and job design are examined in detail.

Compensation practices of organizations are based upon theory, research, and in some instances "armchair" decision making. Edward E. Lawler III in "The Mythology of Management Compensation" attempts to provide a systematic framework for reaching compensation decisions. He looks at the role of pay, pay as an incentive for performance, the secrecy-of-pay issue, and the role of fringe benefits. Lawler concludes the article by proposing what the future of salary administration holds.

Groups are certainly found throughout the organization, and they play a major role in shaping behavior. The now classic Hawthorne studies initiated a lingering interest among theorists, researchers, and practictioners in group phenomena. Maxine Bucklow in her article "A New Role For The Work Group" discusses the role assigned to the work group that leads to positive changes in employee motivation. She suggests that the role proposed by the Tavistock Institute of Human Relations has been more successful than approaches derived from the Hawthorne studies. The Tavistock approach is presented in the form of a discussion of various studies on work groups.

There appears to be a diversity of opinion about the causes, functions, and resolution of conflict among behavioral scientists. There is, however, general agreement that conflict is an integral part of relationships in organizational settings. The existence of conflict in a hospital setting is clarified in an article by Rockwell Schulz and Alton C. Johnson. In their article "Conflict In Hospitals" these authors discuss institutional conflict, individual conflict, interpersonal conflict, administration-medical staff conflict, and nursing conflict. Upon completion of the identification of potential conflict they propose an action program which involves procedures for diagnosing and mitigating conflict. A decision model which identifies conflict participants, some sources of conflict, and some tentative approaches for mitigation is presented in Figure 1.

Most organizations have recognized the importance of leadership in achieving overall performance effectiveness. The leader is certainly an identifiable stimulus which influences to some degree the behavior of people. A recurring problem among managers has been determining the type of leadership that can lead to high levels of individual, group, and/or organizational effectiveness. J. G. Hunt in his article "Organizational Leadership: Some Theoretical and Empirical Considerations" discusses the Fiedler situationally oriented model of leadership together with an empirical test in which it was validated in three business firms. The model is then discussed with regard to its theoretical implications within organizations.

There is a wide range of leadership style which have varying impacts upon productivity. Stephen M. Sales in "Supervisory Style and Productivity: Review and Theory" examines the crucial question of how productivity levels change as a function of different styles of leadership. The two styles which are examined are authoritarianism and democratic. Experimental and survey research on these two styles is presented and discussed by the author.

15

The New Look in Motivational Theory for Organizational Research

J. G. HUNT and H. W. HILL

During the last few years the treatment of motivation with respect to industrial and other formal organizations has more often than not been in terms of models by Maslow or Herzberg.[1] Where theories are apparently so thoroughly accepted, one naturally assumes a fairly substantial amount of data leading to empirical verification. However, as we shall show, there is relatively little empirical evidence concerning Maslow's theory; and while there are many studies bearing on Herzberg's theory, it remains controversial. After comparing these two approaches and reviewing their present status, we will describe a newer motivation theory developed by Vroom, which is similar to those developed by Atkinson *et al.* and Edwards in experimental psychology, and Peak, Rosenberg and Fishbein in social psychology.[2] It is our contention, on both theoretical and empirical grounds,

Source: Reproduced by the permission of the Society for Applied Anthropology from *Human Organization*, Vol. 28, No. 2 (Summer 1969), pp. 100–109.

[1] A. H. Maslow, *Motivation and Personality*, New York: Harper & Row, 1954; "A Theory of Human Motivation," *Psychological Review*, Vol. 50, 1943, pp. 370–96; and *Eupsychian Management*, Homewood, Ill.: Irwin-Dorsey, 1965; F. Herzberg, B. Mausner, and B. B. Snyderman, *The Motivation to Work*. New York: Wiley, 1959; and F. Herzberg, *Work and the Nature of Man*. Cleveland, Ohio: World Publishing Co., 1966, pp. 130–31. V. H. Vroom, *Work and Motivation*. New York: Wiley, 1964.

[2] J. W. Atkinson, J. R. Bastian, R. W. Earl, and G. H. Litwin, "The Achievement Motive, Goal Setting, and Probability Preferences," *Journal of Abnormal and Social Psychology*, Vol. 60 (1960), pp. 27–36; W. Edwards, "Behavioral Decision Theory,"

that Vroom's theory, more than Maslow's or Herzberg's, is in line with the thinking of contemporary psychologists and industrial sociologists and is the best yet developed for organizational use.

THE MASLOW MODEL

Maslow's theory hypothesizes five broad classes of needs arranged in hierarchical levels of prepotency so that when one need level is satisfied, the next level is activated. The levels are: (1) physiological needs; (2) security or safety needs; (3) social, belonging, or membership needs; (4) esteem needs further subdivided into esteem of others and self-esteem including autonomy; and (5) self-actualization or self-fulfillment needs.

The original papers present very little empirical evidence in support of the theory and no research at all that tests the model in its entirety. Indeed, Maslow argues that the theory is primarily a framework for future research. He also discusses at length some of the limitations of the model and readily admits that these needs may be unconscious rather than conscious. While Maslow discusses his model and its limitations in detail, a widely publicized paper by McGregor gives the impression that the model can be accepted without question and also that it is fairly easy to apply.[3] In truth, the model is difficult to test, which is probably why there are so few empirical studies to either prove or refute the theory.

Porter provides the most empirical data concerning the model.[4] At the conscious level he measures all except the physiological needs. His samples are based only on managers, but they cover different managerial levels in a wide range of business organizations in the United States and thirteen other countries. Porter's studies have a number of interesting findings, but here we are primarily concerned with two: (1) in the United States and Britain (but not in the other twelve countries) there tends to be a hierarchical satisfaction of needs as Maslow hypothesizes; and (2) regardless of country or managerial level there is a tendency for those needs which managers feel are most important to be least satisfied.

Annual Review of Psychology. Palo Alto, California: Annual Reviews Inc., 1961, pp. 473–99; H. Peak, "Attitude and Motivation," *Nebraska Symposium on Motivation.* Lincoln, Neb.: University of Nebraska Press, 1955, pp. 148–84. M. Rosenberg, "Cognitive Structure and Attitudinal Affect," *Journal of Abnormal and Social Psychology,* Vol. 53 (1956), pp. 367–72; M. Fishbein, "An Operational Definition of Belief and Attitude," *Human Relations,* Vol. 15 (1962), pp. 35–43.

[3] D. McGregor, "Adventure in Thought and Action," *Proceedings of the Fifth Anniversary Convocation of the School of Industrial Management, Massachusetts Institute of Technology.* Cambridge, Mass.: Massachusetts Institute of Technology, 1957, pp. 23–30.

[4] L. W. Porter, *Organizational Patterns of Managerial Job Attitudes.* New York: American Foundation for Management Research, 1964. See also M. Haire, E. Ghiselli and L. W. Porter, *Managerial Thinking: An International Study.* New York: Wiley, 1966, especially chapters 4 and 5.

A study by Beer of female clerks provides additional data concerning the model.[5] He examines the relationship between participative and considerate or human relations oriented supervisory leadership styles and satisfaction of needs. He also goes one step further and argues that need satisfaction, as such, does not necessarily lead to motivation. Rather, motivation results only from need satisfaction which occurs in the process of task-oriented work. He reasons that a participative leadership style should meet this condition since it presumably allows for the satisfaction of the higher order needs (self-actualization, autonomy, and esteem). Beer found that workers forced to arrange needs in a hierarchy (as required by his ranking method) tend to arrange them as predicted by Maslow. He also found that self-actualization, autonomy, and social needs were most important, while esteem and security needs were least important, although his method (unlike Porter's) did not allow a consideration of the relationship between importance and need satisfaction. Interestingly enough, there was no significant relationship between need satisfaction and Beer's measure of motivation nor between any of the leadership style dimensions and motivation. There were, however, significant relationships between leadership style dimensions and need satisfaction. Beer concludes that the model has questionable usefulness for a theory of industrial motivation although it may provide a fairly reliable measurement of the *a priori* needs of industrial workers.

We have found only three studies that systematically consider the Maslow theory in terms of performance.[6]

The first of these, by Clark, attempts to fit a number of empirical studies conducted for different purposes into a framework which provides for progressive activation and satisfaction of needs at each of the hierarchical levels. The findings are used to make predictions concerning productivity, absenteeism, and turnover as each need level is activated and then satisfied. While the article does not explicitly test the Maslow model, it is highly suggestive in terms of hypotheses for future research that might relate the theory to work group performance.

A second study, by Lawler and Porter, correlates satisfaction of managers' needs (except physiological) with rankings of their performance by superiors and peers. All correlations are significant but low, ranging from 0.16 to 0.30. Lawler and Porter conclude that satisfaction of higher order needs is more closely related to performance than satisfaction of lower

---

[5] M. Beer, *Leadership, Employee Needs, and Motivation.* Columbus, Ohio: Bureau of Business Research, Ohio State University, 1966.

[6] J. V. Clark, "Motivation in Work Groups: A Tentative View," *Human Organization*, Vol. 19 (1960), pp. 199–208. E. E. Lawler and L. W. Porter, "The Effect of Performance on Job Satisfaction," *Industrial Relations*, Vol. 7, No. 1 (1967), pp. 20–28. L. W. Porter and E. E. Lawler, *Managerial Attitudes and Performance.* Homewood, Ill.: Irwin-Dorsey, 1968, pp. 148, 150.

order needs. However, the differences are not very great and they are not tested for significance. For example, correlations of superior ratings for the lower order security and social needs are 0.21 and 0.23, while for the higher order esteem, autonomy, and self-actualization needs they are 0.24, 0.18, and 0.30. Peer correlations are similar. Thus, unlike Lawler and Porter, we conclude that in this study the correlations for lower order needs are about the same as for higher order needs.

A more recent Porter and Lawler investigation seems to provide additional support for their earlier findings by showing that higher order needs accounted for more relationships significant at the 0.01 level than lower order needs. However, they do not report correlations between these needs and performance and so we cannot evaluate their conclusion as we did for their earlier study.

THE HERZBERG MODEL

A second frequently mentioned motivational model is that proposed by Herzberg and his associates in 1959.[7] They used a semi-structured interview technique to get respondents to recall events experienced at work which resulted in a marked improvement or a marked reduction in their job satisfaction. Interviewees were also asked, among other things, how their feelings of satisfaction or dissatisfaction affected their work performance, personal relationships, and well-being. Content analysis of the interviews suggested that certain job characteristics led to job satisfaction, while *different* job characteristics led to job dissatisfaction. For instance, job achievement was related to satisfaction while working conditions were related to dissatisfaction. Poor conditions led to dissatisfaction, but good conditions did not necessarily lead to satisfaction. Thus, satisfaction and dissatisfaction are not simple opposites. Hence a two-factor theory of satisfaction is needed.

The job content characteristics which produced satisfaction were called "motivators" by Herzberg and his associates because they satisfied the individual's need for self-actualization at work. The job environment characteristics which led to dissatisfaction were called "hygienes" because they were work-supporting or contextual rather than task-determined and hence were analogous to the "preventative" or "environmental" factors recognized in medicine. According to this dichotomy, motivators include achievement, recognition, advancement, possibility of growth, responsibility, and work itself. Hygienes, on the other hand, include salary; interpersonal relations with superiors, subordinates, and peers; technical supervision; company policy and administration; personal life; working conditions; status; and job security.

There is considerable empirical evidence for this theory. Herzberg him-

---

[7] Herzberg, Mausner and Snyderman, *op. cit.*

self, in a summary of research through early 1966, includes ten studies of seventeen populations which used essentially the same method as his original study.[8] In addition, he reviews twenty more studies which used a variety of methodologies to test the two-factor theory. Of the studies included in his review, those using his critical incident method generally confirm the theory. Those using other methods give less clear results, which Herzberg acknowledges but attempts to dimiss for methodological reasons. At least nine other studies, most of which have appeared since Herzberg's 1966 review, raise even more doubts about the theory.[9]

While it is beyond the scope of the present article to consider these studies in detail, they raise serious questions as to whether the factors leading to satisfaction and dissatisfaction are really different from each other. A number of the studies show that certain job dimensions appear to be more important for *both* satisfaction and dissatisfaction. Dunnette, Campbell, and Hakel, for example, conclude from these and also from their own studies that Herzberg is shackled to his method and that achievement, recognition, and responsibility seem important for both satisfaction *and* dissatisfaction, while such dimensions as security, salary, and working conditions are less important.[10] They also raise by implication an issue concerning Herzberg's methodology which deserves further comment. That is, if data are analyzed in terms of percentage differences between groups, one result is obtained; if they are analyzed in terms of ranks within groups, another result occurs. The first type of analysis is appropriate for identifying factors which account for differences between events (as Herzberg did in his original hypothesis). The second type of analysis is appropriate if we want to know the most important factors within the event categories (which is what Herzberg claims he was doing). Analyzing the findings of Dunnette and his colleagues by the first method, we confirm Herzberg's theory; but if we rank the findings within categories, as Dunnette *et al.* also

---

[8] Herzberg, *op. cit.*, chapters 7, 8. See also K. Davis, *Human Relations at Work* (third edition). New York: McGraw-Hill, 1967, pp. 32–36; and, R. J. Burke, "Are Herzberg's Motivators and Hygienes Undimensional?" *Journal of Applied Psychology*, Vol. 50 (1966), pp. 217–321.

[9] For a review of six of these studies as well as a report on their own similar findings see M. D. Dunnette, J. P. Campbell, and M. D. Hakel, "Factors Contributing to Job Satisfaction and Job Dissatisfaction in Six Occupational Groups," *Organizational Behavior and Human Performance*, Vol. 2 (1967), pp. 143–74. See also C. L. Hulin and P. A. Smith, "An Empirical Investigation of Two Implications of the Two-Factor Theory of Job Satisfaction," *Journal of Applied Psychology*, Vol. 51 (1967), pp. 396–402; C. A. Lindsay, E. Marks, and L. Gorlow, "The Herzberg Theory: A Critique and Reformulation," *Journal of Applied Psychology*, Vol. 51 (1967), pp. 330–39. This latter study and one by J. R. Hinrichs and L. A. Mischkind, "Empirical and Theoretical Limitations of the Two-Factor Hypothesis of Job Satisfaction," *Journal of Applied Psychology*, Vol. 51 (1967), pp. 191–200, are especially useful for suggesting possible reformulations and extensions of the theory which may help overcome some of the objections voiced in the studies mentioned above.

[10] Dunnette, Campbell and Hakel, *op. cit.*, pp. 169–73.

did, we find no confirmation. If we want to know whether "achievement" is important in job satisfaction we must look at its relative rank among other factors mentioned in the events leading to satisfaction, not whether it is mentioned a greater percentage of the time in satisfying events than in dissatisfying events. This distinction in analytical methods was discussed several years ago by Viteles and even earlier by Kornhauser.[11]

We conclude that any meaningful discussion of Herzberg's theory must recognize recent negative evidence even though the model seems to make a great deal of intuitive sense. Much the same can be said of Maslow's theory.

FURTHER CONSIDERATIONS IN USING THE MASLOW AND HERZBERG THEORIES

Putting aside for the moment the empirical considerations presented by the two models, it is instructive to compare them at the conceptual level suggested in Figure 1. While the figure shows obvious similarities between the Maslow and Herzberg models, there are important differences as well. Where Maslow assumes that any need can be a motivator if it is relatively unsatisfied, Herzberg argues that only the higher order needs serve as motivators and that a worker can have unsatisfied needs in both the hygiene and motivator areas simultaneously. One might argue that the reason higher order needs are motivators is that lower order needs have essentially been satisfied. However, Herzberg presents some evidence that even in relatively low-level blue-collar and service jobs, where presumably lower order needs are less well-satisfied, the higher order needs are still the only ones seen by the workers as motivators.[12]

Another important consideration is the relationship of these models to the accomplishment of organizational objectives. Even if there were unequivocal empirical support for the theories, there is need to translate the findings into usable incentives for promoting such objectives as superior performance, lower turnover, lower absenteeism, etc. If not, they are of little use to industrial organizations. As indicated earlier, there is relatively little evidence empirically relating Maslow's model to performance, or even to psychological well-being. Furthermore, the one Lawler and Porter study seems to show that satisfaction of higher and lower order needs are about equally related to performance, although their later investigation suggests that the former are more strongly related to performance than the latter. But we cannot tell for sure because correlations and differences between correlations are not reported.

Similarly, although Herzberg asked his respondents for effects of job

---

[11] M. S. Viteles, *Motivation and Morale in Industry*. New York: Norton, 1953, chapter 14: A. Kornhauser, "Psychological Studies of Employee Attitudes," *Journal of Consulting Psychology*, Vol. 8 (1944), pp. 127–43.

[12] Herzberg, *op. cit.*, chapters 7–9.

FIGURE 1

Maslow's Need-Priority Model Compared with Herzberg's Motivation-Hygiene Model*

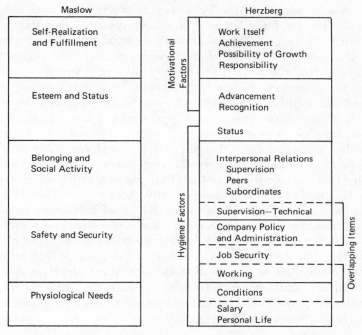

*Adapted from K. Davis, *Human Relations at Work*. New York: McGraw-Hill, 1967, p. 37.

events on their performance, he reports only two studies which attempt to measure performance independent of the respondent's estimate. These seem to show that performance is favorably influenced as more "motivators" are provided in the job.[13] However, insufficient data are presented to permit evaluation of the adequacy of the experimental design and performance measures. A study by Friedlander and Walton that considered employee turnover used a modification of Herzberg's technique and found that employees' reasons for staying on the job were different from their reasons for leaving.[14] The reasons for staying would be called "motivators" while those for leaving were "hygiene" factors.

We conclude that Herzberg's two-factor theory *may* be related to turnover and performance; but present studies are subject to serious criticisms.

---

[13] Herzberg, *op. cit.*, chapter 8.

[14] F. Friedlander and E. Walton, "Positive and Negative Motivations Toward Work," *Administrative Science Quarterly*, Vol. 9 (1964), pp. 194–207.

And we could find only two empirical investigations which related Maslow's model to any of these outputs.

In addition, it should be noted that neither model adequately handles the theoretical problem of some kind of linkage by which individual need satisfaction is related to the achievement of organizational objectives. Given the present formulation, it is entirely possible that there can be need satisfaction which is *not necessarily* directed toward the accomplishment of organizational goals. For example, an important organizational objective might be increased production, but workers might conceivably receive more need satisfaction from turning out a higher quality product at a sacrifice in quantity. They might also be meeting their social needs through identification with a work group with strong sanctions against "rate busting."

Finally, neither of these theories as they stand can really handle the problem of individual differences in motivation. Maslow, for example, explains that his model may not hold for persons with particular experiences. His theory is therefore nonpredictive because data that do not support it can be interpreted in terms of individual differences in previous need gratification leading to greater or lesser prepotency of a given need category.[15] Herzberg, in similar fashion, describes seven types of people differentiated by the extent to which they are motivator or hygiene seekers, or some combination of the two, although he never relates these differences empirically to actual job performance. We turn then to a model which explicitly recognizes these issues and appears to offer great potential for understanding motivation in organizations.

THE VROOM MODEL

Brayfield and Crockett as long ago as 1955 suggested an explicit theoretical linkage between satisfaction, motivation, and the organizational goal of productivity. They said:

> It makes sense to us to assume that individuals are motivated to achieve certain environmental goals and that the achievement of these goals results in satisfaction. Productivity is seldom a goal in itself but is more commonly a means to goal attainment. Therefore, . . . we might expect high satisfaction and high productivity to occur together when productivity is perceived as a path to certain important goals and when these goals are achieved.[16]

---

[15] It should be noted that the Porter and Lawler research reported above extends the Maslow model by providing an explicit linkage between need satisfaction and performance and also implicitly recognizes individual motivational differences. To do these things, their research makes use of Vroomian concepts discussed in the next section.

[16] A. H. Brayfield and W. H. Crockett, "Employee Attitudes and Employee Performance," *Psychological Bulletin*, Vol. 52 (1955), p. 416.

Georgopoulas, Mahoney, and Jones provide some early empirical support for this notion in their test of the "path-goal hypothesis."[17] Essentially, they argue that an individual's motivation to produce at a given level depends upon his particular needs as reflected in the goals toward which he is moving *and* his perception of the relative usefulness of productivity behavior as a path to attainment of these goals. They qualify this, however, by saying that the need must be sufficiently high, no other economical paths must be available to the individual, and there must be a lack of restraining practices.

More recently, Vroom has developed a motivational model which extends the above concepts and is also related to earlier work of experimental and social psychologists.[18] He defines motivation as a "process governing choices, made by persons or lower organisms, among alternative forms of voluntary activity."[19] The concept is incorporated in Figure 2, which depicts Vroom's model graphically. Here, the individual is shown as a role

FIGURE 2

Vroom's Motivational Model°

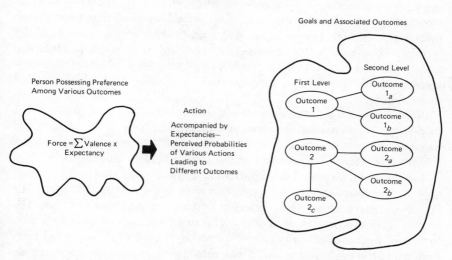

° Adapted from M. D. Dunnette, "The Motives of Industrial Managers," *Organizational Behavior and Human Performance,* Vol. 2 (1967), p. 178. (Copyright, Academic Press, Inc.)

---

[17] B. S. Georgopoulas, G. M. Mahoney, and N. W. Jones, "A Path-Goal Approach to Productivity," *Journal of Applied Psychology,* Vol. 41 (1957), pp. 345–53.

[18] This section is based especially on discussions in Vroom, *op. cit.,* chapters 2 and 7. See also J. Galbraith and L. L. Cummings, "An Empirical Investigation of the Motivational Determinants of Task Performance: Interactive Effects between Instrumentality—Valence and Motivation—Ability," *Organizational Behavior and Human Performance,* Vol. 2 (1967), pp. 237–57.

[19] Vroom, *op. cit.,* p. 6.

occupant faced with a set of alternative "first-level outcomes." His preference choice among these first-level outcomes is determined by their expected relationship to possible "second-level outcomes."

Two concepts are introduced to explain the precise method of determining preferences for these first-level outcomes. These concepts are *valence* and *instrumentality*. Valence refers to the strength of an individual's desire for a particular outcome. Instrumentality indicates an individual's perception of the relationship between a first-level outcome and a second-level outcome or, in other words, the extent to which a first-level outcome is seen as leading to the accomplishment of a second-level outcome.

Valence is measured by instructing workers to rank important individual goals in order of their desirability, or they may rate goals on Likert-type scales. Instrumentality can be measured by rating scales which involve perceived differences in the direction and strength of relationships between various first- and second-level outcomes. Important goals of industrial workers often cited in the empirical behavioral science literature are promotion, pay, pleasant working conditions, and job security. The goals can be ranked by individual workers in terms of their desirability. The resulting scores are measures of valence. In addition, each individual can be instructed to indicate on an appropriate scale the likelihood that a certain job behavior, e.g., high productivity, will lead to each of the four goals described. This score is the instrumental relationship between productivity and a specified goal. Obviously there are alternative methods of measurement available for the concepts; we will leave these for a more detailed discussion later.

Vroom expresses the valence of a first-level outcome to a person "as a monotonically increasing function of an algebraic sum of the products of the valences of all [second-level] outcomes and his conceptions of its instrumentality for the attainment of the [second-level] outcomes."[20]

For example, assume that an individual desires promotion and feels that superior performance is a very strong factor in achieving that goal. His first-level outcomes are then superior, average, or poor performance. His second-level outcome is promotion. The first-level outcome of high performance thus acquires a positive valence by virtue of its expected relationship to the preferred second-level outcome of promotion. Assuming no negative second-level outcomes associated with high performance and no other first-level outcomes that contribute to promotion, we expect motivation toward superior performance because promotion is important and superior performance is seen as instrumental in its accomplishment. Or, to put it in Vroom's terms, performance varies directly with the product of the valence of the reward (promotion) and the perceived instrumentality of performance for the attainment of the reward.

---

[20] Vroom, *op. cit.*, p. 17.

An additional concept in Vroom's theory is *expectancy*. This is a belief concerning the likelihood that a particular action or effort will be followed by a particular first-level outcome and can be expressed as a subjective probability ranging from 0 to 1. Expectancy differs from instrumentality in that it relates *efforts* to first-level outcomes where instrumentality relates first- and second-level outcomes to each other. Vroom ties this concept to his previous one by stating, "the force on a person to perform an [action] is a monotonically increasing function of the algebraic sum of the products of the valences of all [first-level] outcomes and the strength of his expectancies that the [action] will be followed by the attainment of these outcomes."[21] "Force" here is similar to our concept of motivation.

This motivational model, unlike those discussed earlier, emphasizes individual differences in motivation and makes possible the examination of very explicit relationships between motivation and the accomplishment of organizational goals, whatever these goals may be. Thus instead of assuming that satisfaction of a specific need is likely to influence organizational objectives in a certain way, we can find out how important to the employees are the various second-level outcomes (worker goals), the instrumentality of various first-level outcomes (organizational objectives) for their attainment, and the expectancies that are held with respect to the employees' ability to influence the first-level outcomes.

EMPIRICAL TESTS OF VROOM'S MODEL

Vroom has already shown how his model can integrate many of the empirical findings in the literature on motivation in organizations.[22] However, because it is a relatively recent development, empirical tests of the model itself are just beginning to appear. Here we shall consider four such investigations.

In the first study, Vroom is concerned with predicting the organizational choices of graduating college students on the basis of their instrumentality-goal index scores.[23] These scores reflect the extent to which membership in an organization was perceived by the student as being related to the acquisition of desired goals. According to the theory, the chosen organization should be the one with the highest instrumentality-goal index. Ratings were used to obtain preferences for fifteen different goals and the extent to which these goals could be attained through membership in three different organizations. These two ratings were thus measures of the valences of second-level outcomes and the instrumentality of organizational mem-

---

21 *Ibid.*, p. 18.

22 *Ibid.*

23 V. H. Vroom, "Organizational Choice: A Study of Pre- and Postdecision Processes," *Organizational Behavior and Human Performance*, Vol. 1 (1966), pp. 212–25.

bership for atttainment of these outcomes, respectively. The instrumentality-goal index was the correlation between these two measures. But Vroom's theory also involves consideration of expectancy, i.e., how probable is it that the student can become a member of a particular organization? The choice is not his alone but depends upon whether he is acceptable to the organization. A rough measure of expectancy in this study was whether or not the student had received an offer by the organization. If he had received an offer, expectancy would be high; if not, it would be low. The results show that, considering only organizations from which offers of employment were actually received, 76 percent of the students chose the organization with the highest instrumentality-goal index score. The evidence thus strongly supports Vroom's theory.

The next study, by Galbraith and Cummings, utilizes the model to predict the productivity of operative workers.[24] Graphic rating scales were used to measure the instrumentality of performance for five goals—money, fringe benefits, promotion, supervisor's support, and group acceptance. Similar ratings were used for measuring the desirability of each of the goals for the worker. The authors anticipated that a worker's expectation that he could produce at a high level would have a probability of one because the jobs were independent and productivity was a function of the worker's own effort independent of other human or machine pacing. Figure 3 outlines the research design.

Multiple regression analysis showed that productivity was significantly related positively to the instrumentality-goal interactions for supervisor support and money, and there was an almost significant ($p < 0.10$) relationship with group acceptance. The other factors did not approach significance and the authors explain this lack of significance in terms of the situational context. That is, fringe benefits were dependent not so much on productivity as on a union/management contract, and promotion was based primarily on seniority. Thus the instrumentality of productivity for the attainment of these goals was low and the model would predict no relationship. The Galbraith and Cummings study thus supports Vroom's contention that motivation is related to productivity in those situations where the acquisition of desired goals is dependent upon the individual's production and not when desired outcomes are contingent on other factors.

A third study is that of Hill relating a model similar to Vroom's to behavior in a utility company.[25] Hill's model is based upon Edward's subjective expected utility maximization theory of decision making.[26] Here one given a choice between alternatives A and/or B will select that alterna-

---

[24] Galbraith and Cummings, op. cit., pp. 237–57.

[25] J. W. Hill, "An Application of Decision Theory to Complex Industrial Behavior," unpublished dissertation, Wayne State University, Detroit, Michigan, 1965.

[26] Edwards, op. cit., pp. 473–99.

FIGURE 3

Individual Goals and Productivity as Measured by Vroom's

Model in One Industrial Plant°

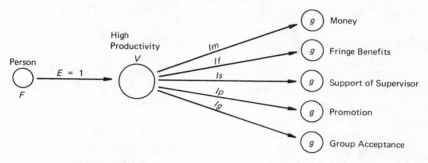

g = Desirability of a particular outcome (rating).

I = Instrumentality of production for particular outcomes (rating of relationship).

E = Expectancy (=1 here because worker sets own pace and is assumed to be capable of high productivity).

V = (Valence) the sum of the cross products of instrumentality and g.

F = (Force) expectancy times the valence of productivity.

Productivity = Objective measures of amount of production in relation to the production standard.

° Based on data from J. Galbraith and L. L. Cummings. See footnote 23.

tive which maximizes his subjective expected utility or expected value. If the outcomes associated with action A are more desirable than those associated with B, and their probability of occurrence is greater than or equal to those associated with B, then an individual will choose behavior A over behavior B. The basic concepts are subjective expectation and subjective utility or valence. Expectation and utility are multiplicatively related and can be measured by the same techniques used to test Vroom's theory. Where a relationship is found between Subjective Expected Utility (SEU) and overt behavior, it can be interpreted as support for Vroom.

The behavior considered in Hill's study is that of job bidding. This behavior is encountered in organizations that post descriptions of job openings on employee bulletin boards and encourage qualified employees to "bid" (apply) for them. Here records were kept of the number of bids made over a three-year period by groups of semiskilled electrical repairmen matched in learning ability, seniority in grade, and age. The men were asked about the consequences of bidding and not bidding on the next higher grade job, and rated the consequence on a seven-point scale of desirability and a similar scale of probability of occurrence. Bidders were those who had bid three or more times during that time.

Fourteen different SEU indices were computed from interview data to determine the relative validity of each in predicting bidding behavior.

Typical of these indices were: (1) the sums of the cross products of expectation and utility for the positive consequences of bidding ($\overset{+}{\Sigma}$ SEU); (2) the same score for the negative consequences of bidding ($\overset{-}{\Sigma}$ SEU); and (3) the

negative consequences $\left(\dfrac{\overset{+}{\Sigma}\,\text{SEU}}{N}, \dfrac{\overset{-}{\Sigma}\,\text{SEU}}{N} \right)$. In addition to these SEU indices,

two traditional attitudinal and motivational measures were used. Semantic differential scales measured each subject's respective evaluation of bidding and the next higher grade job and each subject's need for achievement was obtained.[27]

It was hypothesized that: (1) there would be a positive correlation between the SEU indices and bidding; and (2) the SEU indices would be more highly related to bidding behavior than the traditional measures.

We do not discuss relationships for all of the indices here but do consider results for one of the more comprehensive indices and those from multiple regression analysis. This index is the algebraic sum of the cross products of the positive and negative consequences of bidding minus the same score for not bidding for each individual. The correlation of this index with bidding was 0.26, $p < 0.05$ for a one-tailed test. The correlations between the two semantic differential scales and bidding were -0.09 and -0.25, respectively. Neither of these is significant for a one-tailed test predicting a positive correlation. The correlation between need for achievement and bidding was a nonsignificant 0.17. A multiple regression analysis determined the relative contribution of the SEU indices to the prediction of bidding. A variable was selected for analysis on the basis of its relationship to the criterion and its intercorrelation with the other predictors. The multiple correlation for bidding and seven selected variables was 0.61, $p < 0.05$. This correlation included four SEU indices, all of which had higher beta weights than the semantic differentials or need for achievement. Thus these variables accounted for more variance in the criterion than did the traditional attitudinal and motivational measures. Both hypotheses were therefore confirmed. This study adds support to the usefulness of this type of model in the study of motivation.

Finally, Lawler and Porter report a study that attempts to relate managerial attitudes to job performance rankings by superiors and peers.[28] In it, 145 managers from five different organizations completed questionnaires concerning seven kinds of rewards, and their expectations that dif-

---

[27] For discussions of these measures see C. Osgood, G. Suci, and P. Tannenbaum, *The Measurement of Meaning*, Urbana, Ill.: University of Illinois Press, 1957; A. L. Edwards, *Personal Preference Schedule Manual*. New York: Psychological Corporation, 1959.

[28] E. E. Lawler and L. W. Porter, "Antecedent Attitudes of Effective Managerial Performance," *Organizational Behavior and Human Performance*, Vol. 2 (1967), pp. 122–42.

ferent kinds of behavior would lead to these rewards. The expectations and the ratings of the importance of instrumentality and valence, respectively, were combined multiplicatively to yield multiple correlations which were significantly related to supervisor and peer rankings of the manager's effort to perform his job well. The correlations were higher with effort to perform the job than with the rankings of job performance. Lawler and Porter predicted this result because they reasoned that job performance is influenced by variables other than motivation, e.g., by ability and role perceptions. Of course, Vroom's model is not a behavioral theory but one of motivation only. Motivation is not going to improve performance if ability is low or role perceptions are inaccurate. Vroom's model explains how goals influence effort and that is exactly the relationship found by Lawler and Porter.

CONCLUSION

Taken together, the four studies discussed in the previous section seem to show that Vroom's model holds great promise for predicting behavior in organizations. There still remain some unanswered questions. We do not know all of the goals that have positive valence in a work situation. We do not know how much of a difference in force is necessary before one kind of outcome is chosen over another. Nor do we know what combination of measures yields the best prediction in a given situation. The answers to these and other questions await further research.

One more point should perhaps be made concerning the four studies and their measurement of Vroom's concepts. While it is true that all of them used subjective measures, the model can in fact be tested with more objective devices. Instrumentality can be inferred from organization practices, expectations can be manipulated by instructions, and goals can be inferred from observed approach and avoidance behaviors. Of course, all of these techniques require assumptions concerning their relationship to the worker's subjective perceptions of the situation; but the model is certainly not bound to the methods of measurement used so far. In fact, Vroom specifies in considerable detail the different kinds of techniques that might be used to test his model.[29]

More work must be done before we can make any statements concerning the overall validity of Vroom's model. But the rigor of his formulation, the relative ease of making the concepts operational, and the model's emphasis on individual differences show considerable promise. We are also encouraged by the results of relatively sophisticated studies testing the theory. We believe it is time for those interested in organizational behavior to take a more thoroughly scientific look at this very complex subject of industrial motivation, and Vroom's model seems a big step in that direction.

---

[29] Vroom, *Work and Motivation, op. cit.*, chapter 2.

16

Job Satisfaction Research: The Post-Industrial View

LOUIS E. DAVIS

The study of man at work is exposed to dangerous errors if it does not rest on the study of work itself, on the principles of the unity of its several aspects, and their reciprocal relationship.[1]

Research into job satisfaction has been a focal point of studies on organizational behavior for over 40 years. It has proved a fruitful area of study, and application of research results on job satisfaction has materially affected management practices. However, it is the thesis of this paper that our methods of inquiry into job satisfaction must now be substantially altered. This contention is based on the observation that we are in transition from an industrial era to a post-industrial era. This evolving post-industrial period is ushering in new cultural values and new designs of work organizations, and these changes require coordinate changes in the basic premises of job satisfaction research.

The cultural matrix of the industrial era required organizations to be structured in a certain way with jobs designed to fit that structure. Moreover, the cultural factors that molded organizations and jobs also molded research into these matters along certain lines. That is, the researcher's process of asking questions about job satisfaction depended on the tacit assumptions of the industrial value system.

The coming phase, that of the post-industrial era, will also shape organi-

Source: Reprinted by permission from *Industrial Relations,* Vol. 10 (1971), pp. 176–93.

[1] Alain Touraine, "L'Evolution du travail ouvrier aux Renault," Centre National de la Recherche Scientifique, Paris, 1955.

zational structures and designs for jobs, but these will be markedly different from those of the industrial era. We are beginning, in some industries and some nations, to see quite clearly the new cultural outline. Thus, the kinds of questions that researchers ask about job satisfaction—including the factors they take to be given and the assumptions which constrain their results—will spring from the value system of the post-industrial era.

The concept of job satisfaction, as conventionally drawn, is attacked here because it is almost exclusively concerned with adaptation to jobs that, in the post-industrial context, begin to seem fundamentally unsuited for man. The study of job satisfaction has come to be the study of the minimal gratifications possible under deprived conditions. This has occurred, in part at least, because the opportunities for providing greater satisfaction to organizational members while at the same time meeting organizational objectives are not well understood.

To elaborate, we are witnessing a split between two approaches to the study of job satisfaction. In the first approach, a small concentration of researchers and managers are examining and, in action research undertakings, are changing the structure and content of jobs along post-industrial lines, and thereby materially influencing the motivation and satisfaction of jobholders. In the other approach, researchers who cling to the industrial era model continue to examine all aspects of the work situation but the work itself, while searching for economic, community, group, and personality variables that correlate with measures of job satisfaction. The two sets of endeavors simply exist in different worlds, i.e., they stem from substantially different sets of views, values, and concepts.

In the following sections, we will first describe the relationship between present job satisfaction studies and the cultural values of the industrial era. We will then examine the implications of the changing nature of job design in the post-industrial era for job satisfaction research in the future.

THE INDUSTRIAL ERA

Historically, concern with job satisfaction began when the central conditions of modern industrial organization appeared, about 175 years ago. Industrialism gave rise to, and was most strikingly characterized by, that social innovation called the factory system, under which men were collected, assigned to work (usually at simple, repetitive jobs), and then closely controlled by supervision and by the flow of the work process. The technology of the industrial era was "deterministic." Where it persists today (largely in manufacturing), "deterministic" technology continues to support, and be supported by, the factory system or scientific management. Industrial era technology assumed that cause and effect relationships were known, and that all actions or tasks could be specified to obtain desired results In this context, the building blocks of an organization were taken to be the individual and his tasks. The interdependencies among tasks and among individuals were controlled by strict hierarchical arrangements, systems of payment, and scheduling. When these regulating devices proved inadequate, management tried to reduce variance by tighter task definitions and control of the work rate through pacing (as on assembly lines), or by exercising social control over the individual through external supervision, fractionation of tasks, and increasingly more complex incentive or piece-rate wage payments.

Values

A number of values and beliefs were particularly crucial to the nature of organizations and jobs in the industrial era. First, there is the deeply held belief that the individual can be viewed and treated as an Operating Unit (a phenomenon fully and insightfully described by Boguslaw[2]). As operating units, individuals may be adjusted and changed by training and incentives to suit the needs of the organization. That individuals may have needs is of secondary concern and, at best, simply a constraint.

A second crucial value concerns the reliability of individuals, including the much-discussed concept of responsibility. The societal view that most individuals are unreliable fostered the development of the concept of men as spare parts, and therefore members of organizations were (and are) assigned work in such a manner that they can be treated as interchangeable. That is, as individuals are believed to have only narrow capabilities and limited utility to organizations, they are given narrowly defined tasks and responsibilities. By contrast, in those segments of our society where individuals organize their own work—notably in the professions and some of the crafts—we find the contrasting "requisite-repertoire-of-skills" concept applied. This latter concept postulates that a wide range of capabilities must be available if individuals are to adapt to the changing or evolving requirements of their work situation. Nevertheless, most of our industrial training schemes are based on the spare parts concept.

Three other industrial-era values are relevant here as well. The first is that labor is a commodity to be sold by the individual and purchased by the organization. This stands in contrast to the emerging reality that individuals are organizational members, who may, over time, have changing contributions to make and other needs to satisfy. A second value is that of materialism in its narrow sense, under which the end of achieving higher material comfort justifies the means required to achieve it. Lastly, reflecting the values of the industrial era, many managers view the typical job as a disjointed increment, an isolated event in the life of the individual. This

---

[2] Robert Boguslaw, *The New Utopians* (New York: Prentice-Hall, 1955), chap. 5.

noncareerism syndrome explains how jobs (except those for managers themselves) get to be what they are—fragmentary, unintegrated, and asystemic.

Organization Design

When we examine the industrial era's approach to organization, "scientific management"—which in reality is the machine theory of organization —we find some deeply disturbing omissions. No clear objectives concerning roles for men as men are visible, although objectives are clearly defined for men as machines.[3] When man is considered only as a link in a system, design rules do not exist for allocating appropriate tasks to man. Nor are there design rules for constructing task configurations to make complete and meaningful jobs. Consideration is not given to the unit-of-analysis concept, which is concerned with determining appropriate boundaries of systems containing men, machines, materials, and information needed to pursue specific goals or outcomes in an operating system.

The characteristic organizational structure that we see today can be explained in terms of this theory of organization. The superstructure of the organization is designed to coordinate the elements in which work is done, join them together, counter variances arising within the elements and within the social links created by workers, and adjust the system to variances in either the input or in the output requirements. In such organizations, planning, coordinating, and controlling exist within the superstructure; the performance of activities (most of which are "programmable") occurs at the worker level.

If we turn to how technology is translated into requirements for job designs, we see widespread acceptance of the notion of the "technological imperative," put forth by most engineers and managers. That a substantial part of the technical design of production systems involves social system design is little understood or appreciated. Thus some rather frightful assumptions, supported by our industrial era values, are made about man and are built into machines and processes as system and operational requirements. To a large extent, psychological and social requirements of the work system are considered only as boundary conditions of the technical system. Attempts are then made to reduce these to boundary constants by contractual specifications which define how man must relate to the requirements of the technological system.

---

[3] Charles Perrow, *Organizational Analysis: A Sociological View* (Belmont, Calif.: Wadsworth, 1970), gives us an insight into the strength of industrial culture by reporting an instance in which animals were rejected, partly on compassionate grounds, as appropriate performers of single-purpose, machine-element tasks. Lamentably, the organization found these same jobs acceptable for its personnel to perform.

JOB SATISFACTION RESEARCH IN THE INDUSTRIAL ERA

The preceding section attempted to outline the implicit and explicit values underlying industrialism and the machine theory of organization, and to show how these were manifested in the design of jobs within the industrial framework. A large portion of past and present research into job satisfaction is based on this industrial-era value system. Either explicitly, or by tacit assumption, it shares the values and beliefs of its environmental context.

Technology as a Given

Job satisfaction studies have been and are still undertaken almost exclusively by psychologists and sociologists. Fully acknowledging the difficulty of conducting research on such a complex and multivariate problem, we must still contend that most of these studies have a singular defect—a defect that makes the results difficult to interpret and, in some instances, dangerous to apply: almost universally the studies take technology as a given.[4]

Technology includes the combination of skills, equipment, facilities, tools, and relevant technical knowledge needed to bring about desired transformations in materials, information, or people. But technology often differs significantly from one transformation process to another, and these differences materially affect the entire work situation and the relationship obtaining within it. Consider for a moment the different images that are evoked by the phrases "educational technology," "production-line technology," and "computer technology." It is clear that technology largely determines what the work is about and what demands are placed on the individual and the organization.

Nevertheless, in the psychological and sociological studies of job satisfaction, only the variables not influenced by technology are typically examined.[5] Further, in job satisfaction studies characteristic of the industrial

---

[4] Although it is not directly related to job satisfaction, the comparative analysis of organizations whose conceptual framework has been sketched out by Perrow is a notable exception in the sociological field. Perrow's analysis concerns itself explicitly with technological differences and their impact on roles in organizations. Similarly, much of the work of William F. Whyte, while not focusing directly on job satisfaction, does examine the responses of organization members to the technology of the immediate work place.

[5] Most recently, industrial psychologists have been embroiled in a frequently vicious conflict over whether the two-factor theory of job satisfaction by Frederick Herzberg, *Work and the Nature of Man* (Cleveland: World, 1966), or the traditional undimensional theory in Robert B. Ewen, Charles L. Hulin, Patricia C. Smith, and Edwin A. Locke, "An Empirical Test of the Herzberg Two-Factor Theory," *Journal of Applied Psychology*, L (December 1966), 544–50, George B. Graen, "An Addendum to an Empirical Test of the Herzberg Two-Factor Theory," *Journal of Applied Psychology*,

era there is an unfortunate propensity for treating job satisfaction either as an isolated variable or as an end state in itself. When technology is a given, the use of correlational and factor-analytic research methods ignores the interaction between social and technical systems and thus tells us little about cause and effect relationships.

In sum, the most striking feature of most past and present research on job satisfaction is its failure to study the job itself. One must question how, if the nature of the relevant technology is omitted, the research results can be understood or effectively used. Some of the effects of this omission are illustrated in the following paragraphs.

Job Enlargement Controversy

Psychologists concerned with work content—again, consistently taking technology as a given—have been led off in the direction of examining relationships between repetitive work and monotony, monotony and satisfaction, task length or job size and satisfaction. The recent tempest in a teapot over job enlargement illustrates the dangers inherent in using such research. No sooner was it proposed that "larger" jobs (i.e., more of the same dehumanizing tasks in a job) lead to higher satisfaction then the spurious battle over this fiction was on (MacKinney, et al., Kilbridge).[6] The nonpsychologists purportedly recommending enlargement (Argyris, Davis, Davis and Werling, Guest)[7] were in fact misinterpreted, for they were largely recommending the addition of different tasks—those leading to closure, self-regulation, and autonomy and resulting in fundamentally different relationships of the jobholder to the work process. (This process is now referred to as "vertical enlargement" or "job enrichment" by Herz-

---

L (December 1966), 551–55; Charles L. Hulin and Patricia C. Smith, "An Empirical Investigation of Two Implications of the Two-Factor Theory of Job Satisfaction," *Journal of Applied Psychology,* LI (October 1967), 396–402; George B. Graen and Charles L. Hulin, "An Addendum to an Empirical Investigation of Two Implications of the Two-Factor Theory of Job Satisfaction," *Journal of Applied Psychology,* LII (August 1968), 341–42, explains satisfaction-dissatisfaction. The imbroglio may represent a subconscious playing of games to avoid fundamental considerations of technology and values in determining job content. Herzberg's two-factor theory fortunately raises these issues.

[6] A. C. MacKinney, P. F. Wernimont, and W. O. Galitz, "Has Specialization Reduced Job Satisfaction?" *Personnel,* XXXIX (January/February 1962), 8–17; M. D. Kilbrdge, "Do Workers Prefer Larger Jobs?" *Personnel,* XXXVII (September/October, 1960), 45–48.

[7] Chris Argyris, *Personality and Organization* (New York: Harper, 1957); Chris Argyris, *Integrating the Individual and the Organization* (New York: Wiley, 1964); Louis E. Davis, "Toward a Theory of Job Design," *Journal of Industrial Engineering,* VIII (June 1957), 305–9; Louis E. Davis, "Job Design and Productivity: A New Approach," *Personnel,* XXXIII (March, 1957), 418–30; Louis E. Davis and Richard Werling, "Job Design Factors," *Occupational Psychology,* XXXIV (April, 1960), 108–32; Robert H. Guest, "Job Enlargement—A Revolution in Job Design," *Personnel Administration,* XX (January 1957), 9–16.

berg.) Most of the latter recommendations inferentially raised value questions related to the roles of men *as men* and, consequently, questions about the allocation of tasks between men and machines. Nowhere in this tempest was it recognized by the psychologists that tasks, in addition to meeting the demands of the technical system, also had to satisfy the needs of human systems.[8]

Extrinsic factors. Another body of research differing in purpose and outlook comprises the studies on extrinsic or job-context factors affecting job satisfaction and motivation, including working conditions, pay, supervisory relationships, community, and industry type. Related to this research is that focusing on leadership and managerial style. These studies focus on conditions and factors surrounding jobs and use factor-analytic and correlational methods to identify attitudes of job-holders in existing work situations. This work is represented in studies by Hulin and Smith, Graen and Hulin, Hulin and Blood, Blood and Hulin, Ewen *et al.*, Smith, and Dunnette *et al.*, and—with important modifications—Herzberg and his associates.[9] In terms of methodology, these studies are meticulously executed —with one crucial exception that makes interpretation of results virtually impossible for those who have any concern for the relationships between job content and motivation and satisfaction. In contrast to the careful sampling, control, data collection, and analysis exercised with respect to job attitudes, absolutely no control over or identification of the content of jobs held by the subjects in these studies is undertaken. Completely disregarded are the variables concerned with job boundaries, activities performed, regulation and control of system variations, control of input and output, and access to information within and across job boundaries, all of which have a strong bearing on the satisfaction responses that a job-holder would make. These job content variables clearly are not constant from job to job. The omission of their identification and measurement in the face of their differential effects makes it impossible to interpret such

---

[8] Neither did they recognize the concept of complementarity which Jordan finally stated in 1963 as a systems concept for task allocation in joint man machine systems. See Nehemial Jordan, "Allocation of Functions," *Journal of Applied Psychology*, XLVII (June 1963), 161–65.

[9] Hulin and Smith, *op. cit.*; Graen and Hulin, *op. cit.*; Charles L. Hulin and Milton R. Blood, "Job Enlargement, Individual Differences and Worker Responses," *Psychological Bulletin*, LXIX (February 1968), 41–55; Milton R. Blood and Charles L. Hulin, "Alienation, Environmental Characteristics, and Worker Responses," *Journal of Applied Psychology*, LI (June 1967), 284–90; Ewen, Hulin, Smith, and Locke, *op. cit.*; Patricia C. Smith, "The Cornell Studies of Job Satisfaction" (unpublished, Cornell University, 1963); Marvin D. Dunnette, John P. Campbell, and Milton D. Hakel, "Factors Contributing to Job Satisfaction and Job Dissatisfaction in Six Occupational Groups," *Journal of Organizational Behavior and Human Performance*, II (1967), 143–74; Frederick Herzberg, Bernard Mausner, and Barbara B. Snyderman, *The Motivation to Work* (New York: Wiley, 1959).

findings as Hulin's[10] that community characteristics are predictors of job satisfaction.

Given fractionated, dehumanized jobs, the responses of job-holders are to some extent related to individual differences—to their particular acceptance of and adaptation to, a working life of this quality. Predicting the satisfaction of job-holders in such a working environment is complicated by their state of alienation, which in turn appears to be related to their social environments, i.e., rural, simple vs. urban, or cosmopolitan.[11] These relationships constitute an argument for considering work systems in a social-ecological framework. But almost all of the studies readily accept the requirements seemingly imposed by technology—single-purpose fractionated tasks calling for machine-element responses.[12] That the relationship with the technological system could be otherwise configured has apparently been treated as an off-limits consideration. Fortunately this notion is now being laid to rest by the growing incursion of sophisticated technology that itself performs such tasks and calls for higher order interactions between man and the technical system.

THE POST-INDUSTRIAL ERA

The evolution of technology has been widely studied and described in recent years, as scholars and other social observers have become aware that the new technology is ushering in a new system of social and organizational values. Two trends are particularly relevant in this regard. The first is the continuing substitution of mechanical and electrical energy sources for human energy in the performance of work. The second is the absorption by machines of tasks or activities which are programmable (limited by the particular skills required for the performance of individual tasks). It is not the specific manual or decision-making skills that are relevant here, but whether the sequence in which the activities must be performed can be identified and written down in such a manner as to produce the desired outcome. Future human interventions will largely be of the "nonprogrammable" variety. That is, people will be called on to provide adaptive responses in situations where there are many exceptions, or where a high degree of variability exists (making programming infeasible), or where people provide linkages between programmable segments. Such jobs will

---

[10] Charles L. Hulin, "Sources of Variation in Job and Life Satisfaction: The Role of Community and Job-Related Variables," *Journal of Applied Psychology*, LIII (August 1969), 279–91.

[11] Blood and Hulin, *op. cit.*; Hulin and Blood, *op. cit.*

[12] Robert Dubin, "Supervision and Productivity: Empirical Findings and Theoretical Considerations," in Robert Dubin, George C. Homans, Floyd C. Mann, and Delbert C. Miller, *Leadership and Productivity* (San Francisco: Chandler, 1965), chap. 1.

require skills, contents, and organizational structures quite different from those presently before us.

Values

The values of a society and its institutions slowly evolve in response to social and physical conditions and to the conceptions the society holds of its environment. It is the emergence of some new values and the change in relative importance of others that leads to the recognition that we are witnessing the evolution of new epoch, the post-industrial era. Perhaps the best way of stating the changes in emphasis is to present two tables of Trist's[13] (Tables 1 and 2).

Our social environment is one of continuous irreversible change proceeding at an accelerating rate. Its salient characteristic is that of a turbulent field.[14] As Trist indicates:

This turbulence arises from the increased complexity and size of the total environment, together with increased interdependence of the parts and the unpredictable connections which arise between them as a result of the accelerating but uneven change rate. This turbulence grossly increases the area of relevant uncertainty for individuals and organizations alike. It raises far-reaching problems concerning the limits of human adaptation. Forms of adaptation, both personal and organizational, developed to meet a simpler type of environment no longer suffice to meet the higher levels of complexity now coming into existence.[15]

In response to these environmental conditions, we see growing acceptance of the values of adaptability and composite capability—in Ashby's terms, the possession by individuals of a requisite variety of responses to meet a variety of external demands, or in Emery's terms, a society in which individuals exhibit redundancy of functions rather than being themselves treated as redundant or spare parts.

Developed technology appears to provide limitlessly for material needs and to banish the fear of scarcity. By eroding the bases for the Protestant work ethic this capability of technology reinforces the evolving values of self-actualization and self-expression. Further, advanced technology re-

---

[13] Eric L. Trist, "Urban North America: The Challenge of the Next Thirty Years," *Journal of the Town Planning Institute of Canada*, X (1970), 4–20; Eric L. Trist, "The Relation of Welfare and Development in the Transition to Post-Industrialism," *Proceedings International Seminar on Welfare and Development* (Ottawa: Canadian Centre for Community Studies, 1967), p. 34.

[14] Fred E. Emery and Eric L. Trist, "The Causal Texture of Organizational Environments," *Human Relations*, XVIII (February 1965), 21–32.

[15] Trist, "Urban North America . . . ," p. 6.

TABLE 1

Occupational Structure and Education

Aspect	Salient in 1935	Salient in 1965 (and 1970)
Composition of work force	Blue collar	White collar
Educational level	Not completing high school	Completing high school
Work/learning ratio	Work force	Learning force
Type of career	Single	Serial

TABLE 2

Changes in Emphasis of Social Patterns in the Transition to Post-Industrialism

Type	From	Towards
Cultural values	Achievement	Self-actualization
	Self-control	Self-expression
	Independence	Interdependence
	Endurance of distress	Capacity for joy
Organizational philosophies	Mechanistic forms	Organic forms
	Competitive relations	Collaborative relations
	Separate objectives	Linked objectives
	Own resources regarded as owned absolutely	Own resources regarded also as society's resources
Ecological strategies	Responsive to crisis	Anticipative of crisis
	Specific measures	Comprehensive measures
	Requiring consent	Requiring participation
	Short planning horizon	Long planning horizon
	Damping conflict	Confronting conflict
	Detailed central control	Generalized central control
	Small local government units	Enlarged local government units
	Standardized administration	Innovative administration
	Separate services	Co-ordinated services

moves man's conventional work role and requires of him self-directed decision making to counter unexpected variations, which also supports the value of self-actualization.

Trist's review of occupational structure and education reflects yet another impact of the new technology. Stimulated by the emergent reorganization of society and industry, the view is evolving that the job is an event or stage in an integrated, life-long career—that not only doctors and lawyers but hospital workers, clerks, and machinists are engaged in work that can be viewed as a step on a career ladder. (Some may say this is history turning full circle.) On the part of both managers and workers, new questions are being raised about the opportunities that jobs provide for learning and self-development, and about the career opportunities provided by organizations. The emerging value of careers is reinforced by those of self-actualization, self-expression, and interdependence. Together, these values are forming a comprehensive set that will markedly alter the nature of jobs and organizations.

Socio-Technical Systems

An ecological focus is evolving that provides useful insights for the theory and practice of structuring organizations and determining job content. This focus is a response to changes in the technological and social environment and in cultural values. It led to the development of a conceptual and theoretical framework known as socio-technical systems,[16] and its utility for the post-industrial era lies in its comprehensive view of the interactions among society, its organizations, and the members within them. At the societal level, it takes as central the requirement for organizations and individuals to respond to an environment exhibiting a high rate of change—an environment in which relative uncertainty is high and previous values are being re-examined. At the institutional level, the socio-technical approach takes organizations to be purposive, relating to their surrounding social and technological environments and interacting with them across permeable boundaries. It takes technology as a relevant variable interacting with social and personal variables to *jointly* shape the system for accomplishing the purposes of an organization. At the individual level it takes the organization's members to be purposive, whole human beings reflecting and shaping the values of society, interacting with technology and seeking to satisfy their own and the organization's needs. Socio-technical systems applications lend strong support to the prospect of developing a work world humane in its objectives and satisfying in its consequences to both the individual and the organization. A number of recent developments, both theoretical and empirical, indicate that we can design satisfying, economically efficient jobs which meet these value requirements.

The Norwegian Experience

The evolution of socio-technical systems concepts has taken place over the last 15 years in the course of attempts here and in England to overcome the deficiencies of existing work situations. Furthermore, within the

---

[16] Fred E. Emery and Eric L. Trist, "Socio-Technical Systems," in C. West Churchman and Mildred Verhulst, editors, *Management Science, Models and Techniques*, Vol. 2 (New York: Pergamon, 1960).

last four years Norway has made a national commitment to changing values about man at work through a series of experiments with job and organization design, under tripartite support from the Confederation of Employers, the Confederation of Trade Unions, and the Norwegian government. In these experiments, socio-technical systems theory has been applied with the active participation of both management and labor, and the results have been held up for national examination by the representatives of all interested parties, leading in late 1969 to acceptance of the objectives and modes of organizing as national policy.[17] As might be expected, given the present rapid spread of ideas and its similar values, Sweden is under pressure to undertake a similar form of development.

Socio-technical systems theory is concerned with any organizational setting in which men combine their efforts in cooperative activity with technology toward the achievement of a goal. The theory provides us with two essential concepts basic to the study of man at work. The first is that of open systems and the second is that of correlated but independent social and technological systems operating under joint causation.

Open Systems

The concept of open systems focuses our attention on the relationships between the individual or work group and the external environment. The organizational unit is viewed as operating within and interacting with its environment. It receives inputs, alters them, and exports outputs to that environment. We see that we cannot understand an organizational unit without understanding its environment, that the unit is not independent of its environment, and that there is a mutual permeation of the unit and its environment. We are provided with a theoretical basis for considering spontaneous restructuring of organizational units, growth, self-regulation, and the achievement of a "steady state" at levels permitting work to be done even though there may be disturbances in the environment.

Joint Optimization

Socio-technical systems theory conceives of the working world as consisting of independent technological systems and social systems operating under joint causation. This leads to the central concept of joint optimization, which states that when achievement of an objective depends on independent but correlated systems, such as a technological and social system, it is impossible to optimize for overall performance without seeking to optimize these correlative systems jointly. Among a number of concepts

---

[17] Einar Thorsrud and Fred E. Emery, *Mot en Ny Bedriftsorganisasjon* (Oslo, Norway: Tanum Press, 1969).

that derive from these propositions, the concept of boundary control is of great importance for the design of jobs and of organizational units. Raised are questions of tasks and relationships to be included within the boundary of a job or organizational unit for self-regulation and control of functioning and of functions to be performed by higher levels that will maintain the boundary of a stable organizational unit.

JOB SATISFACTION RESEARCH IN THE POST-INDUSTRIAL ERA

In the preceding section, some of the emergent values of the post-industrial era were sketched out in terms of socio-technical systems theory and the concepts underlying it. The emerging post-industrial value system is stimulating new modes of organizing work and structuring jobs and, correspondingly, it is giving rise to a body of research into job satisfaction that asks new questions and depends on new premises. Here, we attempt to collect a set of references to research that forms part of this new and growing stream.[18]

The Work Itself

Within this group are those who recognize the relationship of motivation and satisfaction to the intrinsic, substantive contents of jobs. The recent work of Lawler, Herzberg, Paul *et al.*, the continuing work of Likert and the Insitute of Social Research at the University of Michigan (Marrow, *et al.*,), and that of Meyers represent significant contributions.[19]

The studies of the organizational behavior group at the Harvard Graduate School of Business Administration provide insights into the technological and environmental conditions of the emerging post-industrial era. Turner and Lawrence examined the impact of technologically determined variations on responses of workers living under differing social and

---

[18] Some of the researchers who have been grouped together here may express surprise that they are being thus clustered. Their relationship is not necessarily one of direct contact and explicit agreement, but rather of unity within the conceptual framework we postulate as being characterisic of the post-industrial "nouveau vague."

[19] Edward E. Lawler, III, "Job Design and Employee Motivation," *Personnel Psychology,* XXII (Winter 1969), 426–35; Herzberg, *op. cit.;* Frederick Herzberg, "One More Time: How Do You Motivate Employees?" *Harvard Business Review,* XLVI (January 1968), 53–62; William J. Paul, Keith B. Robertson, and Frederick Herzberg, "Job Enrichment Pays Off," *Harvard Business Review,* XLVII (March 1969), 61–78; Rensis Likert, *The Human Organization: Its Management and Value* (New York: McGraw-Hill, 1967); Alfred J. Marrow, David G. Bowers, and Stanley E. Seashore, *Management by Participation* (New York: Harper & Row, 1967); M. Scott Meyers, "Who Are Your Motivated Workers?" *Harvard Business Review,* XLII (January 1964), 73–88; M. Scott Meyers, "Every Employee a Manager," *California Management Review,* X (Spring 1968), 9–20.

cultural influences. Lawrence and Lorsch studied the impact on organization design and social relationships of accelerating rates of market and technological change.[20]

Individual vs. Organization

Within this cluster of studies are significant developments that directly confront the issue of values relating to man and organization. In England (Emery) and Scandinavia (Thorsrud and Emery, and Herbst) one stream of these developments has been referred to as democratization of the workplace.[21] In the U.S., the values issue is strongly reflected in the work of Argyris, Davis, Herzberg, and Likert.[22] Another development focuses on the interactions between technology and social organization in shaping the roles of men. In this context, using the socio-technical systems framework, jobs and organizations are being designed that are motivating and satisfying to men and groups and suitable to the organization and its technology. This line of development is reflected in the research of the Tavistock Institute of Human Realtions, London (Emery and Trist, Trist, *et al.*, and Miller and Rice),[23] of the Institute of Work Research, Oslo, Norway (Thorsrud and Emery, Englestad),[24] and Davis.[25] A good deal of this work was stimulated by the early endeavors of Walker and his associates.[26]

Related to the work of these researchers, there has been a somewhat fragmented series of industrial and business applications directed at enhancing the motivation and satisfaction of employees by changing the content of their jobs and extending their responsibilities and authority.

---

[20] Arthur N. Turner and Paul R. Lawrence, *Industrial Jobs and the Worker* (Boston: Harvard Business School, 1965); Paul R. Lawrence and Jay W. Lorsch, *Organization and Environment* (Boston: Harvard Business School, 1967).

[21] Fred E. Emery, "Democratization of the Work Place," *Manpower and Applied Psychology,* I (1968), 118–29; Thorsrud and Emery, *op. cit.;* P. G. Herbst, *Autonomous Group Functioning* (London: Tavistock, 1962).

[22] Argyris, *Integrating the Individual* . . . ; Louis E. Davis, "The Coming Crisis for Production Management: Technology and Organization," *International Journal of Production Research,* IX (London, 1971), 4; Herzberg, *Work and the Nature of Man;* Likert, *op. cit.*

[23] Emery and Trist, *op. cit.;* Eric L. Trist and Kenneth W. Bamforth, "Some Social and Psychological Consequences of the Longwall Method of Coal Getting," *Human Relations,* IV (1951), 3–38; Eric L. Trist, Gurth W. Higgin, Hugh Murray, and Allan B. Pollack, *Organizational Choice* (London: Tavistock, 1963); Eric J. Miller and Albert K. Rice, *Systems of Organization* (London: Tavistock, 1967).

[24] Thorsrud and Emery, *op. cit.;* P. H. Englestad, *Technology and Social Relationships in the Workplace* (Oslo, Norway: Tanum Press, 1970).

[25] Davis, "The Coming Crisis for Production Management . . . ," p. 4; Louis E. Davis, "The Design of Jobs," *Industrial Relations,* VI (October 1966), 21–45.

[26] Charles R. Walker and Robert H. Guest, *Man on the Assembly Line* (Cambridge: Harvard University Press, 1952).

Some of these developments in job enlargement and job enrichment are described by Ford and Foulkes.[27]

Thus, the researchers who reflect post-industrial changes are concerned with the impact of changing technology, social environment, and personal values, and the enormous loss in human resources potential (see Gooding)[28] stemming from continued application of organizational concepts increasingly unsuited to the present era. They see that the sum of the technological and social forces operating on organizations and their members leaves management with no option but to provide satisfying, meaningful work (Davis).[29]

Job design. Depending on the type of industry, state of technology, and characteristics of the environment, an extensive number of propositions for the design of jobs along post-industrial lines can be derived. A number of these have been tested in the socio-technical field studies referred to earlier and are still in the process of evolution and testing in studies currently underway.

A summary report of the English and U.S. socio-technical field studies has been published by Davis.[30] In general, successful job-design outcomes, as measured by various objective criteria, seem to depend on finding an accommodation between the demands of the organization and the technology on the one hand, and the needs and desires of its members on the other, so that the needs of both are jointly maximized. The studies lend support to the general model of responsible autonomous job behavior as the key facet of individual-organization-technological relationships in productive organizations. *Responsible* behavior as defined here implies (1) acceptance of responsibility by the individual or group for the cycle of activities required to complete the product or service, (2) acceptance of responsibility for the rate, quantity, and quality of output, and (3) recognition of the interdependence of the individual or group on others for completion of a cycle of activities. Similarly, *autonomous* behavior encompasses (1) self-regulation of work content and structure within the job (where the job is an assignment having inputs, facilities, and outputs), (2) self-evaluation of performance, (3) self-adjustment in response to work system variability, and (4) participation in the setting of job goals or objectives. Lastly, the studies provide a partial demonstration of the positive effects of responsible autonomous job behavior on objective organizational

---

[27] Robert N. Ford, *Motivation Through the Work Itself* (New York: American Management Association, 1969); Fred K. Foulkes, *Creating More Meaningful Work* (New York: American Management Association, 1969).

[28] Judson Gooding, "Blue-Collar Blues on the Assembly Line," *Fortune* (July 1970), 69; Judson Gooding, "It Pays to Wake Up the Blue-Collar Worker," *Fortune* (September 1970), 133–35.

[29] Davis, "The Coming Crisis for Production Management . . . ," p. 4.

[30] Davis, "The Design of Jobs. . . ."

performances as well as on the attitudes, perceptions, and satisfactions of members of the organization.

FUTURE JOB SATISFACTION STUDIES

Recognizing the emerging value trends of the post-industrial era and their implications for organization and job design, what will, or at least what should, be the shape of future job satisfaction studies? It seems clear that it will be unprofitable to continue static examinations of variations in employee attitudes under deprived work conditions. Instead, meaningful future research in this area will focus on broad, dynamic dimensions of the ongoing process of designing and redesigning the sociotechnical system in line with these new values.

Given this focus, it seems unlikely that job satisfaction will be studied as a distinct phenomenon. Rather, it will tend to focus on the higher systems level and will thus raise new issues about relationships between the individual and his group, requirements for self-sufficiency or autonomy, and the compatibility between these requirements and their associated regulatory or control systems. This new focus will blur the distinction we currently make between organization and job satisfaction. Moreover, the determinants of satisfaction for all jobholders will come to be viewed more like those presently associated with scientists, engineers, teachers, and other professionals working in large complex organizations.

Future Dimensions of Job Satisfaction

To be somewhat more explicit, an extrapolation of the post-industrial trends discussed earlier suggests that the social and technological environments of organizations will hasten the widespread use of various forms of self-sufficient, autonomous work groups. Their primary role, in relation to their transformation technologies, will be that of regulator and controller (or absorber) of systems variances. In organizations where these work groups exist, strict control of members' behavior to achieve organizational objectives is neither particularly useful nor necessary. But at the same time, the organization must ensure that the goals of its units are relevant to those of the organization as a whole and that the organization remains adaptive to the environment. Thus, to a large extent, job satisfaction issues will be centered around the forms and means of goal setting, multiple goal satisfaction (institutional, social, personal), individual and organizational adaptability, self-sufficient operational autonomy, and feedback and rewards. For each of these issues a number of variables will probably be studied in relation to job satisfaction in specific instances and, in addition, as aids in the design of jobs, careers, and organizations.

Some of the variables revolving around careers and organizational adaptability may be concerned with the learning content of jobs, role access to learning, degree and form of self-regulation, control and feedback in operations. Centering around technology are likely to be such variables as man-machine complementarity, access to process variables, congruence of social and technical systems boundaries, scope of process variance regulation authority, and requisite variety of response capabilities, and their accessibility. At the institutional level, variables likely to be studied are participation in goal setting, access to the institution's environment, feedback and rewards, access to total cost data, and permeability of internal boundaries.[31]

New Methods of Job Satisfaction Research

As the focus of future job satisfaction research shifts toward these new dimensions, the methods by which it is undertaken will also shift—in fact, they will be forced to undergo rather dramatic revision. Specifically, researchers will need an in-depth understanding of both the technology used in the transformation process and its related social system. Required, also, will be a relatively complete understanding of the organization's environment.

Understanding both the technology and the environment of the organization requires painstaking analysis in order to determine the variations generated, the means for controlling these variances, the responses called for on the part of the social system, and the apparent structural requirements for its operation. Such information is usually held only by organization members who are expert in the technology, and the researcher must therefore work closely with these people.

Similarly, understanding an organization's social system requires a close association with those who know the values of the participants, their perception of the environment, and their personal concerns, fears, ambitions, and needs. This information cannot be obtained through an arm's-length association—it requires a privileged relationship with those most familiar with the organization. Such an association assumes a position of trust (a position usually regarded with suspicion by "science"), and one that is rarely obtainable in a researcher-researched relationship. In turn, privileged relationships can be won only if the researcher supplies a needed service to the organization and is competent in doing so. In a sense, this means beginning in practice—however imperfect scientifically—working back to theory, conducting more systematic research to test the theory, and moving back again to improved practice.[32] This is the basic model for

---

[31] For interrelated issues of future study requirements of job design, see Davis, "Toward a Theory of Job Design," p. 305.

[32] Louis E. Davis, "Laboratories for Professionals," Graduate School of Business Administration, University of California, Los Angeles, October 1970 (mimeographed);

research in medicine and in organization theory is usually referred to as "action research."

The Action Research Process

Clearly action research is an iterative and developmental process. As it progresses, the researcher tries to make explicit the values of the organization. He assists the organization in ensuring that these values are reflected in the roles and structure of the work situation, and he engages in research into and design of technology so that the issue of joint optimization of social and technical systems is squarely faced and effectively implemented.

To propose that a researcher participate in the creation of the work environment which is the object of his study may strike the reader as an unusual notion. But the richly interconnected nature of the post-industrial domain, and the requirement that organizations and jobs be designed as integrated and interdependent systems, will markedly alter the researcher's role in the future. He will be able to develop the data he needs only if he works in close association with the researched system, and he will be able to achieve this close association only if he provides a valuable service to the organization. The post-industrial job satisfaction studies described above were conducted in this way—that is, they represent combined action-research endeavors carried out in accordance with the socio-technical systems view of integrated organizations, careers, and jobs.

CONCLUSIONS

Evolving technology indicates that we have to prepare people to be adaptable, to hold a number of job sequences in a lifetime, and to be committed to their work situation. In organized work situations, current practices are inimical to achieving such needs. As a nation, we need what Vickers[33] calls a new "appreciation" of the world of work if we are going to prepare for future changes. We need to examine the compatibility between the emerging post-industrial values of our culture and the values of organizations; the autonomy of the individual and control by the organization; the compatibility between demands of the work system and the responses men feel equipped to give; the conflict between demands of jobs and man's needs; the extent to which the technology imposes a rigidity on job content and structure; the requirements, if any, of modern organizational planning and control that impose detailed specification and

---

Social Research and National Policy for Science, Pamphlet No. 7 (London: Tavistock Publications, 1964).

[33] Sir Geoffrey Vickers, *Value Systems and Social Process* (New York: Basic Books, 1968).

restriction on jobs rather than the specification of minimal critical tasks appropriate to the goals of the organization; and the consequences for our society of considering jobs as isolated events rather than stages in a career. Lastly, we must face the consequences of achieving compatibility between man as worker and man as citizen.

Our present national concern with technology has concentrated largely on its impact on skills and on types and number of jobs, and not on the need to evolve new job designs to fit emergent technological configurations. As a consequence, we may miss opportunities provided by the evolution of sophisticated technology to design jobs and organizations that are suited to both men and machines.[34]

A prior condition of future job satisfaction is the development of organizations and jobs that reflect the needs and environmental trends of the post-industrial era. When such organizations and jobs exist, it is likely that job satisfaction research issues will cluster around goal development, multiple goal achievement, and short- and long-term adaptability. Not likely to be seen again are studies of jobs which are created according to mechanistic rules and whose viability is dependent on systems of coercion. Future studies of job satisfaction will be integral with job design.

Future job satisfaction research methods will reflect the realities of studying living organizations characterized by constant large and small changes, by the reality of the impact of both the environment and changes within the organization on its members, and by their adaptations to this reality. At the same time there are crucial research issues of bias, replicability, and post-hoc theory to be guarded against. No longer will the cozy notion hold that organization members are objects waiting to be researched, who in the name of science can be manipulated, so that we can learn something about them. We now recognize that we have to learn through developments which are in the interests of the researched with those of the researcher following.

---

[34] Louis E. Davis, "The Effects of Automation on Job Design," *Industrial Relations,* II (October 1962), 53–71.

17

The Mythology of Management Compensation

EDWARD E. LAWLER III

A host of decisions have to be made every day concerning compensation practices, decisions that are of critical importance in determining the success of any business organization. Unfortunately, relatively little is known about the psychological meaning of money and how it motivates people. Unanswered are such critical questions as:

> How often should a raise be given?
> What are the effects of secrecy about pay?
> How should benefit programs be packaged?

In the absence of systematic knowledge, executives have had to answer these kinds of questions for themselves. Many have drawn primarily from their own and others' experience in arriving at their answers. Unfortunately, common sense derived from experience can be loaded with implicit assumptions which may not be as valid as they seem. It is my purpose here to examine a number of commonly accepted assumptions about pay and to attempt to determine if they are valid.

What are the currently accepted principles and assumptions about how pay should be administered? In order to answer this question, a study was

---

Source: Copyright 1966 by the Regents of The University of California. Reprinted form *California Management Review*, Vol. 9, No. 1 (Fall 1966), pp. 11–22, by permission of the Regents and the author.

conducted among 500 managers from all levels of management and from a wide variety of organizations. The managers were asked to indicate whether they agreed or disagreed with five statements that contained assumptions about the psychological aspects of management compensation —assumptions which have important implications for the administration of pay. The following are the five assumptions and the percentage of managers agreeing with each:

At the higher-paid levels of management, pay is not one of the two or three most important job factors (61 percent).

Money is an ineffective motivator of outstanding job performance at the management level (55 percent).

Managers are likely to be dissatisfied with their pay even if they are highly paid (54 percent).

Information about management pay rates is best kept secret (77 percent).

Managers are not concerned with how their salary is divided between cash and fringe benefits; the important thing is the amount of salary they receive (45 percent).

As can be seen, better than 50 percent of managers participating in the study agreed with the first four assumptions and 45 percent agreed with the last assumption.

Recently, research results have begun to accumualte which suggest that some of the assumptions may be partially invalid and some completly invalid. Let us, therefore, look at each of these assumptions and examine the evidence relevant to it.

WHAT IS THE ROLE OF PAY?

The history of the study of pay shows that we have progressed from a model of man that viewed him as being primarily economically motivated to a view that stresses social needs and the need for self-actualization. Unfortunately, in trying to establish the legitimacy of social and self-actualization needs, the proponents of this view of motivation tended to overlook the importance of pay. In some cases, they failed to mention the role of pay in their systems at all, and in other cases they implied that, because workers and managers are better off financially than they used to be, pay is less important than it was previously.

Because of this failure to deal with the role of pay, many managers have come to the erroneous conclusion that the experts in "human relations" have shown that pay is a relatively unimportant incentive and, as a result, have accepted the view that pay is a relatively unimportant job factor.[1] This is

---

[1] This is not to imply that the leading figures in the "human relations" movement do not understand the importance of pay. But, by emphasizing other rewards and by not dealing explicitly with the role of pay, they have opened the door for others to interpret their writings as implying that pay is unimportant.

illustrated in the results of my study mentioned above. When the managers were asked to indicate how they thought the typical expert in human relations would respond to the statement that for higher-paid managers pay is not one of the most important job factors, 71 percent of the managers thought that the majority of the experts would agree with it, while 61 percent said they agreed with it themselves.

Undeniably, those writers who have stressed social and self-actualization needs have performed an important service by emphasizing the significance of nonfinancial incentives. It is now clear that people are motivated by needs for recognition and self-actualization as well as by security and physiological needs. But does this mean that pay much be dismissed as unimportant? I do not think the evidence justifies such a conclusion.

The belief that pay becomes unimportant as an individual accumulates more money has its roots in an inadequate interpretation of Maslow's theory of a hierarchy of needs. Briefly, Maslow's theory says that the needs which individuals seek to satisfy are arranged in a hierarchy. At the bottom of the hierarchy are needs for physical comfort. These lower-order needs are followed by such higher-order needs as social needs, esteem needs, and finally, needs for autonomy and self-actualization.

According to Maslow's theory, once the lower-order needs are relatively well satisfied, they become unimportant as motivators, and an individual tries to satisfy the higher-order needs. If it is then assumed, as it is by many, that pay satisfies only lower-level needs, then it becomes obvious that once a person's physical comforts are taken care of, his pay will be unimportant to him.[2] But this view is based upon the assumption that pay satisfies primarily lower-level needs, an assumption which I question.

PAY AS RECOGNITION

I would like to emphasize the neglected viewpoint that pay is a unique incentive—unique because it is able to satisfy both the lower-order physiological and security needs and the higher-order needs, such as esteem and recognition. Recent studies show that managers frequently think of their pay as a form of recognition for a job well done and as a mark of achievement.[3] The president of a large corporation has clearly pointed out why pay has become an important mark of achievement and recognition for managers.

---

[2] It should be pointed out that neither Maslow nor any of the leading figures in the "human relations" movement has stated that pay satisfies only lower-order needs. Others make the interpretation that it satisfies only lower-order needs (e.g., Robert B. McKersie, "Wage Payment Methods of the Future," *British Journal of Industrial Relations*, I [March 1963], 191–212).

[3] Edward E. Lawler and Lyman W. Porter, "Perceptions Regarding Management Compensation," *Industrial Relations*, III (Oct. 1963), 41–49; and M. Scott Myers, "Who Are Your Motivated Workers?" *Harvard Business Review*, XLII (Jan.–Feb. 1964), 72–88.

Achievement in the managerial field is much less spectacular than comparable success in many of the professions . . . the scientist, for example, who wins the Nobel prize. . . . In fact, the more effective an executive, the more his own identity and personality blend into the background of his organization, and the greater is his relative anonymity outside his immediate circle.

There is, however, one form of recognition that managers do receive that is visible outside their immediate circle, and that is their pay. Pay has become an indicator of the value of a person to an organization and as such is an important form of recognition. Thus, it is not surprising to find that one newly elected company president whose "other" income from securities approximated $125,000 demanded a salary of $100,000 from his company. When asked why he did not take a $50,000 salary and defer the other half of his salary until after retirement at a sizable tax saving, he replied, "I want my salary to be six figures when it appears in the proxy statement."[4]

It is precisely because pay satisfies higher-order needs as well as lower-order needs that it may remain important to managers, regardless of the amount of compensation they receive. For example, one recent study clearly showed (Figure 1) that although pay is slightly less important to upper-level managers (president and vice-president) than it is to lower-level managers, it is still more important than security, social, and esteem needs for upper-level managers.[5] At the lower management level, pay was rated as more important than all but self-actualization needs.

We can turn to motivation theory to help explain further why pay is important to many managers. Goals that are initially desired only as a means to an end can in time become goals in themselves. Because of this process, money may cease to be only a path to the satisfaction of needs and may become a goal in itself. Thus, for many managers, money and money making have become ends that are powerful incentives. As one manager put it when asked why his salary was important to him, "It is just like bridge—it isn't any fun unless you keep score." In summary, the evidence shows that, although pay may be important to managers for different reasons as the amount of pay they receive increases, pay remains important to all levels of management.

The evidence that is usually given to support the belief that pay is ineffective as an incentive is the finding that a number of incentive plans have failed to produce expected increases in productivity. This view is expressed well by the following statement of a company president: "Wage systems

---

[4] Arch Patton, *Men, Money, and Motivation* (New York: McGraw-Hill Book Co., Inc., 1961), p. 34.

[5] Lyman W. Porter, "A Study of Perceived Need Satisfaction in Bottom and Middle Management Jobs," *Journal of Applied Psychology*, XLV (Feb. 1961), 1–10.

FIGURE 1

Importance Attached to Six Needs by Managers at Three Levels

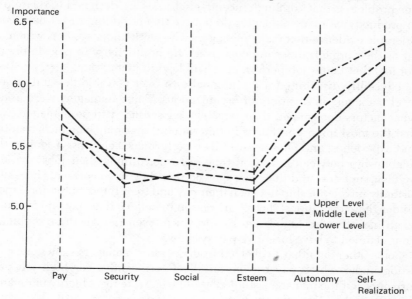

are not, in themselves, an important determinant of pace of work, application to work, or output."[6] That this view is being more widely accepted by managers in industry is reflected in the decline of the use of incentive systems at the worker level. In 1935, 75 percent of a sample of companies replied that they used wage incentive programs. By 1939 the number had fallen to 52 percent and by 1958 to 27 percent. The fact that managers have tended to stop using incentive plans for their workers points up the general disillusionment with the effectiveness of pay as an incentive among managers. This disillusionment is also reflected in my study which showed that 55 per cent of the managers sampled felt that pay is not a very effective incentive at the management level.

MANAGERS' PAY

What experiences have these managers had that might cause them to be disillusioned? I believe that one cause of the disillusionment is in the misunderstanding of how pay functions as a motivator. In current practice, the logic is that if pay is tied to productivity, then productivity should increase. This logic seems to be supported by the law of effect which states

---

[6] Wilfred Brown, *Piecework Abandoned* (London: Heineman & Co., Ltd., 1962), p. 15.

that behavior (productivity in our case) which is seen as leading to a reward (pay) will tend to be repeated.[7] However, recent research shows that one problem is that, although incentive schemes are designed to relate pay to productivity, many managers do not see them as doing this. I have considerable evidence that many managers who work under systems which, as far as their organizations are concerned, tie productivity to pay simply do not feel that better job performance will lead to higher pay.

I recently distributed a questionnaire to over 600 middle- and lower-level managers in a variety of organizations. These managers were asked what factors determined their pay. The consensus of these managers was that the most important factor in determining their pay was their training and experience, and not how well they performed their jobs. A look at the relationship between how well they were performing their jobs as rated by their superiors and their pay showed that they were correct. There was virtually no relationship between their pay and their rated job performance. Under these conditions, there is no reason to believe that pay will function as an incentive for higher job performance, even though these organizations claimed to have incentive pay systems.

Some other data that I collected from the same managers shows one condition under which pay can be an effective incentive for high job performance. Of the managers studied, those who were most highly motivated to perform their jobs effectively were characterized by two attitudes:

They said that their pay was important to them.
They felt that good job performance would lead to higher pay for them.

To return to the law of effect, for these highly motivated managers, pay was a significant reward and they saw this reward as contingent upon their job performance. Thus, it would seem that one of the major limits on the effectiveness of pay as an incentive is the ability of management to design compensation programs that create the perception that pay is based upon performance.

It is not enough to have a pay plan that is called an incentive system. Not only the people who design the plan but the people who are subject to the plan must feel that it is an incentive plan. At the management level, one step in the direction of tying pay more closely to performance might be the elimination of some of the stock option and other deferred payment plans that exist now. Many of these pay plans are so designed that they

---

[7] There is evidence that the law of effect can work where a clearly perceived relationship between the behavior and the reward does not exist. However, the important point is that rewards are maximally effective when they are seen as being clearly tied to the behavior that they are intended to reward. (See, e.g., John A. McGeoch and Arthur L. Irion, *The Psychology of Human Learning* [New York: Longmans, Green & Co., 1952].)

destroy rather than encourage the perception that pay is based upon performance. They pay off years after the behavior that is supposed to be rewarded has taken place, and in many cases the size of the reward that is given is independent of the quality of the manager's job performance.

There are two other factors which suggest that cash payments may be particularly appropriate at this time. A recent study found that managers preferred cash payments to other forms of compensation.[8] Further, the new tax laws now make it possible to get almost as much money into the hands of the manager through salary as through stock option plans and other forms of deferred compensation.

In addition to failing to create the perception that pay is based upon performance, there are two other reasons why incentive plans may fail. Many pay plans fail to recognize the importance of other needs to individuals, and, as a result, plans are set up in such a way that earning more money must necessarily be done at the cost of satisfying other needs. This situation frequently occurs when managers are paid solely on the basis of the performance of their subordinate groups. Conflicts appear between their desire for more production in their own groups, no matter what the organizational costs, and their desire to cooperate with other managers in order to make the total organization more successful.

A second reason why incentive plans fail is that they are frequently introduced as a substitute for good leadership practices and trust between employees and the organization. As one manager so aptly put this fallacious view: "If you have poor managers you have to use wage incentives." Wage incentives must be a supplement to, and not a substitute for, good management practices.

The results of Herzberg's study of motivation have been frequently cited as evidence that pay cannot be an effective motivator of good job performance.[9] According to this view, pay operates only as a maintenance factor and, as such, has no power to motivate job performance beyond some neutral point. However, this interpretation is not in accord with the results of the study. The study, in fact, found that pay may or may not be a motivator, depending upon how it is administered. A careful reading of Herzberg shows that where pay was geared to achievement and seen as a form of recognition by the managers, it was a potent motivator of good job performance. It was only where organizations had abandoned pay as an incentive and where organizations were unsuccessful in fairly relating pay and performance that pay ceased to be a motivator and became a maintenance factor.

---

[8] Thomas A. Mahoney, "Compensation Preferences of Managers," *Industrial Relations*, III (May 1964), 135–44.

[9] Frederick Herzberg, Bernard Mausner, and Barbara Bloch Snyderman, *The Motivation to Work* (New York: John Wiley & Sons, 1959).

INCENTIVE FOR PERFORMANCE

In summary, I think the significant question about pay as an incentive is not whether it is effective or ineffective, but under what conditions is it an effective incentive. It appears that pay can be an effective incentive for good job performance under certain conditions:

When pay is seen by individuals as being tied to effective job performance in such a way that it becomes a reward or form of recognition for effective job performance.

When other needs are also satisfied by effective job performance.

The statement is frequently made that, no matter how much money an individual earns, he will want more. And indeed, as was pointed out earlier, the evidence does indicate that pay remains important, regardless of how much money an individual earns. But the assumption, accepted by 54 percent of the managers in my study, that managers are likely to be dissatisfied with their pay even if they are highly paid does not follow from this point. There is an important difference between how much pay an individual wants to earn and the amount he feels represents a fair salary for the job he is doing. Individuals evaluate their pay in terms of the balance between what they put into their jobs (effort, skill, education, etc.) and what they receive in return (money, status, etc.).[10]

Dissatisfaction with pay occurs when an individual feels that what he puts into his job exceeds what he receives in the form of pay for doing his job. Individuals evaluate the fairness of their inputs relative to their outcomes on the basis of the inputs and outcomes of other employees, usually their coworkers. Managers tend to compare their pay with that of managers who are at the same management level in their own and in other organizations. Thus, dissatisfaction with pay is likely to occur when an individual's pay is lower than the pay of someone whom he considers similar to himself in ability, job level, and job performance. But when an individual receives an amount of pay that compares favorably with the pay received by others who, he feels, have comparable inputs, he will be satisfied with his pay.

However, because an individual feels his pay is fair, it does not mean that an opportunity to make more money through a promotion or other change in inputs would be turned down, nor does it mean that more money is not desired. It simply means that at the moment the balance between inputs and outcomes is seen as equitable.

The results of a recent study of over 1,900 managers illustrates the point that managers can be, and in fact frequently are, satisfied with their pay.[11]

---

[10] J. Stacy Adams, "Wage Inequities, Productivity and Work Quality," *Industrial Relations*, III (Oct. 1963), 9–16.

[11] Lawler and Porter, *op. cit.*

The managers were first asked to rate on a 1 (low) to 7 (high) scale how much pay they received for their jobs. They were next asked to rate, on the same scale, how much pay should be associated with their jobs. As can be seen from Figure 2, which presents the results for the presidents who

FIGURE 2

Attitudes of Corporation Presidents toward Their Pay

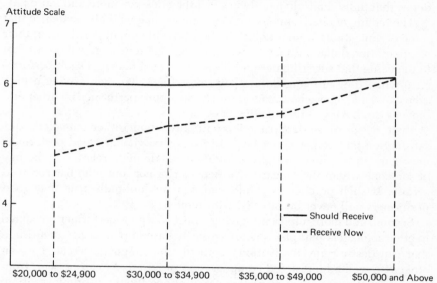

participated in the study, those executives who were paid highly, relative to other presidents, were satisfied with their pay. For this group[12] (earning $50,000 and over), there was no difference between how much pay they said they received and how much pay they thought they should receive. However, those presidents whose pay compared unfavorably with the pay of other presidents said there was a substantial difference between what their pay should be and what it was.

The same results were obtained at each level of management down to and including the foreman level. The highly paid managers at each level were quite satisfied with their pay; it was the low-paid managers at each level who were dissatisfied. In fact, highly paid foremen ($12,000 and above) were better satisfied with their pay than were company presidents who earned less than $50,000.

There is some evidence that managers can, and do, feel that they receive

---

[12] The presidents in this sample tended to come from smaller companies and, hence, the relatively low level of their compensation.

too much pay for their management positions. Of the 1,900 managers studied, about 5 percent reported that they received too much pay for their management positions. These managers apparently felt that their outcomes were too great in proportion to their inputs when compared with those of other managers. Although the number of managers who feel that their pay is too high is undoubtedly small, as indicated by the 5 percent figure obtained in this study, the fact that this feeling exists at all is evidence that individuals do not always feel they deserve more and more pay.

The feeling of overcompensation by some managers is also evidence that some organizations are not doing the best possible job of distributing their compensation dollars. It may be wise for organizations to give more weight to the value that subordinates and peers place on a manager's job performance when they are considering pay raises for a manager. Giving a high salary to a manager who is considered to be a poor performer by other employees can have several negative effects.

First, it can cause dissatisfaction with pay among other managers: dissatisfaction that comes about because managers who are good performers may come to see their own pay as suddenly inadequate relative to the pay of someone whom they regard as a poor performer, but who has received a raise. If such practices are followed, it is undoubtedly true that good performers will never be satisfied with their pay.

Second, and more important, giving a raise to a poor performer is a signal to other managers that pay is not necessarily based upon merit: an attitude that can destroy any motivational impetus that might be created by an otherwise well-administered compensation program. As can be seen from the results of my study of manager's assumptions about pay administration, perhaps the most commonly accepted axiom of good personnel practice is that information about management compensation rates should be kept secret. Many organizations go to great lengths to maintain this secrecy. Information about management pay rates is frequently kept locked in the company safe and the pay checks of top management receive special handling so that the size of the check is not known even by the personnel manager.

The reason typically given to defend the policy of keeping pay information secret is that secrecy helps to reduce dissatisfaction with regard to pay. According to this view, managers who do not know how much others earn are not likely to feel their pay compares unfavorably with that of other managers. Thus, personnel managers are never faced with a situation where Joe thinks he is better than Jack but knows that Jack is making more than he.

PAY RATES SECRET

However, such reasoning fallaciously assumes that secrecy policies eliminate pay comparisons. As was pointed out earlier, the evidence indicates that managers do evaluate their own pay in terms of what other managers earn. What is not clear is what effect the secrecy policies have on the accuracy with which managers estimate the pay of other managers and the effects of the secrecy on how satisfying and motivating these comparisons are.

In order to gather some evidence that might serve as a basis for evaluating the effects of secrecy, I recently conducted an attitude survey. Questionnaires were completed by 563 (response rate 88.7 percent) middle and lower-level managers in seven organizations. Four of the organizations were private companies engaged in a wide variety of activities ranging from rocket manufacturing to supplying gas and electricity. The other three organizations were government agencies also engaged in a variety of activities. The four private companies all had strict secrecy policies with regard to management compensation rates, while the three government agencies did make some information public about their pay rates.

A two-part questionnaire was used. The managers were first asked to estimate the average yearly salary of managers in their organizations who were at their own level, one level above them, and one level below them. The organization provided actual average salaries in order that comparisons could be made. The managers were also asked to indicate how well satisfied they were with several aspects of their organizations' compensation systems. In addition to being asked to express their satisfaction with their own pay, they were asked to indicate whether there was too much or too little difference between their own pay and that of their superiors, and between their own pay and that of their subordinates.

The results of the study clearly showed that the managers did not have an accurate picture of what other managers in their organizations earned. Apparently, the secrecy policies were effective in keeping these managers from knowing what other managers earned. However, rather than committing random errors in estimating other managers' salaries, these managers consistently tended to overestimate and to underestimate. When the managers were asked to estimate the pay of their superiors, they consistently underestimated. When they viewed the pay of their subordinates, they consistently overestimated. One-third of the managers overestimated the pay of their subordinates by more than one thousand dollars. Similarly, they also tended to overestimate the pay of managers at their own level.

Interestingly, the managers in the government organizations were consistently more accurate in estimating the pay of other managers than were the managers in the private organizations. Because the government managers had more information about the compensation programs of their organizations, it was expected that they would be more accurate. However, this finding does serve to emphasize the point that the cause of the managers' misperceptions of other managers' pay was the secrecy policies of their organizations.

The question that now remains to be answered is what effects did these distorted pictures of what other managers earn have on the managers' job satisfaction and job performance. The effects on satisfaction with pay can be seen in the managers' answers to the three questions concerned with satisfaction with pay. They stated that there was too small a difference between their own pay and that of their superiors and also too small a difference between their own pay and that of their subordinates. These attitudes are not surprising since the managers tended to see these differences as smaller than they actually are.

EFFECTS OF SECRECY

Secrecy policies are causing some of this dissatisfaction by giving the managers inaccurate pictures of what others earn. Since managers evaluate their own pay in terms of what others earn, it is not surprising that the data shows that those managers who feel their own pay is too close to that of their superiors and subordinates also feel that their own pay is too low. Undoubtedly, part of the managers' dissatisfaction with their own pay has its basis in unfavorable pay comparisons between what these managers know they make and what they think other managers make. On the basis of this evidence, it appears that *one effect of secrecy policies is to increase dissatisfaction with pay.*[13]

There is another way in which secrecy may contribute indirectly to both increased dissatisfaction with pay and lower motivation to perform a management job effectively. Secrecy allows a manager to avoid the responsibility of communicating to his subordinates his evaluation of their performance.

An example of what can and frequently does happen is that a manager who has to distribute raises capitalizes upon secrecy to avoid what he considers to be an unpleasant task. The manager does differentially distribute raises among his subordinates on the basis of their performance. So far, so good! However, when he explains the raises to his subordinates, if he does this at all, he tells all of them that he has given them as large a raise as he could and that he is satisfied with their performance. The manager may reason that he has done the right thing. "After all," he thinks, "I did reward good performance with higher pay and I didn't cause any unhappiness as I would have if I had told the poor performers how dissatisfied I was with them."

However, the differential raises have no positive effect since they do nothing to encourage the perception that pay is based upon performance. The good performer is not sure he is getting a larger raise than the poor

---

[13] Further support for this interpretation comes from the finding that there was a significant tendency for those managers who had an accurate picture of their subordinates' pay to be more satisfied with their own pay than were those managers who had an inaccurate picture of their subordinates' pay ($r = .35, p = .01$).

performer, and the poor performer may feel he is being rewarded for the type of performance he has been demonstrating. Eventually, of course, the word begins to get around about how much other people got in raises (undoubtedly slightly inflated), and this information is bound to make a number of managers unhappy with their pay, as well as distrustful of their superiors.

The secrecy policies of organizations and the consequent tendency for managers to estimate incorrectly the pay of other managers may also affect the managers' motivation to perform their jobs effectively in other ways. Several studies have shown that accurate feedback about task performance is a strong stimulus to good job performance.[14] People perform better when they receive accurate information about how well they are performing relative to some meaningful standard. For managers, pay is one of the most significant and meaningful pieces of feedback information they receive. High pay is considered a sign that the manager's job performance is good. Low pay is a signal that the manager is not performing his job well and that new behavior is needed.

The results of this study indicate that, because managers have misperceptions about what other managers earn, they are unable to evaluate correctly their own pay. Because of the tendency managers have to overestimate the pay of their subordinates and peers, the majority of the managers see their pay as low and in effect are receiving negative feedback. Moreover, although this feedback suggests that they should change their job behavior, it does not tell them what type of change they should make in their behavior. In cases where managers are not doing their jobs well, this negative feedback is undoubtedly the type of information that should be communicated; in other instances, it gives a false signal to change to those managers who are performing their jobs effectively.

REDUCED MOTIVATION?

Increased pay is one of the most significant rewards that an individual receives in return for taking on the responsibilities and work associated with higher-level management jobs and, therefore, is one of the important incentives in motivating managers to work toward obtaining higher-level jobs. However, as pointed out earlier, our data indicate that managers tend to underestimate the pay of managers at higher levels. This has the effect of making the attainment of higher-level jobs less desirable because it causes managers to underestimate the rewards that are attached to the positions. Thus, the secrecy policies of organizations may be indirectly reducing the motivation of managers to gain higher-level jobs.

If, as the evidence indicates, secrecy policies have significant costs in

---

[14] Victor H. Vroom, *Work and Motivation* (New York: John Wiley & Sons, 1964).

terms of job satisfaction, motivation for effective job performance, and motivation for promotion, does it not seem logical that organizations should alter these policies? Perhaps organizations that now have secrecy policies could give out information on pay ranges and average salaries for all management levels. If they started by giving out only partial salary information, they could better prepare their employees for full disclosure, and eventually the salaries of all members of an organization could be made available to all other members of that organization. It may well be better to provide an individual with accurate information upon which to pay comparisons than to have him make unfavorable comparisons based upon misinformation.

ROLE OF FRINGE BENEFITS

When any organization is asked to determine how much money it spends on compensation, it usually adds the money spent for salaries and fringe benefits. Similarly, an organization determines how much money an individual earns by adding his salary and the costs to them of his benefit package. Union contracts are typically spoken of as settlements involving an x cents per hour compensation package. Implicit in these measures of compensation cost is the assumption that a dollar spent on cash salary is equal to a dollar spent on life insurance or other fringe benefits. From an economic standpoint and in terms of costs to the organization, it seems reasonable that the value of a compensation package is equal to the simple sum of all its parts. It is probably the reason why 45 percent of the managers sampled endorse the view that managers are not greatly concerned with how their pay is divided among various fringe benefits.

However, I would like to suggest that dollars spent on the different parts of the compensation package may not be equal in terms of what they earn in the recipient's perception of the value of his compensation package. Several studies have shown that individuals value some compensation benefits more than others, even though the cost to the company is the same.[15] For example, one study found that employees strongly preferred receiving hospital insurance to receiving additional pension money, even though the insurance and the pension plan cost the organization the same amount. In effect, a dollar spent on compensation can have a different value to the recipient, depending upon the type of benefit the organization chooses to buy with it.

The studies on compensation preferences among both workers and managers show that the preferences of individuals for different benefits vary

---

[15] Stanley M. Nealey, "Pay and Benefit Preference," *Industrial Relations*, III (Oct. 1963), 17–28; Thomas A. Mahoney, *op. cit.*; and I. R. Andrews and Mildred M. Henry, "Management Attitudes Toward Pay," *Industrial Relations*, III (Oct. 1963), 29–39.

greatly, depending upon such factors as their age, sex, number of children, and marital status. For example, older workers value pension plans much more highly than do younger workers, and unmarried men value a shorter work week more highly than do married men. These studies suggest that, at the very least, organizations may need different benefit packages in different locations, depending upon the personal characteristics of the workers in each installation.

A further step that organizations could take would be to design different packages for groups of individuals who have similar characteristics. Indeed, it may be that the optimum solution to this problem of different compensation preferences is for organizations to adopt a "cafeteria" compensation program. A "cafeteria" compensation plan would allow every employee to divide his compensation dollars among the benefits offered by his company. This would allow each employee to select the compensation options that he values most without adding to the compensation costs of the company. Previously, such a program would have been impractical because of the high administrative costs that would be involved. However, with the advent of the computer, it is possible.

"BUFFET" BENEFITS?

"Cafeteria" wage plans would appear to have a particularly bright future among managers where union negotiations and contracts are not likely to be a hindrance. "Cafeteria" wage plans have two additional benefits that strongly argue for their use.

First, they allow employees to participate in an important decision about their jobs. Even among managers, opportunities for actual participation as contrasted with pseudo-participation are rare enough so that in every situation where participation can be legitimately and reasonably employed, it should be.

Second, "cafeteria" wage plans help to make clear to the employees just how much money is involved in their total compensation package. There are many reports of situations where employees do not even know of the fringe benefits for which their organizations are paying. With "cafeteria" wage plans, this situation would be virtually eliminated.

RESEARCH CONCLUSIONS

What are the lessons to be learned from the recent research on the psychological aspects of compensation practices? I believe that the following conclusions are warranted.

Even at the higher paid levels of management, pay is important enough to be a significant motivator of good job performance. However, it will be a motivator only when it is seen by the managers themselves to be tied to their job performance.

Managers can be, and in fact frequently are, satisfied with their pay when it compares favorably with the pay of other managers holding similar positions.

Secrecy policies have significant hidden costs attached to them. The evidence indicates that secrecy may lead to lower satisfaction with pay and to a decreased motivation for promotion.

In order to get the maximum value for money spent on compensation, organizations may have to institute "cafeteria" wage payment systems. Such a system would allow each manager to select the benefits that have the greatest value to him.

WHAT THE FUTURE HOLDS

Will organizations be willing to innovate in the area of salary administration and to implement such programs as "cafeteria" wage plans and openness about salary levels? This question can finally be answered only five or ten years from now when we will know what the wage program of the future looks like. However, there are at least two reasons for believing that organizations will be slow to consider these new programs.

First, as one critic has put it, most organizations seem intent on keeping their compensation programs up with, but never ahead of, the Joneses in a sort of "me too" behavior.[16] It is unfortunate that many organizations got so badly "burned" when they tried to install incentive wage schemes that ignored needs other than that of money. Undoubtedly, this experience has led to the current air of conservatism that exists where innovation with regard to salary administration is concerned.

Second, since none of the implications for practice that have been drawn from the results of this group of studies offers a miraculous cure for the present ills of any organizations' compensation program, slow movement may be desirable. These studies imply that there may be better ways to do things, but they also imply that there may be costs and risks involved in trying these new policies.

For example, the idea of eliminating secrecy, no matter how well handled, will probably cause problems for some employees. In particular, openness will be difficult for the relatively low-paid managers to handle. But I believe that the gains would outweigh the costs and that there would be an over-all gain in motivation as a result of openness with regard to pay. I am led to this belief because, by making pay information public, pay can become an effective satisfier of such needs as esteem and recognition and

---

[16] Marvin D. Dunnette and Bernard M. Bass, "Behavioral Scientists and Personnel Management," *Industrial Relations*, III (May 1963), 115–30.

thereby become optimally effective as a stimulant of effective performance. The same general point is true about "cafeteria" wage plans or tying pay more clearly to performance. There are certain costs that are associated with this type of innovative behavior, but there are also large potential gains possible where the practices are successfully installed.

I have found that the top management of organizations is always questioning and testing the value of their present compensation systems, and I hope that the ideas and research results presented here will be of aid in this process of inquiry and self-correction.

18

A New Role for the Work Group

MAXINE BUCKLOW

This article discusses the role assigned to the work group to bring about desired changes in employee motivation, and suggests that the role proposed by the Tavistock Institute of Human Relations in London has been more successful than earlier approaches which derived largely from the Hawthorne studies.[1] The Hawthorne work directed attention to the existence of small informal face-to-face groups within larger work groups. Members of the informal groups shared in a variety of activities and beliefs common to the group, which were a source of satisfaction, strength, and security, and provided a buffer against the demands of the larger world of department and factory. Elton Mayo extrapolated from these studies to a general social theory centered on the assumption of a basic human need to be gregarious. His influence was largely responsible for the widely held belief that employees were motivated by membership in small primary groups.[2]

Source: Reprinted by permission of publisher and author. From *Administrative Science Quarterly,* Vol 11 (1966), pp. 59–78.

[1] F. J. Roethlisberger and W. J. Dickson, *Management and the Worker* (Cambridge, Mass.: Harvard, 1949).

[2] Elton Mayo, *The Human Problems of an Industrial Civilization* (New York: Macmillan, 1933); *The Social Problems of an Industrial Civilization* (Cambridge, Mass.: 1946); and *The Political Problems of an Industrial Civilization* (Cambridge, Mass.: Harvard, 1947).

THE INFLUENCE OF LEWIN

This interest in small groups was greatly reinforced in the immediate postwar years by the research associated with Kurt Lewin. He defined the group as a dynamic system of interaction between at least two people, and group life as involving a continuous process of adaptation of individuals to one another and to their mutual needs and problems. In this process a structure emerged, which became more stable and organized as the group continued to function. Lewin initiated an era of rigorous laboratory studies into the dynamics of group functioning, designed to reveal fundamental laws of group life. Although much was learned about communication networks, leadership, group cohesion, norms, and so on, empirical results were often conflicting and progress toward basic laws disappointing.

Participation in Group Decision Making

Lewin's influence on industrial practice came largely from the three field studies he directed with children's play groups, housewives, and young-girl pajama machinists at the Harwood Manufacturing Company. The results suggested that involvement in group decision and democratic methods of leadership increased output and member satisfaction. This evidence gave rise to a long period of uncritical adherence to participation and democratic management as means of increasing employee motivation.[3]

In industry, research did not reproduce results as marked as those of the original Lewin studies, and in general, democratic practices were more successful in achieving satisfaction than efficiency. Research workers such as Maier, Likert, and McGregor realized that their techniques had to be linked to the organizational framework. Likert used overlapping group families and linking-pin functions to tie his participation groups to all levels of the organization.[4] Similarly, Maier's new look at organization envisaged participation in problem-solving conferences at all levels, through overlapping membership.[5] Katz and Argyris criticized these proposals because they only softened organizational impact, and made no basic change in the distribution of rewards, and of power and authority. It would also be difficult for the rank and file worker to take part in such proposals.[6]

---

[3] K. Lewin, *Resolving Social Conflict* (New York: Harper, 1948); and K. Lewin, R. Lippitt, and R. K. White, "Patterns of Aggressive Behavior in Experimentally Created Social Climates," *Journal of Social Psychology*, 10 (1939), 271–99.

[4] R. Likert, *New Patterns of Management* (New York: McGraw-Hill, 1961).

[5] N. R. F. Maier and J. J. Hayes, *Creative Management* (New York: John Wiley, 1962).

[6] D. Katz, "The Motivational Basis of Organizational Behavior," *Behavioral Science*, (1964), 131–46; and C. Argyris, *Integrating the Individual and the Organization* (New York: John Wiley, 1964).

The results achieved at Harwood were consistently interpreted in terms of the motivating power of involvement in group decision making, irrespective of the kind of decision or the extent of participation. Maier saw unanimous group decision as the critical motivating device. He considered the type of problems involved as unimportant, and restricted decisions largely to human relations problems.[7] He has more recently been concerned to demonstrate that the quality of decisions need not be lowered by the use of group methods.[8] Likert saw the central role of the face-to-face work group almost through Mayo's eyes. The group motivated members through their need for approval and support and maintained a sense of personal worth. For Likert an important device in building effective groups of this kind was group participation in a limited area of decisions, although decisions did not have to be unanimous. This approach of Likert's is widely held by managers and researchers at the present time.[9]

There has been persistent criticism of the original Lewin studies. Neal Miller and Edith Bennett both criticized the uncontrolled variables in the experiment with housewives. Lawrence and Smith, in an experiment similar to that at the Harwood Company, found involvement in goal setting to be a necessary condition for an increase in output.[10] Argyris criticized the use of decisions of only peripheral interest to workers, and suggested that the experimental conditions created at Harwood by Coch and French were atypical. Normal factory routine had been temporarily set aside and replaced by one in which the employees had vastly increased responsibility for and control over their jobs and work environment.[11] Changes of this kind were omitted in most attempts to reproduce the Harwood results. In French's replication in a Norwegian factory, the original total participation conditions could not be obtained, and problems of only intermediate importance to the workers were used. This limited participation led to improvements in satisfactions and labor-management relations but not in production, and interviews showed that the output had been restricted to standards felt to be safe from rate-cutting.[12]

Gomberg attacked the general human relations movement for its neglect

---

[7] N. R. F. Maier, *Principles of Human Relations* (New York: John Wiley, 1952).

[8] N. R. F. Maier, *Problem-Solving Discussions and Conferences* (New York: McGraw-Hill, 1963).

[9] R. Likert, *op. cit.*

[10] N. Miller, "Learnable Drives and Rewards," in S. S. Stevens (ed.), *Handbook of Experimental Psychology* (New York: Wiley, 1951); E. B. Bennett, "Discussion, Decision, Commitment and Consensus in Group Decision," *Human Relations*, 8 (1955), 251–74; and L. C. Lawrence and P. C. Smith, "Group Decision and Employee Participation," *Journal of Applied Psychology*, 39 (1955), 334–37.

[11] C. Argyris, *Personality and Organization* (New York: Harper, 1957).

[12] J. R. French, J. Israel, and D. As, "An Experiment in Participation in a Norwegian Factory," *Human Relations*, 13 (1960), 3–19.

of trade unions and conflict, since their techniques did not change the basic power relationships, nor challenge management's right to control.[13]

Involvement in T-Groups

Lewin's second major influence was in the development of the training laboratory by those working at the National Training Laboratory at Bethel from 1947 onwards. New psychological knowledge about groups was used to facilitate group and individual learning, largely through the development of the T-group. In the beginning participants came from all kinds of backgrounds, including business and industry. More recently, Bethel and the universities in which laboratories have been set up, such as Texas, California, and Boston, provided training for executive groups and special programs for individual firms. The assumption was that increased self-knowledge and capacity to understand group interrelationships would carry over from the laboratory to the work situation and would be reflected in changed behavior there, but empirical evidence for this was difficult to find. Dubin criticized T-group supporters for overestimating the contribution made by interpersonal relations to organizational effectiveness, which he considered to be largely determined by technology.[14]

Bennis pointed to the shift in emphasis from personal change to organizational development among those anxious to demonstrate impact by the laboratory.[15] In 1957 and 1958, a new training program for staff and action leaders was conducted at Bethel, and special programs were developed and used in firms. The most important was that conducted by the Employee Relations Department of the Esso Company under the leadership of R. R. Blake, J. S. Mouton, and H. A. Shepard from the Southwest Human Relations Laboratory of the University of Texas.[16]

Their long-term program was directed at changing individual cognitive maps through the instrumented T-group, which involved virtual self-

---

[13] W. Gomberg, "The Use of Psychology in Industry: A Trade Union Point of View," *Management Science*, 3 (1956–57), 348–70.

[14] L. P. Bradford, J. R. Gibb, and K. P. Benne, *T-Group Theory and the Laboratory Method* (New York: John Wiley, 1964): C. Argyris, *Interpersonal Competence and Organizational Effectiveness* (Homewood, Ill.: Dorsey, 1962): R. Tannenbaum, I. R. Wechsler, and P. Massarik, *Leadership and Organization* (New York: McGraw-Hill, 1961); and R. Dubin, "Psyche, Sensitivity and Social Structure," in Tannenbaum, *et al.*, *op. cit.*

[15] W. G. Bennis, "A New Role for the Behavioral Sciences: Effecting Organizational Change," *Administrative Science Quarterly*, 8 (1963), 125–65.

[16] R. R. Blake and J. S. Mouton, "The Developing Revolution in Management Practices," *American Society of Training Directors' Journal*, 16 (1962), 29–52; also *Group Dynamics—Key to Decision Making* (Houston: Gulf Publishing, 1961); and H. R. Shepard and R. R. Blake, "Changing Behavior Through Cognitive Maps," *Human Organization*, 21 (1962), 88–96.

direction by participants. This modification was intended to strengthen motivation to transfer learning from the laboratory. For this reason the program was also tied to the organization through the use in laboratories of members from diagonal slices of levels and horizontal units, and superior-subordinate pairs. Special problem-solving groups were also set up within the organization to diagnose needs, clarify goals, and plan for organizational change.

Shepard's evaluation showed that this long-term program had no greater impact than the typical short laboratory. Personal change was widespread through many levels and groups, but this had little impact on organizational practices.[17] As Blake and his associates were more concerned with organizational than individual development, their latest program excluded the T-group and used a more structured seminar approach. This was built around the managerial grid, a device to help participants assess their managerial styles and attitudes, using concepts from Blake's integrated theory of management. The program was tied to the organization through problem-solving groups, which used simulated organizational problems and later real problems of increasingly more critical and long-term significance. An evaluation within a firm showed that managers could learn these new styles and apply them with some effectiveness for the organization.[18]

The evidence suggests that the use of T-group training in industry leads to increased self-knowledge, but that other approaches are needed if organizational development is desired. Blake's ambitious program concentrated on changing managerial behavior and tying the learning process to the organization by considering organizational needs and problems. He failed to consider the limitations imposed by technology and organization structure, and to see that basic changes in these might be necessary.

Argyris has been the only T-group exponent to understand these limitations and to suggest ways to overcome them. He recommends that laboratory training should be used only with management groups, as behavior at the top is considerably influenced by skill in interpersonal relationships. Behavior at lower levels determined largely by technology and control systems, and can be changed only by new thinking about job design, controls, and the authority system.[19]

---

[17] H. A. Shepard, "An Action Research Model," in *An Action Research Program for Organization Improvement* (Ann Arbor, Mich.: Foundation for Research on Human Behavior, 1960).

[18] R. R. Blake, J. S. Mouton, L. R. Barnes, and L. E. Greiner, "Breakthrough in Organization Development," *Harvard Business Review*, 42 (1964), 133–55; and R. R. Blake and J. S. Mouton, *The Managerial Grid* (Houston: Gulf Publishing Co., 1964).

[19] C. Argyris, *Integrating the Individual and the Organization, op. cit.*

THE CONCEPT OF GROUP AUTONOMY

It is difficult to accept the concept of the motivating power of the primary work group in the face of research results. Herbert Thelen in 1954 drew attention to the limitations imposed by technology on the use of T-groups, and suggested the development of small, autonomous work groups. This would involve responsibility for the organization of work, goal setting, and training.[20] This proposal was neglected by the T-group adherents, but taken up by Argyris in *Personality and Organization* in 1957. At the time there were few studies on such groups. George Strauss reported a study in which a group of girls in a paint room was given control over the speed of the conveyor, which resulted in marked increases in output and satisfaction. More recently Non-Linear Systems Inc. in California, carried the implementation of McGregor's Theory Y down to the level of the rank-and-file worker. The assembly line was abolished and workers reorganized into small, self-paced groups of seven members responsible for building complete instruments. The result was an increase of 30 percent in productivity. Motivation was believed to come partly from gregariousness, but largely from the opportunity to use skills, learn and teach, and to take responsibility.[21]

In 1954, Katz cautioned against "the glorification of the primary group as a source of work satisfaction," and suggested the importance of group autonomy. This led to the well-known study by Morse and Reimer in which autonomous groups were compared with hierarchically controlled ones.[22] The autonomy of these groups however, was, largely restricted to decisions about work assignments, length of recess, lunch periods, and so on. It was in no way comparable to the self-direction envisaged by Thelen and Argyris. Workers tried to expand the scope of their decisions, but management refused to delegate more authority, and "the curve of worker decisions soon reached a peak and began to decline." Morse and Reimer concluded that "the granting of 'safe' areas of decision making and the withholding of 'hot' ones is not likely to work for long."[23]

---

[20] Herbert Thelen, *The Dynamics of Groups at Work* (Chicago: University of Chicago, 1954).

[21] G. Strauss, "An Experiment in Worker Control over Pacing," in W. F. Whyte, *Money and Motivation* (New York: Harper, 1955): and A. H. Kuriloff, "An Experiment in Management—Putting Theory Y to the Test," *Personnel*, 40 (1963), 8–17.

[22] D. Katz, "Satisfactions and Deprivations in Industrial Life," in A. Kornhauser, R. Dubin, and A. Ross (eds.), *Industrial Conflict* (New York: McGraw-Hill, 1954), chap. vi; N. Morse and E. Reimer, "Experimental Change of a Major Organizational Variable," *Journal of Abnormal and Social Psychology*, 52 (1956), 120–29.

[23] H. L. Wilensky, "Human Relations in the Work Place: An Appraisal of Some Recent Research," in C. M. Arensberg, *et al.* (eds.), *Research in Industrial Human Relations* (New York: Harper, 1957), p. 42; and Morse and Reimer, *op. cit.*, p. 219.

Disappointment with small groups and employee participation focused attention on the concepts of power and control and on power equalization.[24] Michigan studies of organizational control structures suggested that there was no basis for management's fears that the granting of more control to groups at the bottom would lessen their own authority. Organizational efficiency was found to be related to increased control at all levels, and control was not considered undesirable by low-level workers, when it was a source of involvement for them.[25] Research into communication networks by Guetzkow and Simon, by Trow, and by Mulder has made it doubtful that group performance is related to the degree of centrality in networks, but decision centrality, freedom to exert power, responsibility for the completion of one's task and position autonomy have been found important.[26]

Research at I.B.M. has shown that engineer control of work standards from outside the department was not thought to be legitimate by employees, and correlated negatively with output and satisfactions.[27] Leavitt points out that despite general agreement that power equalization is a key step in organizational change, there is no movement for its achievement at present.[28] In America the problems of the nature and degree of control to be given to employees, including the rank-and-file worker, are little understood, and recent significant English research has either been overlooked or misinterpreted by research workers.[29]

---

[24] George Strauss, "Some Notes on Power Equalization," in H. J. Leavitt (ed.), *The Social Science of Organizations* (Englewood Cliffs, N.J.: Prentice-Hall, 1963); H. J. Leavitt, "Applied Organizational Change in Industry: Structural, Technical, and Human Approaches," in W. W. Cooper, *et al.* (eds.), *New Perspectives in Organizational Research* (New York: John Wiley, 1964); H. J. Leavitt and B. M. Bass. "Organizational Psychology," in P. R. Farnsworth, O. McNemar and Q. McNemar (eds.), *Annual Review of Psychology*, Vol 15 (1964) (Palo Alto, Calif., 1964); and B. M. Bass, *Organizational Psychology* (Pittsburgh: Allyn & Bacon, 1965).

[25] C. G. Smith and A. S. Tannenbaum, "Organizational Control Structure: A Comparative Analysis," *Human Relations*, 16 (1963), 299–317; and A. S. Tannenbaum, "Control in Organization, Individual Adjustment, and Organizational Performance," *Administrative Science Quarterly*, 7(1962), 236–57.

[26] H. Guetzkow and H. A. Simon, "The Impact of Certain Communication Nets upon Organization and Performance in Task-oriented Groups," *Management Science*, 1 (1955), 233–50; D. B. Trow, "Autonomy and Job Satisfaction in Task-oriented Groups," *Journal of Abnormal and Social Psychology*, 54(1954), 204–9; and M. Mulder, "Power and Satisfaction in Task-oriented Groups," *ACTA Psychologica*, 16 (1959), 178–225.

[27] D. Sirota, "A Study of Work Measurement," and S. M. Klein, "Two Systems of Management," both in *Proceedings of the Sixteenth Annual Meeting of the Industrial Relations Research Association* (Madison: Publication No. 32, Industrial Relations Research Association, 1963).

[28] H. J. Leavitt, "Applied Organizational Change," in W. W. Cooper, *et al.*, (eds.), *op. cit.*

[29] B. M. Bass, *op. cit.*

THE INFLUENCE OF BION

W. R. Bion, a psychoanalyst of the Melanie Klein School at the Tavistock Clinic in London, used his wartime experiences with group selection methods and small therapy groups to make an important reformulation of psychoanalytic concepts to explain group as well as individual behavior.[30] He thought that the emotional life of the group could best be understood by the use of psychotic mechanisms, particularly regression. He proposed the concept of work as necessary to keep the group related to reality and to the external environment, in much the same way as the ego functioned to maintain personality and its links with reality.

He assumed a basic capacity for cooperation within the group to achieve its task. He further assumed that the group functioned always at two levels, at the conscious level toward its work task and at the unconscious level toward satisfaction of powerful emotional drives. Bion believed that the group acted as if it had certain basic assumptions about its aims. He termed these assumptions: dependence, fight-flight, and pairing, and felt that they would hinder task achievement. These were the source of emotional drives toward aims far different from the tasks of the group, deriving from a very primitive level and having the characteristics of defensive reactions to psychotic anxiety.

Use of Small Interpretive Groups

Bion had two major influences on the work of the Tavistock Institute of Human Relations in their role of independent consultants in industry. They assumed that the consultant's task was to work with the appropriate small groups within the organization, so that members became aware of the hidden emotional life which hindered the group's work task. This type of group discussion to facilitate change was first used extensively at the Glacier Metal Co. from 1948 onwards. The research team was headed by Elliott Jaques, and included Eric Trist and A. K. Rice.[31] They showed how unconscious mechanisms operated to prevent the effective functioning of the group, and how social institutions were used by members to reinforce individual mechanisms of defense against anxiety, particularly against the recurrence of early paranoid and depressive anxieties first described by Klein.[32]

---

[30] W. R. Bion, *Experiences in Groups and Other Papers* (London: Tavistock, 1961); also "Group Dynamics: A Review," in M. Klein, P. Heimann, and R. E. Money-Kyrle (eds.), *New Directions in Psycho-Analysis* (London: Tavistock, 1955).

[31] Elliott Jaques, *The Changing Culture of a Factory* (London: Tavistock, 1951).

[32] Elliott Jaques, "Social Systems as a Defense against Persecutory and Depressive Anxiety," in Klein, Heimann, and Money-Kyrle (eds.), *op. cit.*

Research was carried out as a collaborative venture between consultant and client firm. Many of the problems for which assistance was sought arose from difficulties with the system of worker-management consultation. This led to extensive use of small groups to work through the problems and to systematic rethinking and reformulation of the functions of worker-management consultation. As a result, according to agreed-upon policy, regular consultative machinery was set up, and employees were involved in a considerable degree of consultation and in making contributions to company policy. The reorganization had also been aimed at the "split at the bottom of the executive chain," the apparently unbridgeable gap between first-line supervisor and rank-and-file discussion between individual and consultant, in which the individual could think aloud and the consultant interpret and feed back.[34]

Autonomous Work Groups

Although interpretive groups did not facilitate change at the level of the rank-and-file worker, Bion's second influence was more successful. In their early studies in coal mining, the Tavistock workers used his assumptions as a guide to the nature of the work group. These related to size, whole task, a basic capacity for cooperation to achieve the primary task, and satisfactions deriving from its effective accomplishments. Their first comparison of the earliest hand methods with those of the conventional longwall production system focused attention on the responsible autonomy of the multi-skilled individual miner, and on the organization of the small, underground work group. Responsibility for the work and for supervision rested with the men themselves, requiring a high level of interdependence between members, rotation of roles and tasks, and sharing in a common paynote. This work organization was productive and did not place undue stress on the men and suggested that industrial production systems were essentially socio-technical systems, in which the social and technical aspects could be causes of stress.[35]

Rice developed the first detailed formulation of the Tavistock's view of the work group in his research in an Indian textile mill.[36] He began with more detailed assumptions about the way in which groups should be organized as to size, skills, status, roles, member control of tasks, opportunity to complete a whole task, and the location of tasks within definite physical boundaries. These were used to develop a theoretical work group organi-

---

[34] Elliott Jaques, "Social Analysis and the Glacier Project," *Human Relations,* 17 (1964), 361–76.

[35] E. L. Trist and K. W. Bamforth, "Some Social and Psychological Consequences of the Longwall Method of Coal Getting," *Human Relations,* 4 (1951), 3–38.

[36] A. K. Rice, *Productivity and Social Organization: The Ahmedabad Experiment* (London: Tavistock, 1958).

zation for an experimental reorganization of the automatic weaving department, in which there had been problems of output and damage following the introduction of automatic looms.

The workers' acceptance of the idea of internally led small groups and their determination to make the new system work, were felt to be some indication of its goodness of fit. After many difficulties and setbacks, quality and quantity were established at higher levels than before the reorganization, so that Rice felt that his assumptions about task organization had some validity. Similar reorganization into small internally structured groups was later introduced into a nonautomatic shed with similar results. Recent evidence from India indicated that the increase in efficiency and decrease in damage had been maintained in both sheds, and that the group system had been extended.[37]

Autonomous Groups in Coal Mining

Rice's Indian study was limited by subjectivity and language difficulties. These were not problems, however, in the Tavistock's rigorous research into problems arising from mechanization in the British coal industry, a study undertaken at the request of the National Coal Board. Comparative studies were made of different stages of technological development, from the early hand methods through the longwall, to more advanced mechanization. The introduction of the longwall had replaced the many different short coal faces throughout the seam with a continuous longwall of coal up to 200 yards long. In its early stage there were no machines and the face was still worked by pairs of men. Later, however, a moving mechanical conveyor belt was introduced to take the coal away from the face. This transformed the whole underground operation. The belt moved along the whole face, so that it had to be treated as a single unit requiring 40 to 50 men.

The operation underground was now rather like a small factory, and managers and engineers drew on factory practice to organize the production of coal under these conditions. The whole coal-getting cycle was broken down into a standard series of operations, each requiring a minimum of skill, and the cycle was finished every 24 hours instead of each shift as before. Men were no longer multiskilled but spent their lives in one job and on one shift. Instead of one rate of payment, there were now five different ones, which brought new differences in pay and status among the men. To keep the cycle running smoothly, close cooperation was needed between the various categories of workers and between the shifts. Responsibility for this now rested with management, not with the men. The men did little to help, so great strains were placed on the managers.

---

[37] A. K. Rice, *The Enterprise and Its Environment* (London: Tavistock, 1963).

There were many problems in this production system. Coal output was below standard and shifts rarely finished their part of the cycle, as the men tended to do only those tasks for which they were paid. Absence rates were high and men were leaving the industry. There was friction between the shifts and many miners were suffering from neurotic illnesses. The research team believed that the factory type of work organization was not well suited to the demands of the longwall situation, judged either by output or by the men's reactions. It went against all the long-standing traditions of British coal mining by eliminating the complete self-supervising miner, taking responsibility for the allocation, coordination, and supervision of the cycle away from the work team, and destroying the small interdependent group.

The research team devised a new composite work organization for the longwall. This was based on their theoretical assumptions, and on changes already introduced by miners dissatsified with the conventional longwall. In the composite organization, a small group of men shared a common paynote and carried out all the production operations in each shift. It was successfully tried out in short faces where 6 to 8 men were responsible for the planning of the total cycle in one shift. There was, however, some doubt that the composite would work with much larger coal faces where 40 to 50 men would be needed to produce coal.

In a face where the conventional system was in use, management, miners, and the union agreed to try the new system. Forty men worked out a new shift pattern, reorganized production operations, and agreed to share equally in a paynote. The men also accepted responsibility for a wider range of jobs, and jobs were rotated. Responsibility for the whole cycle rested largely with the men, and management provided supporting services rather than direct supervision.

A careful comparison was made over one year of a conventional and a composite work organization under very similar underground conditions. The composite work organization rated better in measures of output, turnover, absence, accidents, and stress illnesses. This was important confirmation that the composite, which relied on the characteristics of traditional methods, was a more satisfactory form of work organization. Its strength lay in altering the basis of the task and shift systems, so that miners were again multiskilled, and had responsibility for the cycle. It was later found that with still higher levels of mechanization, the work organization that best fitted the new technology again had much in common with the earlier unmechanized system.

A NEW ROLE FOR THE WORK GROUP

In the most recent reporting of their work, Trist and his colleagues have reformulated their theoretical position.[38] The concept that integrates the

---

[38] E. L. Trist, G. W. Higgin, H. Murray, and A. B. Pollock, *Organizational Choice* (London: Tavistock, 1963).

technological, economic, and socio-psychological aspects of a production system is the primary task: the work it has to perform. Work is the key transaction which relates an operating group to its environment and allows it to maintain a steady state. The concept of organizational choices is introduced so as to direct attention to the existence of a range of possible production systems. The task of management is to choose that which best fits the technical and the human requirements.

Major theoretical importance is now given to the concept of responsible autonomy. The organization of small autonomous work groups has been demonstrated in mining and textile situations. Success with composite longwall groups of forty men would widen the practical implications of the concept.

Responsible autonomy is seen as crucial for the satisfactory design of production systems. It gives the work group a central role in the production system, not the peripheral supporting role envisaged by Mayo and Likert, and has successfully motivated rank-and-file workers to greater cooperative effort than other methods. It also makes more basic changes in the distribution of control and power, by transferring some of the traditional authority of management for the control and coordination of jobs, i.e., the part appropriate to the primary group's task, to the men who actually perform the task. Trist criticizes the proposals of McGregor and Likert to achieve these ends, for failing to understand the difficulties involved, particularly the initial anxiety at relaxing traditional management controls over the primary group.

This real transferring of power and control to the group for the operation of the primary task has other advantages. The coal study supports other evidence that increasing control at lower levels does not decrease control at higher levels nor adversely affect efficiency. As Trist suggests, it exerts an upwards pressure in the managing system which affects all roles, so that all levels have more, rather than less, opportunity to carry out their managerial roles in a broader way. Trist now believes that the transfer of some control to autonomous work groups is the only means of overcoming the split at the bottom of the executive system at Glacier Metal Co.

Emery has recently reassessed the Tavistock work at Glacier, and criticizes the early concern with the working through of problems and with the formal aspects of industrial democracy, without making any basic change in the role of the rank-and-file worker. He now sees the development or autonomous work groups as "the democratisation of the work place" and suggests that industrial democracy, while making decisions more democratic, has not altered the content of a worker's relation to his job.[39]

Herbst who made the first detailed day-to-day study of the interactions

---

[39] F. E. Emery, "Technology and Social Organization," *Scientific Business,* 1 (1963), 132–36.

of a composite group of miners, criticized the Morse and Reimer study for changing only the locus of decision making and not the activities about which decisions were made. He suggested that joint participation in the task may be a necessary prerequisite for joint decision making to be maintained.[40]

It has been argued that the Tavistock concept of the autonomous work group goes far towards solving some of the problems of worker motivation, participation, and power equalization, with which American researchers are preoccupied. The Tavistock concept also provides a new role for the work group different from that advocated by Mayo, Lewin, and Likert. The reorganized groups at Non-Linear Systems, which were virtually autonomous, give further support to the Tavistock concept. King's reorganizations and retraining of women in a Norwegian clothing factory can also be cited as supporting evidence. They were given responsibility for control over their work and work organization, and the result was an increase in output and satisfaction and a broadening of the functions of the unit manager.[41]

IMPLICATIONS

The success of autonomous work groups where other group techniques have failed highlights the failure of research workers and managers to make basic changes in organizational structure, and in the nature and the organization of work. This failure has its roots in unquestioned acceptance of the methods and assumptions of scientific management and the traditional management theorists.

Louis Davis's survey of management practices and assumptions about job design showed the strong influence of scientific management. Adverse effects of greatly reduced job content were thought to be adequately controlled by selection, training, incentives, and working conditions.[42] Miles demonstrated that long exposure to the ideas of democratic management had not changed managers' perceptions and attitudes; these were closer to those of Taylor than to McGregor's Theory Y.[43]

Taylor and the early management theorists believed that their proposals would eliminate the problems of restriction of output, lack of cooperation, apathy, and worker-management conflict.[44] The persistence of these problems over the years led to a succession of new approaches. Hu-

---

[40] P. G. Herbst, *Autonomous Group Functioning* (London: Tavistock, 1962).

[41] D. King, *Training Within the Organization* (London: Tavistock, 1964).

[42] L. E. Davis, R. R. Canter, and J. F. Hoffman, "Current Job Design Criteria," *Journal of Industrial Engineering*, 61 (1955).

[43] R. E. Miles, "Conflicting Elements in Managerial Ideologies," *Industrial Relations*, 4 (1964), 77–91.

[44] F. W. Taylor, *Scientific Management* (New York: Harper & Row, 1947).

man relations and group techniques were part of this pattern, and had only limited success.

There is very little awareness that new thinking about structure and the design of work is a necessary condition for the elimination of apathy, restriction of output, and similar problems. For this reason the Tavistock research and the transformation of Non-Linear Systems are of major significance. They both involve basic organizational changes and suggest that the motivation of rank-and-file workers can be achieved by increasing job content and giving men control of their work environment. Louis Davis has worked toward a new theory of job design which avoids the limitations of scientific management. He has successfully redesigned assembly-line jobs so that the individual carries out a whole task and is responsible for control of quality. The assumptions on which he enlarges individual jobs are similar to those of the Tavistock group.[45]

Also most proposals for joint consultation and worker participation in management do not involve any radical rethinking about organizational design and technology. In Britain, joint consultation has been dominated by concern with the organization and functions of joint committees. The evidence shows preoccupation with welfare problems and little measurable impact on output and satisfaction.[46] American experience with labor management cooperation has been very similar, showing increases in satisfaction rather than in output.[47]

The Scanlon plan is of special interest, because it has raised productivity. Although Scanlon stressed the importance of the incentive aspects of his plan, its success could well come from the role played by the production committees. These operated continuously, were easily accessible to workers, and had a minimum of red tape and machinery associated with them. They also had power to make production decisions appropriate to their level, and this gave some control over production problems. Workers also had direct access to staff men through the committees, which served to break down the traditional barriers and resentments of outside control, particularly engineer control, which has always been a source of restriction of output. Scanlon saw that the machinery for consultation and participation had to provide some control over production decisions.[48]

Milton Derber's report on Israeli industries run by the Histadrut, the trade union federation, provides an excellent example of misunderstanding

---

[45] Louis E. Davis, "Job Design and Productivity: A New Approach," *Personnel*, 33 (1957), 418–30.

[46] W. H. Scott, *Industrial Leadership and Joint Consultation* (Liverpool; Liverpool University, 1952): The National Institute of Industrial Psychology, London, *Joint Consultation in British Industry* (London: Staples Press, 1952).

[47] Ernest Dale, *Greater Productivity Through Labor-Management Co-operation* (New York: American Management Association, Research Report 14, 1949).

[48] F. Lesieur (ed.), *The Scanlon Plan* (New York: John Wiley, 1958).

about worker behavior.[49] The Histadrut expected worker-management relations to be changed by the fact of trade union ownership, by worker representation on boards, and by widespread participation of workers through joint production committees. The familiar problems of restriction of output and apathy remained, however. Labor-management relations were characterized by complaints and misunderstandings and by two-sided bargaining rather than the harmonious family relations expected.

Perceptions of Histadrut managers about industrial relations and their roles as managers were also very similar to those of other managers. Their relations with their subordinates were still based on the dependency built into the organization structure. Trade union ownership had done nothing to soften the impact of the organization.

Extensive training of foremen and workers in the plant and classroom failed to arouse interest in participation, and Histadrut plans to develop plant councils and joint management came to nothing. Derber concluded that we must not expect too much of worker participation in management, but must see that it adds a new dimension to management.

"While workers are capable of making some useful technical contributions out of their work experience, this is most likely to occur at the department or shop level (as illustrated by suggestion schemes), and least likely at the overall plant level. In other words, worker participation in management is not a useful means of tapping the same kinds of talents and ideas which are supplied by managers, but rather is a way to utilize different values and experiences. Worker representatives are most valuable playing a criticizing, modifying role rather than an initiating one."

In Yugoslavia Kolaja found lack of interest among workers in the councils' affairs. There was also resistance to time study, and worker attitudes were generally similar to those found in British and American studies.[50] Blumenthal, studying codetermination in the German steel industry, found that the labor directors who were key figures in the operation of codetermination plans, had made few changes in the procedures and practices they had inherited.[51] They accepted existing industrial organization as a fixed and unchanging framework within which to operate.

Interest in ways of training workers to partake more broadly in management functions and to overcome their resistance to involvement in management, continues in many countries. Swedish experience has been unsuccessful, and this led Eric Rhenman to suggest that an important aspect of industrial democracy for the future is to consider the possibility of giving

---

[49] Milton Derber, "Worker Participation in Israeli Management," *Industrial Relations*, 3 (1963), 51–72.

[50] J. Kolaja, *Workers' Councils, The Yugoslav Experience* (London: Tavistock, 1965).

[51] W. M. Blumenthal, *Codetermination in the German Steel Industry* (Princeton: Princeton University, 1956).

employes a constructive influence over rationalization programs. This kind of insight is rare.[52]

Considerable understanding has also been shown by Hugh Clegg in his plea for a clarification of the aims of industrial democracy. These should relate only to the protection of the rights and the interest of workers. Modern management is now far too complex for workers to share directly in it. There is, however, urgent need to devise ways of providing workers with opportunities for self government at the work level.[53]

CONCLUSION

It has been argued that the Tavistock concept of the autonomous work group has more explanatory power than those concepts deriving from traditional group-dynamic thinking. Their coal and textile studies could well supplement the classical studies of Mayo and Lewin as the mainsprings of thinking and action.

---

[52] Eric Rhenman, *Industrial Democracy and Industrial Organization* (Stockholm: P. A. Norstedt and Soners Forlag, 1964).

[53] Hugh Clegg, *A New Approach to Industrial Democracy* (Oxford: Basil Blackwell, 1960).

19

Conflict in Hospitals

ROCKWELL SCHULZ and ALTON C. JOHNSON

Evidence of conflict in hospitals is readily apparent. Nurse and nonprofessional hospital employee strikes receive wide publicity. Periodically, administrator-medical staff conflicts break into public view. Furthermore, hospital-client conflicts seem to be increasing as consumers of hospital service level charges of inefficiency and inattention to consumer expectations. Internally, the administrator is continually faced with eruptions of personal or departmental conflicts.

The first step in resolving conflict is to identify the underlying forces fostering it. This paper reviews empirical research reported in management, sociological and hospital literature for insight into some of these underlying forces. The scope of this review includes a brief consideration of hospital-client, interpersonal and individual conflicts. Conflicts related to administrators, medical staff and nursing groups are discussed in somewhat greater depth. Finally, some mitigators of conflict are suggested.

Modern management literature describes benefits that are derived from a reasonable amount of organizational and individual conflict.[1] Indeed,

Source: Reprinted with permission from the quarterly journal of the American College of Hospital Administrators, *Hospital Administration*, Vol. 16 (1971), pp. 36–50.

[1] Among them are: Amitai Etzioni, *Complex Organizations*, Holt, Rinehart & Winston, 1961, pp. 124–26; Mason Haire, *Modern Organization Theory*, Wiley, 1965; and Robert L. Kahn, *Organizational Stress*, Wiley, 1964.

confrontation is sometimes necessary in order to achieve overdue reforms. Just how serious, then, is conflict in hospitals?

One might expect conflict to affect quality of patient care adversely. This tends to be confirmed by studies of Georgopoulos and Mann, who found higher quality care in hospitals where physicians and nurses had a greater understanding of each other's work, problems and needs.[2] Studies in mental hospitals report patients are affected adversely by staff conflict.[3] While conflict might foster institutional innovation and progress, the welfare of the individual patient is served more effectively with institutional stability and harmony. Moreover, conflict can be debilitating for participants, rigidify the social system in which it occurs, and lead to gross distortions of reality.[4] Thus, this paper assumes that minimizing conflict is an important goal and it suggests sources and mitigators of conflict.

Institutional Conflict

Evidence of client-hospital conflict is increasing; however, few empirical studies have been conducted to examine this problem. Patients have very little voice in hospital matters, nor, until quite recently, have they seemed to desire one; largely we suspect, because they've assumed that professionals know what's best for them. Etzioni notes that only in public monopolies (e.g., the post office) do clients have less influence than in hospitals.[5] Apparently, he does not see current constituencies of hospital governing boards as an effective voice for the client. The recent report by the Urban Coalition tends to support the view that patients, especially the poor, do not have a proper voice in decision making.[6]

A lack of clearly defined community service goals could be an underlying factor in hospital-client hospital conflict. Etzioni suggests that "sometimes an organizational goal becomes the servant of the organization rather than its master. . . . Goals can be distorted by frequent measuring of organizational efforts, because as a rule, some aspects of its output are more measurable than others."[7] Certainly, hospitals are susceptible to this inversion of ends and means. The hospital financial statement, for example, is

---

[2] Georgopoulos, Basil S. and Floyd C. Mann, *The Community General Hospital.* Macmillan Co., 1962, p. 400.

[3] Stanton, Alfred H., and Morris S. Schwartz, *The Mental Hospital.* Basic Books, 1954, pp. 342–65; and William A. Caudill, *The Psychiatric Hospital as a Small Society.* Howard University Press, 1958, pp. 87–127, as reported by Peter M. Blau and Richard W. Scott, *Formal Organizations.* Chandler, 1962, pp. 53–54.

[4] Walton, Richard, *Interpersonal Peacemaking.* Addison Wesley, 1969, p. 5.

[5] Etzioni, Amitai, *Modern Organizations.* Englewood Cliffs, N.J.: Prentice-Hall, 1964, p. 95.

[6] *Rx for Action,* Report of the Health Task Force of the Urban Coalition. John Gardner, Chairman. Washington, 1969.

[7] Etzioni, *op. cit.,* pp. 4–11.

one of the few easily understood measurements available to trustees and administrators and it usually stresses institutional goals as opposed to patient goals.

Conflict or competition between hospitals is evident from the major programs, such as comprehensive health planning, designed to reduce it. However, there appears to be little empirical research on the seriousness, underlying sources, or measurable effects of such conflict. It can be assumed that displacement of community service goals by institutional goals would be an important factor in such conflicts. What is best for an individual hospital is not always best for the society it serves.

Conflict Within Institutions

Certain internal characteristics inherent in the hospital organization foster conflict. For example, interdependence, specialization and heterogeneity of personnel and levels of authority, all appear to be related positively to conflict.[8] In fact, few organizations are composed of as many diverse skills as the hospital, which generally has nearly three employees for each patient and a heterogeneous health team influenced by over 300 different professional societies and associations.

Individual Conflict

An individual's role in the hospital can have a major effect on conflict to which he is subjected. His personal characteristics and past environment will determine the impact and his coping mechanisms to role conflict. Role theory, including role conflict, has received considerable study, although not in a hospital setting. It is easy to imagine role conflict faced by physicians, nurses and administrators. The physician, for example, functions as an agent for an individual patient, his specialty, his profession, his staff, his institution, his community and his own welfare as an individual practitioner. The welfare of these individuals and groups and obligations of the physician to them and to himself are periodically in conflict. The nurse is frequently caught between multiple lines of authority. The administrator usually functions in a boundary role; that is, he is frequently in a position between the nurse and physician, two physicians, patient and employee, etc.

Role ambiguity is related to role conflict. Role ambiguity can be defined as uncertainty about the way one's work is evaluated by superiors, uncertainty about scope of responsibility, opportunities for advancement, and expectations of others for job performance. A variety of studies have demon-

---

[8] Thompson, Victor, "Hierarchy, Specialization & Organizational Conflict," in *Administrative Science Quarterly*, p. 519, and Corwin, Ronald, "Patterns of Organizational Conflict," *Administrative Science Quarterly*, Dec. 1969, pp. 507–21.

strated that there is frequently a wide disparity between what a superior expects of his subordinate and what the subordinate thinks the superior expects of him. In an industrial setting Kahn found the individual consequences of role ambiguity generally comparable to individual effects of role conflict. They include, "low job satisfaction, low self-confidence, a high sense of futility, and a high score on the tension index."[9]

A Coping Mechanism: Retreat

Surveys in industrial enterprises found that tension and strain increase directly with occupational status. Individuals in professional and technical occupations experienced the most tension followed by managerial, then clerical and sales.[10] However, Kahn found the medical administrator in the industrial plant who works under conditions of high role conflict scored low on tension.[11] In a case study he found the administrator kept potential conflicts in a delicate balance by retreating into his own section of expertise, i.e., statistical and financial management. The obvious implication is that the administrator can minimize conflict and tension by restricting his role. While this represents one case study in a non-hospital setting, one can logically assume a relationship between the scope of an administrator's role and his effort to effect changes and administrative conflict. Such a coping mechanism may aid the equanimity of the administrator but will not help him fulfill his broader obligations and responsibilities. Kahn's studies also relate personality variables to experiences of strain from conflict.[12] He found tension more pronounced for introverts, for emotionally sensitive people, and individuals who are strongly achievement-oriented. Personality characteristics also affected exposure to role conflict and tension. Individuals who are relatively flexible and those who are achievement-oriented are more subjected to conflict pressures.

Interpersonal Conflict

Interpersonal conflict is defined broadly to include both (a) interpersonal disagreements over substantive issues, such as policies and practices, and (b) interpersonal antagonisms, that is, the more personal and emotional differences which arise between interdependent human beings.[13] Both forms are broadly evident in the hospital setting. Interpersonal antagonisms would seem to be more prevalent in hospital operations because by nature

---

[9] Kahn, Robert L., *Organizational Stress*. Wiley, 1964, p. 380.

[10] *Ibid.*, p. 144.

[11] *Ibid.*, pp. 362–71.

[12] *Ibid.*, pp. 225–335.

[13] Walton, *op. cit.*, p. 3.

they deal with emotions. However, no studies were found related to relative frequency, severity or source of interpersonal conflict in hospitals.

Administration-Medical Staff Conflict

Whereas in industry top executives usually enjoy both formal and informal power and status, power and status do not appear to be centered in the same individuals in the hospital organization. This characteristic, rather unique to hospital organization, is a basic source of administration-medical staff conflict.

Power has been defined as the maximum ability of a person or group to influence individuals or groups. Influence is understood as the degree of change that may be effected in individuals or groups. Authority has been defined as legitimate power.[14] In reviewing a variety of authors, Filley and House have summarized the basis of power being derived from (1) legitimacy, (2) control of rewards and sanctions, including money, (3) expertise, (4) personal liking, and (5) coercion.[15] Observation tells us that the hospital administrator usually has (1) legitimacy from delegated authority for hospital affairs from the governing board, (2) effective control of funds, beds, and other resources, (3) increasing expertise, particularly as management information systems improve, (4) personal liking, and (5) ability to coerce through demands of such sources as the Joint Commission on the Accreditation of Hospitals. Studies by Perrow and Georgopoulos and Mann tend to confirm the increasing dominance of the administrator.[16] Recent demands by the American Medical Association and medical staffs in many hospitals for medical staff representation on hospital boards tend to confirm their protestations of declining influence.

The Factors of Status

Other studies are somewhat conflicting; however, they appear to relate more to factors of status. For example, Georgopoulos and Mann, after describing the administrator as most influential, describe his source of influence as delegated authority from trustees, while sources of physicians' influence include their expertise, prestige, status and power among patients and the community.[17] A recent survey reported that "trustees and medical

---

[14] Filley, Alan C., and Robert J. House, *Managerial Process and Organization Behavior*. Glenview, Ill.: Scott, Foresman & Co., 1969, p. 55.

[15] *Ibid.*, p. 61.

[16] Perrow, Charles, "Goals and Power Structure," *The Hospitals and Modern Society*. Eliot Friedson, editor. Free Press, 1963, pp. 112–46, and article in *Handbook of Organizations;* and Georgopoulos, *op. cit.*, p. 567.

[17] Georgopoulos, *op. cit.*, p. 567.

staffs do not view the administrator as a leader, but as a generally passive influence caught between the board and doctors."[18]

Goss suggests that physicians tend to view administration as a less prestigious kind of work.[19]

The hospital administrator's drive for professionalism and his desire for more prestigious titles such as president or executive vice-president, tend to suggest that he believes he needs to improve his status. As physicians attempt to maintain or increase their power, and administrators improve their status, presumably, both tend to feel threatened. Under such circumstances conflict increases.

Physicians and nurses, like professionals in other fields, have primary allegiance to professional status rather than to organizational status.[20] Hence, the potential for professional-instiutional goal conflict is present.

The hospital organization is sometimes referred to as a duopoly with essentially autonomous administrative and medical staff organizations. Croog suggests that each system is oriented to a different set of values, one emphasizing provision of service, one emphasizing maintenance of operation of organization.[21] The Barr report related hospital inefficiences to this dual management authority.[22] Other studies tend to confirm the presence of a conflict between bureaucratic routine and individualized patient care.[23] Perhaps a more flexible organizational structure with emphasis upon project teams would reduce this type of conflict.

Nursing Conflict

Considerable basic conflict in nursing is evident from many studies. Most of these inquiries indicate that nurses are satisfied with their vocation, but dissatisfied with specific conditions of salary, work load, working hours, etc.[24] However, Argyris suggests more basic problems, such as frustration of

---

[18] "Trustee's View of Administrators Told," *Modern Hospital*, October 1968, p. 29.

[19] Goss, Mary E. W., "Patterns of Bureaucracy Among Staff Physicians," *The Hospital*, p. 180.

[20] Argyris, Chris, *Diagnosing Human Relations in Organizations: A Case Study of a Hospital*. New Haven: Yale University, Labor and Management Center, 1965, p. 62; and W. G. Bennis et al., "Reference Groups and Loyalties in the Outpatient Department," *Administrative Science Quarterly*, March 1958.

[21] Croog, S. H., "Interpersonal Relations in Medical Settings," *Handbook of Medical Sociology*, H. E. Freeman, S. Levine, and L. G. Reeder, editors. Prentice-Hall, 1963, p. 256.

[22] Secretary's Advisory Committee on Hospital Effectiveness, Department of Health, Education, and Welfare, 1967.

[23] *Abstracts of Hospital Management Studies*, Vol. IV (June 1968). University of Michigan, pp. 137–40 and 196.

[24] Corwin, R. G., and Marvin J. Taves. "Nursing and Other Health Professions," *Handbook of Medical Sociology*, pp. 187–212, and Argyris, *op. cit.*

the dominant predispositions of nurses.[25] He reports nurses in the hospital he studied were not able to fulfill effectively important predispositions, such as being self-controlled, indispensable, compatible, and expert. Findings of Corwin, Taves and Scott, reported later in this paper, seem to support these conclusions.

Status may be a source of basic conflict among nurses. In years past, nursing was one of the few careers a woman could enter and attain some degree of professional prestige. Today, more vocational opportunities are opening to women as sex discrimination continues to decline. Women can, or at least sometimes believe they can, gain greater recognition in such fields as business, government, medicine and teaching.[26] Whereas nurses had been virtually the only professionals in the hospital outside of the physicians, they are now receiving increasing competition for status from a proliferation of allied health professionals, many of whom have higher standards of education, pay, and autonomy. In his survey of student nurses and personnel in three major hospitals, Taves found that "compared to student nurses who have a relatively high image of nursing on the average, the image that the general duty nurse holds seems to be especially low. . . . Head nurses have a somewhat better image of nursing than general duty nurses." He also found that other hospital personnel had an even lower image of nursing.[27]

Struggle for Professionalism

Frustrations are evident in nursing's struggle for professionalism. Corwin and Taves suggest that "the drive to gain professional status and achieve a unique place of importance within the hospital's division of labor, inevitably brings the group into conflict with the lay administration and physicians who are jealous of their prima donna status within the hospital scheme."[28] Scott states that the nurses' drive for professionalism may be based on carving out a special niche for themselves in which they can operate relatively independently from control by other groups and which allows them some claim to superior status.[29]

Organizational factors present conflicts for nurses. Nurses' career advancement has shifted from an individual to an organizational context wherein a nurse must move through the bureaucratic hierarchy to gain

25 Argyris, *op. cit.*, p. 189.

26 Corwin, and Taves, *op. cit.*, note that studies in two states indicated teaching outranked nursing in prestige (p. 193).

27 Corwin and Taves, *op. cit.*, p. 189.

28 *Ibid.*, p. 206.

29 Scott, W. Richard, "Some Implications of Organization Theory for Research on Health Services," *Milbank Memorial Fund Quarterly*, Vol. XLIV, No. 4, Part 2 (October 1966), p. 52.

recognition. Rewards in this hierarchy, however, do not reflect professional patient care, but administrative duties. Argyris suggests that nurses believe that an administrator is a second-class citizen. He also suggests that the only area where a nurse is free to "blow her top" is in the administrative area and this adds another factor which keeps administration in a low status function.[30] On the other hand, Taves found that nursing personnel who have higher ranking official positions in the organization are more satisfied with their jobs than lower ranking personnel.[31]

The Need to Mitigate and Control Conflict

Others suggest sources of nursing conflict can be a lack of role and job concensus,[32] type of care,[33] and dislike of working with nonprofessionals.[34]

Regardless of the source, it is evident that a considerable degree of conflict exists in hospitals. The problem then, is one of developing ways and means of mitigating or at least controlling conflict. The next section suggests some approaches to the resolution of this problem.

ACTION PROGRAM

Figure 1 presents a decision model related to diagnosing and mitigating conflict. It lists conflict participants and some of the underlying sources of conflicts presented in this paper. A brief description of the mitigators listed in the exhibit follows.

Comprehensive Institutional Goal Setting

Comprehensive institutional goal setting is a formalized program to define goals and objectives *explicitly*. Too often goals are defined implicitly, such as "high quality care at low cost." Explicit goals state measures affecting quality and costs. Often goals can be stated in terms of specially attainable objectives.

Goal definition should begin with a study of the needs of the society the institution intends to serve in order to obviate displacement of goals. Medical staff members and employees, in addition to administrators and trustees, should participate in setting goals. Sociologists, political scientists and economists, as well as planners and citizens of the publics served, can provide

---

[30] Argyris, *op. cit.*, pp. 67–69.

[31] Taves, *op. cit.*, p. 51.

[32] *Ibid.*, p. 74 and p. 205. Georgopoulos, *op. cit.*, p. 398, and Argyris, *op. cit.*, p. 10.

[33] Perrow, *op. cit.*, p. 965. Perrow reported a study by Coser which found nurses giving only custodial care were alienated because they were "unable to implement a single goal."

[34] Argyris, *op. cit.*, p. 70.

FIGURE 1°

Decision Model for Diagnosing and Mitigating Hospital Conflict

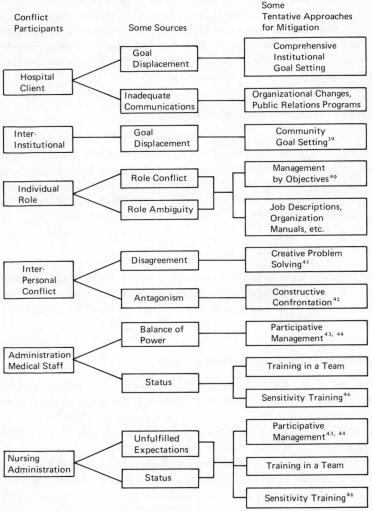

° See text footnotes 39–46 for numbered references in figure.

appropriate resource personnel to deliberations. Explicit institutional goals aid community understanding, assist internal and external evaluation of outputs reducing over-emphasis on inputs such as costs and facilities, help to sublimate personal differences by focusing efforts on end results, and help to marshall required resources for attaining goals.

Organizational Changes, Public Relations Programs

Communications can be improved by broadening official lines of communication with citizens served by the institution. Policies for governing board membership might be revised to represent more appropriately the constituencies served. Or, an advisory board might be established to review expressed needs of constituencies and hospital programs to meet needs. A public relations program based on appropriate client attitude surveys can be beneficial.

Community Goal Setting

While many communities are preparing plans for community health services, few have effectively articulated explicit goals and objectives that plans should serve. The City of Dallas is a notable exception.[35] There, community goals for health services provides a framework for institutions to coordinate individual goals and plans.

Management by Objectives and Role Definition

Management by objectives is the participation between the subordinate and his superior in setting the subordinate's goal.[36] Through interaction and discussion, a subordinate can determine precisely what is expected of him, thus reducing anxiety resulting from ambiguity, while at the same time improving worker independence in task performance and at the same time increasing accountability.

Role definition through job descriptions and administrative manuals can also help to reduce role conflict and ambiguity. These tools are familiar to most administrators.

Creative Problem-Solving

Creative problem-solving utilizes techniques that sublimate antagonistic conflict and fosters creativity in participative problem-solving. Maier notes the distinction between "choice behavior" which is an examination and a selection from the alternatives, and "problem-solving," which is a searching or idea getting process.[37] By turning choice situations into problem-solving

---

[35] *Goals for Dallas,* Dallas, Texas, 1966.

[36] Odiorne, George, *Management by Objectives,* Pitman, 1965.

[37] Maier, Norman F., "Maximizing Personal Creativity Through Better Problem Solving," *Personal Administration,* Vol. 27 (1964) and Filley, Alan C. and Andre Delbecq, "On the Possibility of a Better World," University of Wisconsin (unpublished).

situations, participants are more apt to focus on end results rather than on who is presenting or standing for what. It maximizes creativity and sublimates hostility, self-pity and rigidity. Creative problem-solving promotes end results wherein everyone wins, rather than a choice situation in which there is a winner and loser or a compromise wherein everyone loses.

Constructive Confrontation

Issues of conflict tend to proliferate when there are interpersonal antagonisms between individuals. A manager can take steps to avoid issues that may result in open interpersonal conflict between individuals. However, indirect effects of interpersonal antagonism will frequently persist and in the long run may be more damaging than an open confrontation. Walton suggests using constructive confrontation with third party intervention, particularly by consultants from outside the institution.[38] Components of confrontation include, 1) clarifying the issues with parties, 2) expressing feelings descriptively, 3) expressing facts and fantasies, and 4) resolution and agreement. It would appear, however, that third party intervention should be utilized sparingly.

Participative Management

Participative management is a philosophy of management in which hospital employees and physicians participate in a meaningful way in the administration of the hospital. It is a philosophy espoused by Rensis Likert and by the late Douglas McGregor, who wrote of "theory X and theory Y."[39] Studies by Coleman, Gamson and Corwin support the view that broad participation in authority systems minimizes major incidents of conflict, although minor incidents may be more frequent.[40]

Management by objectives and comprehensive institutional goal setting are examples of participative management. The administrator does not abdicate his responsibility, he shares it. By sharing planning, coordination, control and management information, the administrator can actually gain more control over his responsibilities.[41]

---

[38] Walton, Richard E., *Third Party Consultation*, Addison-Wesley, 1969.

[39] Likert, R., *New Patterns in Management*, McGraw-Hill, 1961; and McGregor, D., *The Human Side of Enterprise*, McGraw-Hill, 1960.

[40] Coleman, James S., *Community Conflict*, Glencoe, Ill., Free Press, 1957; William Gamson, "Rancorous Conflict in Community Politics," *American Sociological Review*, Vol. 31, pp. 71–81; and Ronald G. Corwin, "Patterns in Organizational Conflict," *Administrative Science Quarterly*, December 1969, pp. 507–20.

[41] Tannenbaum, A. S., "Control in Organizations: Individual Adjustment and Organizational Performance," *Administrative Science Quarterly*, September 1962, p. 236.

Sensitivity Training

Sensitivity training, with emphasis on institutional social system development, can help to overcome "hang-ups" related to concerns over status.[42] Laboratory training based on the more traditional group dynamics training is suggested rather than the recent individual self-awareness training which at times borders on therapy. It is the latter, personal development training, that has been maligned recently.

Training in a Team

Health workers are expected to function as a team, yet they are seldom trained for this role. Hospital administrators spend more time with physicians and nurses than any other group. It would be beneficial if they had meaningful dialogue in the formative educational period. This could be easily arranged through seminars or research projects on such subjects as ethics, legal problems, group dynamics, contemporary problems in health, to name just a few. Opportunities for informal as well as formal associations should be arranged. Interdisciplinary study or informal association can also be arranged through the work environment.

Combined degree programs between medicine and hospital administration and/or nursing and hospital administration should be considered seriously. In addition to improving team associations at the educational level, it would help to improve administrative skills of those who actually administer a large part of health service and health team.

In Summary

Conflict in hospitals is an incredibly complex issue. While it deserves considerably more research, much can be done to apply current knowledge of sources and mitigating activities. In general, increased demand for services and attempts to diagnose and lessen conflicts will result in new policies and procedures. Among these will be research studies to identify the impact of various conflict situations. In addition, one can expect to see changes in goal setting, planning, organizational relationships and training programs.

FURTHER READINGS SUGGESTED BY THE AUTHORS

Corwin, Ronald. "Patterns of Organizational Conflict," *Administrative Science Quarterly,* Dec. 1969, pp. 507–21.

---

[42] Buchanan, Paul C., "Laboratory Training and Organization Development," *Administrative Science Quarterly,* September 1969, pp. 466–77; Lewin, Kurt, *Resolving Social Conflicts: Selected Papers on Group Dynamics,* Harper, 1948.

Dodds, Richard W., M.D. "A Framework for Political Mapping of Conflict in Organized Medicine—Especially Pediatrics," *Medical Care Review,* Vol. 27, 10 (Nov. 1970), pp. 1035+.

Kahn, Robert L. *Organizational Stress.* New York: John Wiley & Sons, 1964.

Kelly, Joe. "Make Conflict Work for You," *Harvard Business Review,* July-Aug. 1970, pp. 103–13.

Lewin, Kurt. *Resolving Social Conflicts: Selected Papers on Group Dynamics.* New York: Harper & Bros., 1948.

Perrow, Charles. "Goals and Power Structure," *The Hospitals and Modern Society,* Eliot Friedson, editor. New York: The Free Press, 1963, pp. 112–46.

Pondy, Louis R. "Varieties of Organizational Conflict," *Administrative Science Quarterly,* 14:4 (Dec. 1969), pp. 499–505.

20

Organizational Leadership: Some Theoretical and Empirical Considerations

J. G. HUNT

A recurring problem among managers has been that of determining the type of leader behavior or leadership style necessary to promote effective work groups. Research in this area appears to yield contradictory results. Some studies have shown that leadership styles denoting directive, authoritarian, task-oriented, or similar behavior promote effective group performance; others have shown that human relations-oriented or nondirective leader behavior gives better results. [1].*

To resolve these conflicting results Fiedler has developed the "Contingency Model" theory which proposes that situations be classified in terms of their favorableness for the leader to exert influence over group members. The theory hypothesizes that a task-oriented leader will obtain better performance than a relationship-oriented leader under conditions very favorable or very unfavorable for the leader. On the other hand, the relationship-oriented leader will perform best under "moderately favorable" conditions [2].

This paper discusses the Contingency Model together with a recent empirical test in which is was validated in three business organizations. The model is then considered in terms of its theoretical implications within organizations. Finally, some new research directions are discussed.

Source: Reprinted by permission of *Business Perspectives*, Vol. 4, No. 4 (Summer 1968), pp. 16–24, Southern Illinois University, Business Research Bureau.
* Numbers in brackets refer to references at end of Reading.

DESCRIPTION OF THE CONTINGENCY MODEL

The measure of leadership style used by Fiedler and in the present study is what Fiedler has termed the leader's "esteem for his least preferred coworker" (LPC). A leader is asked to think of the one person with whom he has been able to work the least well (his least preferred coworker) and to describe him on scales such as the following:

Pleasant : 8 : 7 : 6 : 5 : 4 : 3 : 2 : 1 : Unpleasant
Friendly : 8 : 7 : 6 : 5 : 4 : 3 : 2 : 1 : Unfriendly

The least preferred coworker does not have to be someone with whom the leader is presently working but can be someone with whom he has worked in the past; thus he can be a past or present peer, subordinate, or superior. From 18 to 21 adjective scales have typically been included in the LPC measure. The LPC score is the sum of the total number of one to eight point-item scores. A person who describes his least preferred coworker relatively favorably is termed a "high LPC" leader, while one who describes him unfavorably is called a "low LPC" leader [2].

After much research, Fiedler has interpreted the LPC score as a dynamic trait which results in different leader behavior as the situation changes. This behavior is influenced not only by the situation but by the personal needs which the leader seeks to satisfy. The low LPC individual gains need satisfaction from successful task performance, while the high LPC person gains satisfaction through successful interpersonal relations. Thus, high and low LPC leaders seek to satisfy different needs in the group situation, and their behavior varies according to the ease with which a given situation allows them to achieve need satisfaction. Based on the above interpretation, Fiedler has designated high LPC leaders as "relationship-oriented" and low LPC leaders as "task-oriented" [2].

The Contingency Model theory postulates that group effectiveness is contingent upon leadership style and the favorableness of the situation for the leader to exert influence over his group members. While many dimensions might be used to operationally define the leader's situation, Fiedler's earlier research led him to use three: leader-member relations, task structure, and position power.

Leader-member relations have been operationally defined in terms of group member sociometric acceptance of the leader or in terms of the leader's perception of "group atmosphere." This latter measure asks the leader to use the same bipolar adjective format as the LPC scale to describe his work group. According to Fiedler, a leader who describes his group favorably feels well accepted by group members and sees the group as low in tension [2].

Task structure refers to the extent to which task requirements are clearly specified as in routine assembly-line work versus being ambiguous and undefined as in creative research. Four variables developed by Shaw have been used to measure this dimension. These are (a) goal clarity—the extent to which the task's objectives are defined; (b) goal-path multiplicity—whether there is one or more than one way of reaching the goal; (c) decision verifiability—the degree to which the outcome can be evaluated; and (d) solution specificity—whether there is one or more than one possible outcome [3].

Position power denotes the power or authority delegated by the formal organization regardless of the leader's willingness or ability to use it. A simple check list has been used to measure it [2].

Fiedler has arranged these variables in eight different cells to form a "favorableness for the leader" continuum as in Figure 1.

FIGURE 1

Correlations between Leader LPC and Group Performance When Group-Task Situations are Ordered in Terms of "Favorableness for the Leader"

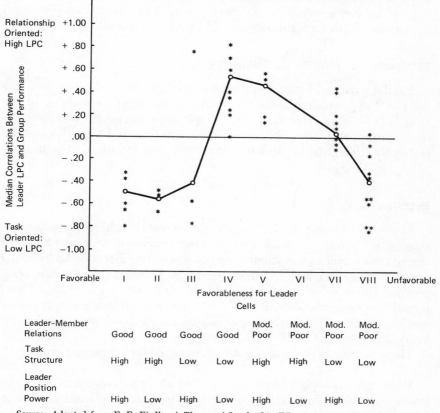

	Favorable	I	II	III	IV	V	VI	VII	VIII	Unfavorable
Leader–Member Relations		Good	Good	Good	Good	Mod. Poor	Mod. Poor	Mod. Poor	Mod. Poor	
Task Structure		High	High	Low	Low	High	High	Low	Low	
Leader Position Power		High	Low	High	Low	High	Low	High	Low	

Source: Adapted from F. E. Fiedler A Theory of Leadership Effectiveness (New York: McGraw-Hill, 1967), p. 146.

Ordering of these dimensions is based on Fiedler's assumption that leader-member relations are most important and position power is the least important. It is assumed that favorable relations will allow a leader to do what would be difficult for a person without favorable relations. A lack of power can be at least partially compensated for by favorable relations or task structure [2].

When the cells are arranged as above and the correlations between leader LPC and group performance within each of them are plotted, the "performance curve" shown in Figure 1 is obtained. This curve is based on twelve years of research and shows the with-in-cell median correlations of 15 different studies representing over 800 groups (2). Thus each median correlation is based on a number of separate samples each of which contains several leaders and work groups.

The curve shows that the correlation between leader LPC and group performance is negative in Cells I, II, III, and VIII, positive in Cells IV and V, and approximately zero in Cell VII. Thus the low LPC, task-oriented leader tends to obtain better group performance under very favorable *and* very unfavorable conditions while the high LPC, relationship-oriented leader does better under moderately favorable circumstances.

TESTING THE MODEL IN BUSINESS

Fiedler conducted one major validation study in cooperation with the Belgian Navy which provided support for the major hypothesis of the model (4). However, this study was an experiment carried out with specially set up groups and tasks. The present study was designed to further test the theory by attempting to validate it in business and industrial organizations [5].

Hypotheses

The model was originally formulated in terms of "interacting groups"—those which require high member interdependence for task completion. It seemed important to test whether or not it could be extended to "coacting groups"—those in which members are relatively independent in task completion. Hypotheses therefore considered both kinds of groups. These hypotheses were also formulated on the assumption that position power would be high in the business organizations sampled and hence data would be available to test Cells I, III, V, and VII.

The following hypothesis was therefore tested for interacting groups:

When group-task situations are ordered along a favorableness for the leader continuum there will be a negative correlation between supervisor LPC and group performance under very favorable leader conditions, while there will be a positive correlation under a situation intermediate in favorableness.

An identical hypothesis was formulated for coacting groups but on an exploratory basis.

Method

To test the hypotheses the following steps were necessary: (a) obtain leadership style data in terms of LPC for work-group supervisors, (b) classify samples into cells considering leader-member relations, task structure, and position power, (c) correlate within each cell supervisor LPC and work-group performance, and (d) test these correlations for statistical significance as indicated below.

Samples

In selecting samples, the main considerations were to find a substantial number of groups performing the same task and to have valid and reliable performance measures. We also hoped to find groups with well-structured tasks as well as those with relatively unstructured tasks so that as many cells of the model as possible could be tested. The following five sets of groups in three organizations met these requirements:

Sample	Number of Groups
1. Company X: Research firm in atomic energy field	
a) Research chemists	18
b) Skilled craftsmen	1
2. Company Y: Grocery chain	
a) Meat departments	21
b) Grocery departments (entire store except meat departments.)	24
3. Company Z: Farm and earth-moving machinery manufacturer Management teams of general foreman or superintendent and subordinate first-line production foremen	15

Measures

Instruments were similar or identical to those described previously. The LPC scale was used to measure leadership style of the work-group supervisors while the group-atmosphere scale was used to evaluate leader-member relations. The task structure and position power measures were modified to fit a business or industrial context.

Samples were classified as primarily coacting or interacting on the basis of an interview with a company official familiar with the extent to which the duties of the sampled units required within-group interdependence. Thus, the research chemists, meat departments, and production management teams were classified as interacting; the shop craftsmen and grocery departments were considered to be coacting.

Performance of research chemists and shop craftsmen was measured by using ratings of three or more officials familiar with their work. Objective productivity figures were available for the supermarket meat and grocery departments as well as the Company Z production foreman sample.

Data Analysis

Each of the hypotheses was tested as follows: (a) Spearman rank order correlations between manager LPC and work unit performance were

FIGURE 2

Correlations between Supervisor LPC and Group Effectiveness Superimposed on a Curve of Median Correlations in Fiedler's Model

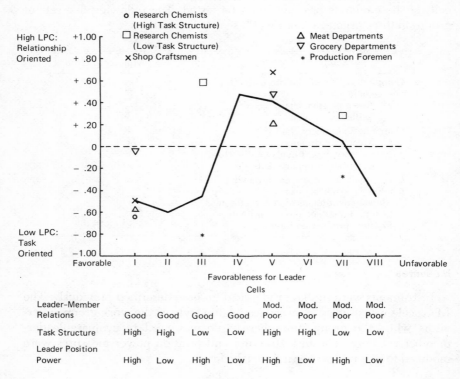

computed for the samples within each cell; (b) for each cell the probability that a correlation of the magnitude and direction found in (a) would occur by chance was determined; and (c) each of these probabilities was combined and tested for over-all significance using a one-tailed test [6].

Results

Figure 2 superimposes the present results on Fiedler's curve of median correlations. Interacting samples are found in Cells I, III, V, and VII, and all correlations except the one for the low-task structure research chemists fall close to the curve. A combined significance test on the correlations of the seven samples in Cells I, III, and V shows them to be significant at slightly better than the .05 level. (Results in Cell VII were not included in the significance test since an essentially zero correlation was predicted. However, their average is zero which tends to support the predicted near-zero correlation even though it has not been tested statistically.) On the basis of these results the first hypothesis was therefore accepted.

Coacting samples are found in Cells I and V, and all four correlations fall close to the curve. These combined correlations are significant at better than the .01 level. This hypothesis was also accepted and it was concluded that the model predicts performance for both interacting and coacting groups in the samples tested here. Although only four cells were tested, if as seems reasonable, position power is generally high in most business and industrial organizations, then these four cells are the really relevant ones for testing the model. Hence we might argue that these four cells constitute a comprehensive test of the Contingency Model in these kinds of firms.

USEFULNESS OF MODEL

While the importance of a "situational" approach to leadership has been recognized for many years [7], this model is the first to provide an operational conceptual scheme for systematically classifying situational as well as other variables. Thus the model provides a badly needed beginning toward reconciling many of the conflicting results found in leadership research. It has also made a significant start toward encompassing the classes of variables that have been suggested by Sanford as being important in a comprehensive theory of leadership. These are (a) the leader and his psychological attributes, (b) the follower with his problems, attitudes, and needs, and (c) the group situation in which followers and leaders relate to one another [8]. The model presently considers leadership style which falls under the first category as does the leader's perception of group atmosphere. Task structure and position power fall under the group situation category. The favorableness for the leader concept, as discussed below, provides a framework which should allow consideration of other variables within the leader and group situation categories as well as a number of variables within the follower category.

The model is an impressive one because of the extensive amount of empirical evidence used in developing it—15 studies of over 800 groups conducted over a 12-year period. Furthermore, the previously discussed Belgian Navy study and the present study lend supporting evidence.

In addition to its theoretical importance, a model such as this has potential usefulness for manager selection and placement as well as training. It also opens up possibilities in terms of organizational design or what Fiedler [2] has termed "organization engineering." Here work unit dimensions would be modified to fit the leadership style of the manager in charge. Thus it may make new tools available for obtaining a better fit between managerial abilities and organizational requirements.

THEORETICAL QUESTIONS

While Fiedler's model as presently formulated is useful for the reasons mentioned above, it also makes a significant contribution in terms of the kinds of theoretical questions it poses. These questions point out new directions which leadership research might take. We consider three of these:

1. An examination of leadership style assuming that the remaining variables are treated as in the present model.
2. An examination of the extension or refinement of the intervening variables of leader-member relations, task structure, and position power with leadership style considered in terms of the presently used LPC.
3. An examination of intervening variables beyond those presently used, assuming LPC is used to measure leadership style.

Leadership Style

An important theoretical problem is that we know little about the behavior of high and low LPC leaders. As previously indicated, Fiedler has interpreted LPC in terms of leader need satisfaction and argues that high LPC leaders achieve need satisfaction through successful interpersonal relations, while low LPC leaders achieve satisfaction through successful task completion. Unfortunately, this interpretation tells us little about the actual behavior of the two kinds of leaders. Fiedler has devoted a great deal of research to this problem, but it is complicated because the behavior of the two kinds of leaders appears to change as the situation in which the leaders are operating makes it easy or hard for them to achieve need satisfaction. Thus, we might expect that sometimes there would be a significant correlation between LPC and measures of leadership style used by other researchers and sometimes not. And, indeed, available studies suggest that this is the case. Typical of these is a study by Meuwese and Fiedler [9] which shows a significant relationship between LPC and the Ohio State dimension of "consideration" (discussed below). An unpublished study by the author shows significant relationships for this dimension in some work-group samples but not in others.

This leader behavior is an extremely important issue because without understanding it we cannot explain why the model "works." We need to have an understanding of the manner in which specified leader behavior interacts with the intervening variables to influence group performance. One approach to this problem is to obtain behavioral data for high and low LPC leaders in each cell of the model. These data could be procured either by observation and classification into different behavior categories or by obtaining group member perceptions of a leader's behavior.

An alternative approach would be to use leadership style measures other than LPC and see the kind of performance curve generated as data are collected for each cell of the model. In other words, "To what extent does the favorableness for the leader concept predict performance when a behavioral measure of leadership style is used?"

Table 1 summarizes leadership style measures used in some of the better known previous research. This table shows that a number of these dimensions appear to be logically related. Furthermore, a study by Argyle, Gardner, and Cioffi gives empirical support to this view [10]. They considered the first five of these dimensions and found significant and fairly substantial intercorrelations between them. Thus, they concluded that "employee centered" supervisors tended to be "democratic," to supervise in a "general way," and to be relatively "nonpunitive." It may therefore be reasonable to consider these variables as subdivisions of a more underlying variable. The "consideration" dimension used in the Ohio State studies appears to include the essence of these other dimensions as well as "human-relations competence." The "differentiation of role" and "administrative competence" dimensions appear to be related; the Ohio State "initiating structure" dimension appears to tap a somewhat similar concept. "Technical competence" appears to be similar to what is termed below "task relevant ability," and hence is considered here in that context rather than as a part of leadership style [11].

The concepts implicit in the "initiating structure" and "consideration" dimensions appear to identify leader behaviors basic to almost any kind of group. Bass [12] further supports use of these dimensions by arguing that they can safely be equated to categories of leader behavior identified by Wherry, Rupe, and Roach. Thus we are interested in considering the kind of performance curve which might result from using "consideration" and "initiating structure" measures of leadership style. These measures would give an indication of the leader's behavior as seen by subordinates.

TABLE 1

Leadeship Style Measures Used in Previous Studies

Study	Dimension	Definition
Michigan* Southern California	Closeness of Supervision	Degree to which supervisor checks up on his men frequently, gives detailed and frequent instructions, and in general limits their freedom to do work in their own way.
Michigan Southern California	Pressure for Production	Degree to which supervisor attempts to keep up production by putting pressure on subordinates, criticizing their efforts, urging them to speed up, and emphasizing deadlines and targets.
Michigan Southern California	Employee Orientation (Production Centered vs. Employee Centered)	Degree to which supervisor emphasizes production as opposed to keeping his employees happy.
Southern California	Democratic vs. Authoritarian	Degree to which supervisor listens to ideas, reasons with his men, explains to them as fully as possible and discusses the work and possible changes with them as opposed to a supervisor who knows his own mind, gives orders crisply, expects men to know what he wants, and relies on his superior knowledge to solve problems.
Michigan Southern California	Discipline	Degree to which supervisor takes punitive action based on the weight and authority of his position as opposed to using tact or persuaasion to correct employee infractions of regulations.
Michigan	Differentiation of Role	Degree to which supervisor performs supervisory functions such as planning, coordination of activities, etc., as opposed to doing subordinate functions.
Mann†	Administrative Competence	Degree to which supervisor performs functions required to coordinate activities of one organization family with another; the ability to think and act in terms of the total system within which he operates. Includes planning, programming, and organizing work; assigning tasks, responsibility, and authority; inspecting and following up work; and coordinating efforts and activities of different organizational members and units.
Mann†	Human Relations Competence	Degree to which supervisor uses pertinent knowledge and methods for working with and through people.
Mann†	Technical Competence	Degree to which supervisor uses pertinent knowledge, methods, and equipment necessary for performance of specific tasks, and for the direction of such performance.

TABLE 1—Continued

Study	Dimension	Definition
Ohio‡ State	Initiating Structure	Degree to which supervisor organizes and defines the relationship between himself and subordinates, defines the role of each subordinate, and establishes well-defined patterns of organization, channels of communication, and ways of getting the job done.
Ohio State‡	Consideration	Degree to which supervisor exhibits behavior indicative of friendship, mutual trust and respect, and "good human relations" between himself and his subordinates.

° For the specific studies conducted by the University of Michigan and the University of Southern California see, Argyle, Gardner, and Cioffi, "The Measurement of Supervisory Methods," in *Human Relations*, Vol. 10 (1957), pp. 295–314.

† See, F. Mann, "Toward an Understanding of the Leadership Role in Formal Organization," in R. Dubin, et al., *Leadership and Productivity* (San Francisco: Chandler, 1965.)

‡ See, Stogdill, R.; and Coons, A., *Leader Behavior: Its Description and Measurement* (Research Monograph No. 88. [Columbus: Bureau of Business Research, Ohio State University, 1957]).

We are faced with an immediate problem, however. There is a question about handling these two dimensions which are often independent of each other [13]. As a starting point, research might be conducted to examine the kind of performance curve generated for each dimension separately. It might be found, for example, that one dimension generated a curvilinear relationship similar to LPC, while the other did not. Or perhaps one dimension would show a sharply changing curve from one cell to another, while the other would show a virtually flat curve. It seems likely, however, that there is an interactive effect between the two dimensions and that they should be tested simultaneously.

One way of simultaneously treating these dimensions when they are independent would be to consider them in the following four combinations: (*a*) high initiating structure—high consideration, (*b*) low initiating structure—low consideration, (*c*) high initiating structure—low consideration, and (*d*) low initiating structure—high consideration. It seems likely that the performance curves for each of these combinations would differ.

This kind of knowledge would allow the model to consider variables used by other researchers. Furthermore, since we could relate perceived leader behavior to other dimensions, we would gain a better idea about why the model shows this kind of relationships.

MODERATOR VARIABLES

As indicated above, a second research direction is to examine some questions concerned with leader-member relations, task structure, and leader position power.

Leader-Member Relations

We are concerned here with the extent to which the leader's perception of group atmosphere and subordinate acceptance of the leader can be considered as interchangeable variables in the model. From a theoretical standpoint they appear different. The former is a leader perceptual variable while the latter is a subordinate perceptual variable or a type of "situational" variable in the sense that it is external to the leader. It is possible, however, that the two kinds of dimensions might play a similar role in the model in terms of their interaction with the other variables in influencing group effectiveness. Therefore we need empirical research to test the interchangeability of these two variables and to provide a basis for further theorizing concerning their influence in the model.

Task Structure

Triandis has suggested that worker "task relevant ability," e.g., aptitude or intelligence, and task structure probably would interact with each other to influence performance [14]. Thus it appears that a different leadership style might be more appropriate where there was a match between ability and structure, for example, high structure—low ability, than where the two were mismatched. We might thus expect some difference in the relationship between different ability-structure combinations and the other intervening variables considered. It is proposed that the following four combinations be examined: (a) high ability—high structure, (b) high ability—low structure, (c) low ability—high structure, and (d) low ability—low structure. The fourth condition would presumably call for more structured behavior from the supervisor than the other conditions, which in turn would appear to differ in the amount of human relations behavior required.

Power

The present concept is concerned with the power the organization grants to a supervisory position. Yet we all know that two managers occupying the same position may have sharply different abilities to use rewards and punishment officially at their disposal. Pelz has referred to this as upward influence—a supervisor's ability to influence his boss so that the supervisor can utilize the power at his disposal. He has shown that helpful and restraining behavior on the part of supervisors has very different effects on employee satisfaction depending upon the supervisor's upward influence [15]. Patchen carries this finding further by showing that, among other things,, upward influence and a supervisor's willingness to use it interact to influence employee productivity norms [16].

Hence it seems reasonable to examine this upward influence concept of power as a Contingency Model dimension. The focus shifts from power inherent in the position to power at the leader's disposal because of his upward influence. This still leaves the question of the extent to which a leader utilizes this power with respect to his employees. It may be obvious to a supervisor's subordinates that because of his upward influence he has much power at his disposal, but he may not choose to use it.

Before this question is considered it would seem wise to examine the relationship between power utilization and leadership style. It might be hypothesized that a low LPC (task-oriented) leader would tend to highly utilize his available power, while his high LPC (relationship-oriented) counterpart would not. Power utilization might also be related to other measures of leadership style. If there is not a strong relationship between power utilization and leadership style, then it would seem reasonable to extend the concept to include it. If, on the other hand, such a relationship does exist, it is suggested that the concept be extended to include upward influence only.

CONSIDERATION OF OTHER DIMENSIONS

A third research direction is to examine other dimensions which might be included in a leadership model. If we think in terms of the favorableness for the leader concept, what intervening variables might be considered?

The present model uses three classes of variables to influence the relationship between leader LPC and group performance. These are group variables—position power, task variables—task strucutre, and leader variables—leader member relations measured by the leader's perception of "group atmosphere." It does not specifically consider subordinate variables such as personality, attitude, or ability which, as indicated above, a comprehensive theory of leadership might contain [17]. This class of variables would include such subordinate dimensions as authoritarianism, need for independence, and task relevant ability which was discussed above in conjunction with task structure. Such variables as group cohesiveness, group member heterogeneity, and group status congruence might be considered as other possible group variables. Task variables, in addition to task structure, might include task complexity as well as technology, e.g., process technology versus small batch or job shop technology can influence the effectiveness of a given leadership style [18].

Leader variables present a problem. It may be that "group atmosphere" is a special case which is only relevant when leadership style is measured using LPC. It would seem that the leader's perception of his acceptance by group members might produce different behavior in a high LPC leader than in one low in LPC and hence influence group performance. If this were the case, it probably would not be a relevant variable when leadership style was measured in terms of behavioral dimensions such as those discussed earlier. Other possible leader dimensions such as personality variables might better be considered as being alternative ways of conceiving leadership style rather than as intervening variables. However, leader task relevant ability would probably be an exception. It does not seem to readily fit into the leadership style category; yet it seems reasonable to classify it as a special kind of moderator dimension interacting with leadership style and other intervening variables to influence group performance.

Thus the model being proposed would use task variables, group variables, subordinate personality, attitude and ability variables, and leader task relevant ability variables to operationally define the favorableness for the leader concept. Now, obviously this is a large number of classes to consider and, of course, the number of individual variables is even larger. What we can expect to find is interchangeability among many of these variables: one variable will interact with leadership style in the same way as another and thus affect group output in the same way. Consequently we might expect, for instance, that group cohesiveness and group member homogeneity might be used interchangeably. In this way it might ultimately be possible to specify a few variables which serve the same functions in the model as a large number of other variables.

COACTING VERSUS INTERACTING GROUPS

The previous discussion concerned itself with interacting (high group member interdependence) groups only. These are the kinds of groups used to formulate the Contingency Model. However, results of the present study introduce one more theoretical issue of importance. That issue is concerned with whether the same kind of model will be useful for interacting as opposed to coacting groups. Results of this study indicate that the same kind of model is applicable to both kinds of groups discussed. However, this finding needs to be examined in future research. Fiedler conducted two studies of coacting groups before his model was developed and found the correlations between LPC and performance to be in the opposite direction from that which would be predicted by the model [2].

We might also theorize that the leader's major functions would be different in the two kinds of groups and therefore require a different leadership effectiveness model. An important leader function in interacting groups would seem to be concerned with coordination of subordinate activities, while a primary function in coacting groups might be stressing psychological support and encouragement and stressing individual motivation.

Perhaps the particular kind of coacting groups is important here. The groups in Fiedler's two studies had, respectively, tension-arousing and highly creative coacting tasks. These kinds of tasks may be so different from the production coacting tasks of this study that a different kind of leadership style is required. The coacting groups examined here do not appear to be involved with particularly anxiety-arousing or creative tasks.

The importance of this issue receives additional support from Dubin. He makes the point that an increasing proportion of jobs will be performed individually rather than in groups; hence group theories of leadership may not be appropriate [19].

REFERENCES

1. For support of the authoritarian position see, for example, C. Hawkins, "A Study of Factors Mediating a Relationship between Leader Rating Behavior and Group Productivity," unpublished doctoral dissertation, University of Minnesota, 1962; M. E. Shaw, "A Comparison of Two Types of Leadership in Various Communication Nets," *Journal of Abnormal and Social Psychology*, Vol. 50 (1955), pp. 127–34. For support of the human relations position see, for example, R. Likert, *New Patterns of Management*. New York: McGraw-Hill Book Co., 1961.
2. F. E. Fiedler. *A Theory of Leadership Effectiveness*. New York: McGraw-Hill Book Co., 1967.
3. M. E. Shaw. "Scaling Group Tasks: A Method for Dimensional Analysis." Gainesville, Florida: Department of Psychology, University of Florida, 1963.
4. F. E. Fiedler. "The Effect of Leadership and Cultural Heterogeneity on Group Performances: A Test of the Contingency Model," *Journal of Experimental Social Psychology*, Vol. 2 (1966), pp. 237–64.
5. For more details of the methodology and results of this study see J. G. Hunt, "Fiedler's Leadership Contingency Model: An Empirical Test in Three Organizations," *Organizational Behavior and Human Performance*, Vol. 2 (1967), pp. 290–308.
6. M. Gordon, E. Loveland, and E. Cureton, "An Extended Table of Chi-Square for Two Degrees of Freedom, for Use in Combining Probabilities from Independent Samples," *Psychometrika*, Vol. 17 (1952), pp. 311–15.
7. See, for example, O. Tead. *The Art of Leadership*. New York: McGraw-Hill Book Co., 1935; W. Jenkins, "A Review of Leadership Studies with Particular Reference to Military Problems," *Psychological Bulletin*, Vol. 44 (1947), pp. 54–79.
8. F. Sanford. *Authoritarianism and Leadership*. Philadelphia: Institute for Research in Human Relations, 1950.
9. W. Meuwese, and F. E. Fiedler, "Leadership and Group Creativity under Varying Degrees of Stress. Urbana, Ill.: Group Effectiveness Research Laboratory, University of Illinois, 1966.

10. M. Argyle, G. Gardner, and F. Cioffi, "The Measurement of Supervisory Methods," *Human Relations,* Vol. 10 (1957), pp. 295–314.
11. These conclusions are similar but not identical to those of D. Bowers, and S. Seashore, "Predicting Organizational Effectiveness with a Four Factor Theory of Leadership," *Administrative Science Quarterly,* Vol. 11 (1966), pp. 238–63.
12. B. Bass. *Psychology and Organizational Behavior.* New York: Harper & Bros., 1960.
13. While often independent of each other, under some circumstances these dimensions appear to be correlated. See, for example, S. Nealey, and M. Blood, "Leadership Performance of Nursing Supervisors at Two Organizational Levels." Urbana, Ill.: Group Effectiveness Research Laboratory, University of Illinois, 1967.
14. H. Triandis. "Notes on the Design of Organizations," in J. Thompson, (Ed.), *Approaches to Organizational Design.* Pittsburgh, Pa.: University of Pittsburgh Press, 1966.
15. D. Pelz, "Influence: A Key to Effective Leadership in the First-Line Supervisor," *Personnel,* Vol. 29 (1952), pp. 3–11.
16. M. Patchen. "Supervisory Methods and Group Performance Norms," *Administrative Science Quarterly,* Vol. 7 (1962), pp. 275–93.
17. There is an exception to this statement if leader-member relations are considered in terms of subordinate acceptance of the supervisor. This would be a form of subordinate attitude.
18. Do not confuse complexity and structure. For example, a missile countdown is highly structured but also highly complex.
19. R. Dubin. "Supervision and Productivity: Empirical Findings and Theoretical Considerations," in R. Dubin, G. Homans, F. Mann, and D. Miller, *Leadership and Productivity.* San Francisco: Chandler Publishers, 1965.

21

Supervisory Style and Productivity: Review and Theory

STEPHEN M. SALES

It is widely assumed that employees will work harder for supervisors who employ given styles of supervision than they will for supervisors who use other styles. This supposition clearly underlies much of supervisory training; it is a basic tenet of the writings of Morse (1953), Likert (1961), and many others. However, the theoretical underpinnings of this assumption are often unclearly stated (when they are stated at all); furthermore, the wide variety of studies investigating the validity of this position are rarely fully described. The present article will sketch a theory which accounts for the predicted differential in productivity and will review and evaluate the literature relevant to this theory.

AUTHORITARIANISM AND DEMOCRACY

The styles to be discussed are the authoritarian and democratic dimensions. The distinction between these orientations has often been made in the literature; it will not be extensively elaborated here. Rather, we shall discuss only the major differences between these styles.

Authoritarian supervision, in general, is characterized by the relatively high degree of power wielded by the supervisor over the work group. As

Source: Reprinted by permission of the publisher from *Personnel Psychology*, Vol. 19 (1966), pp. 275–86.

contrasted with democratic supervision, both power and all decision-making functions are absolutely concentrated in the person of the authoritarian. Democratic supervision, on the other hand, is characterized by a sharing of power and by participative decision making. Under democratic supervision, the work group becomes in some ways co-equal with the supervisor; responsibility is spread rather than concentrated.

DIFFERENTIAL EFFECTIVENESS

It is commonly assumed that, with other conditions held constant, employees will produce more under democratic supervision than they would have produced under autocratic supervision. (Such an assumption, of course, lies behind the entire human relations movement.) There is at least one good reason for this prediction. Specifically, the reinforcing value of work performed under democratic supervision should be higher than that of work performed under autocratic supervision.

It is a basic tenet of experimental psychology that high levels of performance will obtain in situations in which the reinforcement is large, whereas low performance levels will occur in those in which the reinforcement is small. In terms of industrial situations, the more reinforcement an employee receives for production, the higher his production should be. (This is, of course, the assumption which underlies incentive systems, although reinforcement is rather narrowly defined in such programs.) Vroom (1962, pp. 26–43) in particular has explored the ramifications of this argument.

The importance of this point for the present consideration is that production is attended by two different levels of need-satisfaction under the two styles of supervision sketched above. Democratic supervision, by allowing subordinates freedom in determining the specific form and content of their work, implicates the personalities of the employees in the tasks they perform. This means that production, under democratic supervision, becomes a means for satisfying the employees' ego-esteem and self-actualization needs (see Maslow, 1954; Argyris, 1957). That is, the "greater opportunity for regulating and controlling their own activities [provided by democratic supervision] . . . should increase the degree to which individuals could express their various and diverse needs and could move in the direction of fully exploiting their potential while on the job" (Morse & Reimer, 1956). Authoritarian supervision, inasmuch as it makes work merely the carrying out of the supervisor's will, reduces the degree to which such need-satisfaction can be derived from production. Therefore, since productivity is less satisfying under autocratic than under democratic supervision, one would expect that workers would be less productive in the former condition than in the latter. (This effect, of course, should be accentuated for those individuals for whom the needs in question are most important.)

It should be noted that the above considerations do not involve between-style differences which rest upon uncontrolled factors (even when such factors might themselves follow from the style variation). For instance, if turnover were higher under one supervisory style than under the other, one would expect that the method resulting in higher turnover would be accompanied by the lower productivity rate (because of lowered effectiveness during learning periods). Factors of this sort would lead to productivity differences between the supervisory styles; however, such differences would not truly bear upon the question of effectiveness as usually posed. That is, statements about supervisory style center in general about the proposition that employees will work harder for some supervisors than for others. This statement cannot be supported by dependent variable differences which may be shown to result from between-condition variations other than that of supervisory style. The present discussion is concerned solely with productivity differences which follow *directly* from the style of supervision.

RELEVANT INVESTIGATIONS

Any review of the literature on supervision must be in some way limited if both the reviewer and the readers are to escape total exhaustion. For this reason, investigations employing non-production criteria will be excluded from this review as will studies in which methodological looseness clouds interpretation of the findings reported. Thus, investigations which operationalize the effectiveness of the supervisory styles used in terms of "increased acceptance of decisions" (e.g., Coch & French, 1948), morale, or similar criteria will not be reviewed, nor will unstandardized case studies of "participative management" or the Scanlon Plan.

Experimental Investigations

The original and best known study in this area is the experiment of Lewin, Lippitt, and White (e.g., Lippitt & White, 1958, pp. 496–510; White & Lippitt, 1962). These investigators employed as subjects thirty ten-year-old boys who met in six groups which ostensibly were recreational clubs. These groups were supervised by adults who had been trained to act in either a democratic, autocratic, or laissez-faire manner. (The last condition is not considered in the present discussion.) Each club was exposed to each of the three styles for six weeks.

The results of this experiment, in terms of productivity, are extremely difficult to establish. When exposed to autocratic supervision[1] the boys

---

[1] Only the "submissive reaction" to autocracy will be here considered; the "aggressive reaction" is felt to be a function of the subjects and the situation employed by the investigators.

spent more time at work than they did under democratic supervision (74% of the total time as opposed to 50% under democratic supervision). However, the "work-mindedness" of the democratically-supervised boys appeared to be somewhat higher since under democratic supervision the groups engaged in a slightly larger amount of "work-minded conversation." (There were 63 work-minded remarks per child under the democratic condition, whereas in the autocratic condition this figure fell to 52.) However, *no objective measure of productivity is reported by the authors, and therefore it is impossible to determine accurately which of the two styles evoked the higher production* (a fact often overlooked by reviewers of this study).

McCurdy and Eber (1953) examined supervisory style in an investigation on group problem-solving. In this experiment, three-man groups participated in a task in which the group determined the proper setting of three switches. In the authoritarian condition one subject was given the power to order the others at will, making him an "absolute" supervisor. The other subjects were instructed merely to obey orders. In the democratic condition the instructions emphasized equalitarianism, specifying that each subject could offer suggestions and that no individual could order the others in any way. No differences whatever appeared between the two conditions on a productivity criterion.

Shaw (1955), working with communication networks, also used problem-solving as a dependent variable in an investigation of supervisory style effects. Employing three different "nets," he instructed the subjects assigned to the position with the highest independence score within each structure[2] to behave either in an autocratic manner (e.g., by giving orders) or in a democratic manner (e.g., by making suggestions). Shaw found that the autocratically supervised subjects (*a*) required less time to solve the problems, regardless of the communication net in which they were placed, and (*b*) made fewer errors.

Day and Hamblin (1964) trained a female student to employ "close" and "general" supervisory styles in leading groups of female subjects in an assembly-line task. These researchers found that subjects exposed to close supervision produced less than did subjects exposed to general supervision.

Sales (1964), like Day and Hamblin, replicated an industrial assembly-line setting in the laboratory. In Sales's experiment two male supervisors played democratic and autocratic roles over male and female groups. (Both role and sex of the subordinates were fully counterbalanced in this experiment.) Sales reports no differential effectiveness whatever between the two styles; the productivity means for the two conditions were virtually identical.

Spector and Suttell (1957) report a relevant laboratory study with naval

---

[2] The research of Leavitt (1951) clearly suggests that these positions are the ones from which leadership is exercised.

trainees as subjects. These authors trained supervisors to use either "single leadership" or "leadership sharing" styles, patterns which seem to parallel the democratic-autocratic distinction. The task consisted of problems in which team members cooperated in receiving, processing, and recording information. No differences were detected in the productivity of the groups under the two styles.

In the most extensive of the investigations reported in this area, Morse and Reimer (1956) created groups exposed either to democratic or to autocratic supervision by altering the style of supervision used in an ongoing industrial setting. In two divisions ("participative treatment") an attempt was made to push down the level of decision making. Supervisors were trained to employ more democratic supervisory methods, and they were given greater freedom of action than previously had been allowed. In two other divisions an "hierarchically-controlled treatment" was established by an increase in the closeness of supervision and a movement upward in the level at which decisions were made. The treatments were administered for a year's time to approximately five hundred employees.

Morse and Reimer found that both programs resulted in a significant increase in productivity. This increase was slightly higher for the hierarchically-controlled divisions; however, the actual difference between the treatments was quite small.

On balance, then, the experimental studies reviewed above show no consistent superiority of one style over the other in terms of a productivity criterion. Of the six studies for which objective production data are available, one (Day & Hamblin, 1964) reports democratic supervision to be more effective and one (Shaw, 1955) reports authoritarian supervision to be more effective. The other four investigations note no differences of consequence between the two styles.

Survey Investigations

Survey researches applied to the problem discussed herein follow a standard methodology. The supervisory style which exists in each of the work groups in the situation is determined (usually by means of questionnaires administered to the employees), and this variable is then related to productivity. Researchers using this methodology generally have found a clear relationship between style of supervision and work group productivity.

The extensive investigations performed by the Survey Research Center at the University of Michigan during the early 1950s (Katz, Maccoby & Morse, 1950; Katz, Maccoby, Gurin & Floor, 1951; Katz & Kahn, 1951, pp. 146–71) are representative of this approach. In a wide variety of industrial situations (including railway maintenance crews, insurance office staffs, and heavy industry production lines), these authors found (1) that general supervision was associated with high productivity whereas close supervision was associated with low productivity, and (2) that "employee-oriented" attitudes in the supervisor were associated with high productivity whereas "job-oriented" attitudes were associated with low productivity. It is unclear exactly what relationship these independent variables have to the democratic-autocratic dimension; however, it can certainly be assumed that employee-oriented attitudes and general supervision will tend to be associated with democracy (as here used) whereas job-oriented attitudes and close supervision will tend to be associated with authoritarianism. The data of Morse (1953) and Argyle, Gardner, and Cioffi (1957) support these assumptions.

Argyle *et al.* (1958) performed a successful replication of these earlier investigations in a British industrial situation. The authors report that foremen of high-producing work groups tended to use general rather than close supervision and were relatively more democratic in their behavior than were foremen of less productive work groups. Further, the attitudes of the more effective foremen tended to be more "employee-oriented" than those of the less effective foremen. In contrast to experimental findings, therefore, these survey data clearly seem to support the hypothesis that democratic supervision leads to higher production than does authoritarian supervision.

DISCUSSION

The usual explanations offered for the failure of the experimental method to replicate survey findings rest upon either (*a*) the brevity of the experimental sessions or (*b*) the peripheral nature of the experimental tasks. It seems to the present author, however, that these explanations are respectively (*a*) too facile and (*b*) inadequately elaborated for proper handling of the problem.

Of the two, the "brevity" argument is the more open to attack. Experimental sessions are, of course, of relatively short duration. However, the entire science of experimental social psychology rests upon the assumption that experimental periods are sufficiently lengthy for treatments to "take," an assumption which is supported in every significant finding obtained in an experimental laboratory. To argue that the experiments reviewed here failed to demonstrate predicted productivity differences because of inadequate time periods (especially when these same time periods are sufficient to evoke morale differences—favoring the democratic supervisor—between the groups exposed to the two styles) seems somehow an unscientific and unsatisfactory way of explaining the findings. Furthermore, such an explanation fails to account for the quite small productivity differential which existed between the conditions created by Morse and Reimer in an experiment which continued over the course of an entire year.

It appears to the author that, rather than looking to brevity, one may best explain the equal experimental effectiveness of the two supervisory styles by concentrating upon the nature of the tasks involved. (This is, of course, the approach incompletely hinted at in the "peripheral nature" argument.) Specifically, it seems that no differences in effectiveness have been found between the two styles *because the tasks employed wholly fail to meet the conditions under which differential productivity was predicted.*

Democratic supervision, it will be remembered, was expected to be the more effective style because of the greater extent to which it makes productivity a means to need-satisfaction. This prediction rests upon the assumption that democratic supervision allows productivity to be a path to the satisfaction of self-actualization and ego-esteem needs, whereas autocratic supervision does not serve such a purpose.

These conditions do not seem to have been generated by the experimental investigations reported above. Democratic supervision, in these experiments, can hardly be seen as allowing the subjects to see production on the task involved as a path to self-actualization. *The thought is virtually absurd.* Regardless of the intent of the investigators, the decisions allowed by the democratic supervisors (e.g., suggesting possible solutions to simple problems) do not seem to implicate the unique personalities of the subjects in their tasks. This seems to have been true even in the Morse and Reimer investigation, for the authors report that "both groups of clerks indicated that their jobs throughout the course of the experiment did not give them a very high degree of self-actualization." To the extent that experimental studies fail to make productivity under democratic supervision a path to significantly greater need-satisfaction than it would be under autocratic supervision, there is no reason to suspect that they should demonstrate democratic supervision to be more effective. Such investigations simply fail to provide the conditions necessary for a test of the hypothesis in question.

It should not be inferred, however, that survey investigations provide a more adequate test of the hypothesis that workers will work harder for democratic supervisors, in spite of the satisfying direction of the findings. There are at least two reasons for approaching the results of these studies with caution, both of which rest upon the fact that spurious variables which clearly affect work group productivity accompany both these styles. To the extent that the effects of such variables cannot be discounted, survey methodology is incapable of offering convincing evidence concerning the relative effort expended by workers exposed to the styles in question.

In the first place, the supervisory styles discussed herein are accompanied by differential turnover and absenteeism (e.g., Mann & Baumgartel, 1953; Morse & Reimer, 1956; Argyle *et al.*, 1958). These effects do contribute to productivity differences between groups exposed to these styles, since the higher absenteeism and turnover evoked by autocratic supervision would lead to a productivity difference favoring democratic supervision.

However, such a difference would be irrelevant to the hypothesis that democratic supervision leads directly to more concerted effort on the part of the employees involved. The effects of absenteeism and/or turnover could be removed from the analysis by means of simple statistical techniques, although no survey research known to the author has as yet attempted to do so.

A second consideration lies in the fact that supervisors who naturally affect a democratic style of supervision cannot be assumed to be otherwise similar to those who affect an authoritarian style. In particular, the author feels that democratically oriented supervisors can be expected to be more intelligent than are autocratically-oriented supervisors. There are no direct data drawn from industry which bear on this statement. However, the fact that intelligence has clearly been shown to be negatively correlated with measured (F-scale) authoritarianism (e.g., Titus & Hollander, 1957), which in turn has been shown to be highly correlated with authoritarian behavior (McGee, 1955), seems sufficient to make the point.

It may be assumed that the intelligence of the supervisor should be of some importance in determining the productivity of the employees under him. The more intelligent supervisor might be expected to diagnose production difficulties more quickly than the less intelligent supervisor, and he might also be expected to take more effective remedial action. Therefore, inasmuch as authoritarian and democratic supervisors are differentiated on intelligence, one might expect them to be differentiated on their skill in dealing with day-to-day production problems. The advantage, of course, would go to the democratic supervisors.

The effect of this predicted difference between the two supervisory populations would be to make the work groups under democratic supervision more productive than those under autocratic supervision. However, as in the case of the different levels of turnover evoked by the two styles, such a finding would *not* necessarily imply that employees worked harder for supervisors affecting the democratic style. Like the effect of absenteeism, the effect of supervisory intelligence could be removed from the analysis by means of proper statistical techniques, but again there has been no survey research which has done so.

Therefore, in neither experimental studies nor survey investigations has an adequate test of the theory sketched above been made. Experimental studies have not created the conditions necessary for such a test; survey research has introduced at least two contaminating variables which render proper interpretation of the observed relationship extremely difficult. Such studies have not *disproved* the theory in question. They simply have not offered the unambiguous evidence administrative science must have in order to evaluate plans of action (e.g., supervisory training) tacitly based on this theory.

This should not be interpreted to mean that such a test cannot be made. Experimental investigations of the sort attempted by Morse and Reimer

(1956), *using a technology in which self-actualization could occur under democratic supervision,* would provide an adequate test, as would survey investigations in which the intelligence of the supervisors and the turnover (and/or absenteeism) levels existing in the various work groups were assessed and partialled out of the correlation between the style of the supervisor and the productivity of the subordinates. (Research now in progress is directed toward this latter objective.) Without such conditions, however, the hypothesis that democratic supervision will evoke greater effort from employees than will autocratic supervision cannot truly be either supported or rejected.

REFERENCES

Argyle, M., Gardner, G., & Cioffi, F. The measurement of supervisory methods. *Human Relations,* 1957, 10, 295–313.

Argyle, M., Gardner, G., & Cioffi, F. Supervisory methods related to productivity, absenteeism, and labour turnover. *Human Relations,* 1958, 11, 23–40.

Argyris, C. *Personality and Organization.* New York: Harper & Row, 1957.

Coch, L., & French, J. R. P., Jr. Overcoming resistance to change. *Human Relations,* 1948, 1, 512–32.

Day, R. C., & Hamblin, R. L. Some effects of close and punitive styles of supervision. *American Journal of Sociology,* 1964, 69, 499–510.

Katz, D., & Kahn, R. L. Human organization and worker motivation. In L. R. Tripp (ed.), *Industrial Productivity.* Madison, Wisc.: Industrial Relations Research Association, 1951.

Katz, D., Maccoby, N., Gurin, G., & Floor, L. *Productivity, Supervision, and Morale Among Railroad Workers.* Ann Arbor, Mich.: Institute for Social Research, 1951.

Katz, D., Maccoby, N., & Morse, N. C. *Productivity, Supervision and Morale in an Office Situation* (Part 1). Ann Arbor, Mich.: Institute for Social Research, 1950.

Leavitt, H. Some effects of certain communication patterns on group performance. *Journal of Abnormal and Social Psychology,* 1951, 46, 16–30.

Likert, R. *New Patterns of Management.* New York: McGraw-Hill, 1961.

Lippett, R., & White, R. K. An experimental study of leadership and group life. In E. E. Maccoby, T. N. Newcomb, & E. L. Hartley (eds.), *Readings in Social Psychology,* 3rd ed. New York: Holt, Rinehart & Winston, 1958. Pp. 496–511.

McCurdy, H. G., & Eber, H. W. Democratic versus authoritarian: A further investigation of group problem-solving. *Journal of Personality,* 1953, 22, 258–69.

McGee, H. M. Measurement of authoritarianism and its relation to teacher classroom behavior. *Genetic Psychology Monographs,* 1955, 52, 89–146.

Mann, F. C., & Baumgartel, H. D. *Absences and Employee Attitudes in an Electric Power Company.* Ann Arbor, Mich.: Institute for Social Research, 1953.

Maslow, A. H. *Motivation and Personality.* New York: Harper & Row, 1954.

Morse, N. C. *Satisfactions in the White-Collar Job.* Ann Arbor, Mich.: Institute for Social Research, 1953.

Morse, N. C., & Reimer, E. The experimental change of a major organizational variable. *Journal of Abnormal and Social Psychology,* 1956, 51, 120–29.

Sales, S. M. A laboratory investigation of the effectiveness of two industrial supervisory dimensions. Unpublished masters thesis, Cornell University, 1964.

Shaw, M. E. A comparison of two types of leadership in various communication nets. *Journal of Abnormal and Social Psychology,* 1955, 50, 127–34.

Spector, P., & Suttell, B. *An Experimental Comparison of the Effectiveness of Three Patterns of Leadership Behavior.* Washington, D.C.: American Institute for Research, 1957.

Titus, H. E., & Hollander, E. P. The California *F*-scale in psychological research: 1950–1955. *Psychological Bulletin,* 1957, 54, 47–65.

Vroom, V. H. Human relations research in industry: Some things learned. In F. Baristow (ed.), *Research Frontiers in Industrial Relations Today.* Montreal: Industrial Relations Centre, 1962.

White, R., & Lippitt, R. Leader behavior and member reaction in three "social climates." In D. Cartwright & A. Zander (eds.), *Group Dynamics,* 2nd ed. New York: Harper & Row, 1962. Pp. 527–53.

Part V

CLIMATE AND ORGANIZATIONAL DEVELOPMENT WITHIN ORGANIZATIONS

It is general knowledge that organizations differ not only in structural, process, and behavioral dimensions but also in climate. The interaction of people, structure, and technology evidently produces what has been referred to in recent literature as organizational climate. The organization's climate influences to a great extent the efforts of managers to introduce change in structure, process, and behavior. Thus, this section of the reader examines both climate and organizational development since they are so interrelated.

An organization's climate can be described as:

a set of properties of the work environment, perceived directly or indirectly by the employees who work in this environment and is assumed to be a major force in influencing their behavior on the job.

This definition implies that climate is a force that employees react to on the job. It is a force that helps shape the character of an organization.

Another important force that aids in shaping the tone of an organization is commonly referred to as organizational development (OD). The editors interpret OD as:

1. A planned, systematic change process initiated by an organization's management,
2. with the aim of making the organization more adaptable to either present or future change,

313

3. through the use of a variety of methods designed to change skills, attitudes, behaviors, and structure.
4. And based upon the assumption that organizational effectiveness in the sense of adaptability to change is enhanced to the extent that the process facilitates the integration of individual and organizational objectives.

These four statements capture the essence of OD and provide the basis for the selection of articles used in this section.

The first article by Roger Harrison "Understanding Your Organization's Character" focuses upon a climate-type concept. The character of an organization is embedded in its ideological orientation. Harrison postulates four separate ideologies that determine (a) the compatability of an organization's interests with those of its members and (b) an organization's ability to deal with the external environment. He further argues that the failure to comprehend ideological differences often causes conflicts within organizations.

The second article by Michael Beer and Edgar F. Huse, "A Systems Approach To Organization Development" focuses upon an OD effort in an organization. Based upon their investigations the authors reach some interesting conclusions. Some of which are (1) OD efforts must not always start at the top; (2) the organization itself is the best laboratory for learning; (3) structural and interpersonal changes must complement and reinforce each other; (4) adult learning starts with behavioral change rather than cognitive change; and (5) the selection of change leaders as initial targets for the change program is a useful OD strategy.

Paul Buchanan in "Laboratory Training and Organization Development" reviews studies published between May 1964 and May 1968 on laboratory training in human relations. In his discussion such issues as problems of research design, factors influencing learning, types of individuals influenced, and laboratory training as parts of development programs are analyzed.

An important concept in OD involves the durability of the change effort. Stanley E. Seashore and David G. Bowers in "Durability of Organizational Change" examine a change program. The question which they address is whether changes that have been planned, successfully introduced, and confirmed by measurements over but a relatively short span of time, can survive as permanent features of an organization. Such issues as whether the changed organization will become stabilized in its new state or whether it will revert to its earlier state are discussed. To examine these and other change questions data collected at three different points in time are carefully presented and interpreted.

An article by Walter R. Nord, "Beyond the Teaching Machine: The Neglected Area of Operant Conditioning in the Theory and Practice of Management" discusses the issue of reinforcement in change efforts. The objective of the author is to present Skinner's operant conditioning as an approach consistent in many ways with widely accepted and adopted management practices. It is Nord's assumption that the conditioning approach can aid managers in the areas of job design, compensation, organizational design, and training and development. In support of these assumptions Nord discusses the relationship of these areas to conditioning.

The final article by Larry E. Greiner, "Red Flags In Organization Development," cautions readers by examining six trends in OD. The warning signals discussed are placing the individual before the organization, assuming that the informal organization takes precedence over the formal organization, an overemphasis on behavioral change before diagnosis, placing primary emphasis upon improving the behavioral processes of decision making while de-emphasizing or ignoring the content and task issues, placing expert knowledge before managerial knowledge, and imposing programs of OD that have been designed by outsiders who do not know the organization. After discussing these six caution flags Greiner suggests alternative courses of action for those involved in OD programs.

22

Understanding Your Organization's Character

ROGER HARRISON

The failure to recognize the ideological issues that underlie organizational conflict is common among managers and administrators. Usually the issues are recognized only when they are blatant and the lines of struggle are drawn, as in labor-management relationships. But by then the conflict may well have developed to the point where a constructive resolution is virtually impossible.

While the term "organization ideologies" is perhaps unfortunately ambiguous, it is the best name I can apply to the systems of thought that are central determinants of the character of organizations. An organization's ideology affects the behavior of its people, its ability to effectively meet their needs and demands, and the way it copes with the external environment. Furthermore, much of the conflict that surrounds organization change is really ideological struggle (an idea that is certainly not new to political science but one about which behavioral scientists have, until recently, been curiously quiet).

For example, during the commissioning and start-up stages of a U.S. chemical plant in Europe, it became apparent that the Americans and local nationals involved had rather different ideas about decision making and commitment to decisions. Consider the approach of each group.

Source: Reprinted by permission from *Harvard Business Review* (May-June 1972), 119–28; © 1972 by the President and Fellows of Harvard College; all rights reserved.

The Americans tended to operate within what I shall later describe as a task-oriented ideology. In problem-solving meetings they believed that everyone who had relevant ideas or information should contribute to the debates, and that in reaching a decision the greatest weight should be given to the best-informed and most knowledgeable people. They strove, moreover, for a clear-cut decision; and once the decision was made, they usually were committed to it even if they did not completely agree with it.

Some of the nationals, however, came to the project from very authoritarian organizations and tended to operate from a power-oriented ideological base (this will also be described later). Each individual seemed to be trying to exert as much control as possible and to accept as little influence from others as he could. If he was in a position of authority, he seemed to ignore the ideas of juniors and the advice of staff experts. If he was not in a position of authority, he kept rather quiet in meetings and seemed almost happy when there was an unclear decision or no decision at all. He would then proceed the way he had wanted to all along.

The task-oriented people regarded the foregoing behavior as uncooperative and, sometimes, as devious or dishonest. The power-oriented people, however, interpreted the task-oriented individuals' emphasis on communication and cooperation as evidence of softness and fear of taking responsibility.

Each group was engaging in what it regarded as normal and appropriate practice and tended to regard the other as difficult to work with or just plain wrong. The fact that the differences were ideological was dimly realized only by the more thoughtful participants. The remainder tended to react to each other as wrongheaded *individuals,* rather than as adherents of a self-consistent and internally logical way of thinking and explaining their organizational world.

In this article I shall present a theory that identifies four distinct, competing organization ideologies and their meaning for the businessman. But, first, let me attempt to further clarify the concept. Here are the most obvious functions that an organization ideology performs:

Specifies the goals and values toward which the organization should be directed and by which its success and worth should be measured.

Prescribes the appropriate relationships between individuals and the organization (i.e., the "social contract" that legislates what the organization should be able to expect from its people, and vice versa).

Indicates how behavior should be controlled in the organization and what kinds of control are legitimate and illegitimate.

Depicts which qualities and characteristics of organization members should be valued or vilified, as well as how these should be rewarded or punished.

Shows members how they should treat one another—competitively or collaboratively, honestly or dishonestly, closely or distantly.

Establishes appropriate methods of dealing with the external environment—aggressive exploitation, responsible negotiation, proactive exploration.

VALUES AND IDEOLOGIES

An organization ideology, however, is more than a set of prescriptions and prohibitions. It also establishes a rationale for these "do"s and "don't"s. This rationale explains the behavior of an organization's members as well as the working of the external environment (in the latter case, by telling members how to expect other people and organization systems to behave).

The rationale of an organization ideology is similar to what behavioral scientists call "organization theory." The difference is that behavioral scientists try with varying degrees of success to keep their values from influencing their organization theories; people, for the most part, do not try to keep their values from influencing their organization ideologies. (This is one reason why education about organization behavior is likely to be so emotionally loaded; if you change a man's organization theory, he usually ends up questioning his values as well.)

Among people in organizations, ideas of "what is" and "what ought to be" merge into one another and are—or are made to appear—consistent. Here is an example:

The ideology of a large U.S. manufacturer of consumer products prescribed that work should be organized in the way that produced the most profit. If this meant that some organization members had boring jobs which offered little opportunity for satisfaction and pride in their work, then it was unfortunate but ideologically irrelevant. According to the rationale of this ideology, a majority of people did not have much aptitude or desire for responsibility and decision making, anyhow, and those who did would rise by natural selection to more responsible, satisfying jobs.

Some young managers, however, had rather more egalitarian personal values. They uneasily suspected that there were more boring jobs than there were apathetic people to fill them. They were very excited about a group of research studies which attempted to show that giving employees more responsibility and involvement in decision making actually led to improved performance. But in my discussions with the managers, I found that the studies' instrumental value in improving organization effectiveness was not the cause of their popularity; rather, they were welcomed because they helped the managers reconcile their personal values with the dictum of the prevailing ideology that work should, above all, be organized to produce the best economic result. (I have, in fact, found that behavioral research findings are usually accepted or rejected on such ideological grounds instead of on the probability of their being true.)

A CONCEPTUAL FRAMEWORK

There is a considerable body of thought in political science which holds that attempts to resolve ideological struggle are unwarranted interferences with the natural course of history and as such are doomed to be ineffectual.

I do not feel that this theory has been adequately tested, particularly in regard to organization change and development. The first step in testing it is to develop ways of discovering and understanding ideological conflicts when they arise in organizations.

In the remainder of this article I shall present a conceptual framework for doing this. It postulates four organization ideologies: (1) power orientation; (2) role orientation; (3) task orientation; and (4) person orientation. These ideologies are seldom found in organizations as pure types, but most organizations tend to center on one or another of them. I shall describe and contrast them in their pure form to emphasize their differences, and then indicate what I believe to be the strengths and weaknesses of each. After this I shall apply the conceptual model to some common conflicts in modern organization life.

Power Orientation

An organization that is power-oriented attempts to dominate its environment and vanquish all opposition. It is unwilling to be subject to any external law or power. And within the organization those who are powerful strive to maintain absolute control over subordinates.

The power-oriented organization is competitive and jealous of its territory (whether this be markets, land area, product lines, or access to resources). It seeks to expand its control at the expense of others, often exploiting weaker organizations. Even a weak power-oriented organization takes satisfaction in being able to dominate others that are still weaker. Such organizations always attempt to bargain to their own advantage and readily find justification for abrogating agreements which are no longer self-serving.

Some modern conglomerates project images of power ideology. They buy and sell organizations and people as commodities, in apparent disregard of human values and the general welfare. They seem to have voracious appetites for growth, which is valued for its own sake. Competition to acquire other companies and properties is ruthless and sometimes outside the law. Within the organization, the law of the jungle often seems to prevail among executives as they struggle for personal advantage against their peers.

There is, however, a softer form of the power orientation that is often found among old established firms, particularly those with a background of family ownership. Here the employees may be cared for rather than exploited, especially those that are old and loyal. Externally, the proprietors may hold to a code of honor, especially when dealing with others like themselves. This is the power orientation with a velvet glove. But when the benevolent authority is crossed or challenged, from either within or without, the iron fist is very likely to appear again. In such cases, the test of power orientation is how hard a person or organization will fight for power and position when these are at issue.

Role Orientation

An organization that is role-oriented aspires to be as rational and orderly as possible. In contrast to the willful autocracy of the power-oriented organization, there is a preoccupation with legality, legitimacy, and responsibility.

It is useful to see role orientation as having developed partly in reaction to power orientation. Competition and conflict, for example, are regulated or replaced by agreements, rules, and procedures. Rights and privileges are carefully defined and adhered to. While there is a strong emphasis on hierarchy and status, it is moderated by the commitment to legitimacy and legality. The different attitudes of the power and role orientations toward authority might be likened to the differences between a dictatorship and a constitutional monarchy.

Predictability of behavior is high in the role-oriented organization, and stability and respectability are often valued as much as competence. The correct response tends to be more highly valued than the effective one. Procedures for change tend to be cumbersome; therefore the system is slow to adapt to change.

Most commercial organizations are too constricted by market demands to afford the extreme rigidity of a pure role orientation or the worst excesses of its tendency to place procedural correctness before task effectiveness. Some businesses, however, which either control their markets or operate in areas that are highly regulated by law, exhibit a considerable degree of role orientation. The rationality, impersonality, and adherence to procedure of many banks, insurance companies, public utilities, and social work organizations are cases in point. Their role orientation leaves the customer, the public, or the client with little alternate choice in dealing with them.

Task Orientation

In the organization that is task-oriented, achievement of a superordinate goal is the highest value. The goal need not be economic; it could be winning a war, converting the heathen, reforming a government, or helping the poor. The important thing is that the organization's structure, functions, and activities are all evaluated in terms of their contribution to the superordinate goal.

Nothing is permitted to get in the way of accomplishing the task. If established authority impedes achievement, it is swept away. If outmoded roles, rules, and regulations hinder problem solving, they are changed. If individuals do not have the skills or technical knowledge to perform a task, they are retrained or replaced. And if personal needs and social considerations threaten to upset effective problem solving, they are suppressed in the interests of "getting on with the job."

There is no ideological commitment to authority, respectability, and order as such. Authority is considered legitimate only if it is based on appropriate knowledge and competence; it is not legitimate if it is based solely on power or position. And there is little hestiation to break rules and regulations if task accomplishment is furthered by doing so.

There is nothing inherently competitive about task orientation. The organization structure is shaped and changed to meet the requirements of the task or function to be performed. Emphasis is placed on rapid, flexible organization response to changed conditions. Collaboration is sought if it will advance the goal; allies are chosen on the basis of mutual goals and values; and there is little "advantage seeking" in relationships with other organizations.

The task orientation is most readily found in those small organizations whose members have come together because of some shared value, task, or goal. Examples are social service organizations, research teams, and high-risk businesses. Often, however, internal conflict and external stress drive these organizations toward power and role orientations.

Large organizations that operate in highly complex, shifting environments offer more durable examples. Companies involved with dynamic markets or fast-changing, complex technology frequently establish project teams or "task forces." These groups of specialists are selected to solve a particular problem and often operate in a very flexible and egalitarian manner until the problem is solved. The units are then disbanded, and the members join other teams to work on new problems. Although the larger organization in which it operates may be basically role- or power-oriented, the project team or task force often exhibits a relatively pure task orientation. Moreover, these groups have been so successful that some organizations are trying to install a task-oriented ideology throughout their operations.

Some of the aerospace industries have probably gone the furthest in this direction, TRW Systems being a notable example. Although I do not know of any large organization that could be classed as "pure" in its task orientation, the success of such task-oriented programs as MBO is a sign of the growing interest among managers. Parenthetically, the most frequent reason for the failure of MBO is probably that task-oriented managers try to install it in power- or role-oriented organizations.

Person Orientation

Unlike the other three types, the person-oriented organization exists primarily to serve the needs of its members. The organization itself is a device through which the members can meet needs that they could not otherwise satisfy by themselves. Just as some organizations continually evaluate the worth of individual members as tools and accept or reject them accordingly, so the person-oriented organizations are evaluated as tools by their members. For this reason, some of these organizations may have a very short life; they are disposable when they cease to provide a system for members to "do their own thing."

Authority in the role- or power-oriented sense is discouraged. When it is absolutely necessary, authority may be assigned on the basis of task competence, but this practice is kept to the bare minimum. Instead, individuals are expected to influence each other through example, helpfulness, and caring.

Consensus methods of decision making are preferred; people are generally not expected to do things that are incongruent with their own goals and values. Thus roles are assigned on the basis of personal preference and the need for learning and growth. Moreover, the burden of unrewarding and unpleasant tasks is shared equally.

Illustrations of person orientation are small groups of professionals who have joined together for research and development. Some consulting companies, too, seem to be designed primarily as vehicles for members. It is typical of such organizations that growth, expansion, and maximization of income and profit are not primary considerations. Rather, the organizations, hopefully, are conducted to make enough money to survive and provide their members with a reasonable living as well as an opportunity to do meaningful and enjoyable work with congenial people.

There seem to be increasing pressures from the members of modern industrial organizations to move toward person orientation. Young professionals are pushing their companies for opportunities to work on interesting, worthwhile (congruent with their own values) projects. Engineers and scientists, for example, have refused to work on projects for the military and have been successful in getting transfers to nondefense-related activities. Job recruiters find that college graduates are often more interested in opportunities to learn and grow than they are in their chances for organization advancement. Such signs of social change illustrate why the person orientation must be considered an ideological force to be reckoned with, even though there are few contemporary organizations that operate in total congruence with its principles.

STRENGTHS AND WEAKNESSES

An organization ideology obviously has a profound effect on organization effectiveness. It determines how (a) decisions are made, (b) human resources are used, and (c) the external environment is approached. An organization ideology tends to be internally viable when the people within the system want and need the prescribed incentives and satisfactions that reward good performance. It tends to be externally viable when the organization it embodies is a microcosm of the external environment and rewards the same skills, values, and motivations.

External Viability

Usually, as an organization increases in size, its operational environment becomes more complex. Most arenas in which large companies operate change rapidly and/or have many features that require an integrated response. Worldwide markets and rapidly changing technology, for example, make heavy demands on the information-processing and decision-making capabilities of organizations.

The power-oriented organization is not well adapted to flexible response and effective information processing in such environments. Since decisions are made at the top, the information has to pass through many people who screen out the "irrelevant" data. Moreover, some may distort the message to their own advantage (aggressive competition is part of the ideology). And when conditions change rapidly, the time lag introduced by the filtering process may unduly delay organization response.

The role-oriented organization is also insufficiently flexible to easily adapt to rapid external changes. In order to achieve the security that is one of its highest values, it must perpetuate rather rigid roles and reporting relationships. This gives stability but means that even the most powerful individuals may be unable to produce needed changes quickly.

In times of change, established procedures often do not apply, and the information channels become overloaded with problems that require higher-level decisions. Consider what happened in the commissioning and start-up example referred to at the beginning of this article:

Because equipment was not working properly, many actions which ordinarily would have been dealt with by standard operating procedures required top-management decisions. But the ordinary channels would not carry the necessary volume of information, and the quality of decision making and problem solving suffered accordingly. However, when control was shifted to teams of experts clustered around each plant (a task-oriented system) the problems were handled much more smoothly.

Change-Oriented Structures. The task-oriented organization's greatest strength is dealing with complex and changing environments. Decentralized control shortens communication channels and reduces time lags, distortion, and attenuation of messages.

Both the power- and role-oriented organizations associate control with a *position* in the organization; neither provides for rapid and rational reassignment of appropriate *persons* to positions of influence. In contrast, the task oriented ideology clears the way for a very flexible system of control —one that can shift rapidly over time as differing resources are required by external problems.

Probably the best example of this system in operation is the project team or task force that is formed to identify, diagnose, and solve a particular problem. Even some rather bureaucratic organizations make use of these temporary systems for emergency problem solving. The task force leader is selected for his combination of technical expertise and ability to manage a small group in an egalitarian manner.

The temporary work system is a particularly characteristic response of the task-oriented organization to environmental change. These temporary systems can be activated quickly, provided with the necessary mix of skills and abilities, and disbanded again when the need is past. Their use provides what is, in effect, a continuously variable organization structure.

The person-oriented organization, too, is well adapted to dealing with complexity and change. It also features a fluid structure and short lines of communication and control.

Coping with Threat. In a highly competitive environment where organizations are frequently confronted with overt threats and hostility, the strengths and weaknesses of ideological types form a different pattern.

For example, while the power-oriented organization is not well suited to handle complexity and change, its structure and decision-making processes are admirably suited for swift decision making and rapid-action follow-through under high-risk conditions. It tends to promote tough, aggressive people who can lead the organization in a dangerous, competitive environment.

The task-oriented organization usually takes longer to respond, but the response is more likely to be based on adequate data and planning. In contrast to the power-oriented structure, which is aggressively directed from the top, it tends to enlist the full commitment of organization members at all levels.

The role-oriented organization does not deal successfully with sudden increases in threat because it relies heavily on established operational procedures. Consequently, its structure is too cumbersome to react quickly in cases of overt threat.

And the person-oriented organization has difficulty directing its members' activities in unison until the danger is so clear and present that it may be too late. The person-oriented structure, however, does offer some advantages—its members are committed and have a high concern for one another's welfare.

Probably the most viable organization in a hostile, threatening environment would have a combination of the power and task orientations. This is a difficult marriage, however, because the desire for personal power is often incompatible with the required willingness to relinquish control to those with the most knowledge and ability for the task at hand.

Internal Viability

The power-oriented organization is an excellent structure for attaching many eyes, ears, hands, and feet to one brain. It exercises tight internal control and integration. As mentioned earlier, the system works well when problems take the form of overt challenges that can be comprehended and solved by one or a few intelligent, courageous men at the top.

But when the power-oriented organization becomes large and complex, this control tends to break down. Under these conditions the role-oriented ideology is more effective. It provides rules and procedures that allow a high degree of internal integration with little active intervention from the top.

It is obviously more difficult to achieve internal cohesion under a task- or person-oriented ideology. For example, if the work is done by temporary project teams, how are their efforts to be coordinated to a common goal? When a problem-solving team comes up with a solution and then disbands, how is its work to be given impact and continuity in the rest of the organization? Some stable and central structure is needed to provide coordination, long-range planning, and continuity of effort. If it is too stable, however, it may become role-oriented (rigid and hard to change) or power-oriented (recentralizing control). The personal power and security needs of individual members may foster such developments.

These dilemmas of internal structure have led to various compromise solutions such as the "matrix organization." The term "matrix" is used because the actual working groups *cut horizontally across* the normal functional-pyramidal organization, bringing together selected individuals from different functions and different levels to work in a relatively autonomous, egalitarian group. Structural stability is provided by a fixed *role-oriented* framework organized on functional lines. Personnel are readily detachable from the functions for varying periods of time during which they join a *task-oriented* work unit or project team. They are directed by the work unit; but their pay, career prospects, and promotions emanate from the role-oriented part of the system.

Matrix forms of organization have been used with success in highly technical businesses operating in a fast-changing environment. Again, TRW Systems is perhaps the oldest and most comprehensive example. Considerable experimentation with matrix forms has also taken place in the chemical industry, both in the United States and abroad.

Although the matrix system can be effective, it often suffers from attempts of the role-oriented functions to overcontrol the task-oriented functions. The resulting conflict is usually won by the former, which has greater permanence and more resources. One reason for this difficulty is that organizations try to operate partially task-oriented structures without commitments to the ideology. Role-oriented people cannot be plugged into a task-oriented system without conflict.

Effective Motivation. While the power-oriented organization provides a chance for a few aggressive people to fight their way to the top, it offers little security to the ordinary person. It is most viable in situations where people are deprived and powerless and have to accept a bad bargain as better than none. For example, the power-oriented organization thrives in underdeveloped countries.

The power-oriented organization also has the problem of using too much of its energy to police people. Reliance on rewards and punishments tends to produce surface compliance and covert rebellion. Where the quantity and quality of work can be observed (as on an assembly line), inspection and discipline may keep the system working. But if the power does not command loyalty as well, the system usually breaks down. A simple example is the sabotage of hard-to-test aspects of car assembly by disgruntled workers.

The role-oriented ideology tries to deal with the difficulty of supervising complex decision-making and problem-solving tasks by rationalization and simplification. Each job is broken into smaller elements, rules are established, and performance is observed. When conditions change, however, the members are likely to continue carrying out the same (now ineffective) procedures.

The power- and role-oriented organizations simply do not provide for the development and utilization of internal commitment, initiative, and independent judgment on the part of members at other than the highest levels. Nevertheless, in societies where most people's aspirations are just to get by, or at most to achieve a measure of economic security, the power- and role-oriented organizations are able to function adequately.

In affluent societies, however, where security is more widely assured, people begin to look for deeper satisfactions in their work. They attempt to change tightly controlled work assignments and rigid internal structures. When trends toward task orientation ("useful," "meaningful" work) and person orientation (interesting work, self expression, and "doing one's own thing") begin to develop in the wider society, internal pressures for change develop within power- and role-oriented organizations.

Unfortunately, not all people can function productively in a flexible and egalitarian structure. Some people *are* dependent, apathetic, or insecure. They do need external incentives to work and directives or rules to guide their activities.

Furthermore, the task-oriented ideology has its own ways of exploiting the individual. When his knowledge and skills become obsolete for the task at hand, an individual is expected to step gracefully aside to make room for someone who is better qualified. Status and recognition depend almost entirely on task contribution; if the problems facing the organization change suddenly, this can produce cruel reversals of an individual's personal fortune and work satisfaction.

The person-oriented organization seems to be specially created to fit the work situation to the motives and needs of the independent, self-directed individual. It is flexible to his demands, whereas the power-oriented organization is controlling; it gives scope for his individual expression, whereas the role-oriented organization programs every move; it is concerned about his personal needs, whereas the task-oriented organization uses people as instruments for "higher" ends. Unfortunately, as discussed above, the person-oriented organization is less likely to be effective in the external environment than organizations based on the other ideologies.

TOWARD RESOLVING CONFLICT

One basic tension runs throughout the ideologies and organization types discussed thus far. It is the conflict between (*a*) the values and structural qualities which advance the interests of people and (*b*) the values and structural qualities which advance the interests of organizations.

I can identify six interests, all mentioned previously, which are currently the subject of ideological tension and struggle. Three of these are primarily interests of people, and three are primarily interests of organizations. The three interests of people are:

1. Security against economic, political, or psychological deprivation.
2. Opportunities to voluntarily commit one's efforts to goals that are personally meaningful.
3. The pursuit of one's own growth and development, even where this may conflict with the immediate needs of the organization.

The three interests of organizations are:

1. Effective response to threatening and dangerous complex environments.
2. Dealing rapidly and effectively with change and complex environments.
3. Internal integration and coordination of effort toward organization needs and goals, including the subordination of individual needs to the needs of the organization.

These are obviously not all the interests at issue, but in my opinion they are among the most salient.

Exhibit 1 shows the position of each ideology vis-à-vis each interest and indicates, as does the preceding analysis, that the four ideologies have quite dissimilar profiles. Each ideology thus "fits" the needs of a given organization and its members differently. For example, a small organization operating in a rapidly changing technical field and employing people who desire personal growth and autonomy might find its best fit with either the task or person orientation (this depends, of course, on how competitive its markets are and what financial shape it is in). A very large organization operating a slowly changing technology in a restricted market and employing people who desire stability and security might find that a role orientation would provide the best balance.

For most organizations, however, there is no perfect fit with any one of the four ideologies. The "ideal" ideology would possess some power orientation to deal smartly with the competition, a bit of role orientation for stability and internal integration, a charge of task orientation for good problem solving and rapid adaption to change, and enough person orientation to meet the questions of the new recruit who wants to know why he should be involved at all unless *his* needs are met.

But, unfortunately, this mixture of ideologies *and their consequences* for people and organizations will inevitably result in conflict, and its subsequent wear and tear on organizations and their members. Trying to mix ideologies may also prevent each type from producing the advantages that are unique to it.

On the other hand, I do not think that the most viable organizations and the maximum satisfaction of human needs will result from monolithic structures which are ideologically homogeneous. It seems to me that we must learn to create and maintain organizations that contain within them the same diversity of ideologies and structures as are found in the complex environments in which the organizations must live and grow. This means that organizations may have to be composed of separate *parts* that are ideologically homogeneous within themselves yet still quite different from each other.

Such organizations will be very effective in dealing with complex environments and maximizing satisfactions for different types of people, but they will be subject to more internal conflict and ideological struggle than most current organizations could tolerate. For example, instead of a "company spirit" there will be several "company spirits," all different and very likely antagonistic. In this environment of conflicting but mutually interdependent parts, the management—not the resolution—of conflict will be a task of the greatest importance. One can imagine, in fact, that the most important job of top managers will not be directing the business, but instead, managing the integration of its parts.[1]

---

[1] See Paul R. Lawrence and Jay W. Lorsch, "New Management Job: The Integrator" *Harvard Business Review,* November–December 1967, p. 142.

EXHIBIT 1

Interests of People and the Organization under Four Orientations

A. *Interests of people*

	Security against economic, political, and psychological deprivation	Opportunities for voluntary commitment to worthwhile goals	Opportunities to pursue one's own growth and development independent of organization goals
Power orientation	Low: At the pleasure of the autocrat	Low: Unless one is in a sufficiently high position to determine organization goals	Low: Unless one is in a sufficiently high position to determine organization goals
Role orientation	High: Secured by law, custom, and procedure	Low: Even if, at times, one is in a high position	Low: Organization goals are relatively rigid and activities are closely prescribed
Task orientation	Moderate: Psychological deprivation can occur when an individual's contributions are redundant	High: A major basis of the individual's relationship to the organization	Low: The individual should not be in the organization if he does not subscribe to some of its goals
Person orientation	High: The individual's welfare is the major concern	High: But only if the individual is capable of generating his own goals	High: Organization goals are determined by individual needs

CONCLUDING NOTE

Whether men confront or avoid them, ideological issues will continue to sharpen of their own accord, both inside and outside the organization. As long as we continue to raise and educate our children permissively, the pressure from younger members of the organization for greater person orientation will increase. As operational environments become more turbulent and more technical, the attractions of task orientation will make themselves felt. Yet every change in organizations means some degree of power redistribution and with it some shift in rewards—such shifts will always be resisted by those with the most to lose, usually the older members of the organization who have a higher status. Thus I believe that ideological conflict will increase within organizations, whether that conflict is dealt with openly or not.

By dealing with such conflict openly, however, businessmen may find

EXHIBIT 1—*Continued*

B. *Interests of the organization*

	Effective response to dangerous, threatening environments	Dealing rapidly and effectively with environmental complexity and change	Internal integration and coordination of effort—if necessary, at the expense of individual needs
Power orientation	High: The organization tends to be perpetually ready for a fight	Moderate to low: Depends on size; pyramidal communication channels are easily overloaded	High: Effective control emanates from the top
Role orientation	Moderate to low: The organization is slow to mobilize to meet increases in threat	Low: Slow to change programmed procedures; communication channels are easily overloaded	High: Features a carefully planned rational system of work
Task orientation	Moderate to high: The organization may be slow to make decisions but produces highly competent responses	High: Flexible assignment of resources and short communication channels facilitate adaptation	Moderate: Integrated by common goal; but flexible, shifting structure may make coordination difficult
Person orientation	Low: The organization is slow to become aware of threat and slow to mobilize effort against it	High: But response is erratic; assignment of resources to problems depends greatly on individual needs and interests	Low: A common goal is difficult to achieve and activities may shift with individual interests

ways to manage it in the service of both the organization and its members and also to use tension creatively as well as competitively. Hidden conflict, on the other hand, tends to eat away at the strength of an organization and then to erupt when it is most dangerous to organization health.

In writing this article, I have attempted to render these inevitable ideological differences more conceptually clear. The next step is to develop a common language and set of norms that support both the open confrontation of such issues and the strategies for dealing with them in our organizations.

23

A Systems Approach to
Organization Development
MICHAEL BEER and EDGAR F. HUSE

Although the plant has since grown considerably, at the beginning of the change effort there were approximately 35 hourly employees, mostly women; some 15 weekly salaried technical and clerical personnel; and approximately eight professional and managerial personnel, who were paid monthly.

Some particulars about this plant which need to be considered in generalizing the results obtained in this study to other organizations follow: (1) the products are complex; (2) the operation is primarily assembly, as opposed to fabrication; (3) a majority of factory workers are women; (4) the organization is nonunion; and (5) the organization is relatively small. In other words, approaches which might work with female assembly workers in a nonunion plant might not have the same impact with male union workers in a plant utilizing a different technology.

Because the organization was relatively new when this organization development effort started, it did not have a well-established historical culture and set of norms. It was in its formative stages, and crucial decisions were in the making concerning the technology in the plant (means of production), methods of setting production standards and controls, personnel

Source: Reproduced by special permission from *Journal of Applied Behavioral Science* Vol. 8 (January/February 1972), pp. 79–101. © 1972 by NTL Institute for Applied Behavioral Science.

practices and policies, managerial practices and philosophy, and the like. For example, at the time of our entry this was one of the relatively few nonunionized plants in our organization having about 50 geographically separate plants. Thus, an opportunity existed to do work in a plant which had not yet completely internalized the practices and traditions of older plants and of the corporation as a whole.

INTRODUCTION AND HISTORICAL PERSPECTIVE

Since I've been working here, my husband is a much better supervisor in *his* plant. I tell him what he should do to make his people more interested in what they are doing—based on what *our* supervisors do here. *(Assembly Worker)*

I hate to say it, but I think that I could be off the manufacturing floor for a month and my girls would still make the manufacturing schedule. *(First-Line Supervisor)*

The comments above were gathered in one plant of a large company which, for several years, has been the focus of a successful systems approach to organizational development (OD) at all levels. It is important to point out at the outset that no single OD approach was used with this plant. Rather, in the systems approach, a wide variety of behavioral science concepts concerning organizational change and effective management were operationalized.

This article is written to provide the reader with an understanding of the systems organizational model that guided our efforts as change agents; to describe the varied approaches used for organizational change; and to describe the results and what we have learned about the process of change and its prospects in large, complex organizations. Rather than consigning the conclusions to the end, we shall underscore our major findings as we proceed through the sections of the case study.

The organizational development program took place in a plant designing and manufacturing complex instruments for medical and laboratory use.

Through the efforts of the personnel supervisor, enough interest existed initially for our holding a series of seminars which contrasted traditional approaches with newer approaches based on behavioral research findings and theory. Although these seminars never succeeded in getting an explicit decision on the pattern of management that would prevail in the plant (indeed, as will be discussed later, there was considerable resistance to "theory"), they did start to unfreeze the managerial group (which was steeped in the tradition of the parent organization) sufficiently to commit themselves to "trying" some new approaches on a very limited basis. This constituted much less than commitment to a new pattern of management, but it did open the door to experimentation and examination.

Overworked Theories

A number of practitioners of OD stress the importance of top management commitment to OD if such a program is to be successful. As one author puts it, "Without such support, we have found no program of this kind can ever succeed. . . . First, we worked with top managers to help them fully understand. . . . This proved vital, not only in helping their understanding of the concepts but also in earning their commitment to the program" (Roche & MacKinnon, 1970). In the same vein, Beckhard (1969) and Blake and Mouton (1969) stress that OD must be planned and managed from the top down.

Certainly no one would dispute the proposition that top management commitment to OD is highly valuable and helpful. However, our experience in this study [*Finding 1*] indicates that a *clear-cut commitment at the top of the organizational unit to a particular OD approach is not necessary for a development program to succeed.* Indeed, an attempt to obtain too strong a commitment from top management in the early stages may be threatening enough to cause the withdrawal of any commitment to planned change, especially since the concept of OD and its technologies (e.g., Theory Y, job enrichment, sensitivity training, and the like) are foreign and threatening to the established beliefs of many managers.

Moreover, we found [*Finding 2*] that *total top management understanding of where the OD process will lead and the state of the organization at the end is not necessary for successful programs to take place.* Indeed, given the current state of the art, the OD practitioner himself may not have a clear view of the road ahead, except in very general terms.

What *is* necessary is that someone in a strategic position feel the need for change and improvement. In our plant, that person was the personnel supervisor. Although the plant manager was mildly interested in the initial stages, he was mainly submitting to pressures from the personnel man. Throughout his tenure in the plant, the plant manager's commitment and interest mildly increased, but he was never a strong proponent nor the most skilled manager in some of the new approaches. Furthermore, the plant manager's "boss" never fully knew what was going on in the plant nor did he ever commit himself in any way to the OD program. We now believe that it is possible to change a relatively autonomous unit of a larger organization without the total commitment or understanding of top management in that unit and, in larger and more complex organizations, even without their knowledge.

Initial Commitment to New Approaches

In addition to felt need, the second essential condition is that there be, somewhere in the organization, some initial commitment to experimentation, application, and evaluation of new approaches to present problems. A case study report by the second author (Huse, 1965) describes a successful OD program that took place because a middle manager in a large organization felt the need for change and requested help. He could not have cared less about specific OD principles. He simply wanted help in improving his organization. Davis (1967) points out, in his now classic case study, that top management was not really involved at the beginning and that a majority of the effort was expended in "on-the-job situations, working out real problems with the people who are involved with them."

Of course, it is obvious that top management support of both theory and practice makes it easier for the change agent; conversely, the lack of such support increases the risk involved for consultants and managers, and causes other systems problems, as we shall discuss later in this article. Furthermore, the conditions of a felt need, a strong and self-sufficient commitment to change, and relative unit autonomy are needed. What we *are* saying is that the commonly heard dicta that one must start at the top and that top management must be committed to a set of normative principles are overworked. *Change can and does begin at lower levels in an organization [Finding 3]*. If the client system and its management in this case did not (need to) have specific OD concepts in mind, who did? The change agents did.

A CONCEPTUAL MODEL

It is important that the change agent have in mind an organizational model and a flexible set of normative concepts about management with a systems orientation. The organizational model should be general and reflect the complex *interactive* nature of systems variables. The concepts must be updated and changed as new research findings become available and as more is learned about the functioning of the client system, the environment in which the client system operates, and the effects of changes made in the client system. This is, of course, an iterative procedure.

Figure 1 represents the model of organizational change which guided our efforts. This model has some basic characteristics which must be understood if we are to see how it can shape the planning of a change effort. It represents an organization as an open system engaged in a conversion process. Employee needs, expectations, and abilities are among the raw materials (inputs) with which a manager must work to achieve his objectives.

FIGURE 1

Systems Model of an Organization

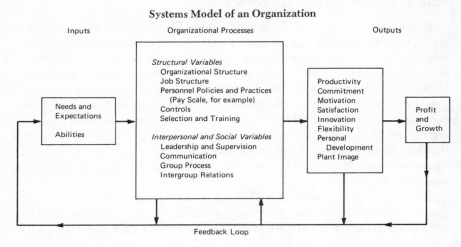

Organizations have many processes. Figure 1 includes only the more important ones in general terms, and these exist at both the structural and interpersonal levels. Leadership and communication, for example, are two of the interpersonal dimensions which serve to pull together, integrate, and shape the behavior of organizational members. They convert into effort and attitudes the potential brought to the organization in the form of needs and abilities of individuals. The structure or formalized dimensions of the organization obviously cannot exist independently of the interpersonal variables, but they are different from the interpersonal variables in terms of their susceptibility to managerial control, the means by which they might be changed, and the timing of their change. Previous literature on organizational change has emphasized interpersonal variables; more recent literature (Lawrence & Lorsch, 1969) has emphasized structural variables. It is our opinion, based upon experience, that both interpersonal and structural variables are crucial to effective organizational change. The effects of organizational design or managerial control systems on employees have been researched and documented but are still insufficiently understood. For example, we are convinced that an operant conditioning model can be used to understand the behavior of managers with respect to controls. "Beating" goals and looking good on standard measures are like food pellets to the manager.

In the output column, we have listed multiple outcomes. These are not completely independent, but they are conceptually distinctive enough in their relationship to the organizational process variables that it is useful to think of them individually. It is the optimization of the organizational outputs that leads to long-term profitability and growth for employees and the organization. Other final outcomes could be listed if we were discussing organizations with different objectives.

Inherent in this model are several basic notions: An organization is an open system which, from the human point of view, converts individual needs and expectations into outputs. Organizational outputs can be increased by improving the quality of the input. An example of this would be the selection of people with higher levels of ability and needs. However, because there are costs associated with selecting personnel of higher quality, we might say that efficiency has not increased. The organization may improve its performance, but this gain has been obtained only because the input, i.e., the quality of personnel has improved, not because there has been a change in the manner in which the organization *utilizes* its human resources.

Since organizations are open systems, organizational performance can also improve by unleashing more of the potential inherent in the human resources. If you will, outputs will increase because we have made the conversion process more efficient. This can be done, for example, by designing organizational processes which better fit the organization's environment or by changing organizational processes so that human resources can be fully unleashed and brought to bear on the task and objectives of the organization. The adjustment of organizational processes to reflect more accurately the needs of the environment and of the persons in it is one of the key objectives of our organizational development program.

Figure 1[1] does not cover some of the more traditional but vitally important concepts of an organization as a total system. For example, capital budgets, the R & D thrust of an organization, overhead or indirect budgets, and the marketing direction of an organization are extremely important aspects which need to be considered. Blake and Mouton (1969) have developed the Corporate Excellence Rubric as a means of assessing the health of the organization through a traditional functional framework. Furthermore, current research (Lawrence & Lorsch, 1969), points up the fact that the differentiation of functional units has a tremendous influence upon the effectiveness of an organization. However, for purposes of brevity, these aspects are not covered in this article.

We chose an eclectic approach to create change in the organizational processes listed in Figure 1, with the basic belief that a variety of approaches to change should be used with the plant in question. The primary mechanism was consulting, counseling, and feedback by a team of four. The primary change agents were the personnel man within the organization (there have been four different ones since the OD effort began); Beer as an external-to-the-plant agent but internal to the organization,

---

[1] Cf. The traditional aspects included in the conceptual model developed by Huse (1969).

and Huse as the outside change agent. The fourth member of the team was a research assistant whose responsibility it was to interview and gather data in the client system for diagnostic and feedback uses by the change agents.[2]

We began a basic strategy of establishing working relationships with individuals at all levels of the organization. We operated as resource persons who could be used to solve specific problems or initiate small experiments in management; we tried to encourage someone or some organizational component to start implementing the concepts inherent in our model of an organization. Managers gained familiarity with these ideas through consultation and, to a much lesser extent and without full understanding, from the initial few seminars that we held. The main ingredients were a problem or a desire to change and improve, combined with action recommendations from the change agents. Soon there were a few individuals throughout the organization who began, with our help, to apply some new approaches. Because most of these approaches were successful, the result was increased motivation to change. To a degree nothing succeeds like success!

Models for Learning

There are at least two basic models for learning. The traditional method, that of the classroom and seminar, stresses theory and cognitive concepts before action. As Argyris (1967) points out, "The traditional educational models emphasize substance, rationality...." However, a number of authors (Bartlett, 1967; Bradford, 1964; Schein & Bennis, 1965) make the point that behavior is another place to start. For example, Huse (1966) has shown that one's own facts are "much more powerful instruments of change than facts or principles generated and presented by an outside 'expert.'" The process of change in this OD effort started with behavioral recommendations, was followed by appropriate reinforcement and feedback, and then proceeded to attitudinal and cognitive changes.

Figure 2 summarizes the basic concept from our experience. *Effective and permanent adult learning [Finding 4] comes after the individual has experimented with new approaches and received appropriate feedback in the on-the-job situation.* This approach is analogous to, but somewhat different from, the here-and-now learning in the T Group.

In other words, a manager might have a problem. Without discussing theory, the change agent might make some recommendations relating to the specific situation at hand. If, in the here-and-now, the manager was successful in the attempt to solve the problem, this would lead to another

---

2 We should like to acknowledge the help and participation of Mrs. Gloria Gery and Miss Joan Doolittle in the data-gathering phase.

FIGURE 2

The Learning Process

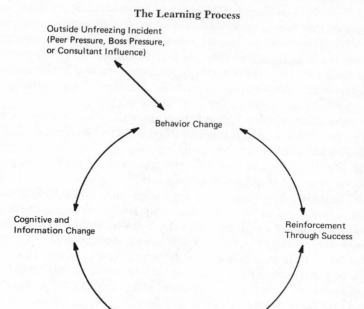

Outside Unfreezing Incident
(Peer Pressure, Boss Pressure,
or Consultant Influence)

Behavior Change

Cognitive and
Information Change

Reinforcement
Through Success

Attitude and Value Change

try, as well as a change in his attitude toward OD. This approach capitalizes upon the powerful here-and-now influence which the job and the organizational climate can have upon the individual. Indeed, such changes can occur without *any* knowledge of theory.

Either model of of learning can probably work to produce change in the individual. However, if one starts with cognitive facts and theory (as in seminars), this may be less effective and less authentic than starting with the individual's own here-and-now behavior in the ongoing job situation. In any case, the process is a cyclic one, involving behavior, attitudes, and cognition, each reinforcing the other. In our case, there was an early resistance to seminars and the presentation of "Theory." However, after behavior and attitude changes occurred, there began to be more and more requests for cognitive inputs through reading, seminars, and the like. It is at this later stage that seminars and "theory inputs" would seem to be of most value.

That learning starts with behavior and personal experience has been one of the most important things we have learned as we have worked to effect organizational change. The process is quite similar to what is intended to happen in laboratory training. What we have found [*Finding 5*] is that *the operating, on-going organization may, indeed, be the best "laboratory" for learning.* This knowledge may save us from an overreliance upon sensitivity training described by Bennis (1968) when he states that "when you read the pages of this Journal, you cannot but think that we're a one-product outfit with a 100 percent fool-proof patent medicine." This finding may also be the answer in dealing with Campbell and Dunnette's (1968) conclusions that "while T-Group training seems to produce observable changes in behavior, the utility of these changes for the performance of individuals in their organizational roles remains to be demonstrated."

The unfreezing process. What triggers an individual to unfreeze and to allow the process to begin, if it is not "theory"? First, there are some individuals who are ready to change behavior as soon as the opportunity presents itself in the form of an outside change agent. These are people who seem to be aware of problems and have a desire to work on them. Sometimes all that they need are some suggestions or recommendations as to different approaches or methods they may try. If their experiences are successful, they become change leaders in their own right. *They then [Finding 6] are natural targets for the change agent, since they become opinion leaders that help shape a culture that influences others in the organization to begin to experiment and try out new behaviors.* As Davis (1967) points out, it is necessary to "provide a situation which could initiate the process of freeing up these potential multipliers from the organizational and personal constraints which . . . kept them from responding effectively to their awareness of the problems." Davis used "strangers" and "cousins" laboratories. In our case, the unfreezing process was done almost exclusively in the immediate job context.

An early example of the development of change leaders in our work with this company was the successful joint effort of an engineer and a supervisor to redesign a hotplate assembly operation which would eliminate an assembly line and give each worker total responsibility for the assembly of a particular product. It resulted in a productivity increase of close to 50 percent, a drop in rejects from 23 percent, controllable rejects to close to 1 percent, and a reduction in absenteeism from about 8 percent to less than 1 percent in a few months. Not all the early experiments were successful, but mistakes were treated as part of the experiential learning process.

As some in the organization changed and moved ahead by trying out new behaviors, others watched and waited but were eventually influenced by the culture. An example of late changers so influenced was the supervisor of Materials Control, who watched for two years what was going on in the plant but basically disagreed with the concepts of OD. Then he began to feel pressure to change because his peers were trying new things and he was not. He began by experimenting with enriching his secretary's job and found, in his own words, that "she was doing three times as much, enjoying it more, and giving me more time to manage." When he found that this experiment in managerial behavior had "paid off," he began to take a more active interest in OD. His next step was to completely reorganize his department to push decision making down the ladder, to utilize a team approach, and to enrich jobs. He supervised four sections: purchasing, inventory control, plant scheduling, and expediting. Reorganization of Materials Control was around product line teams. Each group had total project responsibility for their own product lines, including the four functions described above. We moved slowly and discussed with him alternative ways of going about the structural change. When he made the change, his subordinates were prepared and ready. The results were clear: In a three-month period of time (with the volume of business remaining steady), the parts shortage list was reduced from 14 I.B.M. pages to less than a page. In other words, although he was a late-changer in terms of the developing culture, his later actions were highly successful.

The influence of the developing culture was also documented through interviews with new employees coming into the plant. The perception by production employees that this was a "different" place to work occurred almost immediately, and changes in behavior of management personnel were clear by the second month.

In other words, while seminars and survey feedback techniques were used in our work with this plant, the initial and most crucial changes were achieved through a work-centered, consulting-counseling approach, e.g., through discussion with managers and others about work-related problems, following the model of adult learning described earlier.

So much for the manner in which the unfreezing process occurred and some of our learning about this process. What were some of the normative concepts applied and why? A brief overview of our approaches and findings follows.

A NORMATIVE MODEL

Communications

In this phase we attempted to open up communications at all levels. We started monthly meetings at every level of the organization, as well as a weekly meeting between the plant manager and a sample of production and clerical employees. The aim was to institutionalize the meetings to serve as a means for exchanging information and ideas about what had happened and what needed to happen. The meetings, especially between first-line supervisors and production workers, began primarily as one-way communications downward. Little by little, qualitative changes occurred and the meetings shifted to two-way communications about quality, schedules, and production problems. This effort to communicate (which was also extended through many other approaches) was an entire year in attaining success. It was an agonizingly slow process of change. In retrospect, this was a critical period during which trust was building and a culture conducive to further change was developing. Out of this, we concluded [*Finding 7*] that *organizational change occurs in stages: a stage of unfreezing and trust building, a take-off stage when observable change occurs, and a stabilization stage. Then the cycle iterates.* In addition to the communication type of meeting described above, confrontation meetings between departments were also held (Blake, Shepard, & Mouton, 1964). These, too, improved relationships between departments, over time.

Job Enrichment

A second area of change was in job structure, primarily through the use of job enrichment, or, as it has been called in the plant, "the total job concept." We have already discussed the importance of the job for psychological growth and development—our findings in this area parallel those of Ford (1969). Our first experience of tearing down a hotplate assembly line has already been discussed. This was followed by similar job enrichment efforts in other areas. In one department, girls individually assemble instruments containing thousands of parts and costing several thousand dollars. The change here allowed production workers to have greater responsibility for quality checks and calibration (instead of trained technicians). In another case, the changeover involved an instrument which had been produced for several years. Here, production was increased by 17 percent with a corresponding increase in quality; absenteeism was reduced by more than 50 percent.

The plant is presently engaged in completely removing quality control inspection from some departments, leaving final inspection to the workers themselves. In other departments, workers have been organized into autonomous workgroups with total responsibility for scheduling, assembly, training, and some quality control inspection (the source for the supervisor's laudatory quote at the beginning of this case study). Changes in these areas have evolved out of an attempt to utilize the positive forces of cohesive workgroups. However, like Ford (1969), we have found that not everyone in the assembly workforce responds positively to such changes, although a high majority do so over time.

Mutual goal setting has also been widely adopted. Instead of standards established by engineering (a direction in which the plant was heading when we started), goals for each department are derived from the plant goal, and individual goals for the week or month are developed in individual departments through discussions between the boss and subordinates. Our interview data clearly show that in this way workers understand how their individual goals fit into the plant goal structure and can work on their own without close supervision for long periods of time.

Changes toward a pay process more clearly based on merit (including appraisals for hourly and weekly salaried clerical and technical employees as well as for managerial and professional personnel) were made to reinforce and legitimate an escalating climate of work involvement. More and more employees are now involved in questions of production, quality, department layout, and methods. Assembly workers give department tours to visitors, including vice presidents. Organization-wide technical and product information sessions are held. Concerned more with strategy than with daily problems, the top team has for some time molded itself into a business team, meeting periodically to discuss future plans.

More recently, changes in organizational structure are taking place to move a functionally oriented organization to a matrix organization, using concepts derived directly from Lawrence and Lorsch (1969). This involves, among other approaches, the use of "integrators" at varying levels within the organization.

Systems Interaction

A systems approach requires that mutually consistent changes in *all* subsystems be made in effecting the organizational processes listed in our model. In other words, [*Finding 8*] *multiple changes in the subsystems are needed for the individual employee to change behavior and perceptions of his role.* For example, participative supervison should be accompanied by redesign of jobs to allow more responsibility, by a pay system that recognizes performance, by a communication system that is truly open, and by corresponding changes in other subsystems throughout the organization. Past attempts to change organizations through a nonsystems approach, e.g., through such single media as supervisory training or sensitivity training, have had limited success because other key leverage points have not been changed in the total system. Further, an attempt to change one subsystem too quickly or too drastically can have severely harmful results, as pointed out in the "Hovey and Beard Company" case (Lawrence, Bailey, Katz, Seiler, Orth, Clark, Barnes, & Turner, 1961). Whether structural *or* interpersonal changes should take precedence in a given period of time depends upon the readiness of the system to change and the key leverage points. The key concept [*Finding 9*] is that *structural and interpersonal systems changes must reinforce and legitimate each other.* Figure 3 presents this concept. The change can be in either direction in the model.

We also learned [*Finding 10*] that *systems changes set off additional interactive processes in which changes in organizational functioning increase not only outputs but also develop the latent abilities of people.* We have concluded that the real potential in organizational development lies in setting in motion such a positive snowball of change, growth, and development. For example, as assembly workers took on additional responsibility

FIGURE 3

The Sequence of Organizational Change *

Change in Climate
(Building Trust
through Communication)

Systems and Structural Changes
(Policies, Pay, Controls,
Organizational Structure)

Interpersonal and
Social Changes

they became more and more concerned about the total organization and product. "Mini-gripes" turned into "mega-gripes," indicating a change in the maturity of the assembly workers (Huse & Price, 1970). At the same time, this freed up management personnel to be less concerned about daily assignments and more concerned about long-range planning.

To illustrate this, at the beginning of the OD effort, the organization had a plant manager, a production superintendent, and three first-line supervisors, or a total of five supervisory personnel in the direct manufacturing line. As the assembly line workers took on more responsibility, the five have been reduced to three (the plant manager and two first-line supervisors). The number of inspection and quality control personnel has also been reduced.

A Subsystem Within the Larger Organization

Up to this point in the case study we have been considering the plant as a system in its own right. However, changes set in motion here have also provided the first step in a larger plan for change and development to occur in the parent corporation (consisting of some 50 plants). As a subsystem within the larger system, this plant was to serve as a model for the rest of the corporation—as an example of how change should be planned and implemented. It was our hope that the systems approach to change would create such a clearly different culture in this plant that it would become visible to the rest of the corporation; that people from other segments of the larger organization would visit and become interested in trying similar models and mechanisms of change. Our hopes have been realized. Indeed, both authors are now applying OD concepts to other areas of the organization.

Influence is also exerted upward, with greater acceptance of these concepts by individuals at higher levels in the organization [Finding 11]. It is our perception that changes in organizational subsystems can have strong influences on the larger culture if the change is planned and publicized; if seed personnel are transferred to other parts of the system; if a network of change agents is clearly identified; and if careful planning goes into where and how change resources are to be used. Once again, top management commitment is not a necessary commitment for evolutionary change in a complex, multidivision, multilocation organization. (*Sometimes,* the tail begins to wag the dog.)

Subsystem Difficulties

However, this change process may cause some difficulties in the area of interface between the smaller subsystem and the larger system. For example, the increased responsibilities, commitment, and involvement represented by job enrichment for assembly workers are not adequately represented in the normal job evaluation program for factory workers and are difficult to handle adequately within the larger system. So pay and pay system changes must be modified to fit modern OD concepts. Figure 4 is a

FIGURE 4

Equity Model

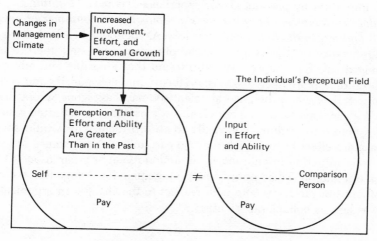

model which shows the effects of change in climate on individual model perceptions of equity in pay.

In addition to the larger system difficulties over wage plans, there still exists a great deal of controversy as to the importance of pay as a motivator (or dissatisfier). For example, Walton (1967) takes a basically pessimistic approach about participation through the informal approach, as opposed to the more formal approaches embodied in the Scanlon Plan (Lesieur, 1958), which "stress the economic rewards which can come from [formal] participation." On the other hand, Paul, Robertson, and Herzberg (1969) review a number of job enrichment projects and report: "In no instance did management face a demand of this kind [higher pay or better conditions] as a result of changes made in the studies." In a recent review of the Scanlon Plan (Lesieur & Puckett, 1969), the authors point out that Scanlon's first application did not involve the use of financial incentives but, rather, a common sharing between management and employees of problems, goals, and ideas. Indeed, Ford (1969) reports on the results of a series of job enrichment studies without ever mentioning the words "pay" or "salary." In the plant described in this case, no significant pressures for higher pay have been felt to date. However, there has been sufficient opportunity for promotion of hourly employees to higher level jobs as the plant has grown.

It is certainly not within the scope of this article to handle the controversy regarding the place of pay as a motivator. We do want to make the point that standard corporate job evaluation plans are only one instance of the difficulties of interface between the client plant as a subsystem and the larger system. In our experience, these and other areas have been minor rather than major problems, but they have been problems.

Changes in Consumption of Research Findings

An important by-product of our experience has been [*Finding 12*] that *the client system eventually becomes a sophisticated consumer of new research findings in the behavioral sciences.* As mentioned earlier, there was early resistance to "theory"; but as the program progressed, there was increasing desire for "theory." We also found that a flexible and adaptable organization is more likely to translate theory into new policies and actions. Perhaps this is where behavioral scientists may have gone wrong in the past. We may have saturated our client systems with sophisticated research studies before the culture was ready to absorb them. This would suggest that a more effective approach may be carefully planned stages of evolution from an action orientation to an action-research orientation to a research orientation. This implies a long-range plan for change that we often talk about but rarely execute with respect to the changes in organizations that we seek as behavioral scientists.

RESULTS OF THE ORGANIZATIONAL DEVELOPMENT PROGRAM

To a great extent we have tried to share with you our results and findings throughout the article. In addition, we are retesting these concepts in several other plants. In retrospect, how much change really occurred at the client plant, and how effective have been the new approaches introduced? We have only partial answers since a control plant did not exist and since the plant was relatively new; no historical data existed against which to compare performance. However, considerable data do exist to support the thesis that change has occurred and that new managerial approaches have created an effective organization. (In addition, the second author is conducting ongoing research in another plant in the organization which has historical data. Before- and after-measures have already shown dramatic change: e.g., red:.ction in manufacturing costs for the plant of 40 to 45 percent.)

Extensive interviews by the researcher and detailed notes and observations by the change agents indicate considerable improvement after our work with this plant. Communication is open, workers feel informed, jobs are interesting and challenging, and goals are mutually set and accomplished.

In each of the output dimensions, positive changes have occurred which we think, but cannot always prove, would not have occurred without the OD effort. Turnover has been considerably reduced; specific changes in job structure, organizational change, or group process have resulted in measurable productivity changes of up to 50 percent. Recent changes in the Instrument Department have resulted in productivity and quality improvements. We have witnessed the significant changes in maturity and motivation which have taken place among the assembly workers. A change to a project team structure in the Materials Control Department led to a reduction of the weekly parts shortages. Following the findings of Lawrence and Lorsch (1969), the use of "integrators" and project teams has significantly reduced the time necessary for new product development, introduction, and manufacture. A fuller evaluation of the integrator role and the project organization as it affects intergroup relations and new product development is reported elsewhere (Beer, Pieters, Marcus, & Hundert, 1971).

Several recent incidents in the plant are evidence of the effect of the changes and bear repeating. An order called for in seven days and requiring extraordinary cooperation on the part of a temporary team of production workers was completed in fewer than seven days. A threatened layoff was handled with candor and openness and resulted in volunteers among some of the secondary wage earners.

New employees and managers now transferred into the plant are immediately struck by the differences between the "climate" of this plant and other locations. They report more openness, greater involvement by employees, more communication, and more interesting jobs. Even visitors are struck immediately by the differences. For example, one of the authors has on several occasions taken graduate students on field trips to the plant. After the tour, the consensus is, "You've told us about it, but I had to see it for myself before I would believe it." Managers transferred or promoted out of the plant to other locations report "cultural shock."

SUMMARY AND CONCLUSIONS

The Medfield Project (as it can now be labeled) has been an experiment in a systems approach to organizational development at two systems levels. On the one hand, we have regarded the plant as a system in and of itself. On the other hand, we have regarded the plant as a subsystem within a larger organization. As such a subsystem, we wanted it to serve as a model for the rest of the organization. Indeed, as a result of this study, OD work is going forward elsewhere in the parent company and will be reported in forthcoming articles.

Although we have shared our findings with you throughout the article, it seems wise now to summarize them for your convenience, so that they may be generalized to other organizations and climates.

Findings

1. *A clear-cut commitment to a particular OD approach is not necessary (although desirable) for a successful OD program to succeed.*
2. *Total top management understanding of where the OD process will lead and the state of the organization at the end is not necessary for organizational change to occur.*
3. *Change can and does begin at lower levels in the organization.*
4. *Effective and permanent adult learning comes after the individual has experimented with new approaches and received appropriate feedback in the on-the-job situation.*
5. *Rather than the T Group, the operating, ongoing organization may be the best "laboratory" for learning, with fewer problems in transfer of training.*
6. *Internal change leaders are natural targets for the change agent, since they become influence leaders and help to shape the culture.*
7. *Organizational change occurs in stages: a stage of unfreezing and trust building, a take-off stage when observable change occurs, and a stabilization stage. Then the cycle iterates.*
8. *Multiple changes in the subsystems are needed for the individual employee to change behavior and perceptions of his role.*

9. *Structural and interpersonal systems changes must reinforce and legitimate each other.*

10. *Systems changes set off additional interactive processes in which changes in organizational functioning not only increase outputs but also develop the latent abilities of people.*

11. *Influence is also exerted upward, with greater acceptance of these concepts by individuals at higher levels in the organization.*

12. *The client system eventually becomes a sophisticated consumer of new research findings in the behavioral sciences.*

Perhaps the most important and far-reaching conclusion is that as organizational psychologists we have viewed our role too narrowly and with an insufficient historical and change perspective. Our research studies tend to be static rather than dynamic. We need to do a better job of developing a theory and technology of changing and to develop a flexible set of concepts which will change as we experiment with and socially engineer organizations. We are suggesting a stronger action orientation for our field and less of a natural science orientation. We must be less timid about helping organizations to change themselves. We must create a positive snowball of organizational change followed by changes in needs and expectations of organizational members, followed again by further organizational change. The objective of change agents should be to develop an evolving system that maintains reasonable internal consistency while staying relevant to and anticipating changes and adaptation to the outside environment. As behavioral scientists and change agents, we must help organizations begin to "become."

REFERENCES

Argyris, C. On the future of laboratory training. *J. appl. Behav. Sci.*, 1967, 3 (2), 153–83.

Bartlett, A. C. Changing behavior as a means to increased efficiency. *J. appl. Behav. Sci.*, 1967, 3 (3), 381–403.

Beckhard, R. *Organization development: Strategies and models.* Reading, Mass.: Addison-Wesley, 1969.

Beer, M., Pieters, G. R., Marcus, S. H., & Hundrert, A. T. Improving integration between functional groups: A case in organization change and implications for theory and practice. Symposium presented at American Psychological Association Convention, Washington, D.C., September 1971.

Bennis, W. G. The case study—I. Introduction. *J. appl. Behav. Sci.*, 1968, 4 (2), 227–31.

Blake, R. R., & Mouton, J. S. *Building a dynamic corporation through grid organization development.* Reading, Mass.: Addison-Wesley, 1969.

Blake, R. R., Shepard, H. A., & Mouton, J. S. *Managing intergroup conflict in industry*. Houston, Tex.: Gulf, 1964.

Bradford, L. P. Membership and the learning process. In L. P. Bradford, J. R. Gibb, and K. D. Benne (Eds.), *T-Group theory and laboratory method: Innovation in re-education*. New York: Wiley, 1964.

Campbell, J. P., & Dunnette, M. D. Effectiveness of t-group experiences in managerial training and development. *Psycholog. Bull.*, August 1968, *70*, (2), 73–104.

Davis, S. A. An organic problem-solving method of organizational change. *J. appl. Behav. Sci.*, 1967, *3* (1), 3–21.

Ford, R. N. *Motivation through the work itself*. New York: American Management Association, 1969.

Huse, E. F. The behavioral scientist in the shop. *Personnel*, May/June 1965, *42* (3), 50–57.

Huse, E. F. Putting in a management development program that works. *California Mgmt Rev.*, Winter 1966, 73–70.

Huse; E. F., & Price, P. S. The relationship between maturity and motivation in varied work groups. *Proceedings* of the Seventieth Annual Convention of the American Psychological Association, September 1970.

Lawrence, P. R., & Lorsch, J. W. *Organization and environment*. Homewood, Ill.: Richard D. Irwin, 1969.

Lawrence, P. R., Bailey, J. C., Katz, R. L., Seiler, J. A., Orth, C. D. III, Clark, J. V., Barnes, L. B., & Turner, A. N. *Organizational behavior and administration*. Homewood, Ill.: Irwin-Dorsey, 1961.

Lesieur, F. G. (Ed.) *The Scanlon plan: A frontier in labor-management cooperation*. Cambridge, Mass.: M.I.T. Press, 1958.

Lesieur, F. G., & Puckett, E. S. The Scanlon plan has proved itself. *Harvard Bus. Rev.*, Sept./Oct. 1969, *47*, 109–18.

Paul, W. J., Robertson, K. B., & Herzberg, F. Job enrichment pays off. *Harvard Bus. Rev.*, Mar./Apr. 1969, *47* (2) 61–78.

Roche, W. J., & MacKinnon, N. L. Motivating people with meaningful work. *Harvard Bus. Rev.*, May/June 1970, *48* (3), 97–110.

Schein, E. H., & Bennis, W. G. *Personal and organizational change through methods: The laboratory approach*. New York: Wiley, 1965.

Walton, R. E. Contrasting designs for participative systems. *Personnel Admin.*, Nov./Dec. 1967, *30* (6), 35–41.

24

Laboratory Training and Organization Development

PAUL C. BUCHANAN

A systematic review of the literature on the effectiveness of laboratory training in industry (Buchanan, 1965) resulted in the following conclusions:

1. Laboratory training is effective as a means of facilitating specifiable changes in individuals in the industrial setting
2. It has been used effectively in some programs of organizational development, but not in others
3. Behavioral scientists associated with the National Training Laboratories are actively engaged in subjecting their theories and methods to systematic analysis, and in developing strategies for organization development
4. Some of these strategies, now being studied systematically, are showing exciting results.

The purpose of this paper is to bring the earlier review up to date and to broaden the focus from industry to all types of organizations.

Interest in laboratory training in human relations has expanded significantly. For example, in 1968, National Training Laboratories were conducting 20 percent more sessions than in the previous year; sensitivity training has become a common activity in workshops and teacher institutes

Source: Reprinted by permission from author and publisher. From *Administrative Science Quarterly* Vol. 14 (September 1969), 466–80.

in the field of education; and the number of professionals in the National Training Laboratories has increased from 159 in 1963 to 289 in 1968.

Research on laboratory training has also expanded. There have been 68 technical articles or books which pertain to some aspect of laboratory training published since the earlier review. (Buchanan, 1965). In a bibliography of research prepared by Durham and Gibb (1960), 49 studies were listed for the period 1947–1960, and 76 for the period 1960–1967. Undoubtedly the best single source of background information on the topic up to 1965 is the book by Schein and Bennis (1965).

Studies on laboratory training during the past four years deal with (1) the methodology of evaluation, (2) theory development, (3) kinds of learning brought about in the laboratories, (4) factors influencing learning in the laboratories, (5) types of individuals who learn from laboratory training, and (6) laboratory training in organization development.

METHODOLOGY OF EVALUATION

The methodology of evaluation continues to be a major problem, yet several recent studies indicate progress.

General Variables in Methodology

House (1967) classified the variables relevant to the problem of evaluation into four categories: objectives of the training, initial states of the learner, initial states of the organization, and methods of inducing change in the learner. Then, considering the methods as input variables, the objectives of the laboratory training as output variables, and the initial states of both the participants and the organization as moderators, he generated a paradigm of relationships that highlighted the issues in planning and assessing organizational development efforts and outlined a specific assessment design to illustrate the paradigm. The result is a clear presentation of relevant types of variables and their interconnectedness, a paradigm that is applicable to the design and assessment of any change in the "person dimension" (Leavitt, 1965) of organization performance. House's study also makes clear that neither the design nor the assessment of any training program is likely to be effective if it does not take into account variables in the *situation* as well as variables in the *person,* a finding highlighted earlier by Fleishman et al. (1955), but still often ignored. Equally important, House shows how theory can be used to make it possible for evaluation studies to contribute to a systematic body of knowledge. However, his paradigm is more adequate in providing for moderator than for output variables. As moderators he lists "the nature of the primary work group," "the formal authority system" of the organization, and "exercise of authority by superior"; yet he doesn't list these organization factors as output variables: he lists only changes in knowledge, skill, attitude, and job performance. But it is on the assumption that such changes in the participant will result in changes in the output of the work unit to which the learner belongs that organizations support training. As important as House's work is, therefore, it omits some important variables.

Problems of Design

While House dealt with general problems of design and evaluation, Harrison (1967) has made a thoughtful analysis of some specific issues. First, as he points out it is seldom possible to assign participants randomly to the treatment and a control group. Usually participants are either self-selected, or are assigned for administrative or other organizational reasons (the personnel officer wants them to attend; they are part of a unit that is to participate; etc.) where control-groups are used for assessment studies. They are usually selected *post hoc* and with little information available about their similarity to the treatment group. For example, in the studies of Bunker (1965) and Bunker and Knowles, (1967), control subjects were nominated by participants, and no data are given for the basis of this nomination, about the experiences the controls had during the period covered by the assessment, or the reasons why participants had attended the laboratory and the controls had not. Only two of the studies reviewed in this paper meet requirements for appropriate control groups (Deep, Bass, and Vaughan, 1967; Schmuck, 1968).

But there is an added difficulty in using a control group which Harrison discusses: the fact that being a member of a group influences expectations and thereby introduces bias, if perceptions of behavior are used as criteria. Because of these difficulties, Harrison encourages (and utilizes) assessment designs that examine the relation between (predicted) processes of training and outcomes from training.

A second problem is that of when assessment measures after laboratory training should be taken to obtain a valid evaluation of the impact of training. As Harrison points out, until one knows the pattern of the impact, he doesn't know what kinds of changes to look for and when. For example, the immediate effect on participants may be uncertainty, discomfort, and experimentation, which may then give way to confidence, new behavior patterns, and stabilization. If this were the case, then measures taken only at the end of the training would be very misleading.

Related to the use of timing of evaluation is that of whether assessment should focus on predicted and/or desired outcomes (what Harrison calls a normative approach), or should be more like a net to catch whatever influences may be apparent. Harrison also discusses difficulties in assessing change on metagoals of laboratory training.

Because of variability in the designs of programs which are called laboratory training it is difficult to specify and apply a design that can be replicated or meaningfully compared with other training methods. As Harrison (1967:6) says, ". . . . we do not yet have adequate enough theory about the effects of different elements of training design even to permit us to classify laboratories according to design."

Miles (1965a, 1965b), for many years an innovator of evaluation designs, met many of the requirements of House's paradigm and Harrison's emphasis on examining process variables. More recently he and his associates have used theory in increasing the rigor of assessment designs (Miles et al., 1965 and 1966; Benedict et al., 1967). This method, which they called a "clinical-experimental approach," has five components: (1) It calls for a clear division of labor between the researcher responsible for assessment, and the change agents responsible for participants. (2) Data are collected both clinically (running account of events before, during, and following the interventions) and experimentally (by preplanned and periodic measurements of the treatment and a control group. (3) The investigators make theory-based general predictions about the impact that the training is likely to have on specific variables of the organization. (4) The change agent obtains information from the participants, and on this basis formulates specific training activities; then he makes short-range predictions about the variables which the intervention would affect. (5) Careful attention is given to the tactical assessment design. (Miles uses a design involving treatment and control groups and several post-training measurements.) In the study reporting their attempt to use this design (Benedict, et al., 1967) were not completely successful in meeting their methodological prescriptions; problems arose around keeping the research members and change agents from influencing each other (especially through the exchange of data); and there was questionable similarity between the treatment and the control groups. Even so, the approach of Miles and associates represents a significant improvement in evaluating change efforts.

The study by Marrow et al. (1967) is of special significance, partly because it exploited the availability of two large organizations with known similarity and with known "states of health." As in Miles' design, the change agents and the researchers constituted two separate teams. Measurements of human factors and management practices were repeated for both the treatment and the control organization. In addition, economic data were also obtained and systematically analyzed in relation to both short-range and longer-range impact on a number of variables. Further elaboration of the measure used is provided by Likert (1967).

Greiner's study of a grid-based organizational-development project was another methodological advance, in that in addition to the researchers' not being part of the change-agent team, information was obtained about conditions that preceded and in fact apparently led to, the intervention (Greiner, 1965; Blake, et al., 1964).

Many of the studies reviewed have attempted, as Harrison and House suggest, to examine hypothesized relations among independent, intervening, and dependent variables (Rubin, 1967 a, b; Harrison, 1966; Kolb et al., 1968; French et al., 1966; Deep et al., 1967; and Friedlander, 1967); Yet in many the basis on which the predicted connection between the training and the measured outcome is not specified (Bunker and Knowles, 1967; Byrd, 1967). Equally important, many do not provide theoretical links between the expected change and improvement in performance on the job.

The practice of assessing the extent of change attributed to a training program by asking participants and their associates to describe any changes they have noted during a specified time after the training (Bunker, 1965; Bunker and Knowles, 1967) has obvious weaknesses such as the demands it makes on memory. But comparisons of responses to questionnaires obtained before and after training also present difficulties. One problem is that the standard of reference used by the respondent may itself be influenced significantly by the training. For example, Blake and Mouton (1968) required participants to rank themselves as to grid styles before and at the end of the seminar, and one of the expected outcomes from the seminar was to increase the use of the "9,9," style by participants. The data (Blake and Mouton,1968:52) from measures before and after the seminar show a *decrease* of around 32 in the percentage of participants who saw themselves having 9,9 as their most characteristic style. And it is a common experience in groups where questionnaires are used to help the group diagnose and assess its progress on, say, openness, to find no increase or actually a decrease on ratings of openness at the same time that members state (and demonstrate) that they are becoming more open with each other.

There is also the problem of test sensitization, which can influence the responses of a control group. Friedlander (1967:305), in interpreting his data which revealed a decrease in effectiveness of the control group, noted:

> The first administration of the [Group Behavior Inventory] queried comparison group members with blunt questions on sensitive issues which they were unprepared to confront at that time. But after six months of observing those inadequacies that did occur, expectations and standards of the leadership role became clearer. Since current leadership practice did not conform to these expectations, comparison group members now perceived significantly greater inadequacies in the rapport and approachability of their chairman.

To the extent that a decrease occurs in the responses of the comparison group after the laboratory training, statistically significant differences between the treatment and the control group will lead to inaccurate conclusions about the impact of the training upon the treatment group. (They will look better due to an apparent decrease in the control group.) It appears that any measurement scheme involving perceptions are subject to error; therefore greater effort to devise other kinds are much needed.

Some additional shortcomings in the design of the assessment studies reviewed are:

1. In several evaluation procedures, changes noted were given equal weight, even though they appeared to vary greatly in importance (i.e., "listens more" was equivalent in the scoring system to "conducts more effective staff meetings").

2. Results from one study could not be compared with results from other studies, since the training programs evaluated varied in length, in the specific design, in the occupational mix of participants, and in the age and sex of participants. Also, the studies varied in the variables examined, the instrument used to assess change in a given variable, and the time at which measures were gathered after the training period. Thus a body of self consistent knowledge is slow to develop.

3. Where laboratory training was part of an organization development program (Blake and Mouton, 1968; Marrow et al., 1967; Miles et al., 1966), it was difficult to know how much any change effected was due to the laboratory training and how much to other circumstances (Greiner, 1965, 1967).

One must conclude, then, that even though much work has been done to devise more effective evaluation designs, the major shortcomings have not been overcome. This means that the findings summarized below are based on inadequate design and can only be tentative.

THEORY DEVELOPMENT

In 1964 eight fellows of the National Training Laboratories presented their views on what happens in a T-group. Several important theoretical papers dealing with this issue have appeared since that time.

Theories

Hampden-Turner (1966) developed "an existential learning theory" which he used to integrate findings from three empirical studies of T-group effectiveness. His theory involved a "developmental spiral," wherein he hypothesized that the participant's initial quality of cognition, clarity of identity, and extent of self-esteem would result in his ordering his experience. This ordering in the context of a T-group, leads the participant to risk his competence in interacting with another person; the reaction of the other person stimulates the participant to a new integration of his experiences. This in turn leads to changes in the quality of the participant's cognition, clarity of identity, and extent of self-esteem, and to a repetition of the cycle.

Harrison (1965) formulated a "cognitive model for interpersonal and group behavior" which was intended as a framework for research, and which he later used as a basis for forming training groups (Harrison and Lubin, 1965) and for designing laboratories (Harrison and Oshry, 1965). Harrison sees learning resulting when a participant's way of construing events is "up-ended" by confrontation with other participants who construe the same event differently, and when the participant also feels sufficiently supported by others that he is able to work through the consequences of the disturbing confrontation. This theory clearly has value as a basis for designing training experiences, and there is considerable support for the belief that the type of learning (change) it emphasizes is important. For example, Harvey (1966) has detected several differences in behavior of people who are high on abstract (versus concrete) thinking, a difference which appears to be compatible with Harrison's emphasis on cognitive structure.

Argyris (1965) stated a theory of individual learning from which he derived implications for designing laboratories. Criticism from several fellows of the National Training Laboratories (Argyris, 1967) should dispel any belief that the National Training Laboratories have became complaisant as a result of their present rapid growth and popularity. Argyris also utilized his theory to identify variables in terms of which change could be assessed, devised measures of these variables, and tested his theory (Argyris, 1965).

Clark and Culbert hypothesized that self-awareness develops as a function of mutually congruent therapeutic relations between participants and trainers (Clark and Culbert, 1965).

Schein and Bennis (1965) set forth a theory of learning through laboratory training which consists of a cyclical interplay of a dilemma or disconfirming experience, attitude change, new behavior, new information and awareness, leading to additional change, new behavior, etc.

Smith (1966) formulated and tested a complex theory of learning based on Kelman's model of influence. Bass (1967) made a critique of T-group theory and concluded that the kinds of learning emphasized can be dysfunctional to job performance. As partial evidence for this view, he cites a study (Deep et al. 1967) in which it was found that intact T-groups performed less effectively on a business game than groups composed of members from different T-groups. (In the study by Deep et al. (1967), the T-group met without trainers and were conducted in what is called "instrumented" laboratory training.)

Laboratory Training and the Improvement of Organizational Performance

Several people have formulated systematic theories about the use of laboratory training in improving the functioning of organizations. Perhaps the most important are those of Blake and Mouton (1964, 1968) in regard to industrial organizations, and Miles and associates (1966) in regard to schools. Blake and Mouton (1968) deal wholly with their plan for organizational development and with guidelines for implementing the plan. Although the basic concepts of planned change which they present are similar to those conceptualized by Lippitt, Watson, and Westley (1958) the value of the study lies in its technology: Blake and Mouton have devised and tested concrete and theoretically sound methods for implementing the concepts.

Miles and his associates (1966) built upon the survey-feedback strategy of planned change, and made a special effort to determine empirically the way in which intervention (or input), intervening, and output variables were interrelated, especially in school systems.

Several other writers have formulated theories about organizations, which are congruent with the values of laboratory training and which emphasize laboratory training as a means of improving the functioning of organizations (Shepard, 1965; McGregor, 1967; Bennis, 1966; Davis, 1967; Schein and Bennis, 1965).

Greiner (1967) speculates systematically about "antecedents to planned change," asking why the Blake-Mouton interventions had the impact they did. He was able to identify "how the consultants made use of roots put down in the unplanned stages many years before [the beginning of the consultant-planned change] to build top management support for Managerial Grid training," and he relates specific events that occurred during the organization development program to these historic roots. His study thus integrates imaginative observation, survey findings, and theory derived from a variety of related fields into a coherent and nonpolemic theory of organization change. He emphasizes the importance of the historical development of an organization in attempts to change it, a conclusion also reached by Sarason (1966) in his statement that the outcome of a *current* change effort is highly influenced by the outcome of *earlier* change efforts. Failure to cope effectively with the organization's earlier experiences with change also appeared to be one of the reasons for the limited impact of a change project in a recent study (Buchanan, 1968).

From this brief overview of recent theoretical developments, it appears that the primary focus has been on how an individual learns in T-groups, and on processes of planned organizational development. Much less attention has been given to the processes of *group* development. Only two studies (Lakin and Carson, 1964; Psathas and Hardert, 1966) attempted to explore patterns of group development.

KINDS OF LEARNING

Persistence of Learning

In summarizing findings from studies of laboratory training it seems appropriate, first, to consider whether the learning from laboratory training persists. Two studies bear on this question. Schutz and Allen (1966) gathered information on the FIRO-B (Fundamental Interpersonal Relations Orientation—Behavioral) questionnaire from participants (and a control group) at the beginning, the end, and six months after a two-week laboratory. They found that participants changed during the training, and that the changes continued after the training. Harrison (1966) collected information from 76 participants at the beginning, a few weeks after, and a few months after they took part in a laboratory. He concluded that there was a change in the predicted direction at both follow-up periods, but that the difference became significant only between the end of the training and the second follow-up measure; thus the training appeared to be progressive. These findings are consistent with those of Bunker and Knowles (1967), who found significant changes in participants (as compared with a control group) 10–12 months following training. Also, Morton and Bass (1964), in a study of 97 participants, found a marked increase in motivation to improve their performance at the end of the laboratory and substantial changes in job performance in a follow-up 12 weeks later. French et al. (1966) also found further changes in participants' self-concepts following the laboratory.

Types of Learning

The next question to be explored concerns what is learned? Here it is difficult to categorize the findings, since researchers rarely look for the same results; and when they do, they typically use different measures, except for the retrospective "behavior change description questionnaire" developed by Miles (1965a) and Bunker (1965) and used in at least three studies.

Reduction of Extreme Behavior

Two studies produce findings, similar in this respect to an earlier study by Boyd and Ellis, which suggest that laboratory training changes people selectivity, depending upon their personality. Schutz and Allen (1966) found that (as measured by FIRO–B) very dominant participants become less dominant, while very submissive participants become more assertive. Using the same instrument, Smith (1964) found that his experimental subjects (108 students in 11 training groups) changed significantly more in the direction of a better match between what they *expected* and what they *wanted* on both the control and the affection scales of FIRO–B. Some of the findings of Bunker can also be interpreted as an indication that reduction of abrasive or otherwise undesirable behaviors occurred. Such studies raise the possibility that laboratory training produces other-directed behavior; but Kassajian (1965) found no change in laboratory participants on an instrument which purported to measure other-directedness.

Openness, receptivity, awareness, tolerance of differences. Changes such as these are most consistently found following laboratory training (and are, of course, among the most commonly stated objectives). Such changes apparently result even from short laboratories. Bunker and Knowles (1967), Morton and Wight (1964), Rubin (1967), Morton and Bass (1964), Schutz and Allen (1966), Smith (1966), and Kolb et al. (1968) all report this kind of learning. Such changes probably occurred in the other studies also, but the measures used did not relate to this kind of change.

Operational skills. This category includes behavior like listening, encouraging the participation of others, use of new techniques, solicitation of feedback, etc. Outcomes of this sort were reported by Bunker and Knowles (1967), Schutz and Allen (1966), Morton and Wight (1964), Sikes (1964), De Michele (1966), and Schmuck 1968).

Because of its design, the study by Schmuck is worth further comment. He studied a four-week laboratory for 20 classroom teachers, where the design included T-groups, problem-solving exercises, and practice in using instruments and procedures for diagnosing classroom problems. Then before the laboratory ended, each teacher formulated specific plans for the following year, applying what she had learned. Follow-up meetings were held bimonthly from September through December. He also met weekly with another set of teachers from the same large school system (and apparently with random assignment of teachers to the two groups), from September to December, covering the same material as in the laboratory except for the T-group work (and of course with much less total time). He found marked differences in the two groups as to the number of practices the participants tried out in their classrooms (5 to 17 by laboratory participants compared with 1 to 2 by the seminar participants), and in the *esprit de corps* among the teachers as indicated by the contacts they made with each other during the fall. What is more significant, he found improvement in the classrooms of the laboratory participants (as compared to both the seminar participants and a small control group), in that the students perceived themselves as having more influence in the class, as being better liked and an integral part of a friendship group in the class, and as being helpful to each other.

Cognitive style. Examples of this type of outcome are findings by Blake et al. (1965) that union and managerial participants reflected predicted differential shifts on a managerial grid questionnaire. Harrison (1966) found shifts on the Role Repertory Test from the use of concrete-instrumental toward inferential-expressive modes of thought. Oshry and Harrison (1966) found that many laboratory participants viewed their work environment more humanly and less impersonally, saw themselves more as a significant part of their work problems, and saw more connection between the meeting of interpersonal needs and the effectiveness of their work.

In some studies, however, changes that were expected were not found. Bowers and Soar (1961) found no differences between a group of 25 teachers who took part in half-day training sessions over a three-week period and a control group, with respect to their use of group processes in their classrooms during the following academic year. This contrasts with Schmuck's finding significant carry-over into the classrooms (but his intervention consisted of four weeks full time, with systematic follow-up during the fall). Bunker (1965) found no differences between his laboratory participants and controls in initiative and assertiveness. Sikes (1964) failed to find predicted differences between laboratory graduates and a control group in their accuracy in predicting the responses of other members in a discussion group. And Oshry and Harrison (1966) predicted, but did not find, significant changes in sensitivity to the interpersonal needs of others or in the importance attributed to the interpersonal needs of others, when participants returned to their jobs.

Where does laboratory training effect change? There is clear evidence that personal growth results for most participants—they feel better about themselves, have new insights, and consider the training one of the important experiences in their life. Furthermore, participants continually report improvement in their family relations as a result of the experience (Winn, 1966). The value of the laboratory experience for job performance, however, is less convincing: fewer extreme behaviors, greater openness and self-awareness, increased operational skills, and new alternatives for viewing situations. These seem small advances compared to the powerful forces that maintain a status quo in organizations. But what such change does represent is an increased readiness for "next steps."

FACTORS INFLUENCING LEARNING

Several recent studies deal with factors that increase learning by participants in laboratory training; those dealing with the value of laboratory training for organizational development are discussed later.

Group Composition

Perhaps the most clear-cut results have emerged regarding the effects of group composition which have been examined in terms of personality and organizational membership of participants. (Harrison (1965:418-9) theorizes about personality factors as follows:

The process of learning is best facilitated when the individual is placed in a learning situation where either the structure produces dissonance or a significant number of others will act, feel, and perceive in ways which create sharp, clear dissonance for the learner or are contrary to his values. The dissonance must, however, be meaningful to the learner in that the alternatives presented by the others have some anchoring points within his current cognitive systems regarding himself and his interpersonal relationships. . . . we propose that a degree of polarization be created on important issues within the group. This polarization provides the battlefield on which learning by the explorations of opposites can take place. "However, if the individual is exposed only to confrontation and dissonance, he is apt to react in extreme ways. . . . For our learning model to operate, the individual should find in the group some relationships which serve as a refuge and support. Persons with similar cognitive systems, values, and perceptions can provide this support and protection against the destructive efforts of a purely confronting experience. This supportive climate is the castle in our analogy.

After reviewing relevant literature, Harrison concluded that personality variables relevant to obtaining his conditions in the formation of groups were of three types: activity-passivity, high-low affect, and negative-positive affect. He found empirical confirmation of his theory, in that groups homogeneous or mixed on one or more of these variables differed predictably in the way the groups functioned and in the kind of learning. More specifically he concluded (1965:431):

1. Learning is facilitated by a group climate which provides support for one's cognitive, emotional, and behavioral orientation and at the same time confronts one with meaningful alternatives to those orientations.

2. Group climate can be manipulated by relatively crude selection procedures.

3. The models and the research findings reviewed here can be applied to the diagnosis of wide ranges of interpersonal learning difficulties and to the design of learning groups which will provide favorable conditions of support and confrontation. A study by Smith (1966) seems to support Harrison's findings about the importance of personality mix of participants.

Morton and Wight (1964) studied differences in organizational membership. They conducted three instrumented laboratories within a company with groups composed so that participants in six of the D-groups (the designation for T-groups in instrumented laboratories) were all from one department, and all members had direct superior-subordinate relations with others in the group; whereas participants in the other six D-groups did not have direct superior-subordinate relationships, and were from separate units of the plant. The three laboratories were conducted according to the same design. On the basis of critical events (critical event was defined as "anything that has happened since the laboratory which would not have occurred had there been no training") obtained from 90 percent of the participants three months after the laboratories, they (1964: 35–36) concluded that

> Participants from the more homogeneous groups reported a significantly greater proportion of critical events. In areas of personal responsibility, such as supervisor responsibility for his subordinates, his responsibility for individual problem solving, for . . . listening, . . . and sensitivity for what was taking place, there was no significant difference in the frequencies with which incidents were reported. When the problems exceeded the limits of the customary personal responsibility and involved the kind of responsibility that results in highly effective team working relations, the homogeneous . . . groups far exceeded the heterogeneous trained groups in the frequencies with which these critical incidents were reported. The post-training activities of the participants have led them into some difficulties. The nature of the difficulties have varied with the homogeneity of the groups. Those who trained in the less homogeneous groups are reporting less accomplished and more resistance of a personal nature. The members of the homogeneous groups, . . . are reporting the greatest number of organizational barriers to applying what they have learned. Whereas the heterogeneous trained groups found their greatest barriers within their primary work group, among those who have not been in the training, the homogeneous trained group report their greatest difficulty in problem solving with those outside their department who have not received training.

These findings must be considered tentative, however, since variables other than the D-group composition could account for the differences between the two types of groups. For example, the report does not make clear the circumstances under which so many members from one department participated in the laboratories; it may have been the supervisor's enthusiasm rather than the D-group composition which accounted for the change. It is also possible that the differences in outcome occurred because many people from the same department had a similar training experience (i.e., participating in a laboratory) rather than that they were in the same D-groups.

Duration of Laboratory

A third variable apparently making a difference in learning outcome is the duration of the laboratory training. Bunker and Knowles (1967) compared the outcomes from two three-week and two two-week summer sessions conducted by National Training Laboratories. They found that the three-week laboratories "fostered more behavioral changes" than the two-week ones; that is, more participants in the three-week ones made changes "toward more pro-active and interactive behavior," while changes made by the two-week participants were in the area of increased receptiveness (i.e., listening, sensitivity, etc.) However, they noted that the laboratories were similar in the amount of time spent in T-groups, but differed greatly in the time devoted to problems relating to their work; thus the differential impact could be due to the design, or interaction between the design and duration, rather than to duration alone. The question of duration merits more study since costs are closely related to duration and almost every study indicates that the trained group shows change.

Trainer Behavior

Interaction effects between trainer and participant orientation on the FIRO–F questionnaire were found to have differential impact upon the "laboratory learning climate" (Powers, 1965) and upon kinds of learning (Smith, 1966). Bolman (1968) also studied the relation of trainer behavior-openness, congruence, and consistency (as judged by participants) to learning by participants. Although the results were inclusive, he succeeded in isolating dimensions of trainer behavior and a way of measuring them. Culbert examined the differential impact of "more" and "less" self-disclosing trainer behavior in two T-groups, and found that although trainer behavior differed as planned, the groups attained the same level of self-awareness (Culbert, 1968).

Goal-Setting and Feedback

Several studies have been conducted to examine the effects of goal-setting and feedback. Kolb et al. (1968) introduced a procedure in T-groups, by which each participant set a specific change goal for himself and was encouraged to work to meet his goal; then they varied the amount of feedback received during the training, and they attempted to heighten each participant's commitment to the goals he set. They found that differences in both the extent of commitment and in the amount of feedback influenced learning. French, et al. (1966) also found that the greater the amount of feedback, the greater the extent of change on self-selected change goals. And Harrison (1966) found that the amount of change in cognitive orientation was significantly related to ratings by participants of how other participants reacted to and utilized feedback during T-group sessions. Those who made it easy for others to give feedback, and who tested the validity of feedback by seeking more, showed the most change. Thus it appears that provision for participants to obtain and utilize feedback is an important factor in laboratory design.

In summary, then, it appears that the climate which develops in the training group, and the kind and/or extent of learning which occurs, are influenced by the personality mix of the participants, the organizational relationships of the participants, and the way the design utilizes feedback. Studies regarding the effect of duration of the laboratory and of trainer behavior are inconclusive.

Type of Laboratory Training and Job Improvement

The question of whether the greatest improvement on the job results from laboratories which focus almost wholly on personal growth or from those which include personal growth, organizational problems, and planning for changes on the job has not been studied with sufficient rigor for meaningful conclusions to be drawn. Bunker and Knowles related their data to the issue; but since the laboratories that they studied varied in duration as well as in the proportion of time spent in T-groups, the differences they found cannot be attributed to the design alone.

Wilson et al. (1968) reported results from a follow-up on two 6-day "off-site" laboratories, one of which utilized "the traditional sensitivity approach described by Weschler" and the other Morton's version of an instrumented laboratory. Six months after the instrumented laboratory and 18 months after the "sensitivity" laboratory, a very high and similar proportion of participants of the two laboratories reported that the experience was of value to them as individuals; participants of the instrumented laboratory showed significantly greater improvement as managers, as members of a team, in building team effort in their organizations, and in communicating with others in the work setting. Although the study design was a weak one, as the authors note, the findings were consistent with their predictions.

There are no studies comparing laboratory training with rational training (Ellis and Blum, 1967), "motive acquisition" training (McClelland, 1965), or other forms of training; yet there is certainly a need for such studies.

TYPES OF INDIVIDUAL INFLUENCED

Personality and Organization Variable

In one of the more thorough analyses of learning processes and outcomes, Miles (1965) explored 595 relations among criterion, home organization, treatment, and personal variables. He found significant relations between on-the-job change and sex (males change more), job security (as measured by years as a school principal, the more secure participant changed more), and power (as measured by number of teachers supervised, the more powerful changed more). He did not find significant differences between on-the-job change and age, ego strength (as measured by Barron's scale), flexibility (as measured by Barron's scale), need affiliation (as measured by French's test of insight), a combination of these personality variables, autonomy on the job (as measured by frequency of meetings with supervisor), perceived power in his work situation, perceived flexibility of his organization, and a combination of these three organizational variables. On the other hand, he found that several of these variables were significantly related to the participant's behavior during the training (specifically to the extent to which he became more communicative, and to the trainer's rating of the extent to which participants changed), and such behavior was in turn related to on-the-job changes.

Unfortunately, there are few replications of Miles' studies. No other study examines age or sex as a factor in learning from laboratories. With respect to personality, Rubin (1967) found that anomy (which as predicted was itself unaffected by laboratory training) significantly influenced the extent of change in self-awareness, which was a factor in the extent of change in acceptance of others. Harrison (1966) found no significant relation between prelaboratory scores on an instrument measuring concrete-instrumental versus inferential-expressive orientation and extent of change as indicated by comparing pre-training with post-training scores on this instrument. He also found no relation between the prelaboratory scores on this instrument and the participants' reactions to feedback during the laboratory—a finding which seems surprising if Harrison's theory about the importance of cognitive orientation is accurate.

In a study of classroom teachers, Bower and Soar (1961) found that an increase in the teachers' use of group processes in the classroom following training was greatest for teachers (a) who were well adjusted and (b) who used group methods before receiving the training. Harrison and Oshry (1965) found that people who were seen as changing most in a T-group were those who were described by colleagues as open to the ideas of others, were accepting of others, and listened well. These two studies suggest that laboratory training develops the participant's interpersonal style further rather than reversing it.

There is rather strong evidence that participants who become involved in the T-group learn more than those who are ranked low on involvement (Bunker, 1965; Harrison and Oshry, 1966). Although Miles did not find the relation between involvement and on-the-job change to be significant, he did find involvement significantly related to trainer ratings of the participants' effectiveness in the group, which was in turn significantly related to on-the-job change. Perhaps involvement in the training group is a function of the amount of dissonance produced or of having "a castle and a battlefield," as Harrison suggests.

The direction that research should take, in the tradition of Miles' study, is exemplified by Smith (1966). Using a complex model of training based on Kelman's model of influence, and four separate measures of learning, Smith explored the relations among group climates (as indicated by the mix of participant orientation, trainer styles, and types of influence underlying the trainer-participant interaction process) and types of learning. He found support for his predictions that (a) the compliant learning pattern, found among groups with authority-oriented participants and trainers, showed highest learning in diagnostic ability, and (b) the internalizing learning pattern, found in groups with data-oriented participants and people-oriented trainers, showed the greatest favorable changes on FIRO scores and on interpersonal awareness. (This study was based on 31 T-groups, but since the laboratories varied in duration, and the participants in age and occupational background, it is difficult to know the extent to which extraneous factors clouded the findings.)

Influence of Background

Bunker and Knowles (1967) found that human relations laboratory participants from religious and governmental organizations showed significant change after a three-week laboratory but not after a two-week one; whereas participants from industry, education, and social service changed significantly after a two-week session, but the differences between the two-week and the three-week sessions were not significant. However, in this study the data on participants' background did not permit more than rough groupings, so little confidence can be placed in the findings.

In summary, these studies provide some support for the prediction that sex, job security, organizational power, anomy of the participant, trainer-participant interaction patterns, the openness of the participant, and the participant's involvement in the T-group make a difference in how much the participant learns; but clearly this is a topic which merits much more systematic exploration.

LABORATORY TRAINING IN ORGANIZATION DEVELOPMENT

The evidence rather clearly indicates that laboratory training has a predictable and significant impact on most participants; yet it is also clear that from the standpoint of organizational improvement, laboratory training by itself is not enough. Several researchers have addressed themselves to facilitating "transfer of learning" (Winn, 1966, Bass, 1967, Oshry and Harrison, 1966). Bass has identified eight different approaches currently being tried as a means of increasing transfer. In varying degrees, these methods involve including in the training people and/or activities associated with participants on the job, while still retaining a focus on behavior in the laboratory. Laboratory training systematically undertaken throughout the company, using combinations of stranger, work, and interface groups, was a major intervention in the program at the Space Technology Laboratories

(Davis, 1967), in Non-Linear Systems (Kuriloff and Atkins, 1966), and in a division of Alcan (Winn, 1966). And the indications are that in all three companies the development efforts were effective.

Laboratory Training as Part of a Development Program

In several strategies, however, laboratory training is one component of a multiphased program, as in Harwood Manufacturing Company's revitalization of Weldon (Marrow, et al., 1967), in Beckhard's work (1966) with a large hotel company, in Blake's and Mouton's work (1968), and in several projects in school systems (Buchanan, 1968; Miles et al., 1966). In all of these cases of organization development, it is difficult to assess how important the laboratory training was in the impact of the total program (and of course it is equally difficult to assess the effectiveness of the total program itself). In an attempt to learn (Buchanan, 1967) what characterized effective programs of organization development eight successful programs and three unsuccessful ones were examined in the hope of finding some crucial variable. The use of laboratory training (or any other formal training) was not a crucial variable. Neither of the two cases (Guest, 1962; Jaques, 1951) where there was the clearest evidence of success involved formal training. One of the variables that did emerge as crucial was the introduction of new and more fruitful concepts for diagnosing current problems of the organization and setting improvement goals. Having new concepts for diagnosing current practices seemed to provide members of the organization with a means of getting from symptoms to variables which provided leverage for change; having new concepts for setting targets was important in working out clear ideas of potentiality and in developing dissonance and thus motivation for change. Information which has become available since that study was made is consistent with the conclusion about the development of new concepts as a crucial issue in organization development. In a project of organization development, analysis of the case reports on work done with two schools indicated that in the more effective of the two projects much more time was given to developing new concepts and the skills of key participants before diagnosis and planning for system change was undertaken (Buchanan, 1968). In the school system where there was more change, the superintendent had participated in a laboratory conducted by National Training Laboratories, and he and the key members of the system took part in a one-week laboratory of their own. In the other system, the superintendent did not have prior laboratory experience, and he and his key staff had a two-day laboratory of their own. In two other cases of organizational development where there was little evidence of effectiveness (Benedict et al., 1967; Miles et al., 1966), diagnosis of current conditions in the system was undertaken before any effort was made to develop new concepts. In contrast, Blake and Mouton (1968) continually stress the understanding of grid theory and the development of skills required in its application as an essential first step in each phase of their strategy. They begin by exposing the key person in the treatment organization to the managerial grid concept and to alternative styles of management and their implications. This is followed by familiarizing a representative sample of participants with the same concepts. Then all members of management are exposed to the same concepts, and only then are needs diagnosed and improvement goals set by individuals and teams for themselves and for the total organization. A case study recently reported by Bartlett (1967), in which the development effort appeared to be successful, also involved development of new concepts and skills as the first step in the program.

Cognitive Changes

Quite clearly formal training is one effective means for developing cognitive changes as an opening step in organizational development. At the same time, it is also clear that there are other means of creating cognitive changes. The question, then, is whether laboratory training and, in fact, what *kind* of laboratory training provides the most useful concepts and skills for organizational development. Answers to this question can be sought from two sources: from theories about effective organization functioning, and from outcomes of organizational development programs that utilize different methods for introducing new concepts and skills. Although the latter method would be more convincing, at this time there is little such information available. One must therefore look to theory for support of the utility of laboratory training as a means of providing relevant cognitive changes in participants in programs of organizational development. Blake and Mouton have made a case for laboratory training based on grid theory; Shepard, Likert, Argyris, Bennis, and McGregor have provided relevant theory in the case of non-grid laboratory training; and Miles has systematically sought empirical data relevant to the question as it pertains to school systems.

One can summarize this review of the literature as to the value of laboratory training as follows:

1. It facilitates personal growth and development, and thus can be of value to the individual who participates.

2. It accomplishes changes in individuals which according to several theories are important in effecting change in organizations and in effectively managing organizations.

3. One study, in which an instrumented laboratory was compared with sensitivity training, provides some indication that more organizational change resulted from the instrumented approach.

4. The findings from this literature search are compatible with the conclusions reached in a similar review made four years ago (Buchanan 1965).

REFERENCES

Argyris, Chris
    1965 "Explorations in interpersonal competence—I and II." *Journal of Applied Behavioral Science*, I:58–83; 255–69.
    1967 "On the future of laboratory education." *Journal of Applied Behavioral Science*, 3:153–83.

Bartlett, Alton C.
    1967 "Changing behavior as a means to increase efficiency." *Journal of Applied Behavioral Science*, 3:381–403.

Bass, Bernard M.
    1967 "The anarchist movement and the T-group." *Journal of Applied Behavioral Science*, 3:211–26.

Benedict, Barbara, Paula Calder, Daniel Callahan, Harvery Hornstein, and Matthew B. Miles
    1967 "The clinical-experimental approach to assessing organizational change efforts." *Journal of Applied Behavioral Science*, 3:347–80.

Bennis, Warren G.
    1966 *Changing Organizations*. New York: McGraw-Hill.

Beckhard, Richard
    1966 "An organization improvement program in a decentralized organization." *Journal of Applied Behavioral Science*, 2:3–26.
    1967 "The confrontation meeting." *Harvard Business Review*, 45:149–55.

Blake, Robert R., and Jane S. Mouton
    1964 *The Managerial Grid*. Houston: Gulf.
    1966 "Some effects of managerial grid seminar training on union and management attitudes toward supervision." *Journal of Applied Behavioral Science*, 2:387–400.
    1968 *Corporate Excellence through Grid Organization Development*. Houston: Gulf.

Blake, Robert R., Jane S. Mouton, Lewis B. Barnes, and Larry E. Greiner
    1964 "Breakthrough in organization development." *Harvard Business Review*, 42:133–55.

Blake, Robert R., Jane S. Mouton, and Richard L. Sloma
    1965 "The union management intergroup laboratory: strategy for resolving intergroup conflict." *Journal of Applied Behavioral Science*, 1:25–57.

Bolman, Lee
    1968 The Effects of Variations in Educator Behavior on the Learning Process in Laboratory Human Relations Education. Doctoral dissertation, Yale University.

Bowers, N. D., and R. S. Soar
  1961 "Evaluation of laboratory human relations training for classroom teachers. Studies of human relations in the teaching-learning process: V. final report." Columbia: University of South Carolina.
Buchanan, Paul C.
  1965 "Evaluating the effectiveness of laboratory training in industry." In Explorations in Human Relations Training and Research. Report No. 1. Washington: National Training Laboratories.
  1967 "Crucial issues in organizational development." In Goodwin Watson (ed.), Change in School Systems. Washington: National Training Laboratories.
  1968 Reflections on a Project in Self-renewal in Two School Systems. Washington: National Training Laboratories.
Bugental, James, and Robert Tannenbaum
  1963 "Sensitivity training and being motivation." Journal of Humanistic Psychology, III:76–85.
Bunker, Douglas R.
  1965 "Individual applications of laboratory training." Journal of Applied Behavioral Sciences, 1:131–48.
Bunker, Douglas R., and Eric S. Knowles
  1967 "Comparison of behavioral changes resulting from human relations training laboratories of different lengths." Journal of Applied Behavioral Science, 3:505–24.
Byrd, Richard E.
  1967 "Training in a non-group." Journal of Humanistic Psychology, VII:18–27.
Clark, James, and Samuel A. Culbert
  1965 "Mutually therapeutic perception and self-awareness in a T-group." Journal of Applied Behavioral Science, 1:180–94.
Culbert, Samuel A.
  1968 "Trainer self-disclosure and member growth in two T-groups." Journal of Applied Behavioral Science, 4:47–73.
Davis, Sheldon A.
  1967 "An organic problem-solving method of organizational change." Journal of Applied Behavioral Science, 3:3–21.
Deep, S., Bernard Bass, and James Vaughan
  1967 "Some effects on business gaming of previous quasi-T-Group affiliations." Journal of Applied Psychology, 51:426–31.
De Michele, John H.
  1966 The Measurement of Rated Training Changes Resulting from a Sensitivity Training Laboratory of an Overall Program in Organization Development. Doctoral dissertation, New York University.
Ellis, Albert, and Milton Blum
  1967 "Rational training: a new method of facilitating management and labor relations." Psychological Reports, 20:1267–84.

Fleishman, Edwin A., E. F. Harris, and H. E. Burtt
   1955   *Leadership and Supervision in Industry.* Columbus: Bureau of
          Educational Research, Ohio State University.
French J. R. P., J. J. Sherwood, and D. L. Bradford
   1966   "Change in self-identity in a management training conference."
          Journal of Applied Behavioral Science, 2:210–18.
Friedlander, Frank
   1967   "The impact of organizational training laboratories upon the ef-
          fectiveness and interaction of ongoing groups." *Personnel Psychol-
          ogy,* 20:289–308.
Greiner, Larry E.
   1965   Organization Change and Development: A Study of Changing
          Values, Behavior, and Performance in a Large Industrial Plant.
          Doctoral dissertation, Harvard Business School.
   1967   "Antecedents of planned organization change." *Journal of Applied
          Behavioral Science,* 3:51–86.
Guest, Robert
   1962   *Organizational Change.* Homewood, Ill.: Dorsey.
Hampden-Turner, C. M.
   1966   "An existential 'learning theory' and the integration of T-group re-
          search." *Journal of Applied Behavioral Science,* 2:367–86.
Harrison, Roger
   1965   "Group composition models for laboratory design." *Journal of
          Applied Behavioral Science,* 1:409–32.
   1966   "Cognitive change and participation in a sensitivity training lab-
          oratory." *Journal of Consulting Psychology,* 30:517–20.
   1967   "Problems in the design and interpretation of research on human
          relations training." In Explorations in Human Relations Training
          and Research, Report No. 1. Washington: National Training
          Laboratories.
Harrison, Roger, and B. Lubin
   1965   "Personal style, group composition, and learning." *Journal of Ap-
          plied Behavioral Science,* 1:286–301.
Harrison, Roger, and Barry Oshry
   1965   "The design of one-week laboratories." In E. H. Schein and W. G.
          Bennis (eds.), *Personal and Organizational Growth through Group
          Methods:* 98–106. New York: Wiley.
   1966   The Impact of Laboratory Training on Organizational Behavior:
          Methodology and Results. Working paper, National Training
          Laboratories.
Harvey, O. J.
   1966   *Experience, Structure, and Adaptability.* New York: Springer.
House, Robert J.
   1965   " 'T-group' training: some important considerations for the prac-

ticing manager." New York Personnel Management Association Bulletin, 21:4–10.
1967 "Manager development: a conceptual model, some propositions, and a research strategy for testing the model." In *Management Development: Design, Evaluation & Implementation.* Ann Arbor: University of Michigan.
Jaques, E.
1951 *The Changing Culture of a Factory.* London: Tavistock.
Kassarjian, H.
1965 "Social character and sensitivity training." *Journal of Applied Behavioral Science,* 1:433–40.
Knowles, Eric S.
1967 "A bibliography of research—since 1960." In Explorations in Human Relations Training and Research, Report No. 2. Washington: National Training Laboratories.
Kolb, D. A., S. K. Winter, and D. E. Berlew
1968 "Self-directed change: two studies." *Journal of Applied Behavioral Science,* 4:453–71.
Kuriloff, A., and S. Atkins
1966 "T-group for a work team." *Journal of Applied Behavioral Science,* 2:63–93.
Lakin, M., and R. Carlson
1964 "Participant perception of group process in group sensitivity training." *International Journal of Group Psychotherapy,* 14:116–22.
Leavitt, H.
1965 "Applied organizational change in industry: structural, technological, and humanities approaches." In James G. March (ed.), *Handbook of Organizations:* 1144–1170. Skokie, Ill.: Rand McNally.
Likert, Rensis
1967 *The Human Organization.* New York: McGraw-Hill.
Lippitt, Ronald, Jeanne Watson, and Bruce Westley
1958 *The Dynamics of Planned Change.* New York: Harcourt, Brace & World.
McClelland, David C.
1965 "Toward a theory of motive acquisition." *American Psychologist,* 20:321–33.
McGregor, Douglas
1967 *The Professional Manager.* New York: McGraw-Hill.
Marrow, A., D. Bowers, and S. Seashore
1967 *Participative Management.* New York: Harper & Row.
Medow, Herman
1967 "Sensible non-sense." *Journal of Applied Behavioral Science,* 3:202–3.

Miles, M. B.
  1965a "Learning processes and outcomes in human relations training: a clinical-experimental study." In E. H. Schein and W. G. Bennis (eds.), *Personal and Organizational Growth through Group Methods:* 244–54. New York: Wiley.
  1965b Methodological Problems in Evaluating Organizational Change: Two Illustrations. Working paper, Columbia University.
Miles, M. B., J. R. Milavsky, D. Lake, and R. Beckhard
  1965 Organizational Improvement: Effects of Management Team Training in Bankers Trust. Unpublished monograph, Bankers Trust Co., New York.
Miles, M. B., P. Calder, H. Hornstein, D. Callahan, and S. Schiavo
  1966 Data Feedback and Organizational Change in a School System. Working paper, Columbia University.
Morton, R. B., and B. M. Bass
  1964 "The organizational training laboratory." *Training Directors Journal,* 18:2–18.
Morton, R. B., and A. Wight
  1964 A Critical Incidents Evaluation of an Organizational Training Laboratory. Working paper. Aerojet General Corporation.
Oshry, B., and R. Harrison
  1966 "Transfer from 'here-and-now' to 'there-and-then': changes in organizational problem diagnosis stemming from T-group training." *Journal of Applied Behavioral Science,* 2:185–98.
Powers, J. R.
  1965 Trainer Orientation and Group Composition in Laboratory Training. Doctoral dissertation, Case Institute of Technology.
Psathas, G., and R. Hardert
  1966 "Trainer interventions and normative patterns in the T-group." *Journal of Applied Behavioral Science,* 2:149–69.
Rubin, I.
  1967a "Increased self-acceptance: a means of reducing prejudice." *Journal of Abnormal and Social Psychology,* 5:233–38.
  1967b "The reduction of prejudice through laboratory training." *Journal of Applied Behavioral Science,* 3:29–50.
Sarason, Seymour B.
  1966 *The School Culture and Processes of Change.* College Park: College of Agriculture, University of Maryland.
Schein, E. H., and W. G. Bennis
  1965 *Personal and Organizational Growth through Group Methods.* New York: Wiley.
Schmuck, R. A.
  1968 "Helping teachers improve classroom group processes." *Journal of Applied Behavioral Science,* 4:401–35.

Schutz, W. C.
1964   An Approach to the Development of Human Potential. Washington: National Training Laboratories, Subscription Service Report No. 6.
1967   Joy. New York: Grove.
Schutz, W. C., and V. Allen
1966   "The effects of a T-group laboratory on interpersonal behavior." *Journal of Applied Behavioral Science*, 2:265-86.
Shepard, H. A.
1965   "Changing relationships in organizations." In James G. March (ed.), *Handbook of Organizations:* 1115-43. Skokie, Ill.: Rand McNally.
Sikes, W.
1964   A Study of Some Effects of a Human Relations Training Laboratory. Doctoral dissertation, Purdue University.
Smith, P. B.
1964   "Attitude changes associated with training in human relations." *British Journal of Social and Clinical Psychology*, 3:104-12.
1966   T-group Climate, Trainer Style, and Some Tests of Learning. Working paper, University of Sussex, England.
Tannenbaum, R., and James Bugental
1963   "Dyads, clans, and tribe: a new design for sensitivity training." NTL *Training News*, 7:1-3.
Wilson, J. E., D. P. Mullen, and R. B. Morton
1968   "Sensitivity training for individual growth—team training for organization development." *Training and Development Journal*, 22:1-7.
Winn, A.
1966   "Social change in industry: from insight to implementation." *Journal of Applied Behavioral Science*, 2:170-185.

25

Durability of
Organizational Change

STANLEY E. SEASHORE and DAVID G. BOWERS

The aim of this article is to add a modest footnote to the growing literature concerning planned change in the structure and function of formal
organizations. The question asked is whether changes that have been
planned, successfully introduced, and confirmed by measurements, over
but a relatively short span of time, can survive as permanent features of
the organization. Will such a changed organization become stabilized in
its new state, or will it continue the direction and pace of change, or perhaps revert to its earlier state?

This report will include a brief review of an earlier effort to change an
organization, a presentation of some new data about the present state of the
organization, and some first speculations about the meaning of the data for
the understanding of psychological and social phenomena in formal
organizations.

BACKGROUND

The earlier events against which our new data are to be set are reported
rather fully elsewhere (Marrow, Bowers, & Seashore, 1967). A brief review
of the essential facts will set the stage.

Source: Stanley E. Seashore and David G. Bowers, "Durability of Organizational
Change," *American Psychologist*, Vol. 25 (1970), pp. 227–33. Copyright 1970, by the
American Psychological Association, and reproduced by permission.

In late 1961 the Harwood company purchased its major competitor, the Weldon company. This brought under common ownership and general management two organizations remarkably similar in certain features and remarkably different in others. Both made and marketed similar products using equipment and manufacturing processes of a like kind; were of similar size in terms of business volume and number of employees; served similar and partially overlapping markets; were family-owned and owner-managed firms; and had similar histories of growth and enjoyed high reputation in the trade.

The differences between the two organizations are of particular interest. The Harwood company had earned some prominence and respect for their efforts over many years to operate the organization as a participative system with high value given to individual and organizational development, as well as to effective performance. The Weldon company had for years been managed in a fashion that prevails in the garment industry, with a highly centralized, authoritarian philosophy and with secondary concern for individual development and organizational maintenance. The two organizations were, in 1962, rather extreme examples from the continuum vaguely defined by the terms *authoritarian* versus *participative*. Measurements in both firms in 1962 confirmed that the difference was not merely impressionistic, but was represented in quantitative assessments of the organizational processes for planning, coordination, communication, motivation, and work performance, and was represented as well in member attitudes. The two firms were also sharply contrasting in their performance in 1962, even though over a longer span of years their business accomplishments had been similar. In 1962 Weldon, in sharp contrast to Harwood, was losing money, experiencing high costs, generating many errors of strategy and work performance, suffering from member disaffection with consequent high absenteeism and high turnover. Weldon, despite its technical, fiscal, and market strengths, was near the point of disaster.

The new owners set out on a program to rebuild the Weldon enterprise according to the model of the Harwood company. The ultimate aim was to make the Weldon firm a viable and profitable economic unit within a short period of time. A rather strenuous and costly program was envisioned, including some modernization of the plant, improved layout and flow of work, improvements in records and production control methods, and product simplification, as well as changes in the human organization. The renewal program concerning the organization itself concerns us here.

The approach to organizational change can be characterized briefly in three respects: (a) the conception of the organizational characteristics to be sought; (b) the conception of processes for changing persons and organizational systems; and (c) the linking of the social system to the work system.

The guiding assumptions or "philosophy" on which the change program was based included elements such as the following:

1. It was assumed that employees would have to gain a realistic sense of security in their jobs and that this security would have to arise basically out of their own successful efforts to improve their organization and their performance, not out of some bargained assurances.
2. The introduction of substantial change in the work environment requires that employees have confidence in the technical competence and humane values of the managers and supervisors; this confidence can be earned only if it is reciprocated by placing confidence in the employees.
3. In a situation of rapid change it is particularly necessary to use procedures of participation in the planning and control of the work and of the changes; such procedures are needed at all levels of the organization.
4. The rebuilding of an organization may require an input of technical resoures and capital on a substantial scale—not unlike the investments required to rework a technology or control system of a factory.
5. Management involves skills and attitudes that can be defined, taught, and learned, and these skills and attitudes need not be confined to high rank staff; each member of the organization, at least in some limited degree, must learn to help manage his own work and that of others related to him.
6. Guidelines such as these are not readily understood and accepted unless they can be linked to concrete events and to the rational requirements of the work to be done and the problems to be solved.

The conception of change processes incorporated in the rebuilding of the Weldon organization emphasized the application of multiple and compatible change forces. The physical improvements in work resources and conditions were to be accompanied by informational clarity, enhanced motivation through rewards, and ample skill training and practice. That is, change was to be introduced simultaneously at the situational, cognitive, motivational, and behavioral levels so that each would support the others.

The linking of the social organization to the work system was to be accomplished through efforts, however limited, to design work places, work flows, information flows, and the like in a manner not merely compatible with but integral with the associated social organization and organizational processes.

The program of rebuilding the organization was carried out by the local management with substantial assistance and stimulation from the new owners and from a variety of consultants, including psychologists. The general planning and guidance of the program were influenced primarily by Alfred Marrow, Board Chairman of the Harwood Corporation and Fellow of Division 14. The role of the Institute for Social Research was not that of change agent, but rather that of observing, recording, measuring, and analyzing the course of events and the change that resulted.

The change program was successful in important respects. Within two years there occurred improvements in employee satisfactions, motivations, and work performance. The organization took on characteristics of an adaptive, self-controlling, participative system. The firm as a business unit moved from a position of loss to one of profit. At the end of 1964, after two years of change effort, the factory was abandoned as a research site, the rate of input of capital and external manpower into the change program diminished substantially, and the factory and its organization were expected to settle down to something like a "normal" state.

EXPECTATIONS ABOUT CHANGE

From the start of this organizational change program there was a concern about the long-run consequences of the program, and there was uncertainty about the permanence of change. The following quotations from our earlier report illustrate the intentions, hopes, and doubts (Marrow et al., 1967):

the whole organization, from the plant manager down to the production workers, were taken into an exercise in joint problem-solving through participative methods in groups, with a view toward making such procedures a normal part of the management system of the plant [p. 69].

The refreezing of Weldon in a new and more effective state is not regarded as a permanent thing, but as another stage in the evolution and continuous adaptation of the organization. Some features of the conversion plan explicitly include the provision of built-in capacities for easier change in the future [p. 232].

Will the changes at Weldon last? The only evidence we have at the present time is that the change from a predominantly "authoritative" to a dominantly "consultative" type of management organization persisted for at least two years in the view of the managers and supervisors involved. Surely there exist forces toward a reversion to the old Weldon form of organizational life; it remains an uncertainty whether they will or will not win out over the new forces toward consolidation of change and further change of the intended kinds [p. 244].

In mid-1969, four and one-half years after the termination of the intensive change program, Dr. Bowers and I invited ourselves back to the Weldon plant for a follow-up measurement of the state of the organization. This remeasurement consisted of a one-day visit to the plant by a research

assistant who administered questionnaires to managers, supervisors, and a
sample of the employees.[1] In addition, certain information was abstracted
from the firm's records, and the views of the plant manager were solicited
as to changes that had taken place and possible reasons for change. We can
turn directly to a few tables and figures representing the changes and the
situation as of 1969.

RESULTS

First, we present some data from the production employees. Table 1
shows selected items from our questionnaire survey bearing on the issue of
whether there has occurred a decline, a rise, or a stabilization of the attitudes, satisfactions, and optimism of the employees. The table shows the
percentage of employees giving the two most favorable responses, of five
offered, to each question. The columns represent the results in 1962 before
the change program began, in 1964 at the conclusion of the formal change
effort, and in 1969.

TABLE 1

Changes in Job Attitudes

Item	1962 %	1964 %	1969 %
Company better than most	22	28	36
Own work satisfying	77	84	91
Satisfied with pay system	22	27	28
Company tries to maintain earnings	26	44	41
Satisfied with supervisor	64	54	54
Like fellow employees	85	86	85
Group cohesiveness	25	23	30
Plan to stay indefinitely	72	87	66
Expect future improvement in situation	23	31	43

The general picture is one of the maintenance of earlier gains in the
favorability of employee attitudes or the further improvement in attitudes.
This observation holds for seven of the nine indicators. The remaining two
deserve brief special comment.

Satisfaction with supervisors declined during the period of the active
change program but has remained relatively high and constant since 1964.
The initial decline is viewed as a consequence of the substantial change in
the supervisors' role during the active change program. During that period,
the supervisors acquired substantially more responsibility and authority as
well as some new activities and duties that are thought to have removed

---

[1] The assistance of Edith Wessner is acknowledged.

the supervisors from a peerlike to a superior status relationship with the operators, which they retain now. This interpretation is, of course, speculative but made before the 1969 data were in hand.

The decline in the proportion of employees planning to stay on indefinitely is rather difficult to assess. The rise between 1962 and 1964 can be attributed to the improvement in pay and working conditions in that period. The subsequent decline is to be accounted for, partly, by the fact of recent production expansion and the presence on the payroll of a relatively larger number of turnover-prone short-service employees. One might also speculate that rising prosperity during the period might have increased the attractiveness of marriage, child bearing, or retirement for these female employees. In any case, the decline in the percentage committed to long job tenure appears to be at odds with the general rise in job satisfactions and in the marked rise in optimism about the future improvement in the Weldon situation. We should add that the decline in percentage committed to long tenure is confirmed by the fact of a moderate rise in actual turnover rates in recent months.

Table 2 shows a few selected items bearing on the question whether the rise in satisfactions and expectations is accompanied by some loss in productivity concern and task orientation. The data, again, are from employee questionnaire responses (except for the last line) and show changes from 1962 to 1964, and then to 1969.

Five of the indicators reflect a rise in level of task orientation and production concern since the end of the formal change program. The remaining items are not negative, but merely indeterminate. There is clearly a rise in recent years in the percentage of employees who say the firm is quick to improve work methods, good at planning, provides efficient services (maintenance, supplies, scheduling), who report that their peers approve of high producers, and who themselves desire frequent and ready access to supervisory help. Two sets of data require special comment.

The data on productivity, three lines in the table, should be considered

TABLE 2

Change in Task-Orientation Indicators

Item	1962 %	1964 %	1969 %
Company quick to improve methods	18	24	31
Company good at planning	22	26	35
Not delayed by poor services	76	79	90
Produce what rates call for	44	67	53
Expect own productivity to improve	63	55	62
Peers approve of high producers	58	58	66
Closeness of task supervision	38	27	47
Desired closeness of supervision	57	52	64
Mean productivity (% of standard)	87	114	?

as a set. The numbers show that the self-report of "Nearly always producing what the rates call for" rose substantially during the active change program, and this is confirmed by the actual productivity records of the firm
as shown in the last line "Mean productivity against standard." During the
same period, the percentage of employees expecting a further gain in their
own productivity declined, as it should have considering that more employees were approaching the firm's hoped-for level of high productivity
and earnings. By 1969 there was some decline in the percentage reporting
high productivity and a corresponding rise in the percentage expecting a
future rise in their productivity; this pair of related changes appears to reflect the presence on the staff of an increasing number of relatively new
employees not yet up to the level of skill and performance they may reasonably expect to attain. There is a crucial item of missing data in the last line
of the table; for technical reasons, we have not been able to calculate the
current actual productivity rate in a form that allows confident comparisons with the earlier figures. Our best estimate is that productivity has
been stable with a slight decline in recent months arising from the recent
introduction of additional inexperienced employees.

Attention is also suggested to the pair of lines in Table 2 concerning
closeness of supervision. At all three times of measurement, these production workers desired more close supervision than they actually experienced;
these employees, unlike those in some other organizations, see their supervisors to be potentially helpful in improving productivity and increasing
piece-rate earnings. The decline in experienced closeness of supervision
during the period 1962–64 matches other evidence to be presented later
that during this period there was a substantial change in the supervisors'
role that diverted the supervisors from immediate floor supervision and
left a temporary partial shortage of this service to production workers. The
figures show that by 1969 this supervisory deficit had been recouped and
more. This sustains our general view that during the years following the
Weldon change program there has been not a decline in concern for task
performance among employees and in the organizational system generally
but rather a further gain in task orientation.

The change in supervisory behavior mentioned earlier is shown in Figure 1. We attempted at the three points in time to measure the extent to
which supervisors, in the view of employees, engaged in behaviors we categorize as "supportive," "goal emphasizing," and "work facilitating." (Two
additional dimensions of leader behavior that we now use in describing
organizations are not represented here because they were not yet identified
in 1962; we chose to continue use of the initial measurement methods
rather than to update them.)

Figure 1 shows that the amount of supervisory supportiveness experienced by employees remained constant during the 1962–64 period and has
risen slightly since then. Goal emphasis and work facilitation both dropped

FIGURE 1

Change in Three Dimensions of Supervisory Leadership Behavior

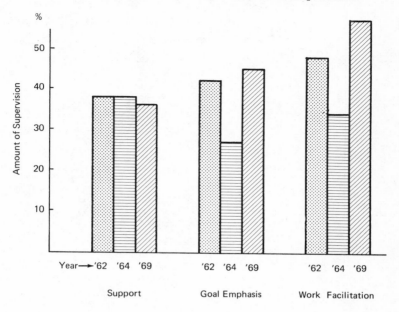

during the active change program, for reasons mentioned earlier, and have since risen above their 1962 levels. These data sustain our belief that the Weldon organization since 1964 has increased its expression of concern for production goals and its provision of conditions for effective work performance, and at no cost of declining concern for employee attitudes and satisfactions.

One more set of data from the employees is pertinent here, namely, their description of the amount and hierarchical distribution of control in the Weldon organization. One of the explicit aims of the change program was that of increasing the total amount of control and of altering the distribution of control so that lower rank people—supervisors and operators—would have some added degree of control. This was accomplished during the change program period to a very limited and nonsignificant degree. Subsequent changes have been in the direction intended and more substantial in degree. The data are shown in Figure 2. In 1969, compared with the earlier periods, there is more control being exercised in total, with a notable increment in the case of the headquarters staff, a further small decline for the local plant management, and increments for the supervisors and for the employees. There appears to have been a change of modest degree, more or less as hoped for, and there has clearly not been a reversion to the original condition of concentrated control in the hands of the plant manager.

FIGURE 2

Change in Amount and Hierarchical Distribution of Control

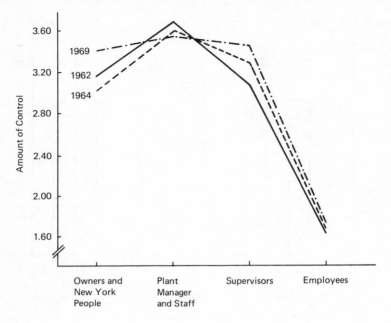

We turn now to some indicators of the state of the Weldon organization from the views of the supervisors and managers. The data presented in Figure 3 are derived from Likert's assessment instrument "Profile of Organizational and Performance Characteristics" (Likert, 1961, 1967). Most readers will have some acquaintance with this instrument and the theory and research data that it expresses, but a brief characterization might be helpful. The instrument used is a 43-item graphic-scale rating form that allows the respondent to describe his own organization as it presently functions and as he ideally would like it to function. The items are so chosen and arranged that the respondent may report a syndrome of organizational characteristics that locates the organization on a scale ranging from "authoritative" to "participative." Likert discerns four regions of this scale, named Systems 1, 2, 3, and 4, with word labels ranging from "Authoritarian" through "Benevolent Authoritarian" and "Consultative" to "Participative." The conception is analogous to McGregor's "Theory X" and "Theory Y" scale, and also to Blake's two-dimensioned matrix. To put it somewhat disrespectfully, the bad guys are thought to have and to prefer System 1 organizations while good guys aspire to and approach the System

4 state. The results for Weldon, 1962, 1964, and 1969 are represented in Figure 3.

At the left of the field are two graph lines showing the state of the Weldon organization in 1962, first as rated by the Institute for Social Research research team from interview protocols and observations, and next and somewhat more favorably as rated by the supervisors and managers on the scene. Weldon at that time was described to be autocratic—in some respects rather harshly autocratic and in some respects more benevolently autocratic. The state of the organization in 1964 and in 1966 is represented in the next two lines. These data are from supervisors and managers; they indicate a pattern of change that is substantial in magnitude and wholly compatible with the intentions embodied in the Weldon change program. There was no regression toward the earlier state during the 1964–66 period. The right-hand line represents the results of our 1969 assessment; it shows that in the view of the managers and supervisors at Weldon, the organization has progressed still further toward their ideal of a participative organizational system.

FIGURE 3

Change in Profile of Organizational Characteristics

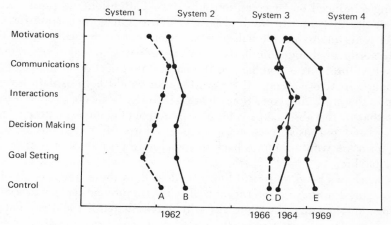

A final remark should be made about measured changes in Weldon before we turn to a consideration of the meaning of these data. Some readers will be interested in business outcomes as well as in the attitudes and behavior of the members of the organization. Briefly, Weldon moved from a position of substantial capital loss in 1962 to substantial return on investment in 1964; this direction of change in profitability has continued through 1968, the last year of record. Employee earnings which rose substantially between 1962 and 1964 have been sustained at a relatively high level. During the period since 1964 there have been substantial gains in efficiency and volume for the factory as a whole. New products and work methods have been introduced. By such business indicators, Weldon is a successful organization.

DURABLE CHANGE

The evidence we must weigh, although somewhat mixed and with a few contrary elements, appears to sustain the conclusion that the Weldon organization, far from reverting to its prior condition, has during recent years made additional progress toward the organizational goals envisoned by the owners and managers in 1962, and envisoned as well by supervisors and production employees at a somewhat later time. This outcome invites speculations about the psychological and social forces that are at work.

We confess a brief regret that there was not an opposite outcome, for we are rather better equipped with ideas about organizational stability and regression than we are with ideas about organizational change and continuing development. For example, before the data became available, we were prepared to make some remarks about the "Hawthorne effect"—about the superficiality and transient quality of organizational and behavioral changes induced under conditions of external attention and pressure; but it boggles the mind to think of a "Hawthorne effect" persisting for over eight years among people half of whom were not on the scene at the time of the original change. Similarly, we were prepared to make wise remarks about cultural forces, habits, and the natural predilection of managers for nonparticipative methods; these we thought would help explain a reversion to the prevailing conditions in organizations. We were prepared to assert that in the absence of contrary environmental forces, external influences, and purposive continuing change efforts of a vigorous kind, an organization would migrate back to some more primitive form of organizational life.

Clearly we need to appeal to other ideas than these. We are, all of us, ill prepared to do so. Two recent and fairly comprehensive reviews of organizational change strategies (Leavitt, 1965; Shepard, 1965) say nothing about the permanence or continuation of change processes except for a remark by Shepard that "change in the direction of collaboration-consensus patterns [participative patterns] . . . facilitates growth, change and adaptation to new environmental challenges and opportunities [p. 1141]."

A first explanatory idea rests on the possibility that the heavy investment of external talent, money, and effort that characterized the original change period at Weldon has been continued during the subsequent years. We are assured that this is not the case. There has indeed been some additional use of external consultants, but at a modest rate that is considered normal and permanent. There has indeed been further improvement and change in the work system and the production facilities, but at no more than a permanently sustainable rate. There has indeed been a continuation of certain organizational activities introduced as part of the original change program, but these are regarded as normal operating procedure and not as special change efforts. Economic conditions have been favorable to the firm, but they were also favorable at the distressed time preceding the change of ownership in 1962.

We believe that there are three other lines of explanation that do bear scrutiny. These thoughts about the Weldon experience are not offered with any sense of great insight or of conceptual innovation. They are offered only as suggestions for lines of inquiry and emphasis in future organizational research. The first concerns the provision of "lock-in" devices that make difficult the reversal of the original change.

It was mentioned earlier that the original change program contained some notions of seeking mutually reinforcing change actions across the psychological, organizational, and technological domains. A central idea was to make structural changes in the organization that matched the work system and that did not violate reasonable assumptions about the values and motives of individual members. For example, the revitalized piece-rate pay system was viewed to be viable only if sustained by the provision of assured services that allowed high earnings, a revision of the record and information flow system that assured instant supervisory response to low earnings, and a moderating of the prior job assignment system so that a production employee could become skilled in the work assigned. The idea of systemic consistency is surely an elementary one, no more than common sense—a habit of thought for those who have learned to view the factory as a total system in which all elements are interdependent. The interdependence of elements tends to preserve, to enhance, and to "lock in" the central characteristics of the system and thus to prevent retrogression.

A second factor in Weldon's continuation of intended change might lie in the earlier legitimation of concern about organizational processes. This is speculative, for we have no ready way to assess the extent to which there was implanted the habit of deliberate and self-conscious examination of the potential side effects of the many policy and operating decisions, usually technical or economic in origin, that arise daily. One of the fragmenting features of many organizations is the tendency to isolate problems, to treat them as if they could be optimally resolved without reference to their broader context. An organization habituated at all levels to think about, discuss openly, and to weigh properly the full range of elements in the organizational system might well have unusual capacities for self-maintenance and self-development.

A third possible explanation of the maintenance of the changes at Weldon and their further development under conditions of limited continuing external influence might lie in the inherent merit of the participative organizational model. Could it be that people who have experienced a taste of it get hooked, know what they want, and lend their effort to maintaining it? A glance at the newspaper headlines on almost any day will suggest that some of our fellow citizens do not like what they are experiencing in formal organizations and have thoughts of having something better, by force if necessary.

REFERENCES

Leavitt, H. J. Applied organizational change in industry. In J. G. March (Ed.), *Handbook of organizations*. Skokie, Ill.: Rand-McNally, 1965.

Likert, R. *New patterns of management*. New York: McGraw-Hill, 1961.

Likert, R. *The human organization*. New York: McGraw-Hill, 1967.

Marrow, A. J., Bowers, D. G., & Seashore, S. E. *Management by participation*. New York: Harper & Row, 1967.

Shepard, H. A. Changing interpersonal and intergroup relationships in organizations. In J. G. March (Ed.), *Handbook of organizations*. Skokie, Ill.: Rand-McNally, 1965.

26

Beyond the Teaching Machine: The Neglected Area of Operant Conditioning in the Theory and Practice of Management
WALTER R. NORD

The work of B. F. Skinner and the operant conditioners has been neglected in management and organizational literature. The present paper is an attempt to eliminate this lacuna. When most students of management and personnel think of Skinner's work, they begin and end with programmed instruction. Skinner's ideas, however, have far greater implications for the design and operation of social systems and organizations than just the teaching machine. These additional ideas could be of great practical value.

While neglecting conditioning, writers in the administrative, management, and personnel literature have given extensive attention to the work of other behavioral scientists. McGregor and Maslow are perhaps the behavioral scientists best known to practitioners and students in the area of business and management. Since the major concern of managers of human resources is the prediction and control of the behavior of organizational participants, it is curious to find that people with such a need are extremely conversant with McGregor and Maslow and totally ignorant of Skinner. This condition is not surprising since leading scholars in the field of what might be termed the applied behavioral sciences have turned out book after book, article after article, and anthology after anthology with

Source: Reprinted by permission from *Organizational Behavior and Human Performance,* Vol. 4 (1969), pp. 352–77.

scarcely a mention of Skinner's contributions to the design of social systems. While many writers who deal with the social psychology of organizations are guilty of the omission, this paper will focus primarily on the popular positions of Douglas McGregor, Abraham Maslow, and Frederick Herzberg to aid in exposition.

Almost every book in the field devotes considerable attention to Maslow and McGregor. These men have certainly contributed ideas which are easily understood and "make sense" to practitioners. Also, many practitioners have implemented some of these ideas successfully. However, the belief in the Maslow-McGregor creed is not based on a great deal of evidence. This conclusion is not mine alone, but in fact closely parallels Maslow's (1965) own thoughts. He wrote:

> After all, if we take the whole thing from McGregor's point of view of a contrast between a Theory X view of human nature, a good deal of the evidence upon which he bases his conclusions comes from my researches and my papers on motivations, self-actualization, et cetera. But I of all people should know just how shaky this foundation is as a final foundation. My work on motivations came from the clinic, from a study of neurotic people. The carry-over of this theory to the industrial situation has some support from industrial studies, but certainly I would like to see a lot more studies of this kind before feeling finally convinced that this carry-over from the study of neurosis to the study of labor in factories is legitimate. The same thing is true of my studies of self-actualizing people—there is only this one study of mine available. There were many things wrong with the sampling, so many in fact that it must be considered to be, in the classical sense anyway, a bad or poor or inadequate experiment. I am quite willing to concede this—as a matter of fact, I am eager to concede it—because I'm a little worried about this stuff which I consider to be tentative being swallowed whole by all sorts of enthusiastic people, who really should be a little more tentative in the way that I am (p. 55–56).

By contrast, the work of Skinner (1953) and his followers has been supported by millions of observations made on animals at all levels of the phylogenetic scale, including man. Over a wide variety of situations, behavior has been reliably predicted and controlled by operant and classical conditioning techniques.

Why then have the applied behavioral sciences followed the McGregor-Maslow approach and ignored Skinner? Several reasons can be suggested. First is the metaphysical issue. Modern Americans, especially of the managerial class, prefer to think of themselves and others as being self-actualizing creatures operating near the top of Maslow's need-hierarchy, rather than as animals being controlled and even "manipulated" by their environment. McGregor (1960) developed his argument in terms of Maslow's hierarchy. Skinner's position is unattractive in the same way the Copernican theory was unattractive. Second, Skinner's work and stimulus–response psychology in general appear too limited to allow application to complex social situations. Certainly, this point has much merit. The application of S–R theory poses a terribly complex engineering problem, perhaps an insoluble one in some areas. Nevertheless, the designs of some experimental social systems, which will be discussed later in this paper, demonstrate the feasibility of the practical application of Skinnerian psychology to systems design. A third possible reason for the acceptance of the McGregor and Maslow school and rejection of Skinner may stem from the fact that the two approaches have considerable, although generally unrecognized overlap. As will be shown below, McGregor gave primary importance to the environment as the determinant of individual behavior. Similarly, although not as directly, so does Maslow's hierarchy of needs. The major issue between Skinner and McGregor–Maslow has to do with their models of man. Skinner focuses on man being totally shaped by his environment. Maslow–McGregor see man as having an essence or intrinsic nature which is only congruent with certain environments. The evidence for any one set of metaphysical assumptions is no better than for almost any other set. Empirically, little has been found which helps in choosing between Skinner's and McGregor's assumptions. Further, since most managers are concerned mainly with behavior, the sets of assumptions are of limited importance. It should be noted, however, that if McGregor's writings were stripped of Maslow's model of man, his conclusions on the descriptive and proscriptive levels would remain unchanged. Such a revision would also make McGregor's ideas almost identical with Skinner's. With more attention to contingencies of reinforcement and a broader view of the possibilities of administering reinforcement, the two sets of ideas as they apply to prediction and control of action would be virtually indistinguishable.

The remainder of this paper will be devoted to three areas. First, the similarities and differences between McGregor and Skinner will be discussed. Then a summary of the Skinnerian position will be presented. Finally, the potential of the Skinnerian approach for modern organizations will be presented with supporting evidence from social systems in which it has already been applied.

McGREGOR AND SKINNER COMPARED

The importance of environmental factors in determining behavior is the crucial and dominant similarity between Skinner and McGregor. As will be shown below, environmental determination of behavior is central to both men.

McGregor (1960) gave central importance to environmental factors in determining how a person behaves. For example, he saw employee behavior as a consequence of organizational factors which are influenced by managerial strategy. In a sense, Theory X management leads to people behaving in a way which confirms Theory X assumptions, almost as a self-fulfilling prophecy. In addition, McGregor's statement of Theory Y assumptions places stress on "proper conditions," rewards and punishments, and other environmental factors. Further, he recognized the importance of immediate feedback in changing behavior. Also, he noted that failure to achieve results is often due to inappropriate methods of control. These are the very terms a behaviorist such as Skinner uses in discussing human actions. Finally, McGregor (1966) noted stimulus-response psychology as a possible model for considering organizational behavior. However, he discarded the reinforcement approach because it did not permit intrinsic rewards to be dealt with. Such a view not only led him to discard a model which describes, by his own admission, important behaviors, but is based on an incomplete view of reinforcement.

McGregor's basic arguments could have been based on Skinner rather than Maslow. The major difference would be the assumption of fewer givens about human nature. In view of this similarity one need not choose either Skinner or McGregor. Rather, there is considerable overlap in that both focus on changing the environmental conditions to produce changes in behavior. Further, both writers place substantial emphasis on the goals of prediction and control. Both are quite explicit in suggesting that we often get undesired results because we use inappropriate methods of control. In fact, the emphasis that McGregor's (1960) first chapter gives to the role of environment in controlling behavior seems to place him clearly in the behavioral camp.

Certainly there are important differences between Skinner and McGregor as well as the marked similarities noted above. For example, McGregor's (1960) use of Maslow's hierarchy of needs implies a series of inborn needs as a focus of the causal factors of behavior whereas Skinner (1953) views environmental factors as the causes of behavior. This difference does not, however, suggest an unresolvable conflict on the applied level. Skinner too allows for satiation on certain reinforcers which will be subject to species and individual differences. Proceeding from this premise, Skinner focuses on the environmental control of behavior in a more rigorous and specific fashion than did McGregor. For example, McGregor (1960) advocated an agricultural approach to development which emphasizes the provision of the conditions for behavioral change as a management responsibility. He noted in a general way that features of the organization, such as a boss, will influence behavioral change. He added that the change would not be permanent unless the organizational environment reinforced the desired behavior pattern. Such a general approach is an assumed basis for Skinner, who proceeds to focus on the types of reinforcement, the details of the administration of reinforcement, and the outcomes which can be expected from the administration of various types of reinforcement. Thus, changes in behavior which are predicted and achieved by Skinnerian methods can be viewed as empirical support for the work of McGregor.

There are other commonalities in the thinking of the two men. Both assume that there are a wide number of desirable responses available to a person which he does not make because the responses are not rewarded in the environment. Both suggest that many undesired responses are repeated because they are rewarded. Both are clearly advocating a search for alternatives to controlling behavior which will be more effective in developing desired responses.

At this same level of analysis, there seems to be one major difference which revolves around the issue of self-control. However, this difference may be more apparent than real. Skinner (1953) wrote "It appears, therefore, that society is responsible for the larger part of the behavior of self-control. If this is correct, little ultimate control remains with the individual (p. 240)." Continuing on self-control, Skinner adds: "But it is also behavior; and we account for it in terms of other variables in the environment and history of the individual. It is these variables which provide the ultimate control (p. 240)."

In apparent contrast, McGregor (1960) stated: "Theory Y assumes that people will exercise self-direction and self-control in the achievement of organizational objectives *to the degree that they are committed to those objectives* (p. 56)." Seemingly this statement contradicts Skinner in placing the locus of control inside the individual. However, this conflict is reduced a few sentences later when McGregor (1960) added "Managerial policies and practices materially affect this degree of commitment (p. 56)." Thus, both writers, Skinner far more unequivocally than McGregor, see the external environment as the primary factor in self-control. While McGregor polemicized against control by authority, he was not arguing that man is "free." Perhaps the more humanistic tone of McGregor's writing or his specific attention to managerial problems faced in business is responsible for his high esteem among students of management relative to that accorded Skinner. While metaphorically there is great difference, substantively there is little. It would seem, however, that metaphors have led practitioners and students of applied behavioral science to overlook some valuable data and some creative management possibilities.

One major substantive difference between the two approaches exists: it involves intrinsic rewards. McGregor (1966) saw a dicotomy in the effects of intrinsic and extrinsic rewards, noting research which has shown intrinsic ones to be more effective. He concludes the "mechanical" view (reinforcement theory) is inadequate, because it does not explain the superior outcomes of the use of "intrinsic" over "extrinsic" rewards. Here, as will be discussed in more detail later in connection with Herzberg, the problem is McGregor's failure to consider scheduling of reinforcement.

"Intrinsic" rewards in existing organizations may be more effective because they occur on a more appropriate schedule for sustaining behavior than do "extrinsic" rewards. Intrinsic rewards are given by the environment for task completion or a similar achievement, and often occur on a ratio schedule. The implications of this crucial fact will be discussed shortly in considering Skinner's emphasis on the scheduling of rewards. For the present, it is suggested that McGregor gave little attention to reinforcement schedules and made a qualitative distinction between external and internal rewards. He seems to agree with Skinner that achievement, task completion, and control of the environment are reinforcers in themselves. Skinner's work suggests, however, that these rewards have the same consequences as "extrinsic" rewards, if they are given on the same schedule.

By way of summary to this point, it appears that more humanistic social scientists have been preferred by managers to behaviorists such as Skinner in their efforts to improve the management of human resources. Perhaps the oversight has been due to the congruence between their values and the metaphysics of people such as McGregor and Maslow. The differences between McGregor and Skinner do not appear to involve open conflict.

To the extent the two approaches agree, the major criterion in employing them would seem to be the degree to which they aid in predicting and controlling behavior toward organizational goals. The work of Skinner and his followers has much to offer in terms of the above criterion. In particular, McGregor's followers might find Skinner's work an asset in implementing Theory Y. The remainder of this paper will develop some of the major points of the Skinnerian approach and seek to explore their potential for industrial use.

CONDITIONING—A SYNTHESIS FOR ORGANIZATIONAL BEHAVIOR

The behavioral psychology of Skinner assumes, like Theory Y, that rate of behavior is dependent on the external conditions in which the behavior takes place. Like Theory X, it stresses the importance of the administration of rewards and punishments. Unlike Theory X, Skinnerian psychology places emphasis on rewards. Like Theory Y it emphasizes the role of interdependence between people in a social relationship and thus views the administration of rewards and punishments as an exchange. For those who are unfamiliar with the work of Skinner and his followers, a brief summary follows. Like any summary of an extensive body of work, this review omits a lot of important material. A more detailed, yet simple, introduction to conditioning can be found in Bijou and Baer (1961) and Skinner (1953). Extensions of this work by social exchange theorists such as Homans (1961) suggest that the conditioning model can be extended to a systems approach, contrary to McGregor's (1966) belief.

Generally, conditioned responses can be divided into two classes. Each class is acquired in a different fashion. The first class, generally known as respondent or classically conditioned behavior, describes the responses which are controlled by prior stimulation. These responses, generally thought of as being involuntary or reflexive, are usually made by the "smooth muscles." Common ones are salivation and emotional responses. Initially, the presentation of an unconditioned stimulus will elicit a specific response. For example, food placed on one's tongue will generally cause salivation. If a bell is sounded and then food is placed on the tongue, and this process is repeated several times, the sound of the bell by itself will elicit salivation. By this process, stimuli which previously did not control behavior such as the bell, can become a source of behavior control. Many of our likes and dislikes, our anxieties, our feelings of patriotism, and other emotions can be thought of as such involuntary responses. The implications of emotional responses are of major importance to the management of human resources and more will be said about them later. However, the second class of responses, the operants, are of even greater importance.

The rate of operant responses is influenced by events which follow them. These events are considered to be the consequences of behavior. The responses, generally thought to be voluntary, are usually made by striped muscles. All that is necessary for the development of an operant response is that the desired response has a probability of occurring which is greater than zero for the individual involved. Most rapid conditioning results when the desired response is "reinforced" immediately (preferably about one-half second after the response). In other words, the desired response is followed directly by some consequence. In simple terms, if the outcome is pleasing to the individual, the probability of his repeating the response is apt to be increased. If the consequence is displeasing to the individual, the probability of his repeating the response is apt to be decreased. The process of inducing such change (usually an increase) in the response rate, is called operant conditioning. In general, the frequency of a behavior is said to be a function of its consequences.

The above description of operant conditioning is greatly simplified. The additional considerations which follow will only partially rectify this state. One crucial factor has to do with the frequency with which a given consequence follows a response. There are several possible patterns. Most obviously, the consequence can be continuous (for example, it follows the response every time the response is made). Alternatively a consequence might follow only some of the responses. There are two basic ways in which such partial reinforcement can be administered. First, the consequence can be made contingent on a certain number of responses. Two sub-patterns are possible. Every nth response may be reinforced or an average of $1/n$ of the responses may be reinforced in a random pattern. These two related patterns are called ratio schedules. The former is known as a fixed ratio and the latter is known as a variable ratio. Ratio schedules tend to generate a high rate of response, with the variable ratio schedule leading to a more durable response than both the fixed-ratio and continuous patterns. A second technique of partial reinforcement can be designed where the consequence follows the response only after a certain amount of time has elapsed. The first response made after a specified interval is then reinforced, but all other responses produce neutral stimulus outcomes. This pattern can also be either fixed or variable. Generally, interval schedules develop responses which are quite long lasting when reinforcement is no longer given, but do not yield as rapid a response rate as ratio schedules do. Obviously, mixed patterns of ratio and interval schedules can also be designed.

A second consideration about operant conditioning which deserves brief mention is the concept of a response hierarchy. All the responses which an individual could make under a given set of conditions can be placed in order according to probability that they will be made. In this view, there are two basic strategies for getting an individual to make the desired response. First, one could attempt to reduce the probability of all the more probable responses. Second, one could attempt to increase the probability of the desired response. Of course, some combination of these two approaches may often be used.

Strategies for changing the probability of a response can be implemented by punishment, extinction, and positive reinforcement. Generally punishment and extinction are used to decrease the occurrence of a response whereas positive reinforcement is used to increase its probability. An understanding of these three operations in behavior control is important, not only for knowing how to use them, but chiefly because of their unanticipated consequences or their side-effects.

Punishment is the most widely used technique in our society for behavior control. Perhaps, as Reese (1966) said, the widespread use of punishment is due to the immediate effects it has in stopping or preventing the undesired response. In this sense, the punisher is reinforced for punishing. Also, many of us seem to be influenced by some notion of what Homans (1961) called distributive justice. In order to reestablish what we believe to be equity, we may often be led to punish another person. This ancient assumption of ". . . an eye for an eye . . ." has been widely practiced in man's quest for equity and behavior control.

Whatever the reason for punishing, it can be done in two ways, both of which have unfortunate side-effects. First, punishment can be administered in the form of some aversive stimulus such as physical pain or social disapproval. Secondly, it can be administered by withdrawing a desired stimulus. The immediate effect is often the rapid drop in frequency of the punished response. The full effects, unfortunately, are often not clearly recognized. Many of these consequences are crucial for managers of organizations.

Punishment may be an inefficient technique for controlling behavior for a number of reasons. First, the probability of the response may be reduced only when the threat of punishment is perceived to exist. Thus, when the punishing agent is away, the undesired response may occur at its initial rate. Secondly, punishment only serves to reduce the probability of the one response. This outcome does not necessarily produce the desired response, unless that response is the next most probable one in the response hierarchy. Really, what punishment does is to get the individual to do something other than what he has been punished for. A third effect is that the punishment may interfere with the responses being made under desired circumstances. For example, if an organizational member attempts an innovation which is met with punishment by his superiors because they did not feel he had the authority to take the step, it is quite possible that his creative behavior will be reduced even in those areas where his superiors expect him to innovate.

In addition to these effects there are some other important byproducts of punishment. Punishment may result in a person's making responses which are incompatible with the punished response. Psychological tension, often manifested in emotional behavior such as fear or anxiety, is often the result. Secondly, punishment may lead to avoidance and dislike of the punishing agent. This effect can be especially important to managers who are attempting to build open, helping relationships with subordinates. The roles of punishing agent and helper are often incompatible. Many line-staff conflicts in organizations undoubtedly can be explained in these terms. Finally, punishment may generate counter-aggression. Either through a modeling effect or a justice effect, the punished person may respond with aggressive responses towards the punishing agent or towards some other stimulus.

The second technique for behavior change, commonly called extinction, also focuses primarily on reducing the probability of a response. Extinction arises from repeated trials where the response is followed by a neutral stimulus. This technique generates fewer byproducts than punishment. However, like punishment, it does not lead to the desired responses being developed. Furthermore, to the extent that one has built up an expectation of a reward for a certain response, a neutral consequence may be perceived as punishing. Thus, extinction may have some advantages over punishment, but has many of the same limitations.

Positive reinforcement is the final technique for changing behavior. Under conditions of positive reinforcement, the response produces a consequence that results in an increase in the frequency of the response. It is commonly stated that such a consequence is rewarding, pleasing, or drive-reducing for the individual. The operant conditioners, however, avoid such inferences and define positive reinforcers as stimuli which increase the probability of a preceding response. Positive reinforcement is efficient for several reasons. First, it increases the probable occurrence of the desired response. The process involves rewarding approximations to the direct response itself immediately after it is made. The desired behavior is being directly developed as opposed to successive suppression of undesired acts. Secondly, the adverse emotional responses associated with punishment and extinction are apt to be reduced, and in fact favorable emotions may be developed. Since people tend to develop positive affect to others who reward them, the "trainer" is apt to become positively valenced in the eyes of the "learner."

By way of summary, Skinner's (1953) approach suggested that the control of behavior change involves a reduction in the probability of the most prepotent response and/or an increase in the probability of some desired response. Punishment and extinction may be used. These means can only reduce the probability of the unwanted responses being made. Also, they may have undesired side effects. The third technique, positive reinforcement, has the important advantage of developing the desired response rather than merely reducing the chances of an undesired one. Also, positive reinforcement is apt to produce favorable rather than unfavorable "side effects" on organizational relationships.

This approach seems to suggest that both or neither Theory X and Theory Y assumptions are useful. This section suggested that conditioning may be both Theory X and Theory Y. Perhaps since the operant view does not make either set of assumptions, it is neither Theory X nor Theory Y. Operant conditioning is consistent with Theory Y in suggesting that the limits on human beings are a function of the organizational setting, but like Theory X, implies something about human nature; namely that deprivation or threat of some sort of deprivation is a precondition for behavior to be controlled. From the managerial perspective, however, the nomonological question is of little significance. The important thing to managers is behavior and the major point of this approach is that behavior is a function of its consequences. Good management is that which leads to the desired behavior by organizational members. Management must see to it that the consequences of behavior are such as to increase the frequency of desired behavior and decrease the frequency of undesired behaviors. The question becomes, how can managers develop a social system which provides the appropriate consequences? In many ways the answer to this question is similar to what Theory Y advocates have suggested. However, there are some new possibilities.

APPLICATIONS OF CONDITIONING IN ORGANIZATIONS

The potential uses of the Skinnerian framework for social systems are increasing rapidly. The approach has far more applicability to complex social systems than has often been recognized. McGregor's rejection of the stimulus-response or the reward-punishment approach is inadequate for management because it does not allow for a systems approach is quite inconsistent with this general trend and his own environmentally based approach. Recent work in the field of behavioral control has begun to refute McGregor's position. The Skinnerian view can be and has been used to redesign social systems.

The most complete redesign was envisioned by Skinner (1948) in his novel, *Walden Two*. In this book, Skinner developed a society based on the use of positive reinforcement and experimental ethics geared to the goal of competition of a coordinated social unit with its environment. In other words, the system is designed to reward behaviors which are functional for the whole society. Social change is introduced on the basis of empirical data. As a result of the success of this system, man is enabled to pursue those activities which are rewarding in themselves. Although the book is a novel, it can be a valuable stimulus for thought about the design of social organization.

In addition, Skinner (1954) has taken a fresh look at teaching and learning in conventional educational systems. He noted that the school system depends heavily on aversive control or punishment. The use of low marks and ridicule have merely been substituted for the "stick." The teacher, in Skinner's view, is an out-of-date reinforcing mechanism. He suggested the need to examine the reinforcers which are available in the system and to apply them in a manner which is consistent with what is known about learning. For example, control over the environment itself may be rewarding. Perhaps grades reinforce the wrong behavior and are administered on a rather poor schedule. It would seem that a search for new reinforcers and better reinforcement schedules is appropriate for all modern organizations.

These speculations suggest the potential for great advances. *Walden Two* is in many ways an ideal society but has been a source of horror to many readers. The thoughts about changes in teaching methods are also a subject of controversy. However, the environment can be designed to aid in the attainment of desired ends. People resist the idea that they can be controlled by their environment. This resistance does not change the fact that they are under such control. Recently, evidence has begun to accumulate that the Skinnerian approach can be employed to design social systems.

Much of this evidence was collected in settings far removed from modern work organizations. The reader's initial response is apt to be, "What relevance do these studies have to my organization?" Obviously, the relationship is not direct. However, if, as the operant approach maintains, the conditioning process describes the acquisition and maintenance of behavior, the same principles can be applied to any social organization. The problem of application becomes merely that of engineering. The gains may well be limited only by an administrator's ingenuity and resources.

Much of the evidence comes from studies of hospitalized mental patients and autistic children, although some has been based on normal lower class children. A few examples from these studies will serve to document the great potential of the conditioning methods for social systems. Allyon and Azrin (1965) observed mental patients' behavior to determine what activities they engaged in when they had a chance. They then made tokens contingent on certain responses such as work on hospital tasks. These tokens could be exchanged for the activities the patients preferred to engage in. The results of this approach were amazing. In one experiment five schizophrenics and three mental defectives served as Ss. They did jobs regularly and adequately when tokens were given for the job. Such performance was reported to be in sharp contrast to the erratic and inconsistent behavior characteristic of such patients. When the tokens were no longer contingent on the work, the performance dropped almost to zero. In a second experiment, a whole ward of 44 patients served as Ss. A similar procedure was followed and 11 classes of tasks observed. When tokens were contingent upon the desired responses, the group spent an average of 45 hours on the tasks daily. When tokens were not contingent on responses, almost no time was spent on the tasks. The implications seem rather clear. When desired behavior is rewarded, it will be emitted, when it is not rewarded, it will not be emitted.

A great deal of related work has been reported. Allyon (1966) and Wolf, Risley, and Mees (1966) have shown how a reinforcement procedure can be effective in controlling the behavior of a psychotic patient and of an autistic child respectively. These are but a few of the many studies in a growing body of evidence.

More important for present purposes are the applications of this approach in more complex social situations. The work of Hamblin et al. (1967) shows some of the interesting possibilities of the conditioning approach for school classes and aggressive children. A token system was used to shape desired behavior. Through the application of the conditioning approach to the school system, gains may be made in educating children from deprived backgrounds. Two examples will illustrate these possibilities.

The first example comes from a recent newspaper story. A record shop owner in a Negro area of Chicago reported seeing the report card of a Negro boy. The owner thought the boy was bright, but the report card showed mostly unsatisfactory performance. He told the boy he would give him $5 worth of free records if he got all "excellents" on the next report card. Ten weeks later the boy returned with such a card to collect his reward. The owner reported that similar offers to other children had a remarkable effect in getting them to study and do their homework. The anecdote demonstrates what everyone knows anyway: people will work for rewards. It also suggests the converse: people will not work if rewards do not exist. The problems of education in the ghetto, and motivation to work in general, may be overcome by appropriate reinforcement. Further support for this statement comes from the work of Montrose Wolf.

Wolf (1966) ran a school for children, most of whom were sixth graders, in a lower class Negro area of Kansas City. The children attended this school for several hours after school each day and on Saturday. Rewards were given in the form of tickets which could be saved and turned in for different kinds of things like toys, food, movies, shopping trips, and other activities. Tickets were made contingent on academic performance within the remedial school itself, and on performance in the regular school system. The results were remarkable. The average school grade of the students was raised to C from D. The results on standard achievement tests showed the remedial group progressed over twice as much in one year as they had done the previous year. They showed twice as much progress as a control group. Other gains were also noted. Wolf reported that a severe punishment was not to let the children attend school. They expressed strong discontent when school was not held because of a holiday. He further noted that when reading was no longer rewarded with tickets, the students still continued to read more than before the training. Arithmetic and English did not maintain these increments. Thus, to some extent, reading appeared to be intrinsically rewarding.

A final point concerns the transferability of skills learned in such a school to society at large. Will the tasks that are not rewarding in themselves be continued? The answer is probably not, unless other rewards are provided. The task then becomes to develop skills and behavior which society itself will reward. If this method is applied to develop behavior which is rewarded by society, the behavior is apt to be maintained. The same argument holds for organizational behavior. It will be fruitless to develop behavior which is not rewarded in the organization.

In summary, evidence has been presented to show the relevance of the Skinnerian approach to complex social systems. Certainly the evidence is only suggestive of future possibilities. The rest of this paper attempts to suggest some of these implications for organizational management.

MANAGEMENT THROUGH POSITIVE REINFORCEMENT

The implications of the systematic use of positive reinforcement for management range over many traditional areas. Some of the more important areas include training and personnel development, compensation and alternative rewards, supervision and leadership, job design, organizational design, and organizational change.

Training and Personnel Development

The area of training has been the first to benefit from the application of conditioning principles with the use of programmed learning and the teaching machine. An example of future potential comes from the Northern Systems Company Training Method for assembly line work. In this system, the program objectives are broken down into subobjectives. The training employs a lattice which provides objective relationships between functions and objectives, indicates critical evaluation points, and presents a visual display of go-no-go functions. Progress through various steps is reinforced by rewards. To quote from a statement of the training method ". . . the trainee gains satisfaction only by demonstrated performance at the tool stations. Second, he quickly perceives that correct behaviors obtain for him the satisfaction of his needs, and that incorrect behaviors do not (p. 20)." Correct performance includes not only job skills, but also the performance of social interaction which is necessary in a factory setting. The skills taught are designed to allow for high mobility in the industrial world. The Northern Systems' method develops behavior which the economic and social system will normally reinforce, and has been successful in training people in a wide variety of skills. Its potential in training such groups as the "hard-core" unemployed seems to be limited only by the resources and creativity of program designers.

The Skinnerian approach seems to have potential for all areas of personnel development, not only for highly programmed tasks. Reinforcement theory may be useful in the development of such behaviors as creativity. The work of Maltzman, Simon, Raskin, and Licht (1960) demonstrated this possibility. After a series of experiments employing a standard experimental training procedure with free association materials, these investigators concluded that a highly reliable increase in uncommon responses could be produced through the use of reinforcement. The similarity of their results to those of operant experiments with respect to the persistance of the responses and the effect of repetitions led them to conclude that originality is a form of operant behavior. Positive reinforcement increased the rate at which original responses were emitted.

Support is also available for the efficacy of operant conditioning to more conventional personnel and leadership development. Three such contributions are discussed below. The first concerns the organizational environment as a shaper of behavior of which Fleishman's (1967) study is a case in point. He found that human relations training programs were only effective in producing on-the-job changes if the organizational climate was supportive of the content of the program. More generally it would appear that industrial behavior is a function of its consequences. Those responses which are rewarded will persist; those responses which are not rewarded or are punished will decrease in frequency. If the organizational environment does not reward responses developed in a training program, the program will be, at best, a total waste of time and money. As Sykes (1962) has shown, at worst such a program may be highly disruptive. A second implication of operant conditioning concerns the content of personnel development programs in the area of human relations. If, as Homans (1961) and others have suggested, social interaction is also influenced by the same operant principles, then people in interaction are constantly "shaping" or conditioning each other. The behavior of a subordinate is to some degree developed by his boss and vice-versa. What more sensible, practical point could be taught to organizational members than that they are teaching their fellow participants to behave in a certain manner? What more practical, sensible set of principles could be taught than that, due to latent dysfunctions generated, punishment and extinction procedures are less efficient ways to influence behavior than positive reinforcement? Clearly, the behavioral scientists who have contributed so greatly to organizational practice and personnel development have not put enough emphasis on these simple principles. The third implication for personnel development is added recognition that annual merit interviews and salary increments are very inefficient development techniques. The rewards or punishments are so delayed that they can be expected to have little feedback value for the employees involved. More frequent appraisals and distribution of rewards are apt to be far more effective, especially to the degree that they are related to specific tasks or units of work.

Job Design

Rcently, behavioral scientists have emphasized the social psychological factors which need to be attended to in job design. McGregor and others have suggested job enlargement. Herzberg (1968) has argued that job enlargement just allows an individual to do a greater variety of boring jobs and suggests that "job enrichment" is needed. For present purposes, job enlargement and job enrichment will be lumped together. Both of these approaches are consistent with the conditioning view if two differences can be resolved. First, the definitions of motivation must be translated into common terms. Second, reinforcers operating in the newly designed jobs must be delineated and tested to see if the reinforcers postulated in the newly designed jobs are really responsible for behavioral changes or if there are other reinforcers operating.

With respect to the definitions of motivation, the two approaches are really similar in viewing the rate of behavior as the crucial factor. The major differences exist on the conceptual level. Both job enlargement and job enrichment are attempts to increase motivation. Conceptually, McGregor and Herzberg tend to view motivation as some internal state. The conditioning approach does not postulate internal states but rather deals with the manipulation of environmental factors which influence the rate of behavior. Actually, some combination of the two approaches may be most useful theoretically as Vinacke (1962) has suggested. However, if both approaches are viewed only at the operational level, it is quite probable that rates of behavior could be agreed on as an acceptable criterion.

Certainly from the practitioners viewpoint, behavior is the crucial variable. When a manager talks about a motivated worker, he often means one who frequently makes desired responses at a high rate without external prompting from the boss. The traditional view of motivation as an inner drive is of limited practical and theoretical value.

If both approaches could agree on the behavioral criterion, at least on an operational level, the operant approach could be employed to help resolve some practical and theoretical problems suggested by the work of McGregor and Herzberg. Since, generally speaking, the external conditions are most easily manipulated in an organization, attention can be focused on designing an environment which increases the frequency of the wanted responses. As a result, practitioners and students of organization could deal with motivation without searching for man's essence. We can avoid the metaphysical assumptions of Maslow and McGregor until they are better documented. The issue of a two-factor theory of motivation proposed by Herzberg, which recently has been severely challenged by Lindsay, Marks, and Gorlow (1967) and Hulin and Smith (1967), among others, can also be avoided. Attention can be confined to developing systems which produce high rates of desired behavior. Thus the conceptual differences about motivation do not cause unresolvable conflict at the present time.

The second area of difference between McGregor–Herzberg and the operant explanation of the effects of job enrichment stems from the failure of Herzberg and McGregor to recognize the great variety of possible rewards available in job design. The Skinnerian approach leads to the development of a more comprehensive discussion of the rewards from enriched on enlarged jobs. In terms of the operant approach, both job enrichment and job enlargement are apt to lead to what would generally be called greater motivation or what we will call higher rates of desired behavior. McGregor and Herzberg suggest feelings of achievement and responsibility explain these results. The reinforcement approach leads to a search for specific rewards in these newly designed jobs.

Job enlargement can be viewed simply as increasing the variety of tasks a person does. Recent research on self-stimulation and sensory deprivation has suggested that stimulation itself is reinforcing, especially when one has been deprived of it. The increased variety of tasks due to job enlargement may thus be intrinsically rewarding due to a host of reinforcers in the work itself rather than to any greater feeling of responsibility or achievement. These feelings may be a cause of greater productivity or merely correlates of the receipt of these intrinsic rewards from stimulation. The evidence is not clear, but the effects of job enlargement can at least be partially explained in operant terms.

Some additional support from this idea comes from Schultz's (1964) work on spontaneous alternation of behavior. Schultz suggested that spontaneous alteration of human behavior is facilitated (1) when responses are not reinforced and/or are not subjected to knowledge of correctness, (2) by the amount of prior exercise of one response alternative, and (3) by a short interval. Low feedback and reinforcement, short intervals between responses, and the frequent repetition of one response are all characteristic of many jobs which need enlargement. Merely making different responses may be rewarding to a worker, thereby explaining some of the benefits noted from job enlargement. It has also been noted that people create variation for themselves in performing monotonous tasks. For example, ritualized social interaction in the form of social "games" is a form of such alternation workers developed noted by Roy (1964).

By way of summary, much of the current work on job enlargement and enrichment has attributed the effects to feelings of achievement or responsibility, without taking into account numerous other possible reinforcers which may be more basic. Further research to determine the efficacy of these various possibilities is needed before definite conclusions can be drawn. Do the feelings of achievement or responsibility operate as reinforcers in an operant manner? Do these feelings come from other more basic rewards as task variety? Present data do not permit answers to these questions.

With respect to the benefits noted from job enrichment, an operant model may provide further insights. Herzberg (1968) maintained that some jobs can not be "enriched" or made more motivating in themselves. It is the contention of this paper that it is not the tasks which are the problem, but it is the reinforcement schedules. For example, what could be more boring, have less potential for achievement and realization of Herzberg's satisfiers than the game of bingo? Yet people will sit for hours at bingo, often under punishing conditions (since the house takes in more than it pays out) and place tokens on numbers. Similar behavior is exhibited at slot machines and other gambling devices. Most operational definitions of motivation would agree that these players are highly motivated. The reason is clear from the operant viewpoint. The reinforcement schedule employed in games of chance, the variable ratio schedule, is a very powerful device for maintaining a rapid rate of response. With respect to job design, the important requirement is that rewards follow performance on an effective schedule.

The type of rewards Herzberg (1968) called satisfiers may be important motivators because they are distributed on a variable ratio schedule. Herzberg's data does not rule out this explanation. Take achievement, for example. If a person is doing a job from which it is possible to get a feeling of achievement, there must be a reasonably large probability that a person will not succeed on the task. Often times, this condition means that some noncontinuous schedule or reinforcement is operating. An individual will succeed only on some variable ratio schedule. In addition, successful completion of the task is often the most important reward. The reward is, of course, immediate. A similar statement could be made about tasks which are said to yield intrinsic satisfaction, such as crossword puzzles or enriched jobs. Thus the factors Herzberg called motivators may derive their potency from the manner in which the rewards are administered. The task is immediately and positively reinforced by the environment on a variable ratio schedule. Often the schedule is one which rewards a very small fraction of a large number of responses. Since behavior is a function of its consequences, if jobs can be designed to reinforce desired behavior in the appropriate manner, "motivated" workers are apt to result. Some of Herzberg's results may be explained without resort to a two-factor theory more parsimoniously in terms of schedules of reinforcement. Herzberg's (1966) finding that recognition is only a motivator if it is contingent on performance further documents the operant argument.

Another suggestion for job design from the operant tradition was suggested by Homans. He explored the relationship of the frequency of an activity and satisfaction to the amount of a reward. He concluded that satisfaction is generally positively related to the amount of reward whereas frequency of an activity is negatively related to the amount of reward the individual has received in the recent past. In order to have both high satisfaction and high activity, Homans (1961) suggested that tasks need to be designed in a manner such that repeated activities lead up to the accomplishment of some final result and get rewarded at a very low frequency until just before the final result is achieved. Then the reinforcement comes often. For example, consider the job of producing bottled soda. An optimal design would have the reward immediately on the completion of putting the caps on the bottles, but the task would be designed such that all the operations prior to capping were completed before any capping was done. Near the end of a work day, all the capping could be done. High output and satisfaction might then exist simultaneously. In general then, the operant approach suggests some interesting possibilities for designing jobs in ways which would maximize the power of reinforcers in the job itself.

A similar argument can be applied to some problems faced in administration and management. For example, it is commonly recognized that programmed tasks tend to be attended to before unprogrammed ones. It is quite obvious that programmed functions produce a product which is often tangible. The product itself is a reinforcer. An unprogrammed task often requires behavior which has not been reinforced in the past and will not produce a reward in the near future. It may be beneficial to provide rewards relatively early for behavior on unprogrammed tasks. This suggestion will be difficult to put into practice because of the very nature of unprogrammed tasks. Perhaps the best that can be done is to reward the working on such tasks.

Compensation and Alternative Rewards

Although whether money is a true "generalized reinforcer," as Skinner suggests, has not been demonstrated conclusively, for years operant principles have been applied in the form of monetary incentive systems. Opsahl and Dunnette (1966) concluded that such programs generally do increase output. However, the restriction of output and other unanticipated consequences are associated with these programs. Many writers have attributed these consequences to social forces, such as the desire for approval from one's peers. Gewitz and Baer (1958), for example, have shown that social approval has the same effects as other reinforcers in an operant situation. Dalton's (1948) famous study on rate-busters may be interpreted to show that people who are more "group-oriented" may place a higher value on social approval and hence are more apt to abide by group production norms than are less "group-oriented" people. Thus, it is not that money in piece-rate systems is not a potential reinforcer, but rather other reinforcers are more effective, at least after a certain level of monetary reward.

The successful use of the Scanlon Plan demonstrates the value of combining both economic and social rewards. This plan rewards improved work with several types of reinforcers, and often more immediately and directly than many incentive systems. The Scanlon Plan combines economic rewards, often given monthly, with social rewards. The latter are given soon after an employee's idea has been submitted or used.

Related arguments can be made for other group incentive programs. Often jobs are interdependent. The appropriate reinforcement for such tasks should be contingent upon interdependent responses, not individual ones. Even if the jobs are independent, the workers are social-psychologically interdependent. Social rewards are often obtainable by restricting output. It is hardly surprising that individual incentive programs have produced the unanticipated consequences so often noted. Further, since rewards and punishments from the informal group are apt to be administered immediately and frequently they are apt to be very powerful in controlling behavior.

In general, then, money and other rewards must be made contingent on the desired responses. Further, the importance of alternative rewards to money must be recognized and incorporated into the design of the work environment. The widely known path-goal to productivity model expresses a similar point.

Another problem of compensation in organizations is also apparent in an operant context. Often, means of compensation, especially fringe benefits, have the unanticipated consequences of reinforcing the wrong responses. Current programs of sick pay, recreation programs, employee lounges, work breaks, and numerous other personnel programs all have one point in common. They all reward the employee for not working or for staying away from the job. These programs are not "bad," since often they may act to reduce problems such as turnover. However, an employer who relies on them should realize what behavior he is developing by establishing these costly programs. Alternative expenditures must be considered. If some of the money that was allocated for these programs were used to redesign jobs so as to be more reinforcing in themselves, more productive effort could be obtained. This idea is certainly not new. A host of behavioral scientists have suggested that resources devoted to making performance of the job itself more attractive will pay social and/or economic dividends.

Another interesting application of conditioning principles has to do with the schedule on which pay is distributed. The conventional pay schedule is a fixed interval one. Further, pay often is not really contingent on one's performance. The response needed to be rewarded is often attending work on payday. Not only is pay often not contingent upon performance, but the fixed interval schedule is not given to generating a high response rate. In a creative article, Aldis (1966) suggested an interesting compensation program employing a variable ratio schedule. Instead of an annual Christmas bonus or other types of such expected salary supplements, he suggested a lottery system. If an employee produced above an agreed upon standard, his name would be placed in a hat. A drawing would be held. The name(s) drawn would receive an amount of money proportionate to the number of units produced during that period of time. This system would approximate the desired variable ratio schedule.

In addition to the prosperity of the owners of gambling establishments, there is some direct evidence that variable ratio schedules will be of use to those charged with predicting and controlling human behavior. A leading St. Louis hardware company,[1] although apparently unaware of the work of the operant conditioners, has applied an approximate variable ratio schedule of reinforcement to reduce absenteeism and tardiness. Although the complete data are not available, the personnel department has reported surprising success. A brief description of the system will be presented below and a more detailed study will be written in the near future.

Under the lottery system, if a person is on time (that is, not so much as ½ minute late) for work at the start of his day and after his breaks, he is eligible for a drawing at the end of the month. Prizes worth approximately $20 to $25 are awarded to the winners. One prize is available for each 25 eligible employees. At the end of six months, people who have had perfect attendance for the entire period are eligible for a drawing for a color television set. The names of all the winners and of those eligible are also

---

[1] The author wishes to thank Mr. C. for making this information available and one of his students, Richard Weis, for informing him about this program.

printed in the company paper, such that social reinforcement may also be a factor. The plan was introduced because tardiness and absenteeism had become a very serious problem. In the words of the personnel manager, absenteeism and tardiness ". . . were lousy before." Since the program was begun 16 months ago, conditions have improved greatly. Sick leave costs have been reduced about 62 percent. After the first month, 151 of approximately 530 employees were eligible for the drawing. This number has grown larger, although not at a steady rate, to 219 for the most recent month. Although the comparable figures for the period before the program were unfortunately not available, management has noted great improvements. It would appear that desired behavior by organization participants in terms of tardiness and absenteeism can be readily and inexpensively developed by a variable ratio schedule of positive reinforcement. The possibilities for other areas are limited largely by the creativity of management.

The operant approach also has some additional implications for the use of money as a reward. First, many recent studies have shown money is not as important as other job factors in worker satisfaction. Herzberg (1968), among others, has said explicitly that money will not promote worker satisfaction. Undoubtedly, in many situations, Herzberg is correct. However, crucial factors of reward contingencies and schedules have not been controlled in these studies. Again, it appears that the important distinction that can be made between Herzberg's motivators and hygiene factors is that the former set of rewards are contingent on an individual's responses and the latter are not. If a work situation were designed so that money was directly contingent on performance, the results might be different. A second point has to do with the perception of money as a reward. Opsahl and Dunnette (1966) have recently questioned pay secrecy policies. They maintained that pay secrecy leads to misperception of the amount of money that a promotion might mean. The value of the reinforcers is underestimated by the participants' suggesting that they are less effective than they might otherwise be. Certainly, alternative rewards are likely to be "over chosen." By following policies of pay secrecy, organizations seem to be failing to utilize fully their available monetary rewards.

In addition to underutilization of money rewards, organizations seem to be almost totally unaware of alternative reinforcers, and in fact see punishment as the only viable method of control when existing reinforcers fail. What are some alternatives to a punishment-centered bureaucracy? Some, such as job design, improved scheduling of reinforcement, and a search for new reinforcers have already been suggested. There are other possible reinforcers, a few of which are discussed below.

The important thing about reinforcers is that they be made immediately contingent on desired performance to the greatest degree possible. The potential reinforcers discussed here also require such a contingent relationship, although developing such relationships may be a severe test of an administrator's creativity. One of the more promising reinforcers is leisure. It would seem possible in many jobs to establish an agreed-upon standard output for a day's work. This level could be higher than the current average. Once this amount is reached, the group or individual could be allowed the alternative of going home. The result of experiments in this direction would be interesting to all concerned. Quite possibly, this method might lead to a fuller utilization of our labor force. The individual may be able to hold two four-hour jobs, doubling his current contribution. Such a tremendous increase in output is quite possible, as Stagner and Rosen (1966) have noted, when the situation possesses appropriate contingencies. Certainly, the problems of industrial discipline, absenteeism, and grievances which result in lower productivity might be ameliorated. Another possible reinforcer is information. Guetzkow (1965) noted that people have a strong desire to receive communication. Rewarding desired performance with communication or feedback may be a relatively inexpensive reinforcer. Graphs, charts, or even tokens which show immediate and cumulative results may serve this function. Some of the widely accepted benefits from participative management may be due to the reinforcing effect of communication. Certainly the "Hawthorne effect" can be described in those terms. In addition, social approval and status may be powerful reinforcers. Blau's classic study described by Homans (1961) on the exchange of approval and status for help is but one example. People will work for approval and status. If these are made contingent on a desired set of responses, the response rate can be increased. At present, often social approval is given by one's peers, but is contingent on behavior which is in conflict with organizational goals.

In addition to these reinforcers, there are certain social exchange concepts such as justice, equity, reciprocity, and indebtedness which deserve attention. Recent research has demonstrated that an unbalanced social exchange, such as one which is inequitable or leaves one person indebted to someone else, may be tension-producing in such a way that individuals work to avoid them. In other words, unbalanced exchanges are a source of punishment. Relationships, such as those involving dependency, which result in such social imbalance can be expected to have the same latent consequences as punishment. Techniques which employ social imbalance to predict and control behavior can be expected to be less efficient in most respects than ones based on positive reinforcement.

The crucial variable in distributing any reward is contingency. Managers have been quick to point out that the problem with a "welfare state" is that rewards do not depend on desired behavior. This point is well taken. It is surprising that the same point has not been recognized in current management practices.

Organizational Climate and Design

Important aspects of human behavior can be attributed to the immediate environment in which people function. The potential then exists to structure and restructure formal organizations in a manner to promote the desired behavior. Once this point is recognized and accepted by managers, progress can begin. The reaction of managers to this approach is often, "You mean my organization should reward people for what they ought to do anyway?" The answer is that people's behavior is largely determined by its outcomes. It is an empirical fact rather than a moral question. If you want a certain response and it does not occur, you had better change the reinforcement contingencies to increase its probable occurrence.

The first step in the direction of designing organizations on this basis involves defining explicitly the desired behaviors and the available reinforcers. The next step is to then make these rewards dependent on the emission of the desired responses. What are some of the implications of such reasoning for organizational design?

Already the importance of organizational climate has been discussed in connection with human development. Some additional implications merit brief consideration. A major one concerns conformity. Often today the degree to which people conform to a wide variety of norms is lamentably acknowldged and the question is asked, "Why do people do it?" The reasons in the operant view are quite clear: conformity is rewarded, deviance is punished. People conform in organizations because conformity is profitable in terms of the outcomes the individual achieves. In fact, Nord (in press) and Walker and Heyns (1962) presented considerable evidence that conformity has the same properties as other operant responses. If managers are really worried about the costs of conformity in terms of creativity and innovation, they must look for ways to reward deviance, to avoid punishing nonconformity, and to avoid rewarding conformity. Furthermore, the way in which rewards are administered is important. Generally, if rewards are given by a person or group of people, a dependency relationship is created, with hostility, fear, anxiety, and other emotional outcomes being probable. Dependence itself may be a discomforting condition. It is therefore desirable to make the rewards come from the environment. Rewards which have previously been established for reaching certain agreed-upon goals are one such means. Meaningful jobs in which achievement in itself is rewarding are another way. In general, to the degree that competition is with the environment or forces outside the organization, and rewards come from achievement itself, the more effective the reinforcers are apt to be in achieving desired responses.

A final point concerns the actual operation of organizations. Increasingly it is recognized that a formal organization, which aims at the coordination of the efforts of its participants, is dependent on informal relationships for its operation. As Gross (1968) noted,

> In administration, also, "the play's the thing" and not the script. Many aspects of even the simplest operation can never be expressed in writing. They must be sensed and felt. . . . Daily action is the key channel of operational definition. In supplying cues and suggestions, in voicing praise and blame, in issuing verbal instructions, administrators define or clarify operational goals in real life (p. 406).

More generally, what makes an organization "tick" is the exchange of reinforcers within it and between it and its environment. The nature of these exchanges involves both economic and social reinforcers. Many of these are given and received without explicit recognition or even awareness on the part of the participants. The operant approach focuses attention on these exchange processes. As a result, it may prove to be an invaluable asset to both administrators and students of administration and organization.

A final advantage of the operant approach for current organizational theory and analysis may be the attention it focuses on planned and rational administration. Gouldner (1966) noted "Modern organizational analysis by sociologists is overpreoccupied with the spontaneous and unplanned responses which organizations make to stress, and too little concerned with patterns of planned and rational administration (p. 397)." The Skinnerian approach leads to rational planning in order to control outcomes previously viewed as spontaneous consequences. This approach could expand the area of planning rational action in administration.

REFERENCES

Aldis, O.   "Of Pigeons and Men," in R. Ulrich, T. Stachnik and J. Mabry (eds.), *Control of Human Behavior*. Glenview, Ill.: Scott, Foresman, 1966, pp. 218–21.

Ayllon, T.   "Intensive Treatment of Psychotic Behavior by Stimulus Satiation and Food Reinforcement," in R. Ulrich, T. Stachnik and T. Mabry (eds.), *Control of Human Behavior*. Glenview, Ill.: Scott, Foresman, 1966, pp. 170–76.

Ayllon, T., and Azrin, N. H.   "The Measurement and Reinforcement of Behavior of Psychotics," *Journal of the Experimental Analysis of Behavior*, 1965, 8, pp. 357–83.

Bijou, S. W., and Baer, D. M.   *Child Development*, Vol. 1. New York: Appleton-Century-Crofts, 1961.

Dalton, M.   "The Industrial 'Rate-Buster': A Characterization," *Applied Anthropology*, 1948, 7, pp. 5–18.

Fleishman, E. A., "Leadership Climate, Human Relations Training, and

Supervisory Behavior," in Fleishman, E. A. (ed.), *Studies in Personnel and Industrial Psychology.* Homewood, Ill.: Dorsey, 1967, pp. 250–63.

"Free Records Given for E's, Pupils Report Cards Improve," *St. Louis Dispatch,* December 3, 1967.

Gewirtz, J. L., and Baer, D. M. "Deprivation and Satiation of Social Reinforcers as Drive Conditions," *Journal of Abnormal and Social Psychology,* 1958, 57, pp. 165–72.

Gouldner, A. W. "Organizational Analysis," in Bennis, W. G., Benne, K. D., and Chin, R. (eds.), *The Planning of Change.* New York: Holt, Rinehart, & Winston, 1966, pp. 393–99.

Gross, B. M. *Organizations and Their Managing.* New York: Free Press, 1968.

Guetzkow, H. "Communications in Organizations," in March, J. G. (ed.), *Handbook of Organizations.* Skokie, Ill.: Rand McNally, 1965, pp. 534–73.

Hamblin, R. L., Bushell, O. B., Buckholdt, D., Ellis, D., Ferritor, D., Merritt, G., Pfeiffer, C., Shea, D., and Stoddard, D. "Learning, Problem Children and a Social Exchange System." Annual Report of the Social Exchange Laboratories, Washington University, and Student Behavior Laboratory, Webster College, St. Louis, Mo., August 1967.

Herzberg, F. "One More Time: How Do You Motivate Employees?" *Harvard Business Review,* January–February 1968, pp. 53–62.

———. *Work and the Nature of Man.* Cleveland: World, 1966.

Homans, G. C. *Social Behavior: Its Elementary Forms.* New York: Harcourt, Brace & World, 1961.

Hulin, C. L., and Smith, P. A. "An Empirical Investigation of Two Implications of the Two-Factor Theory of Job Satisfaction," *Journal of Applied Psychology,* 1967, 51, pp. 396–402.

Lindsay, C. A., Marks, E., and Gorlow, L. "The Herzberg Theory: A Critique and Reformulation," *Journal of Applied Psychology,* 1967, 51, pp. 330–39.

Maltzman, I., Simon, S., Roskin, D., and Licht, L. "Experimental Studies in the Training of Originality," Psychological Monographs: General and Applied, 1960, 74 (6, Whole No. 493).

Maslow, A. *Eupsychian Management.* Homewood, Ill.: Dorsey, 1965.

McGregor, D. *The Human Side of Enterprise.* New York: McGraw-Hill, 1960.

———. *Leadership and Motivation.* Cambridge, Mass.: M. I. T. Press, 1966.

Nord, W. R. "Social Exchange Theory: An Integrative Approach to Social Conformity," *Psychological Bulletin,* (in press).

Northern Systems Company. "A Proposal to the Department of Labor for Development of a Prototype Project for the New Industries Program." Part one.

Opsahl, R. L., and Dunnette, M. D. "The Role of Financial Compensation in Industrial Motivation," *Psychological Bulletin,* 1966, 66, pp. 94–118.

Reese, E. P. *The Analysis of Human Operant Behavior.* Dubuque, Iowa: William C. Brown, 1966.

Roy, D. F. "Banana Time—Job Satisfaction and Informal Interaction," in Bennis, W. G., Schein, E. H., Berlew, D. E., and Steele, F. I. (eds.), *Interpersonal Dynamics.* Homewood, Ill.: Dorsey, 1964, pp. 583–600.

Schultz, D. P. "Spontaneous Alteration Behavior in Humans, Implications for Psychological Research," *Psychological Bulletin,* 1964, 62, pp. 394–400.

Skinner, B. F. *Science and Human Behavior.* New York: Macmillan, 1953.

———. "The Science of Learning and the Art of Teaching," *Harvard Educational Review,* 1954, 24, pp. 86–97.

———. *Walden Two.* New York: Macmillan, 1948.

Stagner, R., and Rosen, H. *Psychology of Union-Management Relations.* Belmont, Cal.: Wadsworth, 1966.

Sykes, A. J. M. "The Effect of a Supervisory Training Course in Changing Supervisors' Perceptions and Expectations of the Role of Management," *Human Relations,* 1962, 15, pp. 227–43.

Vinacke, E. W. "Motivation as a Complex Problem," *Nebraska Symposium on Motivation,* 1962, 10, pp. 1–45.

Walker, E. L., and Heyns, R. W. *An Anatomy of Conformity.* Englewood Cliffs, N.J.: Prentice-Hall, 1962.

Wolf, M. M. Paper read at Sociology Colloquium, Washington University, December 5, 1966.

Wolf, M. M., Risley, T., and Mees, H. "Application of Operant Conditioning Procedures to the Behavior Problems of an Autistic Child," in R. Ulrich, T. Stachnik and T. Mabry (eds.), *Control of Human Behavior.* Glenview, Ill.: Scott, Foresman, 1966, pp. 187–93.

27

Red Flags in Organization Development
LARRY E. GREINER

Many organizations have embarked in recent years on ambitious programs of large-scale change labeled with the high-sounding title of "organization development" (or OD, as it has come to be called by its
devotees). A very special meaning has become attached to OD, usually
referring to the widespread application of an intensive educational program within an organization for the twin purposes of changing managerial
behavior and improving the total performance of the organization.

A basic proposition underlying these OD programs centers around the
notion that if an educational program can cause a large number of individual managers to alter their behavioral styles in working with others,
then the organization as a whole will be transformed—and so will its overall effectiveness.

Although some of these programs have been uniquely designed for a
particular organization, a great majority are prepacked by outside consultants. Such packaged programs include the managerial grid, versions
of sensitivity training, synectics, and a host of lesser known programs designed by small consulting companies and academics who have moved
forward to meet the demand.

Despite the differences between one OD program and the next, there
are some common features that apply to all of them. Basically, they center

---

Source: Reprinted by permission from *Business Horizons* (June 1972), pp. 17–24.

around an educational training program attended by, preferably, a large number of managers and even nonmanagerial employees from a single organization. These training laboratories concentrate on presenting a new role model or behavioral style for managers and employees to emulate back on the job when solving problems in interpersonal settings. The role model tends to be universally prescribed for all who attend the laboratory sessions—that is, if you change your individual styles to this one "best" approach, then you and the organization will perform better.

This learning experience is intensive and intended to be long range; the learning message is not imparted in a one-day session, but begins with a one- to two-week educational laboratory conducted away from the job. It is usually followed by numerous on-the-job learning activities after the initial training session in order to make the reeducation "stick."

NEED FOR PERSPECTIVE

For the last few years, two colleagues of mine, Louis Barnes of Harvard and Paul Leitch, formerly of Harvard, have joined me in studying and learning about the application of various approaches to OD. Out of these efforts has come an increasing concern with some disturbing trends recurring in the design and conduct of many organization development programs.

My purpose in this article is to build on this experience by taking a critical look at these trends and offering some additional perspective on them. To date, this perspective seems to be lacking. Too many organizations have embarked on OD for a number of ill-founded reasons—because it is the "thing to do," or because "change is the watchword of the day," or because "I went to one of their laboratory training sessions; it was good for me, and it will be good for my managers."

To an extent this new initiative has been healthy. A growing number of consultants and companies have at least taken the leap to utilize nontraditional approaches for improving behavioral conditions within their firms. No longer can the behavioral scientist be condemned for sitting in his ivory tower conducting meaningless experiments on his students. Nor can the manager be criticized for forgetting about the human aspects of his organization while drumming away on production at all costs.

But there is also much to be concerned about when examining such an enthusiastic rush into organization development. Numerous methods used in these programs are relatively untested; their deficiencies have not been weeded out through long experience or research.

Moreover, disturbing symptoms of the failure of current brands of OD have been appearing frequently in research studies, in anecdotal comments by managers, and in the literature of organizations. Some skeptics contend that OD is a luxury afforded only by affluent organizations, but which is usually discarded when a major crisis arises. One study has shown that a major OD effort in a government agency failed to make any impact on the climate of the organization, although it did produce small increments in behavioral change.[1] In this case, one wonders how long the individual changes will last.

A thoughtful review of many studies of OD by Dunnette and Campbell has concluded:

> . . . none of the studies yields any evidence that the changes in job behavior have any favorable effect on actual performance effectiveness. Thus, there is little to support a claim that T-group or laboratory education effects any substantial behavior change back on the job for any large proportion of trainees. Whatever change does occur seems quite limited in scope and may not contribute in any important way to changes in overall job effectiveness.[2]

Of considerable concern, in the absence of more convincing research, has been the tendency for consultants and organizations to "freeze" prematurely on particular approaches, indicating that they have already found the one "best" approach. Vested interests no doubt help to explain this absence of self-critique; if I as a consultant design a program, I have a strong commitment and personal interest in its success. Therefore, while I may make small refinements in my methodology, I am not likely to alter its basic approach. Similarly, if I as a manager have committed funds and support to a particular program, I am not likely to treat it as an academic experiment where the chips fall as they may. Rather, I want it to succeed just as I do with any program implemented within my organization.

It is this unhealthy trend toward premature commitment that should be questioned, especially in terms of what has been working and not working. Such a reexamination seems essential if we are to benefit from our experience instead of slipping back into the pitfall of making the same mistakes again.

SIX RED FLAGS

I wish to raise red flags by questioning six trends that may be preventing the very changes that are being sought. For each warning signal, I will suggest an alternative way of thinking that might open up other directions for future OD programs.

---

[1] Larry Greiner, D. Paul Leitch, Louis B. Barnes, "The Simple Complexity of Organizational Climate in a Government Agency," in R. Tagiuri and George Litwin, eds., *Organizational Change: Explorations of a Concept* (Boston: Division of Research, Harvard Business School, 1968).

[2] Marvin D. Dunnette and John P. Campbell, "Laboratory Education: Impact on People and Organizations," in Gene Dalton and others, eds., *Organization Change and Development* (Homewood, Ill.: Richard D. Irwin, 1970).

Flag #1—Individual before the Organization

Many OD programs are characterized by a seemingly logical sequence of learning and behavior change, beginning typically with an exclusive focus on the individual employee and his style of behavior. Next, attention is given to the small group in which the employee works, assuming that if the individual is to change his behavior, there must be support in his immediate work surroundings. Third, once many individuals and small groups are changing, emphasis shifts to intergroup issues, such as resolving conflicts between R&D and production. Finally, after these basic subunits of the organization have been reeducated, consideration is given to issues affecting the entire organization, such as its corporate strategy.[3]

There are two principal reasons why I wish to question this gradually expanding sequence from individual to organization. First, the problems of a particular organization may not fit this exact sequence. It could well be that issues of over-all company strategy are dominant in the beginning and that, until these are more clearly resolved, there can be little clarity of direction for specific changes within basic subunits. A second concern with the "individual first" logic is that spontaneity of problem solving can easily be stifled. I have seen organizations in which certain managers have discovered a serious interdepartmental problem early in their OD program, only to be told by higher management to "cool it" and work on their own team first, since this was the prescribed stage of OD at that time.

To replace the individual-to-organization sequence, I would suggest a more situational and issue-centered approach. That is, if the management of the organization is not using OD to attack major problems affecting a majority of employees, then employees are likely to turn off quite rapidly on OD. For example, if problems center more around formal organization structure, it makes little sense for OD to begin with the behavioral styles of individual managers. Why not change the structure instead of beating around the bush?

Another important guideline is to work simultaneously on both the individual and his surroundings. We know from research on the dynamics of learning and psychotherapy that individuals do not make changes in their behavior entirely on their own initiative. They require strong support from all levels of their environment. Thus, employees in organizations need reinforcement from not only their immediate work groups, but also from the climate of their departments and the formal organization itself. For instance, if a centralized structure is being adjusted to be more decentralized, individual managers will usually have to be assisted in learning through reeducation new behavior skills for acting more autonomously.

---

[3] A clear statement of this sequence is described in Robert R. Blake and Jane S. Mouton, *The Managerial Grid* (Houston: Gulf Publishing Co., 1964).

Flag #2—Informal before Formal Organization

A strong assumption among many OD advocates is that informal organization takes precedence over formal organization. Therefore, they concentrate their educational efforts primarily on the teaching of new "values" or social norms which, if accepted by many colleagues, create social pressure for conformity to new behavior patterns.

Clearly, the informal culture of an organization is a strong determinant of how individuals behave; therefore, it must be addressed in organization change efforts. Yet any manager can tell you that the formal aspects of his organization are also quite important. An OD program may teach the value of participative behavior, but it will not make much headway if managers in this same organization are working under a very rigid and autocratic budget-setting method.

A major reason why formal organization is omitted from many OD efforts is that a taboo frequently exists among OD proponents which says that formal organization is bad or unimportant. This is largely a hangover from the old human relations days when humanistic behavioral scientists preferred to believe that formal organization was only something written on paper or that it was a tool of scientific management to produce mass conformity among employees.

Now we know a great deal more about formal organization, and it is not necessarily as bad as the humanists have contended. Several researchers have shown that formal organization can, indeed, significantly affect the behavior of employees, and that much of this behavior cannot be described as oppressive. For example, Lawrence and Lorsch have shown that formal project teams with considerable delegated formal responsibility can operate in a participative and creative manner. Or advocates of management by objectives have shown how informal participation can be incorporated into formal goal-setting methods.[4]

Therefore, we need to design OD efforts that incorporate a closer connection between formal and informal organization. During the educational phases of OD, managers need to be taught more about formal organization and how it can be used to complement and reinforce changes in their behavior. Many alternative forms of structure are available to managers, not just pyramids with limits on span of control; there are also product, project, and matrix forms of organization. Assumptions that there is one best type of formal organization are as parochial as the mentality that believes in one best type of organization development.

---

[4] Paul Lawrence and Jay Lorsch, *Organization and Environment* (Cambridge: Harvard Business School, 1967); Joan Woodward, *Management and Technology* (London: Her Majesty's Stationery Office, 1958); John Humble, *Management by Objectives in Action* (New York: McGraw-Hill Book Co., 1970).

Flag #3—Behavior before Diagnosis

Most OD programs stress a new behavioral model in reeducating managers. Whether the program be based on sensitivity training, the managerial grid, or management by objectives, the learning content of these programs is based on the assimilation of a new form of work behavior that will supposedly be more effective in decision making.

In other words, they are teaching managers to *act* differently—to be more "participative," "open," "confronting," or "authentic," depending upon the value orientation of the program.

What concerns me about this behavioral emphasis is that the thinking side of managers is frequently overlooked. Where their outward behavior is considered by OD, their conceptual thought process are neglected in terms of how they analyze problems or think about their organizations. This oversight can result in some interesting dilemmas once managers begin to behave differently.

One organization with which I am acquainted began an OD effort that stressed team problem solving and the open confrontation of troublesome issues. This was a big step forward for the organization, whose key managers had previously avoided discussions of important problems because of vested interests among them. However, once these managers took the step and placed the issues on the table, they were not particularly adept at making a thorough intellectual analysis of their problems, which were extremely complicated, interwoven with both emotional and technical aspects.

OD programs need to stress the cognitive along with the behavioral and emotional dimensions of more effective problem solving. For example, at the Harvard Business School, we work very hard in the classroom to teach two important aspects of managerial thinking. First, the student must learn to conceive of an organization as an open system and to think in terms of the important conceptual variables that are relevant to a systemic way of thinking about behavior in organizations.

Second, we see a need to practice over and over again a systematic diagnosis of numerous case situations so that these future managers can more quickly ferret out the problems of a situation and design unique solutions. Sharp and objective intellectual insights into management problems seldom come through brilliant lectures or interesting books on problem solving.

Flag #4—Process before Task

A large majority of OD programs place primary emphasis on improving the behavioral processes of decision making while deemphasizing or ignoring the content and task aspects of operating issues facing the organization. Thus, for example, it is assumed that if a manager can learn to participate more skillfully in team meetings, the content of team decisions will be dealt with more effectively.

While attention to behavioral processes is indeed a worthy focal point, there is a danger that managers will become preoccupied with, and even oversensitive to, their own behavior. As a consequence, meetings will be called to discuss the most trivial of issues in order to avoid affronting people; at the opposite extreme, personal issues will be put on the agenda for team discussion when they might better be discussed privately between two individuals.

This new norm of openness, as taught in many OD programs, is frequently abused in a carte blanche manner without thoughtful attention being paid to questions of whom to be open with, about what, and where and when. In order to make these decisions, one must also keep in mind the task aspects of the job. It makes little sense to call a meeting when knowledge for making a decision rests outside the group or when little content preparation has been done ahead of time to shed light on difficult problem issues.

It is no wonder that some managers are frequently turned off by OD programs that place exclusive stress on behavioral processes. These same managers are often dismissed by the consultants as being afraid or insensitive. Yet another plausible explanation is that these managers are understandably concerned about making progress toward solving difficult operating problems. They want to get on with the work, not just sit around contemplating their navels. Of course, this work-oriented preoccupation can be an obstacle too, since these same managers may ignore the importance of building behavioral commitment to decisions they wish to make.

My suggestion to the OD advocates is for them to strive for a better understanding of how task demands influence the behavioral process, not just the other way around. I have seen great OD progress made in one company when a group of conflicting functional managers were brought together for one day to discuss a single operating problem. Prior to this meeting, they had argued mainly over the telephone or behind the backs of other managers about the problem.

In this situation, the OD advocate with a process orientation might have focused the meeting on the question of "Why are you in conflict?" Yet the consultant involved here made no explicit reference to interpersonal conflicts. Instead, he focused the group's attention on analyzing the particular operating problem and reaching a consensus solution by the end of the day. And this is just what the group did, although it took a great deal of argument and soul searching.

What is fascinating about the outcome of this meeting is that a lot of individual stereotypes about other people were changed, as each manager's preconceived opinions began to break down under a more constructive arrangement for problem solving. In other words, behavioral processes were facilitated by a productive task discussion, even when behavioral problems were not the explicit agenda.

Flag #5—Experts before the Manager

Since the technology of OD is often elaborate, wordy, and known only to outside consultants (or staff personnel responsible for OD), these professionals are tempted to presume more than they know and to "talk down" to practicing managers. It is a reflection of the old dichotomy of we (the consultants or staff) are the experts and you (the Managers) are the doers. Therefore, the "knowledge guys," are here to tell you, the "practitioners," how to improve your organization.

There are understandable reasons for this point of view. The experts will often argue convincingly that OD is such powerful stuff that, if directed by untrained people, it can result in very naïve applications that can hurt rather than help an organization. And managers will often subscribe to this argument too, preferring to believe that the experts know more about their concepts and methods than they do; therefore, we, the managers, who know more about action taking, will confine ourselves to carrying out their recommendations.

Several pitfalls are hidden in this rather arbitrary role division. First, there is the possibility that managers will become overdependent on the experts. As a result, dependent managers do not question or argue with the professionals; they just keep looking to them for direction. Second, the experts seldom know the particular organization as well as the managers themselves. Therefore, the outsiders often end up recommending general methods and techniques that have been useful in prior situations, but which may or may not be relevant to the problems at hand. Third, the experts are removed from responsibility for daily operating decisions, thereby making it difficult for them to respond continuously to the important issues that come up daily while OD is in progress. Finally, and perhaps most serious, the experts usually feel more responsibility for and have more commitment to what they are doing than the managers. The OD program, in essence, becomes the experts' program rather than the organization's.

One way out of this dilemma is to share and develop more expertise and commitment between experts and managers. Organizations which have recognized this need have sought to train not only their own internal staff people but also their line managers for assuming a more active role in the conduct of organization development.

Early in the planning of OD, there is a special need to involve key managers in the diagnosis and planning of the direction and methods for implementing the program. Here the managers must exercise sufficient independence to tell the experts that they are "all wet" when foreign ideas seem irrelevant. To do this requires more knowledge than managers typically have about organization development; hence, their own background should contain an exposure to various methods for introducing OD. This does not mean that they should become OD experts, but that they should have sufficient exposure to see through the jargon that so often pervades the OD field.

In addition, managers should be prepared to make known what they are most familiar with—the specific characteristics of the operation they manage and what they perceive to be the main developmental needs. Here is where the experts would be advised to sit still and listen carefully.

Flag #6—The Package before the Situation

Underlying much of what has been said so far is the deductive fallacy of imposing a program of organization development that has been designed by outsiders who do not know the organization. As a result, there is an insensitive application of a nicely packaged program, based on general theories or misleading past experiences. The organization is asked to fit itself to the package, not vice versa.

This deductive approach is not unknown in the consulting world. Consulting firms, like any other business organization, develop a product to sell. Moreover, they find that the more specific and tangible their product, the more the customer will be attracted to it. Only a few large management consulting firms, such as McKinsey and Booz, Allen & Hamilton, have been able to develop multiple services that can be applied flexibly, though even here each of these firms is frequently identified as being keen on certain solutions which they have grown accustomed to over the years.

I would suggest a more tailor-made approach to the design of OD programs. Here the program is fitted to the situation. This does not mean that a completely new package has to be designed for each customer. Rather, the OD expert must have a large number of tools in his kit so that he can apply a wrench, not a hammer, when only bolts need tightening. Another guideline, as urged earlier, is to encourage managers from within the organization to provide more data and suggestions on what needs to be done. They may have a much more intimate knowledge of company problems than do the outsiders. Their handicap is that they are seldom mobilized to put their heads together, due largely to barriers in communication processes within the organization.

A nice combination of an outsider-insider approach is reflected in the work of Beckhard.[5] He provides a learning structure for managers to get together but does not define their problems and solutions for them.

---

[5] Richard Beckhard, "The Confrontation Meeting," *Harvard Business Review* (May–June 1967).

Rather the managers, by being asked to meet in small groups to confront and identify major issues facing the organization, are the ones who give substance to their organization development efforts. In such cases, Beckhard uses his position as an outside expert to convene the meeting and arrange a focus for productive discussion, but he does not presume to have the answers.

FUTURE ACTIONS

New directions in organization development depend upon a critical assessment of where we are today. I have pointed to six questionable trends that give rise for concern. These include tendencies for OD to begin with the individual before the organization, stress informal values over formal organization, prescribe behavioral actions without diagnostic skills, focus more on behavioral relationships than task accomplishment, adhere to standardized programs over situational needs, and place the expert ahead of the manager. Failure to take account of these other realities of organization life has, I believe, seriously limited the promised impact of organization development. So where do we go from here?

It would be a serious mistake to swing over completely to the other end of the themes; this would only raise six more flags. In doing so, we would prevent the use of the very real expertise that currently resides with experts in the field of organizational development. Instead, I have suggested alternative actions that attempt to build on the strengths from both extremes, since each points to a piece of reality that should be considered in organization development.

First, begin OD with specific and major problem issues founded in the developmental needs facing the organization and many of its employees. These needs may lie in the individual domain with the styles of managers or they may lie in the strategy of the firm. Whichever the case, we know that at some point in any organization change the units of individual, group, intergroup, and organization will have to be addressed, but we should not prescribe the exact sequence ahead of time.

Second, be ready to achieve a more complementary relationship between formal and informal organization during organization development. New informal values will not be accepted for long unless they are reinforced by parallel changes in formal prescriptions. Nor will changes in formal structure be sufficient unless the informal culture is adjusted to accept and encourage the directions implied by new formal designs.

Third, stress a closer integration of diagnostic and action-oriented role models so that we "look while we leap," and we keep on looking as we continue to act. If an educational program is called for, then do not simply stress a single action model, one that, for example, relies exclusively on team problem solving. Instead, sharpen a manager's intellectual insights so that he may choose his actions more appropriately and flexibly.

Yet his action skills should not be neglected, since bright insights are not always equivalent to skillful behavior. Let him know, for instance, that participative behavior can produce certain beneficial results, but also inform him that, under certain conditions, participation can be inappropriate.

Fourth, place more emphasis on the task concerns of managers while educating them in behavioral processes. We cannot ignore the reality of work and the continuing pressure upon managers to deal with the immediate task issues facing them. They may show greater appreciation for the behavioral dynamics in decision making if they can more directly experience task accomplishment at the same time.

Fifth, achieve a more collaborative planning and problem-solving relationship between experts and managers in designing OD programs. Avoid the arbitrary role division of expert as planner and manager as doer. Managers have much to contribute in diagnosing their own ills while experts can provide new tools and fresh perspectives for enlivening managerial insight—without going so far as to recommend one "best" solution.

Sixth, improve the integration of packaged OD materials with the unique demands of each organizational situation. OD tools are just that —handy to have available but applied only when needed. A greater variety of tools must be developed so that they can deal with all points on the continua described in the six flag dimensions. These tools must not be overdesigned, however, since their more important function may be to spade up the data in each situation, not mold the organization or its members in a predetermined fashion.

A little more emphasis on development for OD could head us in a more promising direction.

Part VI

APPLICATION OF
STRUCTURAL, PROCESS,
AND BEHAVIORAL CONCEPTS

INTRODUCTION

The readings in this section of the book differ somewhat from those included earlier in the book in that they are intended to serve as a means to integrate the previous sections of the book. Thus, instead of examining one specific aspect of structure, behavior, and processes in organizations, these readings are actually case study reports which illustrate the various behavioral concepts in actual organizational settings.

The Need for Synthesis

Thus far, the readings in this volume have examined the interdisciplinary field that is concerned with human behavior in organizations. Specifically, the readings have examined behavioral science concepts as they evolve from theory to research. This section attempts to provide on-the-job applications in managing human resources. With the backdrop of the previous selections included in the book, this section provides detailed descriptions of behavioral science applications in three firms of varying sizes and industries. The purpose of this section is to force the reader to attempt to synthesize, in a way that is meaningful to him, the various behavioral concepts and models discussed in the book. The competent manager of tomorrow will be forced to visualize how these various behavioral concepts can be applied in his own organization in order to improve its ef-

427

fectiveness. This is because there is evidence that behavioral science technology is being integrated into the management practices of a growing number of firms and that expertise in human behavior lies within the multidisciplinary field of behavioral science. The selections included in this section of the book support this contention.

The first case report "American Airlines" is concerned with the need for change in organizations, specifically, building flexibility and innovativeness into a tradition-bound organization. When the new president assumed his position in 1968, he recognized the need of a private airline to keep ahead of competition and to incorporate technological advances. He realized that something had to be done to build into the organization the qualities of flexibility and innovativeness. In other words, one of his first objectives was to develop an organization that was responsive to future needs. He felt that the behavioral sciences offered the most promising route. This report summarizes the experience at American Airlines.

The second case report, "The Systems Group of TRW, Inc." examines an organic approach to fostering and managing change within an organization. The principal products of this organization center around advanced technology (satellites, etc.) which requires an atmosphere within the organization to encourage free and imaginative thinking without many of the constraints of traditional organizations. This organization has been a pioneer in the use of behavioral science concepts in designing and maintaining its organization. In many ways TRW Systems is a special company using new organizational approaches to cope with its rapidly evolving and changing environment. The case report included here examines some of these approaches.

The final case report "Genesco, Incorporated," is concerned with the problem of rapid growth, increased size, and its implications for organizational health. Over the past few years, Genesco has evolved from primarily a shoe manufacturer (General Shoe Company) to a diversified organization comprised of 40 operating companies. Like many diversified companies, Genesco has multiplied rapidly by acquiring existing companies, many of which have had long years of closely held ownership. As a result, Genesco has inherited almost every possible style of management. This case report examines the many problems Genesco has had in integrating the many acquired firms into an overall corporate framework.

28

American Airlines

NATIONAL INDUSTRIAL CONFERENCE BOARD

Industries with new and glamorous products and services are not immune to the danger of becoming tradition-bound, the president of American Airlines believes. This danger served as the stimulus for his concern over organizational renewal.

The need of a private airline to keep ahead of formidable competition and to incorporate technological advances at a galloping rate indicated to him that something had to be done to build into the organization the qualities of flexibility and innovativeness. His approach to organizational renewal began with an analysis of what kind of organization American Airlines should be, in light of the new challenges facing the company. When he assumed the presidency at the beginning of 1968, he became the company's fifth president but its third chief executive officer since the firm was founded in 1934. He reports that he found American Airlines a rather tightly structured organization which was exceedingly effective during the early growth period of the company and up to the present time, but which seemed less well suited to the increasingly complex demands of the future in which innovation, change, and long-range planning become of paramount concern.

So one of his first objectives was to develop an organization that was

Source: Reprinted by permission from *Behavioral Science: Concepts and Management Application* (New York: The Conference Board, Inc., 1969), pp. 72–86.

responsive to these future needs. He remarks, "There is no doubt that we have good people—experienced, mature, intelligent, and well trained—but we've got to learn to combine their talents in a manner that will enable us to plan effectively, to secure maximum cooperation between varying disciplines in an inherently complex business, and to experiment and adapt to the challenges that lie ahead."

ACTION NEEDED

He translates these objectives into several action variables:

1. The creation of an atmosphere that will provide every employee with a satisfying experience at work. This means among other things

(a) A democratic organization

(b) A free exchange of ideas—up, down and sideways—and the fostering of constructive dissent

(c) Group participation in decision making

(d) A continuing developmental process on the job; not simply in specialized skills, but most importantly in broadening the outlook and interests of people

(e) Early identification of talent and maximum opportunity for growth

(f) Whenever appropriate, a revision of job content to make the work more satisfying.

2. The establishment of an ideal employer-employee relationship that would, in addition to meeting the employee's material needs, permit the employee to take pride:

(a) In the industry in which he is engaged (Do his friends regard the industry as important and exciting?)

(b) In the company for which he works

(c) In his fellow workers (He wants to be associated with other competent people.)

(d) In the job he holds (He wants a job that has prestige and that demands his full capabilities.)

(e) In the way he performs that job (He wants to do well and he wants his performance to be recognized.)

These points could be condensed to: the enhancement of human dignity, interpersonal relationships, and job enrichment—all within the province of the behavioral sciences as they address themselves to business organizations. Does it follow then, that American Airlines has forsaken its traditional concept of management and replaced it with a wide-scale application of behaviorally oriented management? The answer is no, at least at this point. The president cautions, "Business is still in the stone age when it comes to applying the behavioral sciences. All we have are some beliefs that certain ways of dealing with people are better than others and some rather primitive experiments that seem to confirm these hypotheses."

Nevertheless, he feels that the behavioral sciences offer "the most promising route of the many possibilities available to us for organizational renewal and long-range competitive vigor." He states that he, personally, is willing to experiment with newer management approaches and that he hopes to involve his organization.

EXPERIMENTAL APPROACH

However, he underscores the experimental nature by stressing, "If we try new approaches based on the leads suggested by behavioral scientists, we must do so with conscious recognition that we cannot be sure how they will work out. We must be prepared to accept failures or what may superficially appear to be failures, then change and try again."

His comments might imply that American Airlines is only now beginning to show some interest in behavioral science applications. In fact, behavioral science activity at American Airlines is greater than in the majority of firms. The company has, however, viewed it as a "seeding" operation that only now is beginning to bear fruit in terms of organization–wide impact.

The corporate director of training and development analyzed the situation: "We've been trying to implement behavioral science concepts for quite some time, and we've worked hard at it. But two essential ingredients have been missing: First, we have needed greater commitment at the top of the organization. The second is dependent upon the first, namely, we have not cut across functions and activities enough to develop the entire organization. Instead, our work has been segmented. Therefore, what we have called organization development was little more than managerial development."

American Airlines' organization development program got its stimulus in 1965 when the training and development director and an operating executive attended an outside Managerial Grid Seminar. Later, others in the firm began attending Grid sessions, but in limited numbers. "Until mid-1967 the company's approach to development was, 'send people away to a training course,' but we were unhappy with the minimal return from such training," says the director of training and development. "These outside courses produced no observable change in behavior because people returned from them to the same old environment."

The company made an attempt to relate training to its particular situation by the gradual introduction of group process exercises into its internal managerial development seminars. Eventually the company put together a special management seminar that uses group process to the extent that it has become a type of laboratory training. The seminar is a synthesis of several theoretical schools and uses a variety of techniques. It is called the Managerial Learning Laboratory.

MANAGERIAL LEARNING LABORATORY

The Managerial Learning Laboratory (MLL) is a week-long seminar for middle managers. The labs are conducted by the company's director of training and development and its seven in-house organization development specialists. Usually, two of the specialists work together as trainers. Participants are drawn from a wide range of company facilities and a variety of functional areas, including aircraft maintenance, engineering, finance, sales, personnel, flight and terminal operations, and stewardess services.

From fifteen to twenty managers participate in any given laboratory. They are usually of equivalent rank in the organization, but usually they do not know each other prior to the lab; therefore the format is a "cousins" lab. The company would prefer to bring natural work groups to these labs, but because of the necessity of a 24-hour operation in the airline business, it would not be feasible to take an entire "work family" away from the job for a full week.

Like most laboratory training, the experience is designed to create within the participant an increased sensitivity to his own behavior and to the behavior of others. American Airlines' Managerial Learning Laboratory is designed to "unfreeze" old attitudes and behavior patterns, encourage experimentation with new ones, and "refreeze" new attitudes and behavioral patterns in order to increase interpersonal competence and managerial effectiveness back on the job.

Assumptions

The MLL seminars are based on a set of assumptions or values:

A spirit of inquiry—A feeling of tentativeness and caution, combined with an attitude of experimentation, an openness to new ideas, and a willingness to test them. Feedback is important for learning from everyday experience, although "being a slave to the opinions of others" is not a necessary concomitant to learning from feedback.

A spirit of collaboration—More effective results are obtained through collaborative effort than through individual or independent effort or through authority-obedience modes of managing.

Open resolution of conflict—Interpersonal and organizational conflict is natural and to be expected when people work together. Conflict should be approached honestly and objectively by the parties involved, to seek its resolution, rather then deny or suppress it or allow it to result either in "power plays" or compromise.

The value of awareness—Traditions, inhibitions, and preconceptions all limit human potential and innovativeness. Increased awareness of untried possibilities in each "here-and-now" situation, and of the several choices of a way of acting in each situation, are conducive to experimentation and growth.

The value of candor—Candor begins with an awareness of one's own thoughts, feelings, and motives. The logical progression from this awareness is to develop the courage, conviction, and skill to communicate them, when appropriate, to others.

General Objectives

These values or assumptions about what the laboratory experience ought to accomplish translate into three levels of general objectives:

1. Self-awareness.
2. Group development.
3. Intergroup development.

Carrying the value-centered objectives a step further, the company has developed a model of behavioral patterns for its managers on each of these three levels, in which actual behavior is juxtaposed with optimal or ideal behavior (see Exhibit 5). The MLL experience is designed to aid participants in moving from existing behavior toward the ideals expressed in this model. The content of the MLL includes theory sessions about individual and group behavior, instrumental or systematized feedback, and sensitivity training techniques.

In keeping with one of the cardinal rules of laboratory training, MLL's are conducted on a "cultural island"—a place removed from participant's work and normal environment, where the laboratory behavior becomes the focus of their attention and energies. Prior to attendance, each participant is given a copy of the model of managerial behavior. Once at the seminar, a trainer restates the experimental nature of the learning experience.

Since most of the participants are strangers to each other, the seminar begins with introductions. Sometimes each participant in turn gives his name, his home location, and his work responsibility. Sometimes the trainer will tell them, "You have ten minutes to get to know each other through any means you like, with one exception: you may not speak."

Non-Verbal Encounter

Whenever their first encounter is to be non-verbal, the participants immediately begin to experiment with new modes of behavior. Some managers merely make the rounds of the group and look at their fellow

EXHIBIT 5

Managerial Learning Laboratory

(Course objectives expressed as directional movement at three levels of learning)

Learning Levels

Self-Awareness Level		Group Development Level		Intergroup Action Level	
From	Toward	From	Toward	From	Toward
Being Closed → Being Open		Surface Discussions → Depth Discussions		Competition with Other Groups → Collaboration with Other Groups	
Denying Feelings → Expressing Feelings		Intra-Group Competitiveness → Intra-Group Collaboration		Win/Lose Conflict Resolution → Win/Win Conflict Resolution	
Being Defensive → Accepting Feedback		Guarding Information → Sharing Information		Destructive Inter-Group Relationships → Helping Inter-Group Relationships	
Conventional Approach → Experimental Approach		Denying Feelings → Expressing Feelings		One-Sided Problem-Solving → Shared Problem-Solving	
Suspicion of Others → Trust of Others		Undercutting Other Members → Supporting Other Members		Rejecting Others' Points of View → Accepting Others' Points of View	
Being Guarded → Being Spontaneous		Being Unaware of Group Process → Being Aware of Group Process		Viewing Other Groups as enemies → Viewing Other Groups as Colleagues	
Avoiding Conflict → Facing Conflict		Using Few Group Resources → Using All Group Resources		Suspicion of Other Groups → Trust of Other Groups	
Being Rigid → Being Flexible		Win/Lose Conflict Resolution → Win/Win Conflict Resolution		Commitment Limited to Group Goals → Commitment to Total Organization Goals	
Having a Facade → Being Sincere		Resistance or Apathy to Group Goals → Commitment to Group Goals			
Shallowness of Perception → Depth of Perception		Self-Enhancing Behavior → Contribution to Group Action			
Distorted Self-Awareness → Accurate Self-Awareness					

Managerial Behaviors

participants; others take out family pictures from their wallets; some merely shake hands silently; some offer a challenge like "Indian arm wrestle"; and others use tactile means. According to one trainer, "Simply by observing what mode of communication each chooses, you can tell a lot about the person's willingness to communicate, his ability to do so, and the degree to which he is experimental."

Since there are fifteen or more persons in attendance at any MLL, participants are divided into three teams. The trainers do not assign persons to teams; rather, grouping is based on self-selection. Typically, someone suggests a random drawing or alphabetical divisions. Another method of team selection is for one man to say to another, "I want to be on a team with you." Sometimes a manager may take the initiative and select four or five others to be on "his" team. Whatever the method or criteria used by participants, they eventually form their three teams, thereby solving their first problem as a group.

Once teams are formed, the next step is for the participants to deal with two fundamental questions:

Why did I come to this course?
What are my personal goals for the week?

"Fishbowl"

This exercise, which is considered a key one, is performed in "fishbowl" fashion: one team sits in the middle of the room while each of its members answers these two questions and the team discusses each response. During this discussion, the other teams observe and listen. The fishbowl exercise is repeated with the second and third teams. Following each team's discussion, the other teams give them process feedback on what they have perceived on both an individual and a group level. Each participant also records his observations and reactions, as the first entry in a "diary" that he will keep throughout the laboratory.

TEAM GROUND RULES

Typically, the next sequence in an MLL is for each team to meet to develop its own "policy statements" or ground rules. These ground rules cover eight areas of personal, group, and intergroup relationships that are implied in the behavioral and learning model for the MLL (see Exhibit 5). They are:

(1.) Discussions.	(5.) Process.
(2.) Collaboration.	(6.) Resources.
(3.) Information.	(7.) Conflict.
(4.) Feelings.	(8.) Commitment.

In arriving at its "policies" or ground rules, each team works independently as a leaderless group, and formulation of its responses to the eight areas is based on consensus. The policy statements of one team may vary considerably from those of another team. For example, one team may decide that their ground rule for expressing feelings is "no suppression," while another team may decide "free expression, but controlled." Or under use of resources one team may set as its goal "motivation of individuals in the group"; while another team may decide "to determine what resources are available in the group."

Since the objectives of the laboratory include learning about what encourages or impedes group and team interaction, the teams have complete freedom in defining and supervising their roles and activities. The company trainer neither interferes with nor guides the teams.

Once policy statements are developed, each team presents its ground rules and evaluates how they measure up against the model of effectiveness by answering a question about each of the eight key areas (see Exhibit 6). The team's answers are posted. Then the three teams compete in a simulation exercise—an unstructured but highly competitive business game. Afterwards each team criticizes its performance in the simulation exercise and compares its actual functioning as a team with its policy statements. The fishbowl technique is used again, as each team receives process feedback from the other two teams.

It is hoped that by this comparison of actual behavior with behavioral objectives, the members of a team will become aware of where they succeeded and where they didn't. More importantly, it is hoped that in their identification of successes and failures, the team will analyze the "how and why" of both. This analysis includes feedback on each team member's contribution, on the team as a whole, and on its effectiveness as compared with the other teams. If team "A" sees that team "B" lived up more closely to the objectives it had set than their own team did, appropriate questions for discussion might be, "What factors were at play that made team "B" work together better? What is lacking in our team? How can we interact more effectively? What's holding us back?"

Competition and Collaboration

The simulation exercise, which acts as a stimulus for each team's analysis of its interaction, is designed to encourage and develop team building. The three teams compete in the exercise and one team performs better than the other two. Competing as a team against two groups of "outsiders" will, it is hoped, strengthen intragroup cohesiveness.

The next steps in the MLL exercises are designed to foster intergroup strengths. One widely used exercise in the MLL centers on the Managerial Grid philosophy and its implications for intergroup relations.

EXHIBIT 6

Managerial Learning Laboratory
(introductory team planning session)

Your first tasks as a team are to get to know each other and to exchange views on issues vital to team effectiveness.

In the period of time available, discuss each of the questions below and agree upon a short "policy statement" giving your team's consensus on how your team will function in each of these areas.

Write your short statements on large chart paper and post them in your team area. (If space permits, you may write more than one statement on each sheet of paper.)

1. SURFACE DISCUSSIONS
   DEPTH DISCUSSIONS

How will your team assure that you get beneath surface issues in your discussions?

2. INTRA-GROUP
   COMPETITION
   INTRA-GROUP
   COLLABORATION

How can your team promote a climate in which the members support rather than undercut each other?

3. GUARDING INFORMATION
   SHARING INFORMATION

How will your team see to it that all needed information is made available to the team by the members?

4. HOLDING BACK FEELINGS
   EXPRESSING FEELINGS

To what extent should team members be free to express feelings and emotions while working on a task?

5. UNAWARE OF PROCESS
   AWARE OF PROCESS

How will you assure that your team becomes aware of hangups in the way its members are working together and that it deals with such hangups as needed?

6. USING FEW TEAM
   RESOURCES
   USING ALL TEAM
   RESOURCES

How will your team assure that maximum use is made of the individual and combined resources of all members?

7. WIN/LOSE CONFLICT
   RESOLUTION
   WIN/WIN CONFLICT
   RESOLUTION

To what extent will your team members confront emotional as well as intellectual conflicts? On what bases will conflicts be dealt with?

8. RESISTANCE OR APATHY
   TO TEAM GOALS
   FULL COMMITMENT TO
   TEAM GOALS

How will you assure that members make their maximum contribution to the goals of the team?

The trainer brings all three teams together, shows them a filmstrip on the Grid, then gives everyone a brochure describing typical behaviors as they are plotted on the Grid in fifteen areas of managerial action, including goal setting, boss-subordinate relationships, and managing conflict. Following this plenary session, the participants return to their teams for an hour and a half with the assignment: "Discuss how Grid theory relates to American Airlines management."

Afterwards the teams reassemble to present a visual display of the results of their discussions. It is not uncommon for the reports to reveal that each of the teams had interpreted the assignment differently. A trainer reported that in one session teams "B" and "C" used charts to plot the results of their discussions. Team "B" plotted the perception of each of its members of American Airlines' Grid styles in each area of managerial responsibility. Team "C" 's chart gave the consensus of its members. Team "A" interpreted the assignment as an evaluation of the company's management and a judgment of the Grid styles.

In the plenary session following the presentation of each team's report, typically each team tries to justify its report as the *best* approach to the assignment. Frequently heated arguments break out, but the trainer does not try to intervene. After about 45 minutes, however, he may try to get the participants to analyze what has been going on by asking them to evaluate the "open warfare" that has characterized the competitiveness. He may remind them that they have been so intent upon defending their own team's approach that they have ignored the possibility that all three approaches might be useful in identifying and solving the problem.

In one session the trainer merely went to the blackboard and without comment wrote:

Assumptions

This was a competitive exercise.

There is one best way of relating Grid to American Airlines.

We must *win;* the others must *lose.*
Our interpretation of the ground rules for the exercise is "correct."
To accede to any value in another team's approach is "weakness."

For a while the participants either ignored the trainer's assumptions or failed to grasp their implications, and they continued to argue. Then they grew quiet for a time before attacking the trainer with such remarks as, "You set the tone for the exercise as a competition and now you pull this," and "Do you mean you're trying to tell us it's not competitive when you send three teams to work on a problem and to come back and report the solution?"

As their anger subsided, some of the participants began suggesting alternate assumptions about the teams' activities. Specifically, discussion took the direction of considering the exercise an opportunity for collaborative action in which several valid ways of dealing with the problem could be combined to produce a better solution.

"Win-Lose" Prevailed

The trainer pointed out that the teams had been effective in integrating individuals into teams, had been effective as a team in competition with other teams because of their cohesiveness, but had fallen into a "win-lose" attitude in this last exercise. He drew a diagram to illustrate three levels of development (see Exhibit 7). The teams had demonstrated their success-

EXHIBIT 7

Individual, Team, and Intergroup Levels of Development

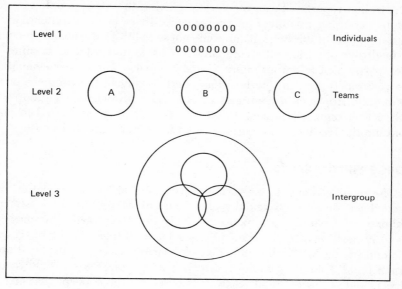

ful development through level 2, but because they had not clarified their objectives for the most recent exercise they had failed to achieve level 3 or intergroup development. He commented, "There seem to be two kinds of competition—one that prevents intergroup productivity and another that enhances it."

Projects and assignments throughout the seminar are designed to illustrate the importance of development on all three levels—individual, team, and intergroup. Each has several built-in features to demonstrate development levels—or lack of development. Following each project, participants increasingly do process evaluation and self-criticism in feedback sessions.

Typically, as participants interact on a team and intergroup basis and as free-flowing feedback becomes the method of learning, many interpersonal factors are brought to the surface. Participants learn to experiment with new modes of behavior on an individual and interpersonal level. American Airlines' director of training and development comments: "It would be desirable to have a pure sensitivity training session before beginning team projects but the MLL lasts only one week. We've found, however, that interpersonal learning does take place and people become sensitized pretty rapidly through group projects. The MLL is, in fact, laboratory training both in content and format."

Interpersonal Feedback

A trainer reports: "From the very beginning the MLL people give and get an increasing amount of interpersonal feedback in team and total group sessions. Some of it is helpful and some not so helpful." Even with the built-in feedback provisions the company sets aside at least one evening for each participant to gather interpersonal feedback. These peer evaluations are performed on a face-to-face basis and usually in the presence of the team only. However, a team may elect to have a miniature T-group with one of the company trainers. In either case, members are asked to make notes on the feedback to be used as a basis for personal goal setting.

FORCE FIELD ANALYSIS

The relevance of training to the participants' ability to be better managers back on the job remains the focus of the Managerial Learning Laboratory. To aid participants in analyzing their own situations and levels of performance, the company uses a special theoretical tool. Toward the end of the MLL, the trainer gives a brief theoretical explanation of Force Field Analysis technique, which is a part of Lewin's "field theory" of personality. Force Field Analysis is based on the concept that any behavior (or level of performance) is the equilibrium between "driving forces," or those factors in the field or contemporary environment which support productive actions, and "restraining forces," or factors that inhibit productive action. Behavior in the direction of productive action (as defined by the individual for himself and based on his perception and motivation) can be raised by one or a combination of the following strategies: (1) Remove or lessen one or more of the restraining forces (2) Add or strengthen one or more of the driving forces.

Field theory posits a given amount of dynamic psychic energy within each field or contemporary environment. The form or direction it takes (driving or restraining) can be modified by the individual through one of the above strategies. Modification in the direction he seeks represents a heightened level of performance (see Exhibit 8).

Using Force Field Analysis, the participants work as teams to answer five questions about the MLL experience in relation to their daily jobs:

1. Which of the things that we learned this week will be valuable to us in our jobs?
2. What restraining forces exist in ourselves and in our jobs that will make application difficult?
3. Which of these restraining forces is under our control to remove or lessen?
4. What driving forces can we add to or strengthen through our own efforts?

EXHIBIT 8

Force Field Analysis

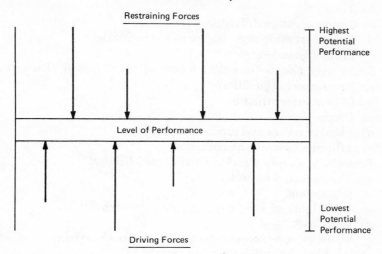

5. What definite actions can each person take when he returns to the job? (Each member makes his own personal list.)

Of course, the responses of one group of managers at an MLL vary from the responses of another, but trainers report that certain answers are typical or representative. The answers to the first question represent the values held by participants at the end of the course:

1. *Learning Valuable for Job Application*
   a) Being aware of group process
   b) Ability to deal with interpersonal and intergroup actions
   c) Realizing importance of other individuals
   d) Value of good, open communication
   e) Value of feedback
   f) Effect of organization's structure on accomplishment of tasks
   g) Understanding motivation and motivational factors
   h) How to work better with people
   i) Resolving conflicts
   j) Self-awareness (as you see yourself, as others see you, as you really are).

Answers to the second, third, and fourth questions represent the participants' awareness of the similarities and differences of the values expressed in answers to Question 1 and those of the workaday world they return to following the MLL:

   2. *Restraining Forces Over Which Major Control Can Be Exercised*
  - a) Old habits
  - b) Time
  - c) Communication difficulties
  - d) Individual inhibitions and personal constraints
  - e) Lack of knowledge

   3. *Restraining Forces Over Which Some Control Can Be Exercised*
  - a) Environment (facilities)
  - b) Organization structure
  - c) Union
  - d) Local practices and procedures
  - e) Attitudes (our own and others)

   4. *Restraining Forces Outside Participants' Control*
  - a) The boss (and his boss)
  - b) Job content
  - c) Availability of others (geographic constraints)
  - d) Workload
  - e) Statistics and information about past performance
  - f) Working difficulties of other people

   5. *Driving Forces That Can Be Added or Strengthened*
  - a) Better relationships with the boss
  - b) Attitudes toward the job
  - c) Setting personal goals
  - d) Measurement of performance and follow through
  - e) Caliber of employees
  - f) Better use of resources
  - g) Better planning and approach to tasks
  - h) Better communication
  - i) Psychological sensitivity or conditioning

The company views this "debriefing," or final, section of the MLL as the most important part of the training. Without it the course may not be seen in perspective as a means of making better managers, a trainer reports. The debriefing is one means of bridging the crucial gap between learning and application.

The answers are clearly subjective and couched in general, sometimes vague terms, but participants are encouraged to use them as a conceptual framework for continuing development as they return to the "real world." The answers to the fifth question are given independently by each participant and they represent a list of *specific* actions he intends to take once he returns to his job.

The company administers an attitude survey to participants at the end of the MLL, as a means of getting systematic feedback on their perception of the learning experience and its relative value to them as managers. Taking the participants' evaluations into account, the corporate training and development staff makes modifications in the course content and methodology to reflect the needs of managers more closely. The seminar normally receives a "seven" rating on a nine-point scale—"nine" equals totally favorable.

POST-COURSE FOLLOW-UP

Six months after the MLL, graduates and their bosses are surveyed to ascertain if they were able to carry over the learning into on-the-job application. The "alumni" almost unanimously report improved work habits and interpersonal relationships; supervisors substantively confirm the response of the participants. But some of the bosses' comments are negative or lukewarm: "I've not observed any particular change in this man's job performance; he has always done an outstanding job"; or, "He has some problems, but he's been making steady progress in overcoming them. Undoubtedly, the course was helpful to him, but I can't point out specific areas of improvement that seem to be related directly to the course."

More typical of supervisor's comments are: "I feel this man has shown improvement particularly in communicating and handling conflict. Much of this I attribute to the MLL"; and, "He has been doing a more thorough job in recent months. He is looking for problems and coming up with solutions and alternatives as a result of his going to the MLL."

So far, about 500 middle managers have gone through a Managerial Learning Laboratory since the first were developed and offered in 1967. Attendance is voluntary, though a manager who has been to an MLL may feel the experience is worthwhile and ask his subordinates to attend. The MLL is one of several management development courses available to middle managers and conducted by the corporate training and development staff. Each year managers receive a prospectus of training courses and make their selections and record them on a data processing card.

Special Labs for Work Teams

As stated earlier, the MLL is looked upon by the company primarily as an initial "unfreezing" exercise. The next developmental step, which American Airlines feels is the logical follow-up to the MLL, is team building with natural work groups. Ideally, the participants in a team building have all had the experience of the MLL and share a common predisposition toward laboratory training. The team-building session, since it involves both boss and subordinate personnel, is a kind of "family lab," though American Airlines builds task-oriented materials into its team-building labs.[1]

Team-building labs are usually conducted by the company's organiza-

---

[1] The task orientation differentiates team building from the pure "family lab," which is concerned almost exclusively with interpersonal competence among natural work groups or "families."

tion development specialists at the request of the operating manager. Most of the requests for team-building labs come from graduates of the Managerial Learning Laboratory. However, the corporate director of training and development concedes that he and his staff try hard to sell the idea of team building to other managers, too. Sometimes they are successful; more managers are using team-building labs; fifteen different work groups have requested them for 1969. Occasionally, the OD specialists report, the concept of team building has caught on within an organizational unit to the extent that the labs represent real organization development, as contrasted with manager development, in that a large number of interfacing groups have undertaken team building as an integral part of their managing.

Early "Seeding"

As early as 1964 the then vice president for line maintenance asked the corporate personnel staff to assist him in upgrading the effectiveness of his managers at the company's large maintenance base in Tulsa, Oklahoma. As a result he attended a Managerial Grid seminar, and later three of his subordinate managers went to Grid seminars to evaluate Grid's appropriateness for the company.

Today that executive is senior vice president for operations at corporate headquarters. As such he is the head of an organizational component that comprises nearly half of American Airlines' work force. Twenty-seven of his top managers have attended Grid labs, and more than 100 of his middle managers have attended the company's MLL seminar.

One large team-building effort is being undertaken at the Tulsa Maintenance Base. The format and direction that it will eventually take are still being decided; the operating managers select the material for team-building sessions. The corporate OD specialists assist in carrying out the *process* of team building, but they are not involved in deciding what the *content* of the meetings entail. In addition to the corporate resources, the Tulsa Maintenance Base has its own organization development staff as internal resources.

Participants in these team-building sessions are drawn from various parts of the division. Managers from the two top levels of management are represented by a "horizontal slice" of the organization that crosses several functional areas and equivalent responsibilities. A "vertical slice" of the organization—representing the same functional areas but with several levels of responsibilities—is used to make up other lab groups.

Behavior and Managerial Style

A large part of these team-building sessions is focused on managerial behavior as it translates into managerial style. The basic concept is like that of the Grid, although these sessions do not use pure Grid terminology. The senior vice president for operations explains: "The Grid tends to stereotype people, and often people spend too much time trying to identify with a spot on the Grid and not enough energy is spent on the change that's needed. It's important to know what operating style you're using and to understand its impact on the problem at hand, but if any development experience is to be relevant to the group it must be spontaneous and related to problems they can see and solutions they can believe in. It's too easy to get bogged down with Grid exercises to the point that method takes precedence over content."

To aid the participants in analyzing the amount and type of participation that takes place in the team-building laboratories, the OD specialists make tape recordings of the groups' discussions. The contributions of each manager, by name, are analyzed so that each may see the nature of his contribution to the groups' effort, as well as the contribution of his fellow participants.

Although American Airlines hopes that some behavioral change in the direction of participative managing will be stimulated by giving managers this detailed feedback, the senior vice president of operations states: "I realize that very little change in basic personality is going to take place as a result of team building. That's not what we're after anyway. But having a democratic organization is, for me personally, the only way to manage. People are all different and they should complement each other with their natural abilities and acquired skills. We don't want a lot of 'carbon copy' managers; in fact, to use Grid terminology, I may hire a 9,1 man to offset a 1,9 man. Hopefully, as they learn to be more goal centered each will become more concerned with people and production; but I don't want a 9,1 man struggling to be a 'Caspar Milquetoast' when it's against his basic nature. If we can just harness the energy of people to identify problems and attack problems instead of the other guy, we've come a long way toward being a real team. But you can't expect people automatically to trust each other and act supportively, and that's why we're setting aside the time and devoting the effort toward building teams."

Role of the Boss

That senior vice president has been in the airline business for nearly thirty years, most of them in a supervisory capacity. How has the relatively recent involvement with behavioral science technology affected his own managerial style? He answers, "I have gone from failure to failure with enthusiasm, but I'm learning all the time, and I believe I'm a better manager. For one thing, I know that participation is the best way to manage people—and sharing responsibility isn't the same as abdicating responsibility. I hope my people will become involved and come up with decisions that will be for the organization's betterment, but if decisions aren't forthcoming I must decide. Then I've got to be strong enough to own up to my responsibility."

Specifically, what managerial skill does he feel he has improved? "I'm learning better to face up to and mediate conflict," he says, "whereas before I tended to suppress or ignore it. I see now that conflict is inevitable sometimes, and it's a fundamental part of my job as a manager to see that conflict is dealt with objectively."

The organization development project being undertaken by the Tulsa Maintenance Base represents one of the first such projects of major scope within American Airlines. The "seeding" of this operation was begun long before the head of the division became a senior officer.

The Tulsa project, however, is not the only recognizable organization development project affecting entire organizational components. There are others, notably the Stewardess College OD project, which have evolved over several years. But neither the Stewardess College nor the Tulsa Maintenance Base projects were initiated because of interest at the top of the firm in applying behavioral science technology to organizational improvement.

DEVELOPING AN OD MODEL

There is one organization development project that was begun by top management. It is a relatively young project which has moved rapidly. If it is considered successful in the long run, it will be used as an OD model for the company. The unit involved, the freight division, has been selected as an experimental model because it is a small division (70 employees) and all its personnel are in one location—factors facilitating observation, measurement, and evaluation.

American Airlines' vice president for freight, attended an indoctrination seminar on the behavioral sciences in the summer of 1967. He reports that this was his first awareness of the contributions of the behavioral sciences to the world of work. The information he got from the seminar "interested and intrigued" him, but he "didn't know what to do with it" because he was unaware of practical applications.

Later in the same year he attended a luncheon for American Airlines' top management. The guest speakers at the luncheon were the vice president for human relations from another company and one of its behavioral science consultants who described their organization development program.[2]

Starting with a T-Group

After the luncheon, American Airlines' vice president for freight sought out the corporate director of training and development and asked, "How

---

[2] The company referred to here is TRW, Inc.

do I get started?" They explored several possible approaches, including sensitivity training, and the vice president asked to go to a T-group. He enrolled in a week-long executive laboratory in January 1968, which was sponsored by the NTL Institute for Applied Behavioral Science.

He described the lab experience as "unique" and stated, "It told me a lot about myself that I didn't know before, and it reaffirmed some things I already knew." In retrospect, he reports that the T-group was not an entirely felicitous experience for him, or for the trainer. "I think my trainer is still pulling his hair over me," reports the vice president. "At the end we weren't even speaking to each other, but that doesn't matter, for it was the other people in my group who were important to my learning!"

Varied Reactions to T-Groups

Despite his difficulties with the trainer, he returned from the lab enthusiastic about his experience, and he sent three of his top managers in the division to three different T-groups. One reported, "I think it was interesting, but I doubt I learned anything viscerally." Another was more enthusiastic: "This is the greatest thing that ever happened to me. I wish I'd gone twenty years ago." It was the consensus that the organization should continue using sensitivity training within the freight division.

To date eleven additional managers have attended labs, either NTL-sponsored or Inter-Company sponsored.[3] As each successive group of managers returns from the lab, the vice president and other "alumni" meet for feedback and evaluation sessions. Eventually, all 24 managers of the division will have attended these "stranger" labs.

Help from Consultant

Rather than wait for all the managers to undergo sensitivity training before proceeding with further organization development, the freight division has already undertaken several projects that touch the entire division. A behavioral science consultant from a New England university has been retained. One of his first tasks, in conjunction with the company's director of training and development, was to perform an attitude survey. This survey was designed to assess the division's perception of the organization, its policies and practices, and the style and effectiveness of its management. Once a profile was developed, based on the survey, management took specific action steps to improve or eliminate problems uncovered by the survey; then it fed back to the entire organization a report of its action. (Notable among the problems revealed by the survey were: (1) unhappiness about inequitable salary structure and methods of pay, and

---

[3] Inter-Company labs are a cooperative effort of American Airlines, EG&G Company, Curtis Wright, DuPont, Union Carbide, Polaroid, Hotel Corporation of America, and the Smithsonian Astrophysical Laboratories.

(2) a great degree of competition and mistrust between the corporate and the field staffs.)

There is evidence of more sharing of information, as a result of the division's new emphasis on openness and better communication. For example, in late 1968 the vice president and the four directors who report to him met with the full division, for the first time in its history, to present the next year's plans and programs, including marketing plans, objectives, goals, and the strategies to reach these goals. This meeting was not just for the purpose of downward communication; instead, each department within the division discussed the reports and a spokesman for each department fed back the department's reactions and critiques.

"Family" Lab

Armed with the feedback from this meeting, the vice president and the four directors held a "family" laboratory off-site, with the director of training and development and the university consultant serving as trainers. As a result of their discussions, the division's top management decided to continue the open communication practice by reporting plans and progress reports to the whole division on a quarterly basis in order to get upward feedback that would serve as the basis for change in objectives and strategies.

Discussing this first "family" lab, the division vice president reported, "It's important to get away from work, put your feet up, and level with each other about the problems that affect us all. It's especially important for a guy like me whose whole manner is somewhat gruff and whom people usually describe as tough. But getting away and taking time out for reflection is a good thing for anybody—away from work where every manager has 'boss' stamped across his forehead, no matter how much he tries to avoid it."

One of the participants found that this "family" lab wasn't as much a high-risk or personal threat as he'd expected. "It was a confrontation," he said "but it was objective, nonincriminating, open and candid." The division plans to continue these off-site team sessions.

Looking Ahead

Additional plans for the future include indoctrination of all division employees in behavioral science findings, and a follow-up attitude survey to see if, as a result of changes made after the initial survey, employee attitudes have modified. The division's top management is also in the process of formulating a set of beliefs to serve as a policy foundation for its activities and goal setting.

The vice president said: "We plan to develop these beliefs not only as a creed but as guidelines for managing and dealing with people. When they are drawn up, we plan to publish them and give them to each employee to use." He reports that not all the beliefs have been identified, but he "has a pretty good idea" about what the list will contain, and he cites as examples:

"The dignity of the individual is to be our foremost consideration. We will not deal with people in terms of age, sex, title, rank, or 'clan.'

"We will be honest with each other. We also will demand honesty with others, and this includes the idea that withholding pertinent information, whether about facts or feelings, is dishonest.

"We will be loyal to each other. This includes loyalty to the organization, to our bosses, and to our peers.

"We will be cooperative, and will give cooperation freely and actively solicit it from others.

"Friendship is not a prerequisite of the above ways of behaving toward each other, but friendly attitudes are prerequisite. (You don't have to *like* everybody.)"

"Tough" but Committed

The vice president for freight has been with American Airlines nearly thirty years. At least two of his colleagues confirm his impression that people perceive him as "tough." Yet he is committed to participative managing. He says: "Anybody can go around using the right words, like 'openness' and 'trust,' but if you really believe that people aren't realizing their potential because the organization restrains and inhibits them, you've got to demonstrate your own commitment." He states that he is willing to experiment with fewer management controls in an effort to release more of the potential in people, but he isn't sure yet what forms the experimentation will take. He says: "There are lots of ways to get more commitment and involvement from people and you don't have to look very far to find some of them. Take, for example, the time clock. The very presence of a time clock says to people 'we don't trust you.'"

He stresses that, despite his concern for human values, his commitment to organization development is predicated on a desire to gain higher productivity. He looks at the time and money expended for organization development as an investment that will pay off for the company.

In fact, when he proposed the freight division's budget for the current year, he took his figures to his boss, the senior vice president for marketing, and said: "I want this budget approved to cover the expense of organization development, and if necessary I'll cut the budget somewhere else. I'll reduce the work force or cut the advertising budget if I have to, but I want the OD money to stay in." (Incidentally, he reports that the entire budget was approved.)

There is evidence that the company's involvement with behavioral science technology is expanding both in existing applications and in initiating new ones. For example, the corporate OD specialists are offering an advanced laboratory workshop for graduates of the Managerial Learning Laoratory who want to do organizational diagnosis in their own work groups.

TOP-DOWN OR NOT?

Organization development frequently begins at the top of the firm and filters down through successive levels of management. Because of the attitude of its former top management toward participative managing, American Airlines started with middle management and is only now involving the top. There is no consensus even among the top, as to whether the top-down approach or the approach the company has taken is a better one in the long run. As the director of training and development put it, "Our work in OD might have been easier if we had started at the top, but we've done what we had to do."

The senior vice president of operations agrees that involvement at the top is important, but he insists, "We can't wait for a model to be developed at the top. We've got to reach people now, and we've got to put out fires of dissatisfaction, discontent, and inefficiency now when it matters." He adds, "I've just been the 'elder statesman' for contract negotiations and a strike settlement that will cost American Airlines many millions of dollars over the next two years. Part of the reason we had the strike is because we've too often ignored the human factors in managing the company, and I'm convinced that the strike partly represented people's asserting themselves to protest the company's lack of concern for their feelings and their lack of involvement in matters that affect them vitally."

Regardless of the direction that American Airlines' organization development program takes from here on, there is some evidence that the very top management is willing to give the behavioral science approach a try. The new chief executive officer has initiated a series of executive seminars for the top team, and much of the content of these seminars is composed of behavioral science inputs. He has also begun to put into practice his belief that a democratic organization is a worthwhile goal by instituting an advisory council composed of the five senior vice presidents and the vice president for planning. While not an "office of the chief executive" as the concept is being applied in some firms, the advisory council is intended to facilitate a better flow of information about the various functional parts of the company and to make major decisions on a participative basis.

What is the role of the chief executive in the company's long-range improvement effort? He answers, "I must set the tone and help to create an atmosphere conducive to change by keeping an open mind and by taking risks myself. I see my role as that of a good dean in a university: I will learn with and from the students."

29

The Systems Group of
TRW, Inc.

NATIONAL INDUSTRIAL CONFERENCE BOARD

"If you want someone to build you a satellite to orbit sixty thousand miles around the earth to detect nuclear earth explosions millions of miles in space, or to make an engine that will cut out five and one-half feet above the moon's surface and gently drop the module carrying two astronauts, then you've got to have an organization that is capable of coming up with highly creative thinking," says a TRW manager.

"The kind of advanced products and service that we provide require that we have imaginative, brilliant minds, and an atmosphere that's pretty open and encourages people to use their minds and imagination without many of the constraints of traditional organizations."

TRW Systems Group is anything but a traditional organization. In fact, one well-known behavioral science practitioner from another firm states that TRW Systems may be "one of the earliest complete models of the industrial organization of the future." Whether or not TRW Systems turns out to be a model of the future organization is yet to be seen, but the firm's total outlook is futuristic. Its products and services are future-oriented, and its mode of managing is geared to constant change and innovation.

In several ways TRW Systems is a special company using new organizational approaches to cope with its rapidly evolving technical and socio-

Source: Reprinted by permission from *Behavioral Science: Concepts and Management Application* (New York: The Conference Board, Inc., 1969), pp. 157–71.

economic environment. It has addressed problems in the strategic missile system, in space exploration and, more recently, in civil systems.

TRW Systems is an operating group within TRW Inc.[1] TRW Systems was formed in 1954; for a time, it was known as Space Technology Laboratories. Since 1958 it has had a part in about 90% of the space projects conducted by the National Aeronautics and Space Administration and the Department of Defense, including NASA's Orbiting Geophysical Observatory, and the Lunar Excursion Module for Project Apollo. Along with its increasing involvement with the nation's aerospace program, TRW Systems has experienced tremendous growth. For example in 1963, there were 6,000 employees; today there are 16,000. More than a third of these are scientists and engineers.

Totality of Systems

The name "Systems" describes the totality of its technological involvement; it is reflected, for example, in the products and services the company provides for space exploration. TRW is involved in basic design and testing of spacecraft; it builds a variety of the operating parts, including engines, valves, sensors, and microelectronic circuitry. The company also conceives its organization as a total system of interfacing jobs, projects, spans-of-control, responsibilities, and the relationships of people who are the embodiment of these organizational variables. Because of its requirements for a high degree of synergy, the company has organized itself in a different way from most other companies, in order to avoid some of the personal constraints and organizational boundaries that have come to be associated with business organizations. There are organization charts at TRW, but they are used primarily to identify the areas of technical competency the firm has represented in its people. These charts do not show how the organization actually functions, because TRW designed what is usually referred to as a "matrix organization."

The Matrix Organization

An internal training document describes the "matrix" or project organization as follows:

"TRW Systems is in the business of application of advanced technology. The company's organization has been expressly planned for

---

[1] TRW Inc., the parent firm, is headquartered in Cleveland. Within the over-all company there are other applications of behavioral science; however, this report deals only with the Systems Groups in Redondo Beach, California. Whenever the name TRW is used in this report, it refers only to the Systems Group.

effective performance of the projects that comprise our business and for flexibility for future shifts in this business.

"The hardware work that we do is awarded by our customers in bid packages that usually involve a number of technical fields and integration of hardware from these into a single end item. We have several hundred of these projects in operation at a time. They range in people assigned from three or four to several hundred. Most of the projects are small—only a few fall in the "large hardware projects" category we are mainly concerned with here.

"From the standpoint of personnel and physical resources, it is most efficient to organize by specialized groups of technologies. To stay competitive, these groups must be large enough to obtain and fully utilize expensive special equipment and highly specialized personnel. If each project had its own staff and equipment, duplication would result, resource utilization would be low, and the cost high; it might also be difficult to retain the highest caliber of technical specialists. Our customers get lowest cost and top performance by organization and specialty.

"For these reasons, the company has been organized into units of individual technical and staff specialties. As the company grows, these units grow in size and fine structure, but a specialty is normally not duplicated in another organization. Our advanced technology capabilities are thus organized into a structure of considerable flexibility and versatility. Each customer's needs call for a different combination of these capabilities.

"A way of matching these customers' needs to the TRW organization elements that can meet them is necessary. The project system performs this function.

"In the project system, a project office is set up for each customer program. The project office reports to a company manager of appropriate rank in the organization with cognizance in the technical area of the project. The over-all project organization is similar for each project. The project manager has over-all management responsibility for all project activities and directs the activities through the project office and substructure described in the following. The project office is the central location for all project-wide activities such as project schedule, cost and performance control; system planning, system engineering, and system integration; and contract and major subcontract management. Assistant project managers are appointed for these activities as warranted by project scope.

"The total project effort is divided into subprojects according to the technical specialty involved, thus matching the TRW Systems' basic organization structure. Each subproject has a subproject manager who takes project direction from an assistant project manager.

The subproject manager is responsible for performance in his specialty area to the supervisor of the organizational element that will perform the subproject work. The subproject manager is the bridge between the project office and this organizational element. The members of the next subordinate level of management in that organization take project direction from him. The work is further subdivided and performed within their organizations.

"The organization of TRW Systems can thus be looked at in a way that is different from that shown by our conventional organization chart. It could be considered as a collection of project organizations. From the customer viewpoint, the project offices are the TRW organizations through which their contract work is accomplished. The project offices fan out into the underlying organization of technical and support specialties, and closely couple the customer projects into the performing structure. This system affords highly effective project performance, as well as flexibility and technical excellence for future work."

An individual may work on a single project for a length of time or he may provide support and expertise for several projects at the same time. In either instance, his assignment will require his working interdependently with a variety of other technical teams or with staff functions needed to support his efforts on the project team.

Project Management with a Difference

Basically the matrix system, as applied at TRW, is a variation of project management, a management system common in other parts of industry. In most project management systems, a work team is put together and each of its members works only with that team until the project is completed. In TRW, a person may belong to several teams at once, or he may start on a project and then move to another project because he has some special expertise that another team needs. This move from one team to another may be because the program manager asked for the individual, or it may be because the employee himself finds the work of the second team more attractive. The employee may have completed that phase of the program for which he was required for his expertise. While the change may have been programmed or initiated by a variety of individuals, the functional manager of the employee's "home" department and the particular project manager on whose project the employee is presently working must concur in the transfer. This concurrence frequently involves the substitution of another individual with necessary skills and experience from the functional department.

Employee Selects Projects

Throughout, the employee's preference is an important and valued input. The matrix organization and the existing 400-plus projects "in-house" facilitate an individual's receiving continually challenging and growthful assignments.

The changing nature of these work "assignments" is further complicated by the fact that, as a result of rapid growth, half of the work force has been with TRW Systems less than two years. Employee turnover, on the other hand, is substantially less than industry averages.

The result of this atmosphere of freedom of movement is a constantly changing organization. A person may work on a project for only a week or for as long as five years. Because of this range of job opportunities, the individual employee can select from a relatively large variety of work assignments. Although each assignment specifies what the employee has to accomplish technically at what cost and time schedule, he can match the opportunity to his needs at that time. It includes an assessment of himself in terms of his total self, his life style, his goals, and his objectives. The company then helps him to translate his goals and objectives into concrete experience. In other words, he begins developing "a way to get there"— to realize his goals.

Sharpening Skills

If he wants or needs further technical or professional training, the company provides liberal tuition reimbursement, as well as 36 after-hours courses in engineering and science which are taught by company personnel. There is also a company sponsored program for "co-op fellows," in which the employee works 24 hours per week while going to school, with the company providing funds for books and tuition. At the doctoral level, it is possible for a select few employees to attend school full time for a maximum of four years.

Training, however, is only one aspect of the company's career development program. The central focus is self-development through interesting and challenging work, which the company hopes to provide for all its employees. For this reason, TRW uses the term "career development" instead of management development, because most people aren't managers and the company hopes to involve the total organization. Moreover, career development implies at the same time both long-range, goal-seeking action and task- or job-centered development. TRW prefers to conceptualize its program as career development, on the assumption that *all* individuals, and not just key employees, have personal career aspirations. The organization is also viewed as having a career with its own goals and aspirations.

The careers of people and the corporation are seen as mutually dependent entities, since the organization cannot grow unless its people grow. It is for this reason that the company tries to avoid "fencing in" people by rigidly labeling individuals and overstructuring jobs and responsibilities; instead, TRW encourages people to be flexible and experimental.

The emphasis at TRW in career development, then, is the creation of a climate that encourages self-actualization for the individual and the utilization of the individual's self-actualization in terms of work for the company.

Difficult to Manage

Allowing this comparatively unusual amount of individual freedom might appear to be contrary to organizational objectives, which in most cases are superimposed on individual objectives. TRW officials admit that it might be an easier organization to run administratively if roles were more permanently defined, and if authority were more rigidly delineated. But TRW believes that the matrix form of organization has important advantages over traditional chain-of-command management systems. As one executive expressed it, "The question is not whether you adopt one type of organization structure or another. The question is whether or not the organization has working relationships that meet the needs of individuals and the objectives of the company. Thus, groups and individuals in TRW derive the necessary discipline from the job itself and the preciseness of the technological and support specialties required to get that job done effectively. We focus on the problem and organize ourselves to solve that particular problem."

"Making the matrix organization really work can be difficult and frustrating; we attempt to reduce the difficulties by encouraging openness and cooperation," comments a training specialist. "If openness exists, a man can devote his time and energies to the real job of making an effective organization, instead of politicking and empire building which dissipate energy and drain off effort that ought to be used constructively on the job." He concludes, "Climate here is important, more so than mere structure. We have a climate that isn't bound to tradition; we create methods and procedures to solve the task at hand. It's permissible here to ask 'why?' or to take risks and do things a different way."

Because people are encouraged to do things "a different way," and because the company has designed a system in which a man's responsibility emerges from the job to be done, he must obtain the cooperation of others over whom he has little traditional, direct authority. The company has created this nontraditional environment in order to increase the effectiveness of the worker. As one employee put it, "Commonly, bosses and procedures circumscribe an employee's behavior; here a man stands up to be counted and takes responsibility. Of course, there are problems. You have to be accountable for what you do, and whenever there are problems you have to work toward resolving them."

The problems he referred to may be technical or personal. TRW sees an inextricable connection between the two. The need for technical teamwork existed before the company tried to build teams through the behavioral science approach. But, in the words of one manager, "Teamwork was needed and we thought of ourselves as a team, but what was supposed to be didn't jibe with what existed. Mainly this was due to unresolved conflict within the team."

Role of Conflict

Whenever people work together there are usually some areas of conflict, regardless of the company. In an organization where people work in well defined functional areas, they are likely to experience contact within a rather narrow field—within their own department or between department heads, for example. In an organization like TRW, where getting a job done cuts across departmental boundaries, contact with a large number of other people is a way of life. At TRW Systems there is no mass production; there is an extremely high technical orientation. Therefore, each job and each individual's contribution is considered unique. Furthermore, because of the necessity for interaction of a technical and a personal nature, the team approach is viewed as the most manageable system. Since the teams comprise a heterogeneous group of technical specialties and individuals, conflict is understandable enough. Add to this the multiple working relationships without clear-cut lines of traditional authority, and conflict often surfaces.

Rather than try to suppress conflict, the company finds that it may even be the source of innovation and creativity if dealt with openly and directly. Therefore TRW isn't seeking an organizational climate in which there is no conflict or interpersonal differences. But if these differences are unexpressed and remain hidden, the company feels, the conflict grows and results in an antagonism and unnecessary competition. One manager called TRW's management approach "a system for managing the hot data," which refers to the inputs from people as they react to each other—and sometimes those hot data are feelings coming out of conflict. For example, an employee may experience difficulty in getting his job done, because of the behavior of someone, including his boss, with whom he has to interact. This difficulty reduces his effectiveness; and it may even intensify and affect the total relationship. In many organizations the culture would require that he not express his feelings openly. In TRW, however, he is encouraged to express his feelings openly about his difficulty so that he and the other person may work out its causes and its implications as regards their working relationship. One manager summed up the firm's approach,

"This organization is set up to make these hot data come to the surface so that they can be used positively." But this doesn't come naturally when people have been conditioned culturally to hide their true feelings. Furthermore, as a TRW personnel executive pointed out: "One of the conditions of effective use of hot data is the ability to deal with them yourself."

Nature of Organization's Problems

In an assessment of the problems facing TRW in 1963, a report identified the situation and the need as follows:

". . . we have in TRW a large number of complex, critical interdependencies. No one technical or administrative group is complete in itself. In getting a particular job done, various resources throughout the company have to be called on to contribute . . .

"This particular feature of the organization requires that there must be continuous open access between individuals and groups within the company.

"It is important to the success of TRW that communication between people be reliable, that we maintain and build upon our interdependencies, that we learn from and help each other, and that we identify and resolve conflict, ambiguity, and duplication."

TRW began experimenting with a process that seeks to increase the effectiveness of interpersonal relationships. The process involved training in off-the-job settings and in-job contexts to:

1. Increase individual, managerial, administrative and technical skills
2. Develop interpersonal and group membership skills
3. Create an environment in the organization which would be even more conducive to individual and group growth, development, and effectiveness.

To help achieve these objectives, TRW has undertaken an organizational change effort that it considers as essential to its particular way of running the firm. The aim of this effort is the creation of an environment that encourages individual flexibility and increased interpersonal competence, which are seen as requisite to the firm's need for constant change and growth. Because of the firm's need for innovation, the change process is centered around problem solving and task accomplishment. The methods and techniques in use at TRW to change the climate are not viewed as a program but rather, as an ongoing process.

Career Development Multi-Faceted

The elements of this process have evolved over the past five or six years, and with that evolution the process has changed and taken on new dimensions to keep pace with personal and organizational growth.

Although the process is designed to improve the entire organization, the degree to which it affects the respective organizational components varies. In the words of the director of career development, "Some individuals and work groups have experimented with and incorporated new ways of relating to each other more than others. Some are in relatively early stages of experimentation. In the learning process, they adopt for themselves the ways of relating what they perceive as effective and useful. Under certain conditions learning occurs more easily than under other conditions. Sometimes things get unlearned, too."

TRW began experimenting with one of the elements of the process—that of sensitivity training—in 1963, and for quite some time the company's involvement included sending a few executives at a time to an NTL or a university laboratory. While the company regarded these "classic" laboratory training sessions as valuable for the men who attended them, there was no "built-in" way of linking the experience into their behavior back on the job. The vice president for industrial relations said, "The laboratory often is an intensive experience, but people can experience tremendous letdowns when they return to their work culture, even if that culture is a highly supportive one."

Task-Oriented T-Group

For this reason, TRW has modified sensitivity training to include job- or task-oriented development. "If people are in a lab and they learn to level with each other about their feelings, they have begun to do something useful," said the same vice president. "But if that's all they do, the experience has relatively minimal usefulness compared to what it could accomplish if people relate to each other within the organizational setting around task issues."

Soon after TRW began running T-groups, it started to attack the problem of having a man go through the experience only to return to a real world environment that was different from—even hostile to—the values of the T-group. The company approach was to zero in on changes in the on-going culture of the organization by encouraging modification of behavior in the on-the-job setting. With respect to participation at company-sponsored leadership laboratories, TRW creates a microcosm of the larger organization in each of the training groups. Thus, engineers, physical scientists, accountants, business managers, computer experts, material specialists, and others interact during the interchange. This form of membership, where individuals from the same company but not the same work group participate, is termed a "cousins" lab.[2]

---

[2] Other forms are the "strangers" lab, which draws its membership from different companies, and the "family" lab, which members from the same group attend. TRW does not use the "family" lab format.

Career Development: Evolving Process

TRW views its involvement with behavioral science technology as an evolving and ongoing process that is designed to match the willingness, readiness, and need of individuals and the organization alike to foster and manage change. Therefore, TRW eschews the idea of a fixed "program"; rather, the company conceptualizes its involvement as a constantly changing process.

Today there are several identifiable applications of behavioral science concepts. A few years ago there were fewer activities on the company's list of career development activities, and in the words of the vice president for industrial relations, "Next year the list may be a longer one—or possibly shorter, depending upon the needs of the organization's culture."

As TRW looks at the current state of its career development activities, there are at least six characteristics or techniques that, it believes, stand out prominently:

A Behavioral Science Consulting Team

Prominent behavioral scientists work with various segments of the organization both off-site and on-site. In addition, to underscore the overlapping nature of both their activities and the groups with which they work, these consultants meet periodically and work as a team.

Team Building

Team building involves a process wherein a manager meets with his work group for extended periods of time to identify and resolve problems directly related to their working as a team.

Intergroup Building

A step beyond team building, in which interfacing and interdependent work groups meet to identify and resolve mutual problems.

Organization Mirror

A method whereby any organization unit actively seeks out its "internal customers" (other units using, or affected by their services) to receive their critique and feedback on the quality of their services.

Diagnostic Techniques

An ongoing process to evaluate the health of the organization its climate and to facilitate communication. Prominent among the diagnostic techniques is a process called *"sensing."* Rather than have an outsider come in to measure attitudes or collect information, appropriate individuals are brought together face-to-face so that an individual or group may get a reading on a particular problem area or segment of the organization. For example, rather than depend on memos or a consultant's report on a particular program, the president might listen while persons directly involved in carrying out the program discuss among themselves its problems and progress. The president does not participate, except to ask questions or request clarification.

Sensitivity Training

A technique for developing greater competence in interpersonal skills.

In reporting TRW's experience, *The Conference Board* has selected certain activities for extensive treatment. There are others which are dealt with only peripherally, if at all. This does not mean that those appearing in this case study are more important than the others. Indeed, TRW views all its activities as interdependent and mutually reinforcing.

Voluntary Participation in Lab Training

TRW's program has always emphasized strongly that each individual should decide voluntarily whether to attend a leadership development laboratory (sensitivity training). In any organization, however, this voluntarism can become reduced, especially after the program gains acceptance. Recognizing this, TRW has evolved a procedure for the selection of participants to ensure that the individual is well aware that he has a choice about attending. The screening process includes interviews by representatives from the personnel department who are trained for that purpose.

While the company reports that sensitivity training speeds up the interpersonal learning process for many people, it does not regard it as a prerequisite to effective management. A TRW manager concluded, "Some people benefit more than others. For those who find the experience meaningful, it has significance in this environment where work content changes rapidly and where most work programs are of relatively short duration."

Linking the personal and learning experience at the leadership laboratory with the application of these insights and skills in the work context begins in a series of follow-on sessions back at the plant. These are held in the week following the lab during the late afternoon and evening hours.

Members of the laboratory compare their post-lab experiences, participate in simulations and skill practice sessions, and test alternatives to job problems with other members of the lab. These postlab bridging sessions number between two and four, depending on the needs and interests of the group members.

This bridging between the laboratory and the work context becomes part of the design format of some of the new experimentation TRW is attempting. Spacing of lab sessions permits participants to test new modes of behavior on the job as well as to use other lab attendees as resources.

Organic and Responsive Program

Individuals central to the process at TRW attribute the effectiveness of the effort to the continued emphasis to keep it organic and responsive: "managers must perceive that this application of behavioral science helps them solve their managerial problems." Thus, features of the TRW "program" constantly change; it is adaptive to emerging needs. Initially, for example, most of the effort focused on the "freeing up" of individuals by means of the sensitivity training techniques; it comprised about 90 percent of the resources devoted to this aspect of training. At the present time, less than 10 percent of TRW's resources apply to lab technology—even though the effort in absolute terms is considerably greater than it was originally.

A project manager noted that the number and complexity of contracts have steadily increased. This trend has considerably heightened technical and organizational interdependencies.

In response to these evolving and developing organizational needs, the process now stresses the improvement of how work groups cooperate. Thus, more than 90% of the resources now available help managers and their work groups to solve their work problems by increasing their skills of adaptability to cope with a rapidly changing environment and technology.

TEAM BUILDING

A statistical manifestation of the shift in the emphasis from sensitivity training to team building is the fact that over the years at TRW nearly 6,000 persons have participated in the team-development process—five times the number of sensitivity trainees.

These employees come from more than 400 work groups, representing all levels of the organization. Thus team building is the major thrust of TRW's involvement with behavioral science principles and technology, and other developmental activities are seen as supportive or an outgrowth of the team-building process. Team-building sessions are designed to bring to light problems that interfere with task accomplishment. Each meeting produces an "action list" of specific items to be worked on back on the job following the meeting. This on-the-job application may range from the airing of differences between two individuals to the resolution of a difficult interface between divisions or even between TRW and a customer.

The team leader can elect to take some time with his team to deal with matters such as: "How can we improve our own effectiveness?" or "Let's take some time and look at our process of working: our staff meetings, how we make decisions, how we relate, how accurately we communicate with each other, and how well we cope with other parts of the company."

Usually in this kind of team building, an outside consultant or a member of the personnel department who is skilled in organization development and who acts as internal consultant would interview each member of the team and say, "We are going to spend a block of time looking at how we can improve our effectiveness. If we are going to do that, what are some things that you think should be looked at and that need to be dealt with?"

The meeting is started by the team leader's explaining the need for the meeting. A typical explanation: "I think we need to improve what we are doing. I believe we can do so if we make the process of improvement a deliberate and joint effort. Let's ask ourselves what can we do better? I have a few ideas and I'm sure you do, too."

The consultant then continues the meeting by feeding back the interview data that he has received and the problems the interviews have uncovered.

These problems are fed back as nearly verbatim as possible from the interviews. The rest of the time is spent dealing with that data.

A number of things that happen in these team meetings are predictable in a general sense. First, the members will deal with what the company terms "accumulated garbage" in the interpersonal system of its particular subculture. That is, things that have gone on over the years that are still bothering them but which have not yet been identified, talked about, dealt with, or worked through. Some of it gets worked through by discussing it, or merely by saying it. Matters of trust are raised. Somehow, just the act of being able to say eye-to-eye that trust levels between two people are low begins to get this problem worked through, according to a company spokesman.

Usually the next "general phase" is an attempt to introduce some specific recommendations for improvement. The range here can be very wide; it can be very personal. In one group, for example, a member was told that he was very competent but extremely cold in dealing with other people. They misperceived his coldness, personally experiencing it as arrogance and rejection. While he didn't warm up towards his co-workers as a result of this confrontation, there was less misperception, and more understanding, of his manner and attitudes.

Matters of an organizational nature often come up: "We need to have more staff meetings. We shouldn't meet once a month. We should meet once a week. The staff meetings should be shorter. We ought to take time in the staff meetings to give a critique of what we are doing."

In a later phrase, the particular team begins to look at how it relates to other teams. And again as in the first phase, usually there is a lot of "garbage" that has accumulated. Quite often there is a lot of wishing that the president of the company would do something to straighten out the other guys: "If he would just go over there and straighten out those purchasing people; or if he would tell the electrical engineers, or say something to personnel. Someone else with more authority should take some constructive action and straighten out the people who are really the problem."

After talking this way for a while (with or without consultant's help) the group usually tires of this approach and begins to question: "Are we a part of the problem?" This is very important insight, because they usually are part of it: the problem is in the relationships. "Can we do something about our troublesome relationships with others and not wait for the president to issue the magic memo, which probably won't work anyway?"

"Some very exciting things take place," says TRW Systems vice president for industrial relations. "I have seen teams completely turn around their relationships with other groups as a result of some insights they gained about their own part of the problem.

"We have conducted team-building sessions along the lines that I have described several hundred times, including the top management team, and have found them to be very useful. There are different degrees of usefulness, but a striking thing to me is that it has *always* been useful to some extent. It does mean that the time spent on our behavioral processes is concentrated: 'Let's stop working for a moment, in a sense suspend what we are doing, and take a look at how we are working, and see if we can do better.'"

INTERGROUP BUILDING

Intergroup building is another key part of TRW's program. This is the effort to do something constructive about the relationship of teams that have to work together. The competitive relationships between groups are potentially destructive. Several years ago, presidents of organizations were writing about how lonely it was to be a president of a company. What they meant, in part, was that when they looked down inside their company, they saw a lot of apparently illogical behavior in terms of the objectives of the organization. The vice president for industrial relations translated it, "People were competing with each other instead of with another company. People were duplicating functions: If you don't really feel that you can trust manufacturing, get your own machine shop; if you don't think you can trust the purchasing people, get your own people to go down into the parking lot and get in your cars and buy the stuff direct; we can't waste time with those clowns.

"People feel that they get their work done in spite of the other groups in the company. If you ask people what is troublesome in their company or organization, they usually bring up these kinds of abrasive relationships between groups. They are usually not very satisfactory. What goes on is a very civilized form of war. It is far short of using rifles, but there is a lot of destructiveness. Much of the energy is used to cope with each other, and what is left is used to really get the work done. Sometimes there isn't very much left.

"There have been situations where people just wouldn't collaborate when obviously that's what they had to do. For example, you may well have a need for reducing costs. A staff group in such an instance can elect to reduce some of the services it provides to the line organizations, and then report dutifully to the president that it has saved the company four hundred thousand dollars. It fails to understand that if you traced the effect of that decision all the way through, real savings were not accomplished. Actually, because the line people could not get needed service they became frustrated and went out and duplicated the service themselves. Result: the staff saved four hundred thousand and cost the company three million. Sometimes, these things never get looked at. They are sub rosa."

Natural Follow-up to Team Building

Intergroup building is a phase beyond team building, in which key people from two groups meet to look at their relationship. "One specific technique we have used quite effectively a number of times," says one manager, 'is to start out by asking each of the two groups to list on paper the things the other group is doing that are bothering them. People in our company tend to get these items quickly identified. Each group is also asked to predict the other group's list of complaints."

The process starts to become constructive, according to a company spokesman, because each group knows what it is doing that the other doesn't like and the prediction lists are usually quite accurate. When they are not, that is instructive, too.

At the end of an hour, the two groups have four lists. Each group has a list of what it dislikes about the other group and a prediction of what the other group dislikes about it. All four are written and put up on the wall, literally, and the rest of the time is spent dealing with the four lists in front of them.

The first assignment is to have a spokesman from one group go through his first list—specific things the other group is doing that bother his group. The other group has the very difficult assignment of listening with empathy: listening to that list from the frame of reference of the people who wrote it.

Empathy can reportedly be acquired in leadership laboratories and improved with practice. To quote one personnel specialist: "Managers in organizations are usually in such an active mode that they are bad listeners. They don't listen from the point of view of the person speaking; they don't fully understand what is going on."

There are, of course, ground rules in the intergroup-building exercises. One can ask questions of clarification but not rebut. For example, if the first group says that the second is technically incompetent, the sought-after reaction is not for the second group to defend its technical competency. A proper response might be, "What have we done to create the feeling of incompetency?" As the spokesman for the first group goes through his list, the assignment for the people in the other group is to suspend judgment, not defend themselves, and understand that there must be a reason for their putting it up there.

The process is then reversed. The spokesman for the second group gets up and goes through his list.

At this point, the two groups have generated the four lists and have a fair amount of understanding. The second group now knows why the first group listed "technical incompetency." They may not agree with this, but at least they may understand the point. The rest of the time is spent in dealing with the issues. They have been identified and each group thinks it understands each other's list.

At that point, some changes have already taken place in the relationship because, perhaps for the first time in a couple of years—sometimes this is literally the case—they are listening to each other. As a manager put it,

"They can deal with some problems that, before this interchange, it was almost impossible for them to think of dealing with. What happens is that there is greater and greater insight. Many of the problems are in the relationship. The second group is not incompetent; there are things that got in the way of efficient work output."

Energy Wasted in Competition

A TRW engineer did a graphic job of explaining the effect a two-group exchange had accomplished. Before the groups got together, they had reached a point approaching open warfare. The energy they were using up in their relationship was expended in coping with each other. He reported that only a minute part was used in getting the real work done, because 'it does take energy to have a bad relationship."

He went on to say they decided that in the future when the interpersonal "garbage" began to build up, they wouldn't wait until it got too high but they would sit down and talk with each other.

CONFRONTATION AND "TOUGHNESS"

Throughout the laboratories and the on-the-job programs, TRW stresses the principle of confrontation. Confrontation involves leveling about issues and behavior that relate to the job, or surfacing the "hot data" and dealing with it in an open manner. Writing in a professional journal,[3] TRW Systems' vice president for industrial relations decried the lack of emphasis on direct confrontation in much of behavioral science literature and in the application of behavioral science in organizations. He wrote, "The values that Douglas McGregor stood for and articulated . . . have within them a very real toughness: 'In dealing with one another, we will be open, direct, explicit. Our feelings will be available to one another, and we will try to problem solve rather than be defensive.' These values have within them a very tough way of living—not a soft way." He went on to submit that for any behavioral science program to help the organization function more effectively, it must eschew the "sweetness and light" or sentimental approach to human relations and adopt a goal-centered, task-oriented approach that includes leveling and direct confrontation.

One hoped-for application of the confrontation principle takes the form of face-to-face feedback from one employee to another in the course of their workaday contacts. However, TRW cautions that candid feedback can be a destructive process unless it is done in an atmosphere of "confrontation with caring," meaning that there is already a climate of mutual trust

---

[3] See "An Organic Problem-solving Method of Organization Change" in *Journal of Applied Behavioral Science*, Vol. 3, No. 1 (1967).

and supportiveness established between the parties involved. A TRW manager said, "Each of the persons should be sure that the feedback is given objectively, without any intent to hurt the other person. Unless persons are sure of this rapport, confrontation often does not occur, although it may be needed to help persons improve and to further the interaction of the group. Sometimes feedback is withheld for a long time because one person is afraid that the recipient cannot deal with the data."

At TRW the whole emphasis on confrontation is based on the assumption that people ought to be able to carry back to their jobs the atmosphere of trust, leveling, and candor that they developed in the laboratory. However, the company recognizes that not everyone has had the "unfreezing" experience of a lab, and that the strength of the face-to-face relationships which were established in the lab may be diluted in the daily work culture.

THIRD-PARTY FACILITATORS

The company utilizes "third-party facilitators" as social mirrors in mediating conflict in workaday situations, on the assumptions that a third party will have more ego and social distance from the persons involved in conflict and, therefore, be more dispassionate and objective in reflecting on and evaluating the interactions. This third-party facilitator may be a professional from the personnel staff who is assigned to a project group or to a functional area of the company, or he may be a consultant.

The use of outside consultants for follow-up is an unusual and important part of TRW's approach to the company-consultant relationship. A vice president said, "There's something bordering on the unethical about a consultant who comes in, puts on a sensitivity training workshop, and then rides off into the night." Therefore, the company uses consultants as part of its total approach to career development. In the laboratory a consultant acts as a trainer, but he is always coupled with a co-trainer from the company. And he doesn't "ride off into the night" afterwards. Rather he continues to work with the laboratory "graduates" back on the job in the capacity of helping to further team development, or in on-the-job consulting or coaching, or as a third-party facilitator in confrontation sessions. He has a continuing assignment to a specific organizational unit.

Internal Catalysts or Change Agents

Those members of the organization who are third-party facilitators act in the capacity of internal catalysts and change agents. They remain physically with their work groups or departments to serve as behavioral consultants, as well as to perform routine personnel services for the group.

"In a real sense we must wear two hats," said one of these personnel managers who is attached to an operating team. "We have to be a member of the team, while standing back and observing the team's activities for the purpose of objective feedback. It's a delicate balance to maintain."

As already indicated, most of these third-party facilitators are personnel specialists or outside consultants. But there is a third kind of internal facilitator, a person who has been a part of the operating team and who assumes that role to work with his colleagues. One of these, for example, is a senior staff physicist whose regular job is assistant to the director of the physical research center, an organizational unit composed of 140 scientists and 140 back-up personnel (technicians, journeymen, and clerical employees). The physical research center is divided into five basic laboratory groups, which may be working on 50 different projects at any given time.

Because of the highly technical and scientific nature of the center's work, this man was freed from his research responsibilities to provide liaison with the multiple departments and project teams that interface with the center. He explained, "I see a lot of people throughout this organization, and in my present capacity I can move about the company freely as a contact liaison on technical matters, but I can also consider and bring into action interpersonal and communication variables, along with technical considerations."

Why does a research physicist find dealing with people variables useful? He comments "Scientists are particularly hard to work with in the interpersonal areas. I realized this and felt strongly enough about it to want to do something actively to channel their technical expertise into a synergistic relationship with the rest of the operation. It's the only way we could use our potential for innovation. We've got to be innovative in this organization."

Physicist in Role of Change Agent

Capitalizing on his desire to work with his colleagues, the company enabled him to attend U.C.L.A.'s Learning Community in Organization Development[4] in 1967. Today, among his other responsibilities, he serves as co-trainer for off-site team-building sessions (in conjunction with an outside consultant), and he is a third-party trainer or facilitator for the full-time members of the professional training staff. However, the bulk of his work is concerned with day-by-day problems within the physical research center.

Typical of problems he deals with is one involving interpersonal conflict

---

[4] The Learning Community in Organization Development at U.C.L.A.'s graduate school of business is a ten-week residential seminar, limited to sixteen participants who are responsible for organization development in a variety of fields including industry, government, community, religion, and education, with representation from each field. It is an intensive program that depends heavily upon group process.

over allocation of funds for research. "Scientists tend to be independent," he said, "and by virtue of the nature of the work they perform, each sees his research as the most important. Each man insists his pet project takes priority over all others. There's just so much money available for research, and it has to be divided fairly among the five laboratories in the research center. You can imagine how much win-lose is operative at the allocation of funds." Previously, the company had felt that funds could be allocated on a priority basis by a committee of laboratory chiefs. It found, however, that each member of the committee fought for the lion's share. The research physicist recalls "putting scientists on a committee—especially one that called for empathy and cooperation among the members—really produced a 'can of worms.' After all, most scientists aren't people oriented. In fact, many of them chose to be scientists because they wanted to *avoid* people and emotional contacts." He also reported that each lab director tended to blame the committee for his failure to get the funds that his people requested. By blaming the committee, he was, in effect, refusing to accept any personal responsibility for the committee's decisions, even though he was party to them. Each would return to his group with his "slice of the pie" and say something like, "The committee decided that we don't get the money we need to proceed with a couple of our projects."

Setting of Priorities

Over the years, the physical research center has evolved an allocation process, that includes an awareness of "people" variables, whereby funding of research is handled quite differently. Each researcher is asked to set priorities on each of his projects. Then he meets with his fellow researchers in his laboratory to compare his list with theirs. As a group, they make a list of priorities for the entire laboratory, discussing in detail—using direct confrontation—the projects that are marginal. Once the group has decided which projects are *really* high priority, their laboratory director meets with the four laboratory directors, representatives of the operating divisions, and the head of the research center to work out the granting of funds. In these sessions this senior staff physicist, the center's internal change agent, acts as third-party facilitator and encourages the scientists not only to present their requests but also to level, positively and negatively, whenever there are disagreements. To aid them in being objective, the internal consultant asks them each to prepare a plan of action against foreseeable and unforeseeable contingencies. For example, each is asked to set priorities among the projects he has already listed if total funds were cut 80%, then to revise the list on the basis of a reduction of 50% of available funds.

With the continuing evolution of the process, there is a widespread feeling that the new way of deciding who gets what funds for what purpose has helped to make the research center's people more effective. Among the benefits cited:

1. There is better communication from bottom to top about what everyone else is working on.
2. There is a basis for agreement on center-wide priorities.
3. There is now an objective basis for allocating funds in keeping with over-all company objectives.
4. A lot of win-lose competition is eliminated as group members view each priority in terms of the total group's objectives (for example, sometimes during the decision-making meetings some priorities emerge as having so much impact on the total organization that a laboratory director will volunteer to postpone a pet project of his in order for the funds to be spent for more urgent research).

Although each of the laboratory directors participates in the decision-making conference, the final decision on how funds are allocated is made by the research center director, who is accountable for the operation. After allocations are made, he meets again with the total group to feed back his decisions. The senior staff physicist observes, "It is necessary that he give his report before all the laboratory heads, for then he is accepting responsibility for his actions, and there is no opportunity to blame anyone else for any dissatisfaction that may result. Also, in the face-to-face setting, each man in the group has an opportunity to express his feelings about how the money is finally divided and to work through any resentments he may have."

"Working with an aggregation of brain power isn't easy," reports the physicist, but he has found that scientists *are* concerned about the maintenance of the total operation, and they *do* want to be involved in managing their own affairs, including money, when they are exposed to the total picture.

Multiplier Effect

The company hopes that the men who have undergone sensitivity training will have a multiplier effect on the parts of the organization where they work. TRW stresses the catalytic or multiplier effect also in its use of internal facilitators or organizational consultants, but it is realized that no matter how hard these professionals work in their "third-party facilitator" capacities, there is a limit to what they can accomplish. One company goal, therefore, is to develop in each manager the skills to be a "trainer" for his own work group. The training manager reported, "A manager needs human development skills as much as he needs technical and management know-how. We must develop in them the ability to do problem solving and to facilitate interpersonal competence among their people to the extent that work groups themselves can become more cohesive and effective."

As the alumni of the sensitivity sessions fan out throughout the organization, TRW hopes, an informal network of interacting people will develop to provide the fluidity and openness the firm feels it must have to remain innovative. Considering the matrix organization and the multiple interfaces within the firm, it views this goal as realistic and necessary.

There is widespread optimism at TRW Systems that this new kind of organization is coming into being. Yet the behavioral-science approach to managing is not yet a complete way of life. There are those within the organization who feel that the effort expended on unfreezing, changing, and refreezing attitudes is a waste of time and money. For this reason, the company refuses to "send" someone who is reluctant to attend. Some employees report, however, that because of the company's in-depth involvement with sensitivity training, there is unofficial social pressure to attend a T-group. TRW, as indicated earlier, tries to offset these social pressures.

Loose Structure Sometimes Frustrating

Some people who come to the company from other organizations are frustrated by the culture of TRW Systems. A member of the personnel staff says, "People who come from more rigid organizations initially often feel confused and lost here. They don't find elaborate procedures or rules or "tight" organization structures to direct them. It's not uncommon for a new hire to see what appears to be freedom of movement and open interaction going on and not believe what he sees. But *most* people will behave as Theory Y assumes. It just takes some people a while to react to an organization that's trying to live up to Theory Y assumptions."

Some people, because of their personality structures or developmental experience, never adjust to the rather free-wheeling style of TRW Systems. A Ph.D. engineer recalls such a person, "We had a guy in the program management office who was brilliant but 105% aggressive and 300% hostile. People were scared to death of him, and they asked for an off-site team meeting to tackle the problem among others. We held the session and began to get at the 'how and why' of his mode of operating, along with the group's feelings and reactions to him. After the meeting the group didn't end up liking him any better—he was still a thoroughly unlikeable guy—but they understood better the dynamics of his behavior and their reactions. The result was that they learned to work together as a task-oriented and goal-centered group."

Sometimes the "hold-out" is the head of a program involving a large number of people. What happens if this situation exists? A program manager answered, "There are some people who don't take well to the laboratory approach; they prefer to operate in a more formal hierarchical manner. If a guy is like that, he is free to run the project his way as long as he is effective. But if he is not, something will have to be done about it." This is not a hypothetical case, that program manager admits, for there have been some such men. His behavior would probably have been spotted by the personnel manager serving as consultant for the group; or perhaps some member of the group would discuss the program manager's behavior with the personnel man, who would then probably suggest presenting these data about the impact of his behavior to the program manager directly.

Rationale for Stress on Group Process

TRW Systems is committed to the group process in developing an organization, and they report that their efforts have, so far, been mainly successful. A personnel man comments, however, "We couldn't do everything at once; we chose the laboratory approach to develop the organization by attempting to change the climate first, on the assumption that if people could bring to the organization's objectives their own self-actualizing behavior in an atmosphere that encourages them to be honest and authentic, the problems of maintaining the organization would take care of themselves." He adds that all the "maintenance problems" haven't taken care of themselves, but the firm is now adding more traditional management and skills to its career development. Like other types of training in TRW Systems, this new program is organic. Although it will draw upon outside professional help, the program is still geared to the culture, norms, and values of the organization.

The company's career development program would seem to be an expensive proposition, considering the overhead charges and the man-hours allotted to the program. It is expensive, a vice president agrees, but he adds that company studies show that TRW Systems spends just about the same amount per employee for training as do other industrial firms. The point is that TRW Systems doesn't spend as much on traditional types of training as other firms do. The director of training explains the company's approach, "We are basically trying to create an atmosphere of openness that prevents win-lose. If win-lose is the life style of a company, the problems it causes can create all kinds of expense in terms of needless competition and draining of people's energies that ought to be channeled into their jobs. We feel it is cheaper to work to prevent the kind of organizational dry rot that can degrade an organization."

Evolving and Intensifying Effort

Whatever TRW Systems has already accomplished in its effort to achieve an open system, it is not content with merely maintaining the level it has reached. The company's approach to its ultimate objective is not to relax its effort, but to intensify it. The substance of the company's optimistic attitude toward continuing change is summed up in a paper by one of its behavioral science consultants and TRW Systems' vice president for industrial relations:[5]

> Introducing change into a social system almost always involves some level of resistance to that change . . . we are not fully satisfied with the here and now, because the limits of man's potential have certainly not been reached. All we know for sure is that the potential is vast. . . . Belief in these values must lead to a bias towards optimism about the human condition; 'Man does have the potential to contribute to that effort.' . . . But in addition to this bias towards optimism, there has to be a recognition of the fundamental fact that we will continuously have to be dealing with resistance to change, including resistances within ourselves. People are not standing in line outside our doors asking to be freed up, and upended. Cultures are not saying 'change us; we can no longer cope, we are unstable.' Commitment to trying as hard and as well as we can to implement these values is not commitment to an easy, safe existence. . . . On the other hand, the rewards we experience can be precious, real, and profound. They can have important meanings for us individually, for those with whom we work, and for our organization. Ultimately, what we stand for can make for a better world—and we deeply know that this is what keeps us going.

---

[5] "Values, Man, and Organizations," by Robert Tannenbaum and Sheldon A. Davis. *The Industrial Management Review,* (MIT), Vol. 10, No. 2 (Winter 1969).

30

Genesco, Incorporated

NATIONAL INDUSTRIAL CONFERENCE BOARD

A few years ago Genesco was the General Shoe Company and its operations were almost exclusively in the Southeast. Today Genesco has a wide range of apparel products and services, and its facilities are spread throughout the country and abroad. Shoes still represent an important aspect of the total operation, but about 60% of Genesco apparel business is non-footwear.

The new diversified Genesco comprises 40 operating companies, with many divisions within these companies. The firm has 160 manufacturing plants, and distributes its products through more than 44,000 retail outlets, including approximately 2,000 stores that are owned and operated by Genesco. These organizational components include facilities for the manufacture of all types of men's and women's apparel, distribution of Genesco-made products, and retail outlets ranging from the "five-and-dime" variety store (Kress) to some of the smartest fashion stores (Bonwit Teller, I. Miller, Henri Bendel). Probably the most succinct description of Genesco is its own corporate slogan, "Everything to Wear."

Like many diversified firms, Genesco has multiplied rapidly by acquiring existing companies, many with long years of closely held ownership. As these firms became part of Genesco, the company inherited almost every

Source: Reprinted by permission from *Behavioral Science: Concepts and Management Application* (New York: The Conference Board, Inc., 1969), pp. 99–105.

conceivable style of management; and Genesco has had its share of problems in integrating the many acquired firms into an over-all corporate framework. Member companies of Genesco still bear their original names, and a great deal of latitude is allowed in the day-by-day operation of the companies, in keeping with the corporation's concept of decentralization. The corporate offices and staff maintain central control over the wide-range and long-range functions, including marketing, finance, insurance and legal matters, taxes, accounting policies, and top management selection, compensation, and development.

Diversity and Growth

It is precisely because of the diversity within the company and the nature of the company's expansion that Genesco has embraced some of the concepts of behavioral science. Genesco's vice president–organization planning states that he is familiar with recent findings of behavioral scientists and that he is committed to the "behavioral-science approach," although he scrupulously avoids the tag "behavioral science." (See box: Candor from a "Practicing Behavioral Scientist" at Genesco.) But his de-

---

Candor from a "Practicing Behavioral Scientist" at Genesco

"I think there is too much emphasis placed on identifying an individual in a corporation as a behavioral scientist. I personally would be horrified to have such a title hung on me, for it would hamper greatly my work in implementing behavioral science concepts with operating managers, who tend to distrust or dislike theoreticians. . . .

"Some of them (behavioral scientists) believe the title puts them in some special category or enhances their importance, and some of them work full-time at trying to convince people that behavioral science concepts are mysterious and can be understood only by a chosen few. I think this is wrong. It undermines practical efforts to implement behavioral concepts."

---

sire to avoid being labeled "behavioral scientist" has in no way deterred him from trying to apply behavioral science concepts within the company. In fact, he feels that the behavioral-science approach to managing is particularly relevant to a company of the nature and size of Genesco. He explained, "We are an organization composed of many different kinds of businesses and, certainly, a variety of personalities, and it is in the understanding and acceptance of individual differences that the company has its strength."

He added, too, that these individual differences may also give rise to many problems that usually don't exist to the same extent in more homogeneous organizations. One of them is the problem of integrating the goals and objectives of individuals into the larger long-range objectives of the corporation. It is because of this need for fuller integration of efforts and the need for keeping in mind the over-all objectives of the corporation that Genesco has tried to utilize the findings of behavioral scientists in several instances.

Early Involvement with Behavioral Science

There has been evidence of interest in behavioral science within Genesco and its parent company for nearly twenty years. Many in Genesco's senior management group keep abreast of behavioral science literature and continuing developments in the field. The company has maintained an informal relationship with behavioral scientists since Rensis Likert, Douglas McGregor, and other pioneers in the field began working with industrial organizations. These behavioral scientists and others have spoken at top management seminars, and the company today continues in-house behaviorally oriented briefing sessions. When asked how much interest in the behavioral sciences exists within Genesco, one senior executive reported that top management's interest in behavioral science applications had stabilized at a moderate level for a long time, though there was an intellectual awareness of behavioral-science findings. More recently, under the firm's new chief executive, the interest has accelerated. There are indications of increased behavioral-science activity to back up the intellectual commitment, and the chief executive has evidenced a willingness to experiment with newer techniques.

The new chief executive had attended the Menninger Foundation's executive seminar. Soon after he became president he participated in an advanced seminar at the Levinson Institute.[1] His concern with mental health on the job and increased managerial effectiveness within the company prompted him to bring in Dr. John Wakefield, a psychiatrist with experience in industry as a resource person and consultant, to work with Genesco two or three days a month.

Where Is Interest?

Interest in the behavioral sciences at Genesco is clearly stronger at headquarters than in the operating divisions; specifically, the greatest interest is among the corporate manpower group and the organization planning section. But, spearheaded by the corporate manpower specialists, this interest is spreading to the operating divisions and interest among middle and lower managers is reported on the rise. Part of this spread is

---

[1] The Levinson Institute in Cambridge, Mass., is headed by Dr. Harry Levinson, who originally developed and led the Menninger seminars, and who is continuing the work he began at Menninger with his own institute. The Levinson seminars, "On Leading Men," have been offered since mid-1968.

traced to the training of divisional manpower specialists at corporate headquarters before they are sent to their respective divisions. Their orientation and training at the central office has some input from behavioral research. (See box: "Four Types of Personnel Men.")

"Four Types of Personnel Men"
(observations for the Vice President–Organization Planning at Genesco)

"There are at least four categories for the people whose job is in personnel. As I see them, they fall into one of the following:

Type I

"The old fashioned personnel man, whose job is considered a 'necessary evil' by the company. He's the 'records keeper' who is always trying to find the magic gimmick to revitalize the organization. In other words, he's the 'hack.' I think most personnel men fall into this category. That's one reason we avoid the term 'personnel' at Genesco, preferring to call ourselves 'Manpower.'

Type II

"Type II is someone who may do all the jobs that Type I does, but he perceives himself as a part of the management of the company—not an appendage or a luxury. He usually, in turn, is treated as a part of management and he has some influence in management decisions.

Type III

"This type has the same outlook as Type II, except that he knows something about how and why people behave as they do. In other words, he is the *professional* in the field of human resources management. He draws on sound management theory and practice to back up his behavioral science efforts, and he integrates them into his management style.

Type IV

"This is the 'true believer' or convert to the behavioral sciences. He usually latches onto one approach or view of man, and he holds it tenaciously—even if it ignores everything we know about the nature of people, and long after the theory is proven impractical for a given situation. In his way, he's as bad as Type I.

"*At Genesco we are trying to develop Type III. We are no more interested in turning out manpower specialists who are 'starry-eyed' Type IV's than we are in having Type I—the hacks.*"

In addition to the training of professional manpower specialists who will be assigned to the operating divisions, the corporate manpower group is concentrating its behavioral science activity on line or operating managers within the divisions. In fact, the focus of behavioral science at Genesco is clearly in the area of managerial development for the middle management of operating divisions.

To expose those managers to behavioral science, Genesco uses a variety of programs and techniques. This, according to Genesco, is necessary, because of the wide spectrum of management styles, growth histories, value systems, and practices that now exist in the company. Therefore, the general approach to management—indeed to development—is geared, insofar as possible, to the peculiar needs of each manager in a given situation. The corporation makes use of many outside organizations and programs that draw upon behavioral research for their substance. Among them are the

Menninger Foundation, The Levinson Institute, the Foundation for Research on Human Behavior, the Managerial Grid, and The National Training Laboratories.

In addition to these outside organizations and programs, Genesco makes use of its consulting psychiatrist in at least three areas of internal management concern:

(1) *Acquisitions*—Diagnostic interviews and counseling are conducted on an individual and group basis with top executives of established firms acquired by Genesco, as well as with the former entrepreneur's new corporate colleagues. Genesco feels that the numerous psychiatric implications of acquisition have largely been ignored. The company's analysis has shown that the heads of acquired firms are often demoralized by loss of status and the fear of becoming "lost" in the bigger company. Furthermore, managers already in the organization often show a lack of sensitivity and of understanding of the "acquired" manager and his style of operating. Both the "old" and "new" manager tend toward polarized positions and perceptions about their responsibilities, thus causing conflict and sapping of energies.

(2) *Assessment*—On the assumption that basic personality traits are rarely changed, the company is putting increased emphasis on greater understanding of the individual personality and motivation of top managers. Without trying to modify behavior appreciably, the firm is using psychiatric diagnosis to assess managers in terms of placement in the organization where their abilities can be used most advantageously and where they can produce most effectively.

(3) *Planning*—The psychological implications of long-range and manpower planning, as well as individual career planning, as adjuncts to the total management system aimed at future growth.

Restricted Use of Laboratory Training

Since 1960, Genesco has used sensitivity training as a part of its development program and the company feels the lab experience has, for the most part, been useful for the fifty key executives who have been to T-groups. However, Genesco is highly restrictive in its use of sensitivity training. In the first place, only laboratories conducted by National Training Laboratories are used; secondly, only "high potential" managers may attend a T-group. Furthermore, before any manager registers for a T-group or before he is sent by his superior, the corporate director of management development and the vice president—organization planning must approve the request to attend. Even then, a person may go to a lab only after a counseling session.

"A lab may be a most effective technique to assist a manager in his personal and professional development, and we are convinced of the value of the laboratory experience for a great many persons," states a member of the organization planning section who has, himself, attended two T-groups, "but the lab is not a substitute for therapy and it should not be used as such."

Another executive agreed: "Like so many things that can aid a person, only those persons who are already stable and productive are likely to reap any real benefit from the laboratory experience." This executive insists, "The marginal ones may only be harmed by participating in a T-group." Therefore, if a manager is, for example, too timid and withdrawn, the company probably would not send him to a lab, for fear of driving him further into his shell. For these reasons, although a request may be generated from the individual or his boss to attend a T-group, the corporate office insists upon final say, as a control.

The company estimates that 50 key executives have "graduated" from sensitivity training labs, and it plans to continue using this type of interpersonal training for selected high potential managers in the future.

The use of pure laboratory training within Genesco is restricted to off-site labs or "stranger" labs. There have been no labs conducted internally or composed only of Genesco personnel.

The company's use of the Managerial Grid follows much the same pattern. Genesco has used the Grid for some managers, though to a lesser extent than NTL; but, so far, attendance at Grid sessions has been limited to Phase 1, which is conducted by Scientific Methods, Inc., and composed of representatives or "strangers," from several companies. There is a possibility that Genesco will delve further into the Managerial Grid and try the "team building" Phase 2 within the company, but so far it has no definite plans in this direction.

Aim Is Development of Generalists

Although laboratory training, organizational diagnosis, counseling, and many of the other development programs are broad based and extend through many levels of management, what Genesco considers one of its most pointed applications of behavioral science technology is restricted to the younger middle managers of the company. This effort is aimed at developing managers for *general* management—as opposed to specialists —and only those with the highest managerial potential are included in the program. Not only is Genesco interested in developing men and women who are generalists with the flexibility to perform a wide range of managerial functions, it also hopes to develop *personal* flexibility and interpersonal competence in dealing with peers, superiors, and subordinates. As one official put it, "The truly successful manager today must have interpersonal skills, as well as a knowledge of his job, and of the principles of responsibility, accountability, etc. Furthermore, management is now a profession, and it will become even more professional in the near future, so we feel it is absolutely necessary that our young managers—who will someday be at the very top of the organization—know something about the "how and why" of human behavior. This is at least as important as knowing how to read a profit and loss statement, for example."

DEVELOPMENT COUNCILS

To accomplish these objectives, Genesco has put together an in-house training device to expand and develop both the managerial and the interpersonal skills of its most promising middle managers. This device is called a Development Council. There are three such councils in constant operation, one for each of the company's major divisions: manufacturing, wholesaling, and retailing. The underlying rationale for the councils and the mode of operating them have firm roots in behavioral science research.

Each of the development councils is composed of the very best of its division's high producers. Nomination to membership on a council most often comes from the young manager's peers; these nominations are given informally to the immediate supervisor (who may, himself, nominate one of his most promising managers). After the supervisor has screened the nominations within his unit, he submits them to his supervisor; and the screening/filtering process continues upward to the president of the respective division. Then the division presidents submit a list of the managers nominated and approved to the corporate manpower group, who make the final selection. Although a new council is formed only once each three years, the nomination process continues, and employees are encouraged to submit nominations at any time, because a member of a council may be "washed out" or may leave the company. In this case, the reserve list serves as a source for a replacement.

Twelve men or women are eventually granted membership on each of the councils, making a total of 36 of the more promising young managers who are undergoing this intensive management development at all times. Persons who are granted membership know that they have been pegged for greater responsibility.

Coordination of the entire council's activity, from final selection to replacements for persons who, for whatever reason, leave the council is the responsibility of the corporate manpower development group. This amounts to a great deal of control, which, on the surface, may appear to be inconsistent with the principles of freedom of movement and participative management. One executive points out that this control is necessary because the council and its work are integrated with Genesco's long-range (and corporate-wide) manpower planning and managerial succession program; therefore, the "big picture" of the total corporation must be considered, along with the individual manager's development.

So far, there is little about the development councils, as discussed here, that would set them off as "behavioral science," with the exception of the initial nomination by a manager's peers. However, there is evidence of both behavioral concepts and applications in the more substantive aspect of the councils: namely, how they operate.

For the Young and Promising

After a candidate passes all the screening for membership on one of the development councils, he meets with eleven other high potential members from other units in his division. Members of his group usually come from a variety of locations and represent a fairly wide spread in levels of responsibility, e.g., one may be a store manager, another a junior buyer. The two things all twelve have in common are their exceptional performance as managers and their age—usually not over 35, although occasionally one is around 40.

Members belong to their respective councils for three years. There are four "formal" meetings at a central location each year, but the councils may elect to meet more often—indeed, Genesco hopes they will meet informally in between scheduled meetings.

When a council first convenes, it is unlikely that the members even know each other, let alone have worked together. Yet they will see each other for at least 12 times in "official" sessions, and probably more often in "nonofficial" sessions, in the next three years, and some of them may soon be working together as a team within a specific unit of the corporation. Each group is composed of individuals with diverse backgrounds and individual career aims. Moreover, the members' own motivations, ideas, and preferences about leadership styles, ways of dealing with problems, and mode of decision making may, in part, reflect the climate of their respective operating units. How does such a heterogeneous collection of people begin to function as a working team? The first problem, obviously, is communication. Genesco uses a common task to start the communication process. The task is usually a problem that is assigned to the group, and they are asked in their roundtable sessions to come up with a solution that reflects the best thinking of the group.

"How do you develop good retail executives?" might be the task/problem. Sometimes the problem is more specific and the group's final recommendations are sent to the executive committee. The executive committee may or may not act on their recommendations. The solution really doesn't matter, however. Rather the problem serves as a means of uniting the group to accomplish a task, and, in the process of doing so, the group learns something of the value of sharing ideas, concerted effort, and teamwork.

Genesco hopes that the group members also learn about themselves and how they affect others. This effort to improve interpersonal and inter-group competence is what one executive called "a structured laboratory." In fact, the methodology is, in many ways, related to a pure laboratory, in the sensitivity training sense. With the exception of the initial "kick off" problem assignment, there is no agenda—and not infrequently the group disposes of the assigned task rapidly, either by agreeing on a solution or by deciding that the problem is not worth further attention. There is no designated leader in the group—though, as in T-groups, there may be attempts to elect a leader; and self-appointed leaders may be "de-throned." The corporate director of management development meets with the council, but he does not direct or teach. He serves a function, like that of a lab "trainer," by being nondirective, and by reflecting occasionally on what is happening within the group. (He may even be asked to leave while the group works out a particular difficulty.) And, finally, the "lab experience" nature of the meetings is underscored by the ground rule that instantaneous and completely candid feedback is the method of procedure. This atmosphere of openness and candor includes interchange of feedback among the members about their ideas, their contribution to the group, and how they each affect the others. There is also a systematic peer evaluation—both written and oral—of each member's developmental progress throughout the three years.

Flexibility for Mobility

So far as Genesco is concerned, it is the no-holds-barred atmosphere in the group that sharpens the members' skills in dealing with people. "We are trying to develop managers who can function under any kind of situation at any place, and by creating an atmosphere of open and free exchange we feel that we are helping the individual manager to understand his own reactions to very different kinds of persons, as well as help him to understand and cope with a variety of reactions that others may have toward him," reports a "trainer" for one of the councils. "Sometimes the frankness that characterizes these sessions can be pretty raw, but among the more experimental members one can observe personal growth as a result of it." He continues, "Although we hope to develop generalists, we are not seeking to develop people in one mold. In fact, the councils, if anything, point out individual differences rather than play them down. If development is to be the growth experience that it is supposed to be, individual differences become the strength of the company, for we have to depend upon the special talents of each member of the management team in order to maintain the upsurge Genesco has been experiencing. But being different doesn't have to result in exclusiveness or competitiveness. If we deal openly and honestly with our differences, we learn to respect the other person and work better with him on a team. The time and effort put into these councils are worthwhile, even if they accomplished nothing else."

Genesco views the three development councils as valuable for reasons other than improving interpersonal competence. The company feels that the councils help to sharpen basic decision-making skills, as well as broaden the individual's view of the total corporation. This latter consideration appears to have a direct relationship to the emphasis on mobility that currently characterizes Genesco. Managers may be transferred from division to division and from one location to another many times in their rise to the top. In fact, one officer put it this way: "Anybody who expects to get ahead in this company must be willing to do any job and move anywhere at any time."

As one corporate executive looks into the future, he predicts a deeper penetration of behavioral research and its applications within Genesco. He commented, "Our younger managers—both line and staff—are on the threshold of larger responsibility. They have been exposed to the findings of behavioral research, and we expect them to try newer approaches to their managing and observe the results as they move into the top jobs. I think they are aware that change in the business climate, change in the work force, and change in the entire world is a fact of life. The behavioral scientists have a lot to say about managing change—and that's really the essence of the manager's job, isn't it?"